Robert A. Calvert

FULLNESS OF LIFE FOR ALL

CURRENTS OF ENCOUNTER

STUDIES ON THE CONTACT BETWEEN CHRISTIANITY AND OTHER RELIGIONS, BELIEFS, AND CULTURES

GENERAL EDITORS

REIN FERNHOUT
JERALD D. GORT
HENRY JANSEN
LOURENS MINNEMA
HENDRIK M. VROOM
ANTON WESSELS

VOL. 22

FULLNESS OF LIFE FOR ALL

Challenges for Mission
in Early 21st Century

Edited by
**Inus Daneel, Charles Van Engen
and Hendrik Vroom**

Amsterdam - New York, NY 2003

Festschrift in Honour of Jerald D. Gort
on the Occasion of his 65th Birthday

This volume has been made possible by generous grants from the Haak
Bastiaanse-Kuneman Foundation and the Van Coeverden Adriani
Foundation, both of which are connected to the Vrije Universiteit at
Amsterdam.

On the cover: The Last Supper, by Sadao Watanabe.
(With permission from the Asian Christian Art Association, from: Masao
Takenaka and Ron O'Grady (eds.). (1991). *The Bible in Asian Eyes*.
Auckland (N.Z.). Pace Publishing.)

The paper on which this book is printed meets the requirements of "ISO
9706:1994, Information and documentation - Paper for documents -
Requirements for permanence".

ISBN: 90-420-1095-9
©Editions Rodopi B.V., Amsterdam - New York, NY 2003
Printed in the Netherlands

Table of Contents

PART III
THE CHALLENGE OF RELIGIOUS FREEDOM

PART IV
THE CHALLENGE OF RECONCILIATION

PART V
THE CHALLENGE OF INTERRELIGIOUS DIALOGUE

1 Introduction

1 CHALLENGES FOR MISSION

At the end of the nineteenth century the name of American Methodist layman John Raleigh Mott (1865-1955) became associated with the watchword of the Student Volunteer Movement and the World Student Christian Federation: "The Evangelization of the World in this Generation"—a formula that found enthusiastic support along with criticism at the first World Missionary Conference at Edinburgh in 1910.[1] The members of those movements felt themselves responsible to offer the Good News to everyone on earth, so that all people would have the possibility of hearing the Gospel. It was the high tide of colonialism, belief in progress, and unrestrained optimism concerning the benefits of Western civilisation and culture. Admittedly, the churches and missions were not in full agreement with the colonial powers and did not approve of all the military methods. Many, "constrained by Jesus' love" (the title of Van den Berg's groundbreaking study, 1956), took great risks to bring the Gospel of God's mercy to those who could be comforted by the message that the Messiah had come and that people of all cultures could be saved in the name of Jesus.

A century later the situation has dramatically changed. The enthusiasm to preach the Gospel to everyone who has not heard has been tempered by a century with two world wars, the end of colonialism, an oppressive communist era, the supremacy of the free market economic system, the rise of global uncertainty, and the growth of religious relativism. Eighty years ago, Hegel's phrase about Christianity as the "absolute religion"—only surpassed by Reason—was popular. Ernst Troeltsch said that, as a religion of personal salvation, the Christian religion was the highest and most effective development in the religious world that we know of so far (Troeltsch 1969: 2). Troeltsch believed that Christian salvation fulfills the aspirations that are present in the Jewish and Islamic religions of Law and in the higher polytheistic religions as well (ibid.:187). The idea of progress was not only a cherished belief of

---

[1] See Stephen Neill 1964: 393f. and Jerald Gort 1989: 359-365.

Hegelians, but was also shared by positivists: science, and not superstition would bring progress.

For a long time the Christian mission could relate quite well to this atmosphere, assuming that Christianity would help to remove superstitious heathenism. However, in our time the cultural forces of empirical research, scientific technique, and economic life have left the Christian religion bereft of its plausibility; those who critique superstition no longer exempt Christian faith. We have to acknowledge the fact that the object to reach all people with the Gospel in one generation has not succeeded.

Former secretary-general of the World Council of Churches, Emilio Castro, remarked that not every person in the world has heard the Gospel, and especially the poorest have not been reached. It may be said as well that in a country like India the percentage of Christians from among the poor *dalit* is so high, that we recognize that missionaries have reached poor people as well. It should also be pointed out that missionary workers have often protested against the worst policies of colonialism. Not everything has gone wrong, otherwise it would simply not be true that today two-thirds of all Christians live in non-Western countries.

Cultures have changed. Former Christian countries have been secularized, especially those in Europe. After the fall of communist reign in Russia and its satellite countries in 1989, people of Western cultures hoped for a more peaceful, just and sustainable society. But the attack on the World Trade Center in New York on September 11th, 2001, has become a sign that new tensions are alive and new dangers have come from new corners of the world. Wars today ravage big parts of the world. Poverty and hunger are the daily life of hundreds of millions of people. The hope that the Christian church could fix a broken world is dim at best. The idea of progress has faded into a shadow in the darkness of the ambiguities of development. Increased wealth in many of the world's cities means more traffic; more traffic causes more pollution. Better health-care implies more people living longer, and a larger population implies (under the present conditions) more hunger, and more loneliness in the large mega-cities of poor countries. Not all hope for a better future is lost. Many people are involved in many significant efforts to change the world in which we live. But the optimism of the early twentieth century has faded away.

The observations above have been written from a Western perspective. In the future, much will be shared, we trust, from the southern and Asian perspectives. Poverty, lack of trust in the economic advantage of the free market, the need to rethink Modernity, and the limitations imposed by a narrow conceptions of reason—are existential issues confronting Christians the world over. People long for a post-colonial theology and a post-colonial way of reading the Bible.

In many places in the world church members are involved, not only in conflicts, but in the work of reconciliation as well. For a long time now, ecumenical organizations have pleaded for a just economic order, based less on greed and endless economical growth then on the real needs of people.

We could say that during the past three decades many of the larger mainline churches have paid more attention to political and diaconal issues than to evangelization. From the sixties on political issues have been very prominent. Who would question the efforts to overcome racism, apartheid, discrimination, to help to prevent a nuclear war and further peace, and to bring equality between women and men? However, the relative neglect of evangelization has other reasons as well. One of them is the religious relativism that questions the idea that one religion could be superior to others. Such relativism is not brought about by sheer laxity. On the contrary, for a great many people its roots spring from self-critique and respect for others. As John Hick once asked in a discussion in his class: "Do you really think that we are right and 'they' are wrong?" (cf. Hick 1980: 1989).

The discovery that our opinions are determined to a large extent by our context, has roots in the critiques of Marxists, in anthropological studies, and in the hermeneutical philosophy of those who read and followed Wittgenstein. Increasingly the idea of equality of all human beings and their cultures has been accepted. As has been indicated already, the value of mutual respect has been brought forward as one reason not to think that I am right and you are wrong. However, it can be argued that the values of respect, love and dialogue do not presuppose a kind of individualistic isolation—everyone holding his or her own beliefs—but rather a humble and friendly sharing of resources, values and ideas (Vroom 1996).

Truth and the acknowledgment of the value of the insights of others are presuppositions for dialogue. But this does not assume the equal value and truth of all ideas. The presupposition of the statement that a belief is true, takes into account the fact that we have reconsidered it and have become aware of what other people believe. Reflection, reconsideration and dialogue are necessary conditions for the confirmation of beliefs. Those conditions are not consistent with the relativisation of all beliefs, because such relativisation is the end of the search for truth and as such the end of respect for the beliefs and values of other people as well. A real sharing of beliefs is not a superficial exchange of points of view (see Gort 1992).

A woman from India once spoke on Christmas Eve in Coventry Cathedral in a televised service. She said that real sharing is the sharing of things that we really need. She reminded her audience about the Samaritan woman who after having been told by Jesus about grace and truth and having been known by him as she really was, went to her village to tell people that she had met someone who knew all she had done (John 4:39). That is a real sharing: honest and plain. The woman from India pointed out the fact that real sharing is concerned with life issues, both practical life and insights into life. Should we keep our richness to ourselves? Do we keep our hopes and fears to ourselves? Do we hold for ourselves the Gospel of grace, freedom, forgiveness, and reconciliation?

The idea of the equality of cultures and religions is a formidable challenge for the church's mission in this new century. There are many others. This volume is dedicated to several of those challenges. Its focus is on the Christian message in a secular and plural world. In this volume we deal with some of the main challenges for the mission of the churches: evangelization in a secular and plural culture (Part I); contextualization and liberation (Part II); the defence of freedom of religion (Part III); reconciliation (Part IV); interreligious relations (Part V); and ecumenical cooperation (Part VI).

2   THE CONTEXT OF THIS VOLUME

The title of this volume is derived from the theme of the 24th General Assembly of the World Alliance of Reformed Churches (W.A.R.C.), at Accra in August 2004. The theme of that assembly is "hat All May Have Life In Fullness." One of the central issues is the missionary presence of the churches in societal life. W.A.R.C. has a history of social involvement. It opposed apartheid and took many initiatives in the ecumenical program for Peace, Justice, and the Integrity of Creation. Since the General Assembly at Debrecen (August 1997) this emphasis has continued to be a strong element in a convenanting process in which churches bind themselves to foster economic justice, the preservation of natural resources, and environmental balance. The world is God's creation, entrusted to humankind to live in and share.

The biblical theme of fullness refers to the presence of God, who after the erection of the tabernacle filled the building: he filled it with his glory (Exodus 40:34). Just as once the tabernacle was filled with the presence of God, so the human heart may be filled by God's Spirit. The letter to the Ephesians prays that the readers "may be filled with all the fullness of God" (3:19). This prayer follows after the acknowledgment that the love of Christ surpasses knowledge. It is especially the love of God that cannot be understood fully. The author of Ephesians does not refer to intellectual discussions about the existence of God, but to God's faithfulness in Jesus Christ. A heart filled with the fullness of God is a heart filled with love.

This longing for fullness was combined in the Gospel of John with the notion of life. Eternal life has been realized in Christ, who is the Way, the Truth and the Life. Such a life is guided by the Spirit of God, with its fruits of love, joy, peace, patience, kindness, generosity, faithfulness, gentleness, and self-control (Galatians 5:22ff.).

Such Christian life itself is a witness. Christian witness is more than humanness, because it arises from the fullness of God's grace: forgiveness, reconciliation, and hope that God may reign. Therefore, works are not enough, and the proclamation of God's salvation is an ongoing task of the Church. Christian presence will make God's presence known. Such fullness of life permeates the heart, mind and actions of Christians. The editors of this volume hope that this commission of truth will challenge us all to reflect upon the missionary presence of the churches in society and on the communication of the Gospel in our secularized, religiously plural world with its struggles, violence and rumours of war. Fullness of life, that is the Kingdom of God, already present but not complete in this existence, constitutes Christian expectation and hope.

The contributions in this volume have been written in honour of Jerald D. Gort's 65th birthday and retirement. He has a warm passion for mission, both global and local. His work reflects a deep concern about the implications of relativism for mission and the lack of dedication as regards the full exposure of people to the Gospel message. He is an enthusiastic supporter of a liberative ecumenism that gives concrete form to Christian unity, mercy and justice.

Jerry Gort studied theology at Calvin Seminary (Grand Rapids, Michigan) and specialized in missiology with Johannes Verkuyl with whom he worked closely for many years. Since that period he has taught missiology at the Vrije Universiteit in Amsterdam. He has been involved in projects of interreligious dialogue on the academic level along with the organization of interreligious workshops and the publication of their papers: *Dialogue and Syncretism* (1989); *On Sharing Religious Experience* (1992); *Human Rights and Religious Values* (1993); *Holy Scriptures and Society* (1995); *Religion, Conflict, and Reconciliation* (2002); and *Religions View Religions. Toward a Comparative Theology of Religions* (2003). Jerry Gort's own specialization—next to being a fine editor—is the development of theology in the ecumenical movement. He has written many articles on the development of ecumenical thought. Together with other colleagues, helped by the expertise of Henry Jansen, Gort edited the series Currents of Encounter, in cooperation with the publisher, Fred van der Zee.

Jerry Gort loves meeting colleagues from many parts of the world and he made many friends at missiological conferences. A number of them are among the authors of this volume. African theology and the development of African churches have been of special interest to him. Six contributions in this volume stem from the context of Africa.

All the chapters in this volume have been written from a common concern about the task facing the churches in their witness to the Gospel, their efforts to further respect for all human beings, to preserve the freedom of belief, and to help people to reconcile. Some contributions are case studies of episodes of missionary work and they end with some lessons to be learned from those experiences. Others survey the teaching of churches in relation to other religious traditions, and examples of individuals who have met in dialogue and witness with persons of faiths other than their own. All the contributions seek to help clarify contemporary missionary challenges.

3 THE CONTRIBUTIONS

Part I deals with the task of evangelization in a secularized, pluralistic culture. *Gerald Anderson* (New Haven) stresses the need for the church to voice an explicit confession of Jesus Christ as Messiah. The title Messiah relates directly to the promise of the Kingdom of God. Therefore this Christian witness does not exist only in "words, words, words," but is related intrinsically to the fullness of life and the image of God. *Roger Greenway* (Grand Rapids) describes the ministry of evangelists as a specialized function of the church for people with gifts in the communication of the Gospel to those who do not know it. If everybody in the church has a missionary task, in fact nobody has! Yet the essential task of the church requires not only a warm faith but also special capabilities and a special ministry. *Henry Jansen* (Opperdoes, Netherlands) asks what the Gospel has to offer secularized people. He answers the question with reference to the fact that people seek to know what makes their lives meaningful. God accepts people and gives their lives a value in a broader context. A fully secular life without transcendence has no higher meaning than that found in things people possess that quickly pass away. He illustrates the consequences of the lack of transcendence in some novels, and shows some of the practical opportunities in which the churches can reach out to people in secularized areas. *André Droogers* (Amsterdam) describes the new context of modern pluralist cultures from his perspective as a cultural anthropologist. In anthropology a great deal of attention has been paid to the ways in which patterns and, in a sense, recipes are used by people for behaviour in certain situations. People employ repertoires and Droogers explains what that entails. Missiology needs to be conscious of the ways in which people in a plural culture assemble their own 'bricolage' on the basis of repertoires and insights derived from various cultures. *Henk Vroom* (Amsterdam) applies these ideas and gives some examples people participating in rituals of different religious traditions and making their own assemblage of beliefs, chosen from various sources. Until recently this phenomenon was known in Asian countries like Japan. Today it has become a world-wide phenomenon. He evaluates this appropriation of religion and suggests some of the consequences it has for the churches.

    The contributions in Part II take up the challenges of contextualization and liberation. *John Mbiti* (Bern) describes the discussions that emerged during a conference of the members of the Ecumenical Association of Third World Theologians (EATWOT) with Western theologians, in Geneva in 1981. With a strong focus on liberation and the struggle to overcome different forms of oppression, the conference participants acknowledged the need for new formulations of the church's doctrines like that of christology. Mbiti is sympathetic with the emphasis on liberation but feels uncomfortable when other themes and issues are neglected. He pleads for a continuation of dialogue between theologians from the South and the North. *Marc Spindler* (Leyden) deals with local ideas on the "sweet" fullness of life in the culture of Madagascar. In the process of inculturation the church should use native categories. Spindler describes the fundamental-theological method of some Madagascarian catholic theologians and their use of indigenous ideas as a kind of natural theology. *May ny aina* (life is sweet) is a saying people are fond of using in Madagascar. Aina has other meanings than the Germanic words for life: harmony and solidarity are included. Spindler concludes his contribution with a discussion of the starting-point for a true contextualization. From his rich experience in southern Africa *Frans Verstraelen* (Leyden / Zimbabwe) describes the way in which missionaries have adapted to local customs and ideas—or often just tried to replace them by (Western) Christian forms of Christianity. After Vatican II and amid analogous developments in the World Council of Churches, the climate changed and missionaries became more open to local cultures. Verstraelen describes the consequences of these new approaches, their relation to African traditional religion, and the question of local leadership. He distinguishes among three types of Christian African religiosity. He concludes his contribution with the contemporary challenges the churches face in Africa. *Anne-Marie Kool* (Budapest) describes the challenges faced by Hungarian churches after the liberation from Communism and the turn to democratic societies which are forced to find their way in a free market society, into which many missionary groups enter as well. They have to learn to cooperate, to overcome discrimination against gypsies. In short, the churches encounter at the same time nearly all the challenges with which this volume is concerned.

Both contributions in Part III are concerned with the challenge to preserve freedom of religion. *Jan van Butselaar* (Bennebroek, Netherlands) describes the newly created Dutch forum for religious freedom and its work. Churches struggle to build compassionate societies and are involved in a great many institutions of education, healthcare and care for homeless, drugs addicts, and other persons in need. Mission also requires of persons to change their religious affiliation. Therefore the mission of the church presupposes freedom of religion: and the preservation of religious freedom in the broadest sense of the word is itself a missionary task of the church. In the same vein *Jan Jongeneel* (Utrecht) deals with the freedom of persons to change their religious affiliation or to relinquish it altogether. He describes different forms of apostasy and pleads for the freedom of conversion.

Part IV has two contributions on another challenge of the church, reconciliation. God has given us "the ministry of reconciliation" (1 Corinthians 5:18). The proclamation that God has reconciled himself with us through Christ has as a consequence, and perhaps as a presupposition, that the church helps people to reconcile with each other and live in peace. Christians should help to build just and merciful societies, to overcome discrimination and poverty in our broken societies. One of the most important aspects thereof is the work of reconciliation and forgiveness. *Bob Schreiter* (Chicago / Nijmegen, Netherlands) describes the nature of reconcliation as a missionary and diaconal project. Reconciliation cannot undo the wrongs and injustices that people have suffered. Yet it can enable them to forgive and to establish better relations. This work is reminiscent of the reconciliation that God Himself has brought. *Piet Meiring* (Pretoria) describes the work of the South African Truth and Reconciliation Committee. The detailed and very moving stories that the women told in the hearing of the Committee and the reactions of these women to the confessions of the perpetrators, some of whom longed for forgiveness, gives the reader a sense of the urgency, necessity and pathos of reconciliation in today's broken world.

Part V contains the contributions on interreligious relations and the challenge of witness and dialogue in the encounter with people of other religious traditions. From his expertise in both the missionary history and the theology of religions *Arnulf Camps* (Nijmegen) describes the missionary approach of three early Jesuit missionaries in their encounter with various religious traditions: Xavier, Ricci and De Nobili. He explores the thought of these three pioneers in Asia, and concludes that the contemporary world "asks for further courageous steps." *Willi Henkel* (Rome) gives a clear summary of the more recent teaching on interreligious dialogue by the Vatican. He starts with "Ecclesiam Suam"

(1964), and goes through the Vatican II documents up to the documents of John Paul II. Henkel summarizes the teaching on dialogue and proclamation and concludes that views of the Catholic Church spring from a spirituality that is based on belief in God as the Holy Trinity. In his turn, *Kenneth Cracknell* (Fort Worth) describes the development of the theology of religions within the thought of the World Council of Churches. He begins with the Guidelines on Dialogue with People of Living Faiths from 1979—recently revised and updated—and shows how evangelization is an integral part of dialogue. Referring to dialogue in the New Testament and to the work of the apostle Paul, he then describes the nature of dialogue, and shows how the communication of the Gospel takes a great many forms. It may take a lot of time to bear fruit. In the second part of his contribution he turns to the views of a few of the pioneers of the encounter with people of other religious traditions: Bartholomaeus Ziegenbalg, Henry Martyn, Thomas Ebenezer Slater, Hendrik Kraemer and Wilfred Cantwell Smith. Cracknell concludes that dialogue and witness go hand in hand. *Karel Steenbrink* (Utrecht) draws from his expertise in Christian-Muslim relations in Indonesia for a case study about the encounter of Indonesian Muslims with North-American Christians. He concentrates on Haji Abdulmalik bin Abdulkarim Amrullah, known as Hamka, who has been the chair of the High Council of Muslims in Indonesia in his relationship with his half-brother Willy Karim Amrullah, who has been baptized a Christian, and Abdul Mukti Ali. Steenbrink shows how the North-American forms of Christianity more and more determine the ideas about Christianity of a great many Muslims. *Rein Fernhout* (Amsterdam) translates the classical Catholic and Protestant views on grace in Theravada Buddhist terms. He describes precisely the classical distinctions between Catholic and Protestant thought on grace, faith, merit and sin, and the Buddhist view of *puñña* and *papa* in order to make Christian views understandable to Buddhists showing the commonalities and the differences. He demonstrates a way to compare and discuss each other's beliefs, one of the urgent challenges of comparative theology and religious philosophy.

The subject of Part VI is the relationship between mission and ecumenism. In the Protestant missionary movement all Western denominations have been transported to other parts of the world, and an important challenge for Christian witness now is to show a degree of harmony and unity. *Inus Daneel* (Zimbabwe and Boston) discusses Jerry Gort's concern for ecumenical cooperation and his emphasis on liberation as a starting point for interreligious encounter and cooperation. He concretizes Gort's views on sharing and dialogue with a survey of developments within the African Independent Church Conference (founded in 1972) and the Association of African Earthkeeping Churches, telling the story of how ecumenical and interreligious cooperation emerged. *Wilbert Shenk* (Pasadena, California) retells the story of a Mennonite couple, Edwin and Irene Weaver, who upon invitation by a local Mennonite church in 1959 were sent to Nigeria. There they discover the dividedness of Protestant Christianity in that area, and experience how difficult it was to organise ecumenical cooperation. The warning that they had read entering their town, "Go Slow Through Uyo," became a metaphor of their work in which dialogue, reconciliation and cooperation were central.

A survey of the contributions in this volume demonstrates how intertwined are the various challenges facing the Christian churches in mission in this new century. Both on a global scale as well as on the smaller scale of cities and villages religious pluralism is a fact, with secularization, an atmosphere of relativity, freedom of religion, and bricolage as consequences. Christian churches and missions are challenged by the task to find a friendly and faithful approach to the cultures and religious traditions in the various contexts in which they live, and a common search for a believable presentation of the Gospel in a world searching for true faith, hope and love.

The Editors

BIBLIOGRAPHY

Gort, Jerald D. (1998). "Van Edinburgh 1910 naar San Antonio 1989: Een doorlopend verhaal". In: *Wereld en Zending* 18. No.4 Pp. 359-365.

Gort, Jerald D., Hendrik M. Vroom, Rein Fernhout, Anton Wessels (eds.). (1992). *On Sharing Religious Experience*. Amsterdam: Rodopi /Grand Rapids: Eerdmans.

Hick, John. (1980). *God Has Many Names*. London.

—. (1989). *An Interpretation of Religion*. Harmondsworth: Macmillan.

Neill, Stephen. (1964). *A History of Christian Missions*. Harmondsworth: Pelican.

Troeltsch, Ernst. (1969). *Die Absolutheit des Christentums*. Tübingen: Siebenstern. (1902).

Van den Berg, Jan. (1956).*Constrained by Jesus' love. An Inquiry into the Motives of the Missionary Awakening in Great-Britain in the Period 1698-1815*. Kampen: Kok.

Vroom, Hendrik M. (1996). "Judging and Respecting the Beliefs of Others". In: Vincent Brümmer and Marcel Sarot (eds.). *Revelation and Experience*. Utrechtse Theologische Reeks Nr. 33. Utrecht: Faculteit der Godgeleerdheid Utrecht. Pp. 109-130.

PART I

THE CHALLENGE OF A SECULAR AND PLURAL CULTURE

2 "You are the Messiah" (Mt. 16:16)[1]

Gerald H. Anderson

1 INTRODUCTION

The question posed by Jesus in Mt. 16:15, "Who do you say I am?", is the essential question of the Church and its mission. Peter's confession, "You are the Messiah, the Son of the Living God" (Mt. 16:16; also Mk. 8:29), is the essential answer.

Jesus affirms Peter's answer, and indicates that this is more than just Peter's personal opinion; it has been revealed to Peter by God the Father, and with this confession Peter becomes the "rock" on which Jesus will build his Church (Mt. 16:17-19). This confession is essential for the Church; the recognition that Jesus is the Messiah, the Son of the Living God, is the heart of the Church's message and mission. F. Dale Bruner says that in Matthew 16:13-28, "Jesus teaches us what makes a church a church" (Bruner 1990:II, 568). Peter's confession, according to Joseph E. Monti, is the single, normative, foundational confession of faith that "grounds all Christological reflections in their attempt to give some coherent and cognitive theological content—some sensible explanation—to and for this faith experience" (Monti 1984:11).

Other opinions ("some say... and others say...", Mt. 16:14) were not acceptable to Jesus, because they pointed to alternative figures in answer to his question, "Who do people say that the Son of Man is?" Peter's confession was clear and unambiguous, "You are the Messiah", and it was without qualification.[2]

---

[1] This essay is revised and reprinted from Colzani, *et al.* 2001: 91-100.

[2] Cf. Jesus' acknowledgment that He was the Messiah in Mk. 14:62 and John 4:26. This was the understanding of the disciples and others. Andrew told his brother, Simon Peter, "We have found the Messiah" (John. 1:41); Peter, in his sermon in Jerusalem on the day of Pentecost to "fellow Jews," spoke of Jesus as the fulfilment of God's promise to Israel, and said, "Men of Israel, listen to me:... Let all Israel accept as certain that God has made this Jesus, whom you crucified, both Lord and Messiah" (Acts 2:36); Paul, speaking in the Jewish synagogue in Thessalonica on the sabbath, said, "This Jesus, whom I am proclaiming to you, is the Messiah" (Acts 17:3-4). The author of John's Gospel says he is writing "so that you may come to believe that Jesus is the Messiah, the Son of God, and that through believing you may have life in his name" (John. 20:31). Andrew told his brother, Simon Peter, "We have found the Messiah" and "he brought Simon to Jesus" (Acts 1:41f.). In Acts 8:5 it is reported that "Philip went down to the city of Samaria and proclaimed the Messiah

Jesus "ordered the disciples not to tell anyone that he was the Messiah" (Mt. 16:20), but that was temporary. The scope of Jesus' mission strategy was progressive (Acts 1:8), first to his disciples; then to the house of Israel (Mt. 10:6; 15:24; cf. Acts 11:19); and, after the resurrection, to all the nations (Mt. 28:16-20; Acts 1:8).[3] As the Catholic bishops of the United States said in their pastoral statement on world mission, "Jesus was a missionary" (1986:1). He instructed his disciples, "As the Father has sent me, so I send you" (John. 20:21; cf. John. 17:18). He was unique, ultimate, and universal.[4]

2   THE CHALLENGE

The Church in mission today faces serious obstacles and challenges, both external and internal. These include persecution, secularism, resurgent world religions, communism, totalitarian regimes, post-modern skepticism, and "religious indifference" as mentioned by Pope John Paul II in *Tertio Millennio Adveniente* (36). These external factors and forces, however, are not the greatest threat to the Church in mission. The Church has dealt with these in the past and has prevailed. It will continue to overcome them, although in some situations it will be at great human cost in struggle, suffering and sacrifice, even possible martyrdom.

The most serious threat to the Church's mission today comes not from outside the Church, but from inside the Church itself. Once again Jesus poses the question, "Who do you say I am?" and today many opinions and options other than Peter's confession are heard in the Church. They can only be described as deviations from the revelation of God the Father to Peter, a revelation that was affirmed by Jesus and is part of the historic teaching of the church. After all, "Jesus Christ is the same yesterday and today and forever" (Heb. 13:8).

In *Redemptoris Missio* (RM) Pope John Paul II pointed to this problem when he spoke of "widespread indifferentism... based on

---

to them." For discussion and literature on "Jesus as Messiah," see Davies and Allison 1991: II, 594-601.

[3] Manson says, "The limitations imposed [by Jesus] were imposed on the apostles alone, and were not meant to apply for all time... the matter is one of priorities: the first, but not the only, task of the Messiah is concerned with Israel," 1955: 3f.

[4] Cf. *Redemptoris Missio* (RM): 6, 13; *Ecclesia in Asia* (1999): 14. See also *International Theological Commission* 1997: passim.

incorrect theological perspectives... characterised by a religious relativism which leads to the belief that 'one religion is as good as another'" (RM 36). This is a theological virus that is very widespread; it infects all churches, and in this sense it is an ecumenical virus that has reached global epidemic proportions. Strong medicine and strategic steps are needed to deal with the problem.

3   JESUS CHRIST: LORD OF ALL AND FOR EVERYONE

I want to address briefly three aspects of the Christian claim to universality and its missiological implications.

First, the New Testament is clear that Jesus is Lord of all and for everyone. There are no exceptions or exemptions to the universal Lordship of Jesus Christ. Either everyone needs the Gospel, or no one needs it. This begins, as noted above, with the Jews, and then expands to include everyone. This is summarized most clearly in the Great Commission of the risen Christ, which is generally considered to be the premier text for the world mission of the Church. Adolf von Harnack spoke of the Great Commission as a "manifesto" that was a "masterpiece." He affirmed, "It is impossible to say anything greater and more than this in only forty words" (in: Bosch 1991:56). Karl Barth said, "The Great Commission is truly the most genuine utterance of the risen Jesus." It is the great turning point in history, Barth said, when the temporary restriction of going only to the house of Israel (Mt. 10:5) is lifted after the resurrection, and the apostles are sent to make disciples of all nations (Barth 1960:67). According to David Bosch, "There can be little doubt that Matthew himself understood the last verses of chapter 28 to be the key to his entire gospel" (Bosch 1983:223).

However, and secondly, the expansion of mission to include "all nations" (Mt. 28:19), in no way cancels the original mission to the Jews. "You are the Messiah" is still where mission begins—"to the Jew first" (Rom. 1:16; cf. Rom. 2:9-10). Unfortunately, there has been a trend since the 1950s among some Roman Catholic and Protestant theologians to suggest that the Jewish people do not need to acknowledge Jesus as the Messiah. In this view the Jewish people have their own covenant with God through Abraham which renders faith in Jesus as the Messiah unnecessary. Some Christian theologians have even suggested that Jesus was not the Messiah, or was a failed Messiah (e.g. Brockway 1988:351). Apparently, in this view, Jesus was confused and Peter's confession was a mistake.

Nowhere in the New Testament or in official statements of the Roman Catholic Church or of the World Council of Churches have I found any exemption of the Jews, or anyone else, from the universal claims of the Gospel. To the contrary, Jesus sends his disciples—then and now—to all nations and peoples: to proclaim the Gospel, to make disciples, to baptize them, and teach them all that he commanded. Obviously, this must be done with sensitivity, respect, humility, and repentance for sins of omission and commission. This is the position, as I understand it, that has been affirmed consistently by the Roman Catholic Church under the pontificate of John Paul II. *Redemptoris Missio* states that "for all people—Jews and Gentiles alike—salvation can only come from Jesus Christ" (RM 5), "the universality of this salvation in Christ is asserted throughout the New Testament" (RM 5), and "the Church calls all people to this conversion" (RM 46). This is reaffirmed in the apostolic exhortation *Ecclesia in Asia* and in the declaration *Dominus Iesus* from the Congregation for the Doctrine of the Faith.

The main point here is that the relation of the Gospel to the Jewish people is foundational for a theology of religions. If mission to the Jews is denied, then denial of mission to people of other faiths easily follows. Christian theologians who say that the Jewish people do not need the Gospel are also likely to deny that people of other faiths need the Gospel, and we end up with a rampant, radical relativism and rejection of the Christian mission to all people of other faiths. For while the relation of the Church to the Jewish people is distinctive, it is not totally different or separate from the relation of the Church to people of other faiths. A theology of religions begins with the relation of the Church to the Jewish people.

And yet, thirdly, suggestions like that of Professor Claude Geffré that "the relation of the Church to Judaism has the value of a paradigm for the relation of Christianity to other religions," pose a theological leap that is intriguing but problematic (Geffré 2001:47-63). Is there biblical support for placing other religions, and presumably other covenants, side by side with Israel in our understanding of salvation history?[5]

In John's Gospel we are told, "Salvation comes from the Jews" (4:22). Commenting on this formula, Joseph Cardinal Ratzinger says:

This heritage remains abidingly vital and contemporary in the sense that there is no access to Jesus, and thereby there can be no entrance

---

[5] This position was advocated by Choan-Seng Song 1976: 211-222.

of the nations into the people of God without the acceptance in faith of the revelation of God who speaks in the sacred Scriptures that Christians term the Old Testament (Ratzinger 1994:624).

This perspective was also advanced in "The Jewish People and Their Sacred Scriptures in the Christian Bible," a document prepared by the Pontifical Biblical Commission chaired by Cardinal Ratzinger and published in 2001. The Jewish scriptures, it says, "occupy a place of extreme importance in the Christian Bible… Without the Old Testament, the New Testament would be an indecipherable book, a plant deprived of its roots and destined to dry up."[6] It goes on to say that "The Jewish wait for the Messiah is not in vain… We [Christians], like them, live in expectation. The difference is in the fact that for us, he who will come will have the same traits of that Jesus who has already come and is already present and active among us." Thus Jews and Christians share the wait for the Messiah, though Jews are waiting for the first coming and Christians for the second.[7]

None of this is inconsistent or contradicts earlier authoritative Vatican teaching, especially in *Redemptoris Missio* and *Dominus Iesus*, that Jesus Christ is the sole saviour of all humankind, including the Jews.[8]

---

[6] The document was released in Italian and French in December 2001. This writer has relied on news articles about the document, with quotations in English that appeared in *Catholic News Service Document*. U.S. Conference of Catholic Bishops. December 6, 2001; *Christian Century*, February 13-20, 2002:14f.; Cf. Melinda Henneberger, 2002.

[7] This is reminiscent of the story told by a Jewish person in which the Messiah comes at the end of days. Jews and Christians rush out to greet him and establish his reign. Finally, they ask him if this is his first or second coming, to which the Messiah replies, "No comment."

[8] The journal *Inside the Vatican*, published in Rome, said that the *New York Times* news article about the content of the Pontifical Biblical Commission document just mentioned was "misleading" for two reasons; first because it called it "a Vatican document," and said that it was now "official church doctrine," which is not true. "The document was issued by a commission of the Vatican… a low-level commission… *with no doctrinal authority whatsoever*" (italic in the original). "It is a document of little authority." Secondly, the *Times* news article was misleading because it implied that this document represents "the beginnings of a reversal of the teaching of *Dominus Iesus*, which had nearly the highest level of authority that a Church document can have." See: "A Misleading Article." *Inside the Vatican*. February 2002:54f.

4   TWO STREAMS: DISCONTINUITY AND CONTINUITY

Even for those who affirm with Peter, "You are the Messiah," there are difficulties today in describing and defining the relation between God's redemptive activity in Jesus Christ, people of other faiths, and those faiths themselves. Indeed, this has become one of the most difficult, divisive, and controversial areas of missiological discussion. On the one hand, we want to be faithful to the witness of Holy Scripture and the authoritative teaching of the Church, and—at the same time—we want to be sensitive to the context of religious pluralism and to those with whom we seek to witness in dialogue and proclamation.

In Scripture and in the history of Christian doctrine there are two major streams or traditions regarding the relationship of God's redemptive activity in Jesus Christ and God's activity among people of other faiths.[9] One tradition, while recognizing the uniqueness and universality of Jesus Christ, emphasizes the continuity of God's revealing and redeeming activity in Christ with God's activity among all people everywhere. It views Christian faith as the climax of a divine revelation that began long before human history and has been available to everyone.

Jesus Christ in this view is crucial, normative, and definitive, but not exclusive. What is true of Jesus Christ in a focal way is pervasively true of the whole cosmos. He is the key or clue to the rest of God's working. But the Word of God is not limited to and did not end with the revelation in the historic person of Jesus, yet it is also not apart from Christ in the Spirit. There is much biblical and patristic testimony in support of this tradition. John's Gospel affirms that the same light which was in Jesus enlightens everyone (John. 1:1-9). Paul said that a thousand years before the birth of Jesus, "Christ" was with the Israelites in their wanderings in Sinai (1 Cor. 10:4). And Acts 14:17 assures us that God "has not left himself without witness" among all nations, even those who had no knowledge of the biblical revelation. In this view, the *logos spermatikos* is active everywhere, sowing seeds of truth, and thus preparing the way for the Gospel.

The other tradition emphasizes a radical discontinuity between the realm of Christian revelation, which is unique, and the whole range of non-Christian religious experience. In this view, the non-Christian religions are the various efforts of human beings to apprehend their

---

[9] I have written on this subject many times, most recently Anderson 1996 and 1999. Some of what I have said elsewhere is included here.

existence, whereas Christianity is the result of the self-disclosure of God in Jesus Christ. God has spoken to humanity only in the person of Jesus Christ, and "there is salvation in no one else" (Acts 4:12). This tradition—which is the narrow, exclusivist tradition—is equally, if not more strongly, represented in Scripture and the history of Christian doctrine.

These two streams of teaching and tradition are hard to reconcile, and seem almost contradictory. Yet both are part of the Christian tradition. Both are found in Scripture and patristic teaching. Both are represented in the history of Christian missions. Both must be maintained in a balanced tension. This is hard to do when those from one tradition offer continuity with doubtful uniqueness, and those from the other side urge uniqueness without continuity. Needed in our theological understanding about mission and religious pluralism is uniqueness with continuity.[10]

In *Redemptoris Missio*, John Paul II spoke about the truth of these two elements in tension when he affirmed "the real possibility of salvation in Christ for all mankind" (RM 9) and explained that for individual non-Christians "salvation in Christ is accessible by virtue of a grace which... enlightens them in a way which is accommodated to their spiritual and material situation" (RM 9, 10). How does this happen? The Second Vatican Council said this salvific grace comes to individual non-Christians from God "in ways known to himself" (Ad Gentes 7).

There is a passage in *Redemptor Hominis*, John Paul II's first encyclical, that is important for this discussion. The pope says, "The human person—every person without exception—has been redeemed by Christ; because Christ is in a way united to the human person—every person without exception—even if the individual may not realize this fact" (RH 14). May I ask: If everyone without any exception whatever is already redeemed by Christ and united with Christ, even when they are unaware of it, why is there any urgency or need at all for persons of other faiths to hear the Gospel, to proclaim their faith in Jesus Christ, to be baptized into membership in the visible church and to partake of the sacraments?

If I could ask Cardinal Ratzinger just one question, it would be this: "Your Eminence, why did you never mention *Redemptor Hominis*, with this important statement from the Holy Father, in *Dominus Iesus*?"

---

[10] This formulation was first suggested by Soper 1943:225-27.

To his credit, Cardinal Ratzinger does say in *Dominus Iesus*, "Theologians are seeking to understand this question more fully. Their work is to be encouraged, since it is certainly useful for understanding better God's salvific plan and the ways in which it is accomplished" (DJ 21).

5   A NEW PARADIGM?

Today there is an effort on the part of some missiologists to propose a new paradigm for mission that would replace evangelization with reconciliation and healing as the goal of mission. I will illustrate this effort with the proposal from a well-known Protestant missiologist, S. Wesley Ariarajah from Sri Lanka, who is now a professor at Drew University in the United States.[11]

Ariarajah proposes that Christian mission should be seen as a common cooperative enterprise with people of other faiths for reconciliation and healing, rather than to seek for the conversion of people to faith in Jesus Christ. Non-Christians, in his view, do not need faith in Jesus Christ, because God is already with them and using them in much the same way that God is present among Christians. With a convoluted argument about the declining status of the churches in Europe being preferable to the growing churches in Africa, Latin America, Asia and Oceania, he makes a curious identification of "evangelization" with the cause of Mammon. Finally, he urges that in mission we should give up "doctrinaire Christology," including "the claim to uniqueness," because it is irrelevant. This should be replaced, he says, with an emphasis on "an authentic spiritual life that is centered in God."

Ariarajah claims to have shaped his new pluralist paradigm for mission as a result of dialogue with Hindus and Buddhists, and clearly there is nothing here that a Hindu or Buddhist would disagree with. It is also likely that if the early missionaries to Sri Lanka had his theological views, Ariarajah would not be a Christian today. It is not clear if this would matter to him. There appears to be an underlying assumption that

---

[11] S. Wesley Ariarajah, "Christian Mission: The End or a New Beginning?" My comments are based on the full text of his address given in October 1998 to a meeting of the United Methodist General Board of Global Ministries. An abbreviated and sanitised version, with his most egregious statements deleted, was published in Ariarajah 1999: 10-14.

the various religious traditions are equally valid in the divine plan of salvation.

I must confess that I find Ariarajah's relativism no less doctrinaire than the Christology to which he objects. According to his dogma of relativism, everything is relative except relativism. And his caricatures of traditional missionary thinking are no less objectionable: conversion, he says, "has come to mean... an activity aimed at dragging persons from one community to another," and the traditional goal of mission, he alleges, "is to make everyone accept Jesus Christ," which implies coercion. I cannot find statements from any reputable missiologist in the last fifty years that would match these characterizations. Such radical theological relativism and derision regarding the Christian mission illustrate the threat to mission from inside the Church.

Carl E. Braaten reminds us that anytime there is discussion about the salvific contribution of other religions, it is important to ask "if it is the same salvation that God has promised the world by raising Jesus from the dead. The resurrection gospel is the criterion of the meaning of salvation in the New Testament sense" (1980:6). While reconciliation and healing are certainly part of the Christian message and mission, they cannot take the place of evangelization in a paradigm for mission. As Pope John Paul II stated in *Redemptoris Missio*, "Proclamation is the permanent priority of mission," and "the proclamation of the word of God has Christian conversion as its aim" (RM 44, 46).

Christianity's claim to universality is based on the universality of Jesus Christ which the Church proclaims, starting with the confession, "You are the Messiah."

6   THE TEACHING OF MISSIOLOGY: ONE STEP IN MEETING THE CHALLENGE

Earlier I suggested that strategic steps are needed to meet the internal challenge to mission if the Church is to be effective in presenting the uniqueness and universality of Jesus Christ. Let me mention one of the most important steps that could be taken for the advancement of mission.

There is an urgent need to re-establish the place of missiology in theological faculties. There has been a decline of mission studies and professors of mission/world Christianity in some seminaries, especially in Europe and North America. In the 13 official United Methodist seminaries in the United States in 2002, only three had a full-time professor of missiology or world Christianity. Even some well-known

American Evangelical seminaries and Bible colleges, which earlier had a strong program of mission studies, with full-time professors and required courses for all students, now have little in this field, and do not require mission courses for graduation. Of course, there are pockets of vitality in some Evangelical centers, such as Asbury Theological Seminary, Fuller Theological Seminary, and Trinity Evangelical Divinity School, where there are graduate schools of mission and evangelism. Boston University School of Theology, Princeton Theological Seminary, and Yale Divinity School are among the mainline ecumenical seminaries that have distinguished professors and courses in mission studies.

I believe I am correct that only one of the diocesan-sponsored Catholic theologates in the United States today has a professor or anyone else who regularly offers courses in missiology to those who are preparing for the priesthood, but no such course is required for graduation and ordination. I am told that a similar situation prevails in Europe. How can those who are going to be pastors of congregations communicate a vision and understanding of world mission, with commitment and passion, if they do not have it themselves? And where will they get it if they do not get it as part of their theological education? Is it possible that the absence of missiology in the curriculum of many Catholic diocesan theologates may contribute to the imbalance in mission theology and the decline in missionary vocations, despite the specific call in *Redemptoris Missio* (83) for missiology to be included in the teaching of seminaries and houses of formation?[12]

There is a rich, unequivocal understanding of mission at the heart of the Catholic Church in the Magisterium of the last half-century, from the Dogmatic Constitution on the Church, *Lumen Gentium*, and the Decree on Missionary Activity, *Ad Gentes*, of the Second Vatican Council, to Pope Paul VI's apostolic exhortation on evangelization, *Evangelii Nuntiandi*, to Pope John Paul II's encyclical *Redemptoris Missio* and his apostolic exhortation *Ecclesia in Asia*—always with priority given to proclamation and evangelization. Therefore it is difficult for this Protestant ransomed sinner to understand why only one diocesan

[12] Catholic Theological Union in Chicago and Washington Theological Union in Washington, D.C., which are sponsored by several religious congregations and orders, with notable professors and programs of mission studies, are the main Catholic academic programs for mission studies in the U.S.A. But they are not (with few exceptions) training the diocesan clergy in the nation.

seminary in the United States would feel it is necessary to include the subject of missiology in the curriculum. For a seminary faculty to say that this is included in ecclesiology or historical or biblical studies, is inadequate, even dubious. As Stephen Neill once observed, "If everything is mission, then nothing is mission," and similarly, "If everyone is responsible for mission, then no one is responsible."

In 1986 the Catholic Bishops of the United States, in their pastoral statement on world mission "To the Ends of the Earth," said, "Theological studies should include a strong missionary emphasis, so necessary for the formation of future priests and leaders" (1986:70). In *Redemptoris Missio*, John Paul II said, "Theological training cannot and should not ignore the Church's universal mission, ecumenism, the study of the great religions and missiology. I recommend that such studies should be undertaken especially in seminaries and in houses of formation for men and women, ensuring that some priests or other students specialize in the different fields of missiology" (RM 83; cf. 79). But nothing changed; it made little difference. A few years ago I asked a Catholic archbishop in the United States why his archdiocesan seminary offered no course in missiology. This was obviously a painful topic for him since his personal commitment to world mission was well known and he held a prominent position in a pontifical mission organization. He said to me, "You have to understand that I have very little influence with the seminary faculty and I have to be careful not to interfere with the curriculum." At that moment my Protestant preconception about the power of Catholic bishops was shattered.

There are some hopeful signs, however. In an eloquent address to the International Association of Catholic Missiologists in Rome in February 1999, Chicago's Francis Cardinal George, O.M.I., spoke about "The Promotion of Missiological Studies in Seminaries," in which he identified missiology as being "at the center of theological exploration of some of the most critical theological questions facing us today" (1999: 20f.). He urged that "the study of mission is intended for all seminarians, diocesan and religious alike," and he expressed the hope that in "the new millennium, missiology should be taken up with new vigor and sense of purpose" (ibid.:22, 25). In particular, he noted the need for some scholars with advanced studies in missiology "who are trained fundamental and dogmatic theologians, who can bring the mission focus to bear on the articulation of the issues in fundamental and dogmatic theology."[13] This is an extremely important strategic step for the mission of the Church and needs to be addressed by all those with responsibility for theological education and ministerial formation.

Despite the decline of mission studies in some seminaries in the West, there is the development of strong academic programs of mission studies in some parts of the non-Western world. Two impressive examples are the graduate school of Mission and Evangelism at the Presbyterian Theological Seminary in Seoul, Korea, and the Akrofi-Christaller Memorial Centre for Mission Research and Applied Theology in Akropong-Akuapem, Ghana.

We can also be encouraged by the growth and vitality of several professional associations for the advancement of mission studies, such as the American Society of Missiology, the Evangelical Missiological Society, the British and Irish Association for Mission Studies, the Deutsche Gesellschaft für Missionswissenschaft, the Nordic Institute of Missiology and Ecumenism, the Ecumenical Francophone Missiology Association, the Southern African Missiological Society, the International Association for Mission Studies, and the International Association of Catholic Missiologists.

7 CONCLUSION

There are good reasons to hope that the Church will be ready to reap the harvest with "the dawning of a new missionary age" in the Third Millennium which Pope John Paul II has envisioned as a time when "God is preparing a great springtime for Christianity" (RM 92, 86). The Church will again respond to Jesus' question, "Who do you say I am?" with Peter's answer, "You are the Messiah."

---

[13] Francis Cardinal George 1999:24. In 2000, the Mission Committee of the Conference of Major Superiors of Men's Institutes in the United States offered to provide one-day workshops, weekend workshops, and a basic course in mission theology for use in seminary formation, "given that electives in missiology are seldom chosen by seminarians for the priesthood because it is not now required by the Program of Priestly Formation and is seldom a perceived need [emphasis in the original] by students or deans" ("Some Proposals for One-Day Workshops, Weekend Workshops, and a Basic Course in Mission Theology for Use in Seminary, Formation," Conference of Major Superiors of Men, Silver Springs, MD, 2000:2).

BIBLIOGRAPHY

Anderson, Gerald H. (1996). "Theology of Religions: The Epitome of Mission Theology". In: Willem Saayman and Klippies Kritzinger (eds.). *Mission in Bold Humility: David Bosch's Work Considered*. Maryknoll, N.Y.: Orbis Books. Pp.: 113-120.

—. (1999). "Christian Mission in Our Pluralistic World". In: David W. Shenk and Linford Stutzman (eds.). *Practicing Truth: Confident Witness in Our Pluralistic World*. Scottdale, Pa.: Herald Press. Pp. 31-45.

Ariarajah, S. Wesley. (1999). "Christian Mission: The End or a New Beginning?". In: *New World Outlook*. May-June. Pp. 10-14.

Barth, Karl. (1960). "An Exegetical Study of Matthew 28:16-20". In: Gerald H. Anderson (ed.), *The Theology of the Christian Mission*, New York: McGraw--Hill. Pp. 55-71.

Bosch, David J. (1983). "The Structure of Mission: An Exposition of Matthew 28:16-20". In: Wilbert R. Shenk (ed.). *Exploring Church Growth*. Grand Rapids, Mich.: Wm. B. Eerdmans Publishing Co. Pp. 218-248.

—. (1991). *Transforming Mission: Paradigm Shifts in Theology of Mission*. Maryknoll, NY: Orbis Books.

Braaten, Carl E. (1980). "Who Do We Say That He Is? On the Uniqueness and Universality of Jesus Christ". In: *Occasional Bulletin of Missionary Research* 4, no. 1. Pp. 1-8.

Brockway, Allan R. (1988). "Learning Christology Through Dialogue with Jews". *Journal of Ecumenical Studies* 25. Pp. 347-357.

Bruner, F. Dale. (1990). *Matthew: A Commentary*. Vol. 2. Dallas: Word Publ.

Catholic Bishops of the United States. (1986). *"To the Ends of the Earth," A Pastoral Statement on World Mission*. Washington, D.C.: U.S. Catholic Conference.

Colzani,G. and P. Giglioni, and S. Karotemprel (eds.). (2001). *Cristologia e missione oggi*. Rome: Urbaniana University Press.

Davies, W.D., and Dale C. Allison. (1991). "Excursus XII". In: *A Critical and Exegetical Commentary on the Gospel According to Saint Matthew*. Vol. 2. (The International Critical Commentary). Edinburgh: T&T Clark. Pp. 594-601.

Geffré, Claude. (2001). "La prétention du christianisme à l'universel: Implications missiologiques". In: G. Colzani, P. Giglioni, S. Karotemprel (eds.), *Cristologia e Missione oggi*. Rome:Urbaniana University Press. Pp. 47-63.

George, Cardinal Francis (O.M.I.). (1999). "The Promotion of Missiological Studies in Seminaries". In: *Mission Studies* XVI-2. Pp. 13-27.

Henneberger, Melinda. (2002). "Vatican Says Jews: 'Wait for Messiah is Validated by the Old Testament'". In: *The New York Times*. January 18.

International Theological Commission. (1997). *Christianity and the World Religions*. Vatican City: Libreria Editrice Vaticana.

Manson, T.W. (1955). *Only to the House of Israel? Jesus and the Non-Jews*. London: Athlone Press. Reprinted Philadelphia: Fortress Press 1964.

Monti, Joseph E. (1984). *Who Do You Say That I Am?* New York: Paulist Press.

Ratzinger, Joseph Cardinal. (1994). "Reconciling Gospel and Torah: The Catechism". *Origins*. February 24.

Song, Choan-Seng. (1976). "From Israel to Asia: A Theological Leap". In: Gerald H. Anderson and Thomas F. Stransky (C.S.P.) (eds.). *Mission Trends*. No. 3: *Third World Theologies*. New York: Paulist Press. Pp. 211-222.

Soper, Edmund Davison. (1943). *The Philosophy of the Christian World Mission*. Nashville: Abingdon-Cokesbury Press.

3 Evangelists: Recovering a Lost Gift

Roger S. Greenway

1 INTRODUCTION

Evangelism of a confrontational kind first came to my attention when I was a young boy. My Uncle Case (Cornelius VanderJaagt) was the grandson of nineteenth century Dutch immigrants to America, and there never was a man with more zeal for telling people about Jesus than he. In his youth, he rebelled against his upbringing in a Christian home and church (Reformed Church in America) and for some years lived an immoral life. But one day the Lord took hold of him and he was radically converted. His repentance and contrition were so profound that he cried for three days. When finally he gained assurance of God's forgiveness, he set out to witness and evangelize everywhere he went. His zeal for confronting people with the good news of Jesus Christ knew no bounds. For example, his daily employment required that he travel throughout the State of Michigan, and he always carried with him a bucket of paint and a brush. He left his telltale mark—"Jesus saves! Are you saved?"—on rocks and bridges along every highway. Eventually the State authorities made him stop. He pleaded with the Reformed Church to become more active in evangelism, but the church did not know what to do with an evangelist like him. The consensus was that he should cool his enthusiasm. When his pleas for more evangelism were ignored, he turned away from the Reformed Church and for the remainder of his life worked as an independent evangelist.

There was little doubt that Uncle Case was an effective evangelist. Though he has been dead for four decades, I still hear stories about his boundless love for sinners and his marvelous way of explaining the gospel of God's liberating grace in Christ. Some of the stories are about the sensational methods he used to capture an audience. One method was to climb a lamp post in a sleazy part of town, shouting "Fire, Fire!" Soon a crowd would gather and shout back, "Where's the fire?" That question would launch him into preaching on "Hell—where you are all going unless you repent and turn to Jesus!" There are stories about Uncle Case's powerful voice (frankly, his voice scared me as a child), which served him well in open air preaching before electronic sound systems became common. A ninety-year old woman told me that when she was a young girl, her family could sit on the front porch of their house two blocks away from the Fulton Street Market (Grand Rapids) where Uncle Case was preaching and could hear every word he said.

Person after person has told me about a father, a grandfather, an uncle or some friend from years past, whose life was changed as a result of Uncle Case's ministry. But sadly, he left some bad stories behind him too, and invariably they had to do with money. As an independent evangelist, he was not accountable to a church or agency for the money he received from donors. He did not spend money on himself, but he failed to keep accurate records of the money he received or how he spent it. It was said that wherever he went he left a trail of unpaid bills behind him. To Uncle Case, raising money came easily. A favourite method was to warm up his supporters with tales of his evangelistic activities and then pull off a shoe, hold up a foot and expose the gaping holes in his socks. Then he roared: "Those holes were made doing the work of the Lord, but I don't have money for new socks!" As was expected, dollars poured in and donors asked no questions.

All my life I have asked myself the question: If instead of pushing Cornelius VanderJaagt aside, the Reformed Church had recognized in him the precious gift of evangelism, and had supported him in his efforts to spread the gospel, encouraged him to balance his zeal with discretion, helped him with financial accounts, and drawn the converts from his ministry into the church, how many rich benefits there might have been for the church, for him, and for other evangelistically gifted people who took him as their model? That is the question which I will address in this chapter. My contention is that the biblical gift of "evangelist" has been neglected by western churches and denominations and needs to be recovered.

2   WHO WERE THE EVANGELISTS?

Our study begins with a search for clarification concerning the meaning of the term "evangelist." The word "evangelist" appears only three time in the New Testament. In Acts 21:8, it is recorded that Paul and his party of missionaries arrived at the city of Caesarea and "stayed at the house of Philip the evangelist, one of the Seven."In Ephesians 4:11, which is a key verse for our present study, the Apostle Paul wrote that the ascended Christ bestowed gifts upon the church, giving " some to be apostles, some to be prophets, some to be evangelists, and some to be pastors and teachers." In Paul's final instructions to Timothy, recorded in 2 Timothy 4:5, he told Timothy to "do the work of an evangelist." There is no universal agreement as to the precise nature of these five categories of church leaders—apostles, prophets, evangelists, pastors and teachers. The absence of the article before "teachers" may imply that pastors and teachers formed a single group, as they both ministered to individual congregations (TDNT:VI,497). Early Christians understood the different charismata because they knew people who functioned in these ministries, spreading the gospel and developing churches. But in the course of time the distinctions became less clear, especially as ministries that began as vital functions in a dynamic spiritual environment became formal, institutionalized offices.

The role of evangelist as a distinct charismata given by Christ to his church has been relatively neglected among scholars. Far more attention has been given to the office of pastor than to that of evangelist, even though the New Testament refers to congregational leaders as pastors only once (Eph.4:11). The disregard for evangelists can be seen in the Belgic Confession, one of the basic standards of Reformed churches, which speaks of ministers, elders and deacons but says nothing about evangelists as having an office in the church. Today, the office of evangelist is almost unheard of in major denominations in the west. Evangelists such as Billy Graham are respected for what they have contributed to world evangelization. Billy Graham in particular has done a great deal to improve the work of evangelists. Nevertheless, evangelists do not fit the official scheme of things as far as most churches and denominations are concerned. Consequently, the gift of evangelist has been neglected, and churches have been preoccupied with internal matters at the expense of outreach.[1]

The word "evangelist" (*euangelistès*) means "preacher of the gospel." It is rooted in the Greek words *euangelion* (gospel, good news) and *euangelizomai, euangelizesthai* (to gospelise, preach the gospel, bring, announce good news), which are used a total of 132 times in the New Testament. The basic meaning of "evangelist" is a teller, a bringer of good news, particularly to people who have not heard it before. In that sense Jesus was an evangelist (9 occurrences in the four Gospels, and also in Eph. 2:17 and 1 Peter 4:6). The archangel Gabriel acted as an evangelist (Luke 1:19 and 2:10). John the Baptist was an evangelist (Luke 3:18), as were the twelve disciples (Luke 9:6). Members of the early church proclaimed good news, as did the apostles. God himself is

---

[1] It should be noted that the Christian Reformed Church of North America took a major step toward correcting this "misplacement" in 1978, when it established a fourth office, that of evangelist. This decision came after nearly 70 years of serious study and debate. The report adopted by the synod of that year contains valuable material on the subject.

described as an evangelist (Acts 10:36; Heb. 4:2; 4:6; Rev. 10:7). An angel is depicted in Revelation 14:6 as flying through the sky proclaiming an eternal gospel to those who live on the earth. Besides the numerous uses of *euangelion* and *euangelizesthai*, the New Testament contains scores of synonyms to describe the range of activities that fall under the rubric of evangelism (Barrett 1987:15). It is, however, in the New Testament description of Philip's ministry that we learn specific details about a man who functioned as an evangelist and bore the title.[2]

3   PHILIP THE EVANGELIST

In Acts 21:8, Philip is called "the evangelist," and the description found in Acts regarding Philip's character and ministry provides a vivid example of an early evangelist and his work. Compared with Peter and Paul, Philip played a secondary role. Nevertheless, Philip's role was crucial for the spread of the gospel, which makes it puzzling that New Testament scholarship has virtually ignored Philip (Scott Spencer 1992). Could this neglect be somehow related to the misplacement of the role of evangelist in the churchly scheme of things? For our purposes, Philip the evangelist deserves careful attention.

The first reference to Philip is Acts 6:5, where he is listed among the first "deacons," men chosen to administer the daily distribution of food to the widows affiliated with the church in Jerusalem. These men were known to be persons of faith and integrity. Their work of humble service to needy women freed the apostles to concentrate on "prayer and the ministry of the word" (v.4), thereby providing a basic structure for the word-and-deed witness of the church. After they were chosen by the group of believers (v.5), the seven men were presented to the apostles, "who prayed and laid their hands on them" (v.6). Under this arrangement, "the word of God spread" (v.7).

Philip appears again in Acts 8, where the record shows that Philip demonstrated a great passion for bringing the liberating message of Jesus Christ to people bound by religious traditions that did not offer salvation (John 4:22). The people were Samaritans, close neighbours of the Jews who despised and avoided them. Jesus had commanded the disciples to take the message of the kingdom to the Samaritans (Acts

---

[2] Barrett lists 153 current English meanings of 42 New Testament Greek verbs related to evangelize. He states that down through the centuries the English usage of the term has come to connote most closely six synonyms, which he calls The Big Six—the words preach, bring, tell, proclaim, announce, declare (1987:18f.).

1:8), and Jesus himself had left an example of ministry to Samaritans (John 4:40f.). Nevertheless, Philip's bold initiative of going to a city in Samaria and preaching Christ there was a breakthrough in New Testament evangelism. Later, the Apostle Peter would preach the gospel to the Gentile centurion, Cornelius (Acts 10), but that event had not yet occurred when Philip evangelized Samaria. Philip's actions were an indication that he possessed the evangelist's special gift, in that he carried the gospel where others had not yet gone.

God blessed Philip's efforts in evangelism. Philip "proclaimed the Christ" in Samaria, and when the crowds heard him, many responded, with the result that there was "great joy in that city" (Acts 8:7f.). In addition to many conversions, God showed his approval of what Philip did and said in Samaria by granting miraculous signs, healings and exorcisms. In contrast to some so-called evangelists today, Philip did not have to "advertise" himself as an effective evangelist because the evidence of divine empowerment was plain for everyone to see. Philip's nemesis, Simon the sorcerer, was astonished by the miracles he saw and tried to buy the power for himself (Acts 8:19).

When Philip crossed the ethnic and cultural borders that separated Jews and Samaritans and preached the gospel in Samaria, he did so as a spokesman for Jesus Christ without a direct mandate from the church authorities in Jerusalem. At the same time, he and his ministry were not independent from the church and its apostolic leaders. In Acts 8:14-17, we read that when the apostles in Jerusalem heard that Samaritans had accepted the word of God through Philip's work, they sent Peter and John to evaluate what had happened. When the apostles saw what had taken place, they were pleased. They recognized what was lacking in terms of the baptisms Philip had performed, and they prayed that the Samaritans might receive the Holy Spirit. They placed their hands on the converts who then received the Holy Spirit (Acts 8:15-17). On their way home, Peter and John showed they had learned from Philip's example. They did a new thing for apostles to do: they themselves evangelized Samaritans (Acts 8:25).

Philip the evangelist was gifted in such a way that he could bring the gospel effectively to large crowds, as he did in Samaria, and also to lone individuals, including people of different races and stations in life. When an angel sent him, apparently with no explanation, to a desert road and told him to approach a stranger from another country riding in a chariot, Philip made no "fuss," nor asked questions, but obeyed the angel's order eagerly (Acts 8:29f.). The stranger turned out to be an "Ethiopian eunuch," a man of power and high social status from a country beyond Egypt, whom God in some mysterious way had prepared for an encounter with Philip and the gospel. Philip "ran" to fulfill his calling (Acts 8:30), for he had a passion for people whoever they might be. Sitting beside the Ethiopian, Philip did what evangelists do: he explained the Scriptures, led the man to Christ, and later baptized him (Acts 8:26-39). In this case, there was no further contact between them, nor between the Ethiopian and the apostles. The Ethiopian went on his way rejoicing, and Philip went back to evangelizing city people (Acts 8:39f.). Among many lessons, the story teaches us that the Holy Spirit works in peoples' lives long before sacred encounters occur when they hear evangelists speak of Christ. True evangelists respond obediently to the Spirit's promptings even though at the moment they cannot explain why.[3]

We should note also that Philip was not always itinerating. At a certain point in his life he became resident in the city of Caesarea, a largely Roman city on the Mediterranean coast. As a port city with a varied population and connections with other ports around the Mediterranean, Caesarea was an excellent location for an evangelist to live and work. Acts 21:8-9 says that Paul and his party, *en route* to Jerusalem, "reached Caesarea and stayed at the house of Philip the evangelist, one of the Seven. He had four unmarried daughters who prophesied." The fact that at this stage in his ministry Philip was resident in a particular place did not change his calling as an evangelist. He was still "the evangelist," and residency in a city like Caesarea probably enhanced his effectiveness. Philip's ministry in Caesarea included being faithful as a husband and father, the fruit of which appeared in the form of four godly daughters who bore witness to Christ as their father did.[4]

---

[3] Scott Spencer 1992:158. Spencer contrasts Philip's ready response to Peter's initial indignation at the thought of mingling with "unclean" Gentiles. Philip, says the author, "acts more like Isaiah in his willing compliance with the Lord's purpose" ("Here am I! Send me").

[4] Rev. 19:10 indicates that pointing to Jesus Christ is the very essence of prophecy. In the early days of the church there were numerous prophets, and Christians perceived that their faith was verified by the presence of prophets among them. Jesus was the great prophet promised long before in Deut. 18:18. With his coming, prophecy was fulfilled and revived, as Peter made clear on the day of Pentecost, when he interpreted what was happening by quoting the prophet Joel: "This is what was spoken by the prophet Joel, I will pour out my Spirit on all people. Your sons and daughters will prophesy, your young men will see visions, your old men will dream dreams. Even on

4   TIMOTHY, THE PASTOR-EVANGELIST

In his two letters to Timothy, the Apostle Paul counselled Timothy regarding the duties and responsibilities of pastoral leadership in a local church. Timothy had been Paul's helper from the time of Paul's second missionary journey, he was relatively young and somewhat timid, and now he was working, probably on an interim basis, as the principal leader and teacher of the church at Ephesus. Timothy had plenty of difficulties to deal with: false teachers, immoral people, women who caused trouble, an absence of good organization in the church, slaves whose attitudes discredited the Christian faith, rich people who were proud and domineering, quarrels and controversies of many sorts and the inner temptation to give up the ministry. After many words of instruction and warning, Paul adds: "Keep your head in all situations, endure hardship, do the work of (an) evangelist, discharge all the duties of your ministry" (1 Tim. 4:5).

After reviewing all the things Timothy was expected to do as a church leader, it would seem cruel for Paul to add yet another array of responsibilities, things associated with the work of an evangelist. Pastoring a church like that of Ephesus was more than enough work. Dare Paul expect Timothy to do more? It is not clear in my mind whether Paul, now in prison, regarded Timothy as primarily an evangelist who for a time was resident in Ephesus for the purpose of setting the young church in order, or whether Paul now saw Timothy as a pastor in a local congregation. We need not settle the question, because the instructions Paul gave are applicable to leadership situations in churches and mission situations everywhere. When God's blessing on evangelists' work results in converts being won and new groups of believers formed, the evangelists very often must remain with them for some time. Evangelists in that situation function as pastors of new believers who need to be established in the faith, protected from false teachers and introduced to the many dimensions of discipleship. For this reason, evangelists require some pastoral skills, and if they are church-planting evangelists, they require the skills of group leadership

---

my servants, both men and women, I will pour out my Spirit in those days, and they will prophesy." The content of true prophecy was none other than the prophet, Jesus himself. The great proclaimer was also the message proclaimed. Cf. Green 1970: 200, who also describes the prominent role that women played in the spread of the gospel during the early centuries, 175-178.

and church organization. As one who has served as an evangelistic missionary in Asia, a church planter in Latin America and an inner city pastor in North America, I attest to the contemporary relevance of everything Paul wrote to Timothy.

What, then, is the force of Paul's statement to Timothy, "Do the work of (an) evangelist, discharge all the duties of your ministry?" A clue to the answer may be the absence in Greek of the definite article before the word evangelist. This suggests that it was not Paul's intention to assign Timothy a second job, but instead to stress the evangelistic character of all pastoral duties. It is as if Paul were saying: Timothy, your pastoral work should reveal an evangelistic flavour throughout. You are a gospel-preacher wherever you go, and even though you currently minister to a congregation you must keep your eyes open for lost sheep. You must expect to experience opposition just as evangelists do. Above all, the message of the gospel must be central in your ministry. Let nothing stop you, but with the commitment and perseverance that characterize evangelists, discharge your gospel-ministry to the full. Remember that you are never a pastor without being an evangelist as well.[5]

Many Christian leaders are calling for missionary (or missional) congregations, churches that look outward toward a world in deep distress instead of being preoccupied with internal matters. However, missionary congregations are not likely to develop until pastors take seriously Paul's instruction to Timothy and give evangelism the place it should have in their ministries. Pastors fulfill their leadership in evangelism in three ways: by teaching and preaching evangelism from the Scriptures, by modelling evangelism in their lives and ministries, and by organizing (or allowing gifted evangelists to organize) the congregations for evangelistic ministries in their communities. When church members are motivated and instructed by their leaders' words and example, they are more likely to live, serve and speak in ways that draw others to Christ and the church.

Show me any place in the world where the gospel is advancing and churches are growing, and I will show you leaders, however humble

---

[5] Hendriksen 1957:312. Richard Stoll Armstrong exclaims: "Evangelism is not just one thing among many that a pastor does. It is the heart of everything a pastor does! If we have no concern about, no interest in, no sense of responsibility for sharing the good news, what are we doing in the ministry? How can we fulfill our ministry if we are not doing the work of an evangelist?" (1990:13).

they may be by human standards, who take seriously Paul's instruction to Timothy to make evangelism a vital part of their ministry. By the same token, show me churches that are in decline and I will have no difficulty pointing out breakdowns in pastoral leadership and failure to discharge the evangelistic dimensions of the pastoral office. It is a sad fact that many churches that are in serious decline are located in places of great spiritual need, but their leaders and members lack the vision and will to evangelize. Charles Goodell's book, now long out of print, has been to me a source of inspiration and instruction. In it, Goodell says the following about the pastor as evangelist:

> Lost people, like lost sheep, do not come home of themselves. They have to be sought. It is not enough to build your church and to stand in your pulpit and say 'Come.' You have to go out and seek, if you would save. When the passion for souls dies out, then all sense of the reality of religion perishes. It is when we see Him healing people that we have faith in the great physician; it is when we see the lost being saved that we believe in Christianity, and when the passion for the lost dies out in the pulpit, people will shiver around its cold ashes instead of warming their souls at the blaze of a light that was kindled in the heavens. Let us get then a clear conception of what the pastor is. The pastoral function is nothing more nor less than to watch over the sheep and to bring those who are straying back into the fold. Is it not time to go back to the one business for which the Church of God was organized and inspired? (Goodell 1922:110).

5   PASTORS' COMPLAINTS

At a consultation held in Thailand I heard pastors from various parts of the world complain that they felt victimized because they lacked the time and training to engage in various special ministries, particularly evangelism, that church members demanded. They complained especially about para-church mission agencies that could offer better programs, hire the staff they needed, and focus on evangelism in a way that churches could not do. The pastors pointed out that para-church organizations are structured differently than churches, they focus on a few things that they learn to do very well, and they often enjoy great success in achieving their goals. Pastors of churches, on the other hand, have to accept a broad range of tasks from preaching two or three times a week, to counseling troubled families, conducting weddings and funerals, teaching ladies' societies, comforting the sick and elderly, working with youth and fulfilling denominational responsibilities. Having been a pastor myself, I could sympathize with the pastors

gathered in Thailand. Though few of them realized it, they were victims
of a blunder that churches made long ago when the office of evangelist
was eclipsed, and the responsibility for promoting both the internal
health of the church and its external witness to the world came to rest on
the pastors. When Christ's gift of evangelists was ignored, or redefined
to mean something else, the stage was set for a series of things to
happen.

One of the consequences was the growth of para-church mission
organizations staffed by gifted men and women who found in these
organizations opportunities to use their gifts in ways that churches did
not provide. I do not agree with some who have virtually given up on the
church as far as evangelism is concerned. Forty-three years of ministry,
most of it in missions and evangelism, have strengthened my conviction
that when local churches enjoy the leadership of pastors who are committed to evangelism, and the pastors have the necessary training and
assistance, churches take back seat to no other organizations in drawing
sinners to Christ and nurturing them over the long haul to faithful and
responsible discipleship. What is needed in the churches is the recovery
of a precious, spiritual gift.

A second complaint that I heard from the pastors gathered in
Thailand was that they did not know how to increase evangelism in their
personal ministries or in their congregations. Many of them felt guilty
over the decline of their churches. They resented it when evangelism-
minded church members poured their energies into para-church missionary organizations. But the pastors did not know where to turn. Their
dilemma could be traced in part to the schools where they had been
trained for the ministry. Evangelism tends to have the same importance
in churches that it has in the seminaries where pastors are trained. For
that reason, our concern for church-based evangelism takes us to the
schools where church leaders are formed. What is needed in most
seminaries is the recovery of the importance of evangelism and the place
Christ intended it to have in the church and its ministry.

In the latter part of the 20th century, few people knew more about
seminaries around the world and how well they do in producing
pastor-evangelists than James F. Hopewell, who was associated with the
Theological Education Fund from its beginning in 1958. In his official
position with the Fund, Hopewell visited hundreds of theological
institutions around the world with the specific purpose of evaluating
their effectiveness. Defining "mission" as the witness Christians make
outside the normal circle of churches and "candidate" as persons being

prepared by theological institutions for a career in Christian service, Hopewell wrote the following:

> The problem is that surprisingly few candidates are prepared to engage in that mission with any consistency or accuracy. And while this fault may be attributed to most any aspect of modern church structure, it seems particularly encouraged by the pattern of theological education now practised in most seminaries around the world...Most of the factors that comprise our understanding of typical theological education have been unconsciously designed, to avoid, and therefore to hinder, the basic Christian intention of mission. And I do not mean to beat the anti-intellectual drum against higher learning. What rather concerns an increasing number of critics is that the very tool of higher learning has been misappropriated to perform a third-rate job for a second-rate church structure. In a time when our understanding of the ministry more and more implies its dynamic, missionary function, we continue to rely upon a system of preparation which at its roots is essentially static and isolationist (Hopewell 1956:158-63).

I have lectured in seminaries in many parts of the world, and what I observed leads me to agree with Hopewell's assessment. Few candidates for the pastoral ministry receive the kind of training they need for effective leadership in evangelism, and the results are plainly visible in the churches. However, I believe the problem is not simply the deficiencies in seminary curriculums. The problem lies in a one-sided emphasis on the office of pastors to the neglect of the role of evangelists. What would it take for the training of evangelists to be put on the same level of importance as the preparation of pastors? To begin with, it would require re-educating churches and denominations regarding the gift of evangelism and its importance in Christian ministry. Pastors would have to take more seriously the two-sided nature of their calling, to feed and care for their members and with equal fervour to carry the gospel to the world beyond. Seminaries would have to re-work their curriculums to give proper emphasis to evangelism. But such changes will not take place until the lost gift is rediscovered, Christ's gift of evangelists, which like the finding of a pearl of enormous value has the potential for affecting everything, from the churches' vision to their structures, priorities, ministries and budgets.

6   THE OFFICE OF EVANGELIST

In 1978, the synod of the Christian Reformed Church in North America established a "fourth office," that of evangelist, besides the three traditional offices of minister, elder and deacon. This decision came after four decades of struggle over the place of layworkers in evangelism in the structure of the church. Years of study and countless reports clarified the need for giving ecclesiastical authority to those who do the work of evangelism on behalf of the churches. Evangelists now are able to bring the Word and administer the sacraments in emerging congregations and also in organized congregations alongside the pastors. (Special concessions are made for organized churches among the Native American population.) A concern expressed in the study committee reports which led up to synod's decision was that gifted evangelists should focus on evangelism. Evangelists might be appointed to work at some distance from the churches that called them, or they might work in and through those very same churches. In the latter case they would complement the work of the pastors and lead church members in witnessing to unsaved neighbours. The form used by the CRCNA for the ordination of evangelists describes their work clearly:

> The work of an evangelist is to preach the good news. He calls people to heed the voice of the good Shepherd, who laid down His life for the sheep, and urges them in the name of Christ to be reconciled to God. He also gathers new believers into an emerging congregation, where he ministers the Word and sacraments. Evangelists are treated as elders by the congregations that call and ordain them. Although every believer is called to bear witness to Christ, and every elder, deacon, and minister is called to engage in the work of evangelism, the evangelist is called to this work as his primary task, under the supervision of the consistory.

The Church Order (Article 23) of the CRCNA adds to the duties of an evangelist an important element: they should equip the believers, young and old, to participate in the work of evangelism.[6] There may be no

---

[6] The decision by the CRCNA Synod 1978 was a major step forward in terms of recovering the evangelistic gift in the churches. In line with this decision and in cooperation with the Board of Home Missions of the CRCNA, Calvin Theological Seminary, introduced in 2001 a Masters program for persons preparing for evangelistic church planting, with courses offered in Spanish as well as English. Unfortunately, a subsequent denominational study committee has given in to pressures from church staff workers to receive more recognition by ordaining them as evangelists. Synod 2001 gave its initial approval to this, pending a final decision by a future synod. If approved, it would mean that almost everyone working for the churches, directors of youth ministries, music directors, worship leaders and other staff positions could potentially be authorized to administer the sacraments under the title

better way to overcome the evangelistic sterility of many churches than the calling of trained and gifted evangelists, to work in, around and beyond established congregations, inspiring and instructing members of all ages to reach out and draw people to Christ. The challenge for churches like the CRCNA that recognize the "fourth office," will be to keep the focus of evangelists on their primary task, namely, evangelism. Many pressures will appear to pull them in other directions.

7 REQUIREMENTS FOR EVANGELISTS

Churches and denominations can be expected to differ as to the requirements for the ordination of evangelists. Like Philip the evangelist in Acts, evangelists must be active church members with a proven record of faithful service. They should be recommended without reservation by their consistory or council. In addition they should have enough general education and specialized training to be able to function effectively among the people with whom they will be working. I do not believe that churches should be rigid on the matter of educational qualifications. Requirements should be "contextualized" to fit each situation. For example, I know of an effective evangelist working in Michigan who has only a high school education. He relates easily with the "blue collar" people among whom he goes calling daily. He knows the Bible, loves the people, and over the years has drawn scores of people to Christ and the church. In urban populations evangelists need to qualify in special ways. It is more important that urban evangelists speak the language of the people and understand their culture than that they have achieved a certain academic level. In connection with this point I see great wisdom in the guidelines given by the CRCNA Synod of 1973, which state:

> Because the Scriptures do not present definitive, exhaustive descriptions of the particular ministries of the church, and because these particular ministries as described in Scripture are functional in character, the Bible leaves room for the church to adapt or modify its

---

of "evangelists." Just about any staff worker could be ordained as an "evangelist." While it is true that every church worker, as every church member, is a witness for Jesus Christ and there are evangelistic dimensions to every service performed in Christ's name, when everyone is an "evangelist," very soon no one is an evangelist. Then the particular focus of the office of evangelist, which is outward toward the unsaved, unchurched and uncared for, is soon lost.

particular ministries in order to carry out effectively its service to
Christ and for Christ in all circumstances (Guideline 12).

In most cases, evangelists will need and want some specialized training.
Even those who already hold academic degrees will probably need
further training in communication, intercultural understanding, major
non-Christian religions, practical ministry skills and the kind of insights
that can be acquired only by working alongside seasoned evangelists.
No one should equate formal, academic training with preparedness for
evangelism. Missions at home and overseas have suffered too often
because of ill-prepared workers with prestigious diplomas. Before
evangelists are approved and ordained they should prove themselves to
the churches in terms of their faith and godliness, their knowledge of
Scripture, Christian doctrine and the Church Order. They must present
recommendations from people who have known them for considerable
time and who testify that indeed they have the character and gifts
expected of evangelists. They must have their personal lives in order.
Candidates for ordination as evangelists must be able to communicate
the gospel orally before audiences and in one-to-one situations. They
must love people, and have a passion for working with unbelievers with
a view to making them disciples of Christ. Whether seminaries as we
know them are fit to train evangelists remains an open question in my
mind. If seminaries want to be used in this way, they will have to
develop special programs in close conjunction with people who
understand evangelism, as Calvin Theological Seminary has recently
done.

8   TWO MEN ON THEIR KNEES IN THE SNOW

When I attended Calvin Seminary in the 1950s, Professor Henry
Schultze was our professor of New Testament. He was an old man by
that time, and his voice was so feeble that we literally had to sit at his
feet in order to catch his words. One day he was speaking to us about 2
Timothy 4. When he came to the words, "Do the work of an evangelist,"
he launched into a story that went like this: "Boys (he always called us
boys), some years ago I attended an all day meeting about some church
matters at the Manor House (a downtown hotel in Grand Rapids). It was
February, and there was a lot of snow outside. Late in the afternoon we
concluded the meeting, put on our coats and about five us went out the
side door to the street. Suddenly, we stopped and stared at what we saw.
In front of us, their knees in the dirty wet snow, were two men praying
by the running board of a car. One man was sobbing, and the other had

his arm around him and was praying for him. I recognized the man praying. He was an evangelist by the name of Case Vanderjaagt. (The professor had no idea Case was my grandmother's brother.) Boys, we ministers were all dressed in fine woolen suits, and we didn't move for a full minute. The same thought went through all our minds: 'I've never done that. I wouldn't do that, get my suit wet and dirty kneeling in the snow with a stranger.' Quietly, we moved away. None of us ever forgot what we'd seen. Boys, don't neglect evangelism! It's been our churches' weak point too long. With everything else they expect of you, do the work of evangelists!"

If Uncle Case were alive today, maybe he wouldn't have to go independent.

BIBLIOGRAPHY

Barrett, David B. (1987). *Evangelize! A Historical Survey of the Concept.* Birmingham, AL: New Hope.
Hendriksen, William. (1957). *New Testament Commentary: Exposition of the Pastoral Epistles.* Grand Rapids, MI: Baker Book House.
Goodell, Charles L. (1992). *Pastor and Evangelist.* New York: George H. Doran.
Green, Michael. (1970). *Evangelism in the Early Church.* London: Hodder and Stoughton Ltd.
Hopewell, James F. (1956). "Preparing the Candidate for Mission". *International Review of Missions* 56. Pp. 158-63.
Scott Spencer, F. (1992). "The Portrait of Philip in Acts: A Study of Roles and Relations". In: *Journal for the Study of the New Testament, Supplement Series* 67. Sheffield, England: Sheffield Academic Press Ltd. P. 13.
Stoll Armstrong, Richard. (1990). *The Pastor-Evangelist in the Parish.* Louisville, Ky: Westminster/John Knox Press.
Theological Dictionary of the New Testament. Vol.VI. Gerhard Friedrich (ed.). (1968). Grand Rapids, MI.: Wm.B. Eerdmans Publ. Company. (TDNT).

4   A Contemporary Window to Eternity: Christian Faith and the Search for Meaning in Contemporary Secularized Culture

Henry Jansen

1   INTRODUCTION : CHRISTIAN FAITH AND CONTEMPORARY CULTURE

Religious perspectives and worldviews in general have to do with answering fundamental questions of human existence (see Vroom 1989:329). If a religion succeeds in gaining converts, it does so in the conviction that it conveys the truth in a way that cannot be found in other religions, however much the adherents of that religion may respect other religions for the truth that they have to offer. In relating the story of how Christianity came to Northumbria (York), St. Bede records a speech reputedly made by one of King Edwin's thanes during the debate on whether to accept or to reject the Christian faith:

> Your Majesty, when we compare the present life of man on earth with that time of which we have no knowledge, it seems to me like the swift flight of a single sparrow through the banqueting-hall where you are sitting at dinner on a winter's day with your thanes and counselors. In the midst there is a comforting fire to warm the hall; outside, the storms of winter rain or snow are raging. This sparrow flies swiftly in through one door of the hall and out through another. While he is inside, he is safe from the winter storms; but after a few moments of comfort, he vanishes from sight into the wintry world from which he came. Even so, man appears on earth for a little while; but of what went before this life or of what follows, we know nothing. Therefore, if this new teaching has brought any more certain knowledge, it seems only right that we should follow it (St. Bede 1955:II.13,127).

This speech proved to be the turning point in the debate and the occasion for the conversion of the population of this part of ancient England. Obviously, it was clear to the council that Christianity gave "more certain knowledge" of "what went before this life [and] of what follows."

The theme of this volume is the fullness of life for all. The above quotation certainly has to do with this fullness of life. According to this speech, the lives of the Anglo-Saxon inhabitants of England were enriched by this new teaching. Can Christianity do the same in our contemporary secularized culture? The word "secularized" is most significant in attempting to provide an answer to this question. The people of the culture in which the thane made his speech were asking questions about the finitude of human life and the meaning of human life in light of this finitude. It was open to the answers provided by Christianity because it shared the latter's belief in the transcendent: something that went beyond that which could be experienced in empirical existence here and now. In contrast to that situation, contemporary society seems to have succumbed to the triumph of empiricism: if human life is meaningful, that meaningfulness needs to be elucidated in terms of here and now, in terms of results that can be measured and seen, as opposed to "what went before this life [and] of what follows."

How do we convey the fullness of life that the Gospel has to offer to our contemporary, secularized society? What points of contact can be found in society for the Gospel? Ironically, perhaps, it is this very empirical approach to existence that can provide an opening for churches in our society today. The stress on the here and now of human (and creaturely) life creates a vacuum that is felt in contemporary society. The fundamental issue here is similar to that expressed by the thane in Northumbria more than a millennium ago: can we find more certain knowledge of the mystery surrounding our lives? In many respects, though not exclusively so, a search for meaning is present in our society as well. This is not to say that this is the only question with which our society is concerned. There are different points of contact to be found, such as the question of guilt and responsibility, also present in contemporary society. Nonetheless, the search for meaning is an important question and one that provides a point of contact as well. Moreover, these various questions are often interrelated. As we will see below, the issue of atonement, understood as "at-onement" in the world with respect to the issue of meaning, is also one that has to do with responsibility. To understand "meaning" one must also have a notion of "responsibility"; to understand "responsibility" one must also be able to ascribe "meaning" to one's actions.

In this essay I will first describe certain manifestations of the search for meaning that we encounter in contemporary society. In this description I will have recourse to contemporary literature, since the stories that are told and heard in our society also deal with these fundamental questions of human existence. The stories we tell and wish to hear are often those that interpret reality and through which we ascribe a place to our own lives (on this see Jansen 2001:13). I will then attempt to provide some practical guidelines as to how the church can use this search as a point of contact for the communication of the fullness of life for all that is the offer of the Christian Gospel. Precisely because the search for meaning is not merely a theoretical concern, but a question of here and now; the Christian church can use this here and now.

2   THE SEARCH FOR MEANING IN CONTEMPORARY SECULARIZED SOCIETY

The mood or habit of mind of contemporary society can be characterized in many respects as postmodern.[1] By this we mean a relativism with respect to all truth claims and, by extension, all claims to finding meaning in existence. Postmodernism rejects the idea that there is a purpose that guides history as a whole. If there is a purpose that guides the individual life, this purpose is initiated by individuals or the circumstances in which they find themselves. This distinguishes the postmodern mood from that of the pre-modern and the modern: there is no external (God, revelation) or internal (self-evident truths derived through experience or reason) authority which can provide such a master plan or even the idea of one. Many postmodern thinkers, be they novelists, philosophers and or theologians concur in rejecting this notion.[2] Though this idea may seem theoretically acceptable, the concept has profound implications for society as a whole.

What has been lost in this rejection is any consensus or certainty as to the direction in which society is to develop. Because there is no longer a common vision for society, there is also no place within the whole for an individual human life. People are thus at a loss to find purpose for their lives. This has had a twofold effect on the lives of individuals. On the one hand, one can speak of an effect with respect to ethics. The increasingly sole moral principle operative in the contemporary period is that one should not harm others. Cruelty determines the bottom line of what is permitted. In a liberal society cruelty constitutes the worst that one can do (Rorty 1989:xv). In popular language, anything is permitted as long as nobody gets hurt and the ones

---

[1] I am using the term postmodern here in a loose sense and not in reference to a particular school of thought, whether philosophical, theological or literary. Certainly, any use of the term will have some reference to these areas and their representative thinkers. Nonetheless, the term can also be used to describe a general mood in society, as can also be done with the terms modernity and Romanticism, with reference to questions and positions that are more or less assumed.

[2] On her rejection of the idea of larger purpose or goal to existence, see Iris Murdoch 1971:78.

involved are consenting adults. On the other hand, many also display a dissatisfaction with the direction that their lives have taken. Some become involved in other religions or new religious movements such as New Age in a search for purpose in their lives. Others make radical adjustments in their priorities. One hears stories of people who, having been successful in their careers, suddenly give up their careers to work in the care sector of society, devoting themselves to volunteer service in a hospital, care facility, or hospice. The phenomenon of the immense popularity of the Harry Potter books and the film version of J.R.R. Tolkien's *Lord of the Rings* cannot be ignored. One possible explanation for this could be that in these books and films people find a way of admitting the notion of transcendence into their lives, even if it is only restricted to the world of the imagination. This too, however, may also be indicative of a fundamental need in contemporary society. Many people appear to be dissatisfied with a purely empirical view of their existence and are searching for ways in which they can find meaning and purpose.

This search for meaning can also be detected in contemporary novels. Contemporary authors like the Dutch writer Cees Nooteboom, the American writer John Irving, as well as the English writer Ian McEwan demonstrate a struggle with the significance of what they write. This is a profound change from the conception of the author in the Victorian novel or of pre-modern literature, who was fully capable of transcribing the innermost thoughts and feelings of his or her characters, deciding, willy-nilly, what the outcome of a story could be. In a pre- or anti-modern setting, such an omniscient and omnipotent stance of the writer could be attributed to revelation.[3] The writer was given insight into the reality of the human situation and the end of human history through God's revelation. In modernity (understood here as the philosophical and ideological tradition flowing from the Enlightenment), the notion of revelation disappeared and an increasing emphasis was placed on the ability of human beings, on the basis of reason and/or empirical evidence, to discover the plot of history itself and how human stories could end. One of the primary examples of the change in the conception of the author in the contemporary period was the publication of John Fowles' *The French Lieutenant's Woman* in 1969. In this novel the author constantly distances himself from influencing the outcome of the novel by juxtaposing three different endings, the first of which is

---

[3] See Spark, and the discussion in Jansen 2001:50.

completely Victorian (the omniscient and omnipotent author), the second more in line with the early twentieth century and the last post-modern. The Victorian ending has the novel end happily with a marriage between the two main characters. The second ending does not include marriage, but this development seems to be in the offing. In the last ending, the main character rejects the possibility of marriage and chooses freedom, which for Fowles represents the main theological principle of our time as opposed to the notion of authority. The author cannot influence the ending of his novel: the characters must remain free. Novels, therefore, like the future, remain open-ended. Authors must yield their control of the outcome of the story and not succumb to the temptation to omniscience and omnipotence.

Fowles' novel is powerful in bringing this freedom to expression. But now, more than thirty years later, what is the outcome of this change? An important consequence of this development can be seen in McEwan's novel *Atonement*. Towards the end of the novel we find the main character, Briony Tallis, a successful author herself, musing:

> No one will care what events and which individuals were misrepresented to make a novel. I know there's always a certain kind of reader who will be compelled to ask, But what *really* happened? The answer is simple: the lovers survive and flourish. As long as there is a single copy, a solitary typescript of my final draft, then my spontaneous, fortuitous sister and her medical prince survive to love.
>
> The problem of these fifty-nine years has been this: how can a novelist achieve atonement when, with her absolute power of deciding outcomes, she is also God? There is no one, no entity or higher form that she can appeal to, or be reconciled with, or that can forgive her. There is nothing outside her. In her imagination she has set the limits and the terms. No atonement for God, or novelists, even if they are atheists. It was always an impossible task, and that was precisely the point. The attempt was all (371).

This passage concerns an act which Briony performed as a thirteen-year-old girl, which resulted in her sister's lover being sent to jail on a rape conviction and, indirectly, in the early deaths of her sister and her lover in World War II. Briony has written a manuscript which tells, finally, the truth about the events in question. But the manuscript cannot be published until all parties directly involved are dead because otherwise the publishing company and Briony could be sued. It is because of this delayed publishing of the manuscript that Briony wonders whether it will make any difference.

In referring to herself as God, Briony seems to be regressing to the Victorian mode of thinking about the novelist. The novelist can influence what the characters do and can have insight into the thoughts her characters have. However, here it is a decidedly different view of the author as God that comes to the fore. This is not the author who, on the basis of her omniscience, writes what is the case. Rather, this is the author who reconstructs the events to make something else of the story. Briony thus rewrites the story to make some attempt at atonement for what she has done, revising the plot and recasting Robbie and Cecilia to resemble the main characters in a play, The *Trials of Arabella* (a play which appears to have been written as a standard Victorian romance), which she had written as a thirteen-year-old girl to celebrate her brother's homecoming. The writer's task, it seems, is to rewrite the story in order to save the characters.

One also finds this perspective in McEwan's American contemporary, John Irving, a postmodern writer who, like Briony, has a penchant for the nineteenth-century novel. In "Trying to Save Piggy Sneed," Irving relates a story from his youth in which a mentally handicapped man, Piggy Sneed, was burned to death in his barn where he lived with his pigs. Irving, a teenage volunteer fireman, feels a certain amount of guilt in relation to Piggy for the way in which he, along with other children, had laughed at and teased Piggy while he was still alive. Unable to face the fact of Piggy's death, Irving begins to invent other endings: Piggy had gone to Florida or to Europe. In other words, he begins to imagine ways in which the situation could be made right again. Irving's grandmother advises him that he could have saved himself a lot of bother if he had treated Piggy with a certain amount of decency and sympathy. However, Irving ends this story with, "Failing [decency and sympathy] I realize that a writer's business is setting fire to Piggy Sneed *and* trying to save him again and again; forever" (Irving 1996:21).

The use of the term "atonement" is also significant in this context. Originally, the term meant "reconciliation" itself, "at-onement" with another. This term has gained a particular meaning in the history of Western thought through its very close association with Christianity, whereby it has come to mean the means by which one is reconciled with God through Jesus Christ. In the context of this novel, however, the meaning of the term has shifted. In one sense, it still retains the old meaning: Briony seeks atonement for what she has done to her sister and her sister's lover. But especially in the second paragraph cited above, one senses that the term has come to refer to one's "at-onement" with the world that one has created. For Briony and (one suspects) McEwan and John Irving, reality (the world out there) remains something foreign and strange with which the writer strives to become reconciled through his or her writing.

But this kind of atonement is impossible because it is the author's imagination that sets the limits for the story. All responsibility ends with the author. There is no higher court to which the author can appeal. All responsibility ends with the author. In this sense the passage can be seen as postmodern in the sense that the only criteria that can be seen to be justified lie with the author him- or herself. The author is the final judge and all criteria are subjected to the notion of "attempt". It is no longer the truth that constitutes the meaning of the novel but the attempt on the part of the author. The novelist has become God, not perhaps in the sense of Fowles' authority, but certainly in the sense that the novelist is now free to do as he or she pleases.

Is this a problem which concerns writers only? Is it a particular issue that arises only in connection with the creative process? This problem does not belong solely to the domain of writers or artists. It has its complement in society as a whole. We have dispensed with God, removing the transcendent not only from the public square but also from hearth and board as well. This is perhaps the triumph of secularism in that it has now reached the private realm. We could live for a long time with the notion of a secular, neutral state, even perhaps with the idea of neutral education, so long as religious values and norms were conveyed within the environs of the family and church. Those norms and values are for the most part no longer taught within the environs of the home. Church attendance has dropped dramatically in most countries in Western Europe (see Halman and De Moor 1993:44, Table 3.1). This is not the place to go into the reasons and roots of this thorough secularization. Perhaps it was as inevitable development.

Whatever the case may be, we have dispensed with God both in the public and in the private realms. Parallel to displacing God is the movement to make ourselves God. We have ourselves become the center of our universe. This entails that we suddenly have taken the burden for the universe upon ourselves. It is up to us to solve the problems of the world with which we are now confronted: environmental questions, territorial and religious disputes (e.g. Israel and the Palestinians), political issues, etc. To want to be God implies the burden of God (the burden of "at-onement") as well as responsibility for the world: not only for what it has become but also for what it can be or should be, according to whatever values and norms we might espouse.

In dispensing with God, however, we have also dispensed with any notion of meaning for human society beyond our empirical existence. We have therefore also dispensed with the possibility of "at-onement" with our existence in the world. In the postmodern situation, in contrast to the modern situation, we have become disillusioned about human beings taking on the role of God. In a recent editorial in *Centraal Weekblad*, the weekly paper of the three uniting Protestant churches of the Netherlands, the editors commented that with the disappearance of God, total nihilism threatens. At first many people no longer believed in God but still in humankind. What is left if one no longer believes in humankind? If one no longer lives up to one's own norms, then a great black hole threatens. In a neutral society all must figure it out for themselves.[4] With the absence of God, God is no longer there to blame for the things that go wrong. We ourselves are to blame, and when we have lost the illusion about ourselves, we have nothing left except ourselves.

The editorial is concerned in the first instance with the question of responsibility. But a link with the issue of meaning can also be seen. Like the novelist, humans have chosen freedom. But this freedom leaves humans having no "at-onement" with a world that increasingly strikes them as strange and foreign, a world in which humans do not seem truly to belong. It is a world in which life often goes contrary to expectations, a world in which dreams are destroyed or run aground on the realities of everyday life. It is a world in which human beings find that they cannot be all that they can be. Personal satisfaction and dignity give way to the social demands of success (often measured in monetary terms). We feel responsible for the suffering of the world but also helpless in the face of the suffering that confronts us. This is also the absence of "at-onement" with the world and with ourselves. To right the wrongs of this world seems to be beyond human ability and therefore we are faced with the meaninglessness of what one does to alleviate these wrongs. If the emphasis is on the here and now, no human being and, quite possibly, no human society can ever arrive at the point where people feel at one with their existence. Should they even try? That is the question with which humans are left.

---

[4] "Hoe God en de mens verdwenen uit… [How God and humankind disappeared from …]." *Centraal Weekblad* 50/18 (May 3, 2002):2. This article was written in response to several violent acts that have recently occurred in Europe.

We can continue to make the attempt, in the sense that "the attempt was all," as Briony Tallis says, however fruitless it may be. Another solution for this problem of "at-onement" in the contemporary world is much more radical: the refusal of responsibility. We can, in other words, take the position that human life is not worth the attention we have paid to it and say with the Dutch writer Cees Nooteboom that we desire nothing more than "to be alone, merely born and not created, existing on [our] own like any otter, buzzard or grasshopper" (Nooteboom 1991: 110). Or we could adopt the attitude of dilettantism that emerges from Nooteboom's novel *Rituals* (1992).[5] This is the world into which we are born and die. The world that we experience as strange and foreign is, in fact, the only world there is. There is nothing else, nothing to which we can aspire. Our freedom from God has left us alone in the world. This manifests itself also in the extreme individualism that we are witnessing today: the retreat to one's private world (the home and private interests), as opposed to activity in the community, as an attempt to find meaning and pleasure in life.

And thus we return again to the issue of meaning as it is expressed in the practical concept of "at-onement" with the world and with the larger community of which one is member: voluntarily or involuntarily?[6] How can churches and ministers of the Gospel use this as a point of contact in the communication of the gospel?

3   THE RESPONSE OF THE CHRISTIAN CHURCH TO THE CRISIS OF
      MEANING

As we saw above, the question of meaning is one that has theoretical and practical sides. The Christian faith can use this crisis of meaning as a fruitful point of contact in conveying the Gospel to contemporary society on both the theoretical and practical levels, with the result that one can feel "at one" with one's existence in the world.

The kernel of truth in the postmodern position lies in its reaction to the Enlightenment and nineteenth-century idea that human beings had some kind of innate, natural access to the divine mind. The postmodern position is correct in insisting that final, complete truth is beyond us.

---

[5] See the discussion of Nooteboom in Jansen 2001.

[6] This is not to say that meaning can only be found in the Gospel and not in other religions or in a secularized worldview. Of course, meaning can be found there as well (on this see Stoker 1996). My concern here is only to present the possibilities for meaning as found in the Christian faith.

Gone is the time when we believed that all problems could be solved from within history (historical idealism: the dream of the nineteenth century). Gone is the time as well when we thought that science could provide all the answers we needed. Instead, postmodernity has rightly laid stress on the subjectivity and relativity of human knowledge. With this the Christian can readily agree. We do not have innate insight into the divine mind. Our knowledge remains partial and obscure and whatever knowledge we may have remains a question of revelation.

But the solution offered by Nooteboom of this postmodern mood (the refusal of responsibility) does not satisfy. We seem to be left with the skeletal remains of what it means to be human and how human life can be meaningful, denying what seems to be a general human characteristic. Granted, we know little about the psychology of buzzards and otters, but human beings, at least in general, seem to need to ascribe meaning to their lives, to find significance in what they do and how they do it. We could refer to this, in Calvin's terms, as the *semen religionis*. That this is a general human trait may indicate that we need to take this need much more seriously. That humans seem to have a *psychological* need for this has no bearing on the existence of a corresponding fulfilment of this need (God, the transcendent) any more than the biological need for food has bearing on the question of whether this food exists. If human beings have this trait, can they be at all content with existence in the same way that a buzzard or otter apparently is?

On the theoretical level, the Christian churches can respond to this need in the first place by stressing with the *Shorter Westminster Catechism* that the chief end of all human beings is "to glorify God and enjoy him forever." Thereby Christians emphasize that only through belief in God may human beings be everything that God intended them to be. Only through faith can human beings find personal satisfaction and purpose in their lives. Meaning in one's life is thus a question of faith. In connection with this, churches need to stress the givenness or gift-character of meaning. Here we might be helped by imaginative uses of, for example, the first answer of the *Heidelberg Catechism*; i.e. "that I am not my own but belong, body and soul, to my faithful Saviour Jesus Christ." As human beings, we do not need to create meaning for ourselves or for what we do. The meaningfulness of what we do is given to us freely. As human beings, we are caught up in God's movement toward a new creation, where the world will no longer seem strange and foreign to us, where we will no longer feel the tension between work and leisure, where we will be what we were meant to be. We do not need to settle for the mere existence of otters and buzzards, for the meaning is given: we belong, body and soul, to that movement of God towards a new creation.

The meaningfulness of one's actions need not be seen thus as having, in the first place, an impact on the whole world at once. The problem faced by Nooteboom's characters in his novels is that they cannot save the world; therefore they retreat to their own as a means of self-protection. Instead, one may speak here of several levels or circles of meaning. The first circle of meaning is that the meaningfulness of what one does in one's immediate environment, with the challenges and issues that come one's way. What does one do with the refugees that live in one's neighbourhood or with the beggar one encounters on the street? Inspiration may be drawn here from the book of Ruth in the Old Testament. Ruth and Boaz were not in the first place concerned with saving all of Israel, let alone the world. Both were faced with the very specific question of Naomi, Ruth's mother-in-law, who had no means of supporting herself. Out of compassion Ruth and Boaz respond to her need. And what they do for Naomi are, in themselves, small acts of mercy and kindness. Nonetheless, through their acts they become the great-grandparents of David, the greatest king of Israel and in a very specific way the chosen servant of the Lord. This is a second and larger circle of meaningfulness. They thus also become the honoured human ancestors of the Messiah, Jesus Christ, thus playing a definite role in the salvation of the world, the final circle of the meaningfulness of their acts. Neither Boaz nor Ruth could have foreseen what significance their acts would have in the larger history of God's movement. Nor can we see what significance our acts will have. We have only what we can see in front of us and to that we are called to respond. We are thus also carried beyond the claim of Briony Tallis, "The attempt was all," for the meaning of the attempt is in the attempt itself.

On the practical level, the Christian churches need to present themselves, in view of this movement of God, as communities which offer alternatives to the present, harassed pace of society. There are several points which come to mind here. Protestant churches, at least in major urban centers, should perhaps take a hint from Catholic churches and be open at certain times during the week for people to enter to meditate, a place of retreat from their busy schedules. The churches also need to provide space for people to rest and experience silence. The decor of the interior of the churches can be so arranged as to remind the visitors visually of the greater story in which they are caught up. Churches could thus also reflect on how the interiors of our churches help to convey that sense.

More importantly, the various Christian communities need to be active in their larger communities by presenting themselves as a foretaste of that new creation. In the first place, they need to be active in their communities in the diaconal sense as well as the evangelistic sense. If they are situated in an economically depressed area, they need to attend to the physical needs of the community as well as the spiritual needs. Something as practical as organizing young people to fix up homes (painting, wallpapering) can be a vital means of conveying the message of God's new creation. The deacons in churches can also organize social events in order to invite people who suffer loneliness. In a mobile society in which people, especially younger people, often move away from the neighbourhood or city or town where they grew up, organization of activities can help to draw these younger people into the church. This requires hands-on ministry and not simply the facelessness of another charitable organization. Who knows what effect such acts will have in the coming of God's new creation? If various church communities are present in such an area, they need to display a certain solidarity with respect to such activities, above and beyond the organizational level, so that their witness will attain unity with respect to proclamation and deed. The activities in which the churches engage will be those demanded by the communities of which they are a part.

Churches in small villages will have different challenges and hence different tasks. Yet in some respects the task will be the same. One of the fall-outs of a mobile society is that people often move to villages in order to escape the hectic pace of their vocational lives in the city, although it must also be stated that even many villages are no longer the slow-paced restful places they used to be. Here too the churches can be a presence by organizing activities in which people can once again feel part of a community. There are many other ways in which churches in village communities can be active. One of the major concerns in my area is the agricultural industry. A regional committee is in place to give support and advice to the farmers in this area, even though there could be much more involvement by churches in this matter.

Closely connected with this diaconal activity of the church (and in essence one with it) is the openness of the church as a community. Theologically, this can be grounded in the doctrine of the Trinity, where terms such as oneness, interpenetration, and unity in word, work and service are central (see Plantinga 1988 and 1989). Services on Sunday need to be much more open. Whereas the liturgy for a church service may be more or less standard, with appropriate deviations where necessary, the service itself can contain much more. A sign outside the church (large enough to be seen by those in passing cars) advertising the theme for the coming Sunday is a good idea. People will possibly come to the realization that the church is there for them. Moreover, offering coffee or tea before and after the service will enhance the feeling of community among the members (especially if they are engaged in their community in an active way). In conversation with one another, people can give and receive meaning as part of the Christian message. Within the church community, they should be free to express their fears, insecurities and loneliness without fear of censure or ridicule. They should feel accepted.

In these activities the churches will engage in concrete attempts toward "at-onement" in the world, based on the theoretical considerations (doctrine) of God's reconciliation of the world with himself in Jesus Christ. The concrete engagement of the Christian churches in meeting the concrete manifestation of meaning as expressed in the concrete need of "at-onement" will thus help to provide meaning in the lives of the people to whom they minister and thus communicate the fullness of life for all as expressed in the Gospel.

4   CONCLUSION

The question of meaning in contemporary society presents itself in theoretical and practical concerns. Theoretically, many people can no longer find meaning in their lives: their lives and what they do appear to have little significance in the world at large. This has had practical implications for their lives: retreat into private worlds and, more radically, the rejection of responsibility. But this does not suffice to respond to the human need for meaning. Human beings cannot be satisfied with the skeletal remains of what it means to be human.

On this issue churches can engage in fruitful ministry by theoretically and practically addressing the issue of meaning. Through what they have to offer as representatives of the Gospel of Jesus Christ in this world, the Gospel can, through attention to issues of here and now with which people are concerned, provide more certain knowledge of what went before this life [and] of what follows.

BIBLIOGRAPHY

St. Bede. (1955). *A History of the English Church and People*. Transl. Leo Sherley-Price. Harmondsworth: Penguin Books.

Christian Reformed Church. (1987). *Ecumenical Creeds and Reformed Confessions*. Grand Rapids: CRC Publications.

Fowles, John. (1969). *The French Lieutenant's Woman*. London: World Books. Reprint 1971.

Halman, Loek, and Ruud de Moor. (1993). "Religion, Churches and Moral Values." In: Peter Ester et al. (eds.). *The Individualizing Society: Value Change in Europe and North America*. Tilburg: Tilburg University Press.

Irving, John. (1996). "Trying to Save Piggy Sneed." In: John Irving. *Trying to Save Piggy Sneed*. New York: Arcade Publishing. Pp. 5-21.

Jansen, Henry. (1995). *Relationality and the Concept of God*. Currents of Encounter 10. Amsterdam/Atlanta: Editions Rodopi.

—. (2001). *Laughter among the Ruins: Postmodern Comic Approaches to Suffering*. Frankfurt a.M.: Peter Lang.

McEwan, Ian. (2000). *Atonement*. London: Jonathan Cape.

Murdoch, Iris. (1971). "The Sovereignty of Good over Other Concepts." In: Iris Murdoch. *The Sovereignty of Good. Studies in Ethics and the Philosophy of Religion*. New York: Schocken Books.

Nooteboom, Cees. (1991). *In the Dutch Mountains*. Transl. Adrienne Dixon. Harmondsworth: Penguin.

—. (1992). *Rituals*. Transl. Adrienne Dixon. Harmondsworth: Penguin.

Plantinga, Cornelis, Jr. (1988). "Images of God." In: Mark A. Noll and David. F. Wells (eds.). *Christian Faith and Practice in the Modern World: Theology from an Evangelical Perspective*. Grand Rapids: Wm. B. Eerdmans. Pp. 51-67.

—. (1989) "Social Trinity and Tritheism." In: Ronald J. Feenstra and Cornelius Plantinga, Jr. (eds.). *Trinity, Incarnation, and Atonement: Philosophical and Theological Essays*. Library of Religious Philosophy. Vol. I. Notre Dame: University of Notre Dame. Pp. 21-47.

Rorty, Richard. (1989). *Contingency, Irony and Solidarity*. Cambridge: Cambridge University Press.

Spark, Muriel. (1957). *The Comforters*. New York: New Directions Books Reprint 1994.

Stoker, W. (1996). *Is the Quest for Meaning the Quest for God? The Religious Ascription of Meaning in Relation to the Secular Ascription of Meaning*. Currents of Encounter 11. Amsterdam/Atlanta: Editions Ropodi.

Vroom, Hendrik M. (1989). *Religions and the Truth*. Currents of Encounter 2. Transl. Johan Rebel. Grand Rapids: Wm. B. Eerdmans Publishing Co.

5   Changing Culture and The Missiological Mission

André F. Droogers

1   INTRODUCTION

Missiologists cannot exercise their tasks without paying attention to culture and the Christian religion has its own diverse cultural roots. In addition to its history, there is a permanent confrontation with cultures other than the one in which this religion originated. The need for contextualization is one of the *raisons d'être* of the discipline of missiology. Because the Christian message must be subjected to a process of inculturation, culture is a crucial concept for missiologists. Moreover, missiologists appear to some degree to count on the possibility of steering cultures in a desired direction, because they want the Christian message to be implemented in church praxis and the daily lives of the converts. Here again knowledge of the concept of culture and the ongoing debate on culture is appropriate.

Anthropologists sometimes behave as if they are the proprietors of the domain of culture. Though obligated by *noblesse oblige,* they do not always take the trouble to explain to the interdisciplinary audience the debates that occur within the walls of their special area. The result is sometimes a kind of information lag in that other disciplines, including missiology, use ideas that were fashionable one or two decades ago in anthropology but are not reconsidered today or no longer play a central role. In this article I will provide an update of the discussion on culture, with the inevitable restriction that it is, of course, my personal and subjective version of that update.

I will first describe the vicissitudes of the term in the short history of anthropology, as it moved from a phenomenon that was supposed to be limited and autonomous to a view of culture as a human capacity that produces an open and flexible way of living in a world that is becoming increasingly globalized. One approach, inspired by cognitive studies, which views culture as the human capacity to produce and use repertoires composed of schemas, will be discussed in somewhat more detail. The consequences for missiology will be considered throughout. A brief conclusion takes stock of the current trends.

2   A CONCEPT WITH A HISTORY

In the last century, the concept of culture has been subjected to a tidal wave of intense discussions. One of the parameters that colored the debate was that for a long time British and Amercian anthropologists differed in their way of doing anthropology. The British saw themselves as a special kind of sociologist and were influenced by sociological theories, particularly those of French origin, such as the approach that Durkheim and his followers had developed. They preferred to call themselves social anthropologists, thereby indicating that they had little use for the term "culture." The American anthropologists, on the contrary, made the concept of culture their trade mark and accordingly labeled themselves cultural anthropologists. In continental Europe each country had its own approach, sometimes oriented to Britain or the United States or both (as in The Netherlands), sometimes developing a style of its own (as in France and Germany). Dutch anthropology also assimilated French innovations, such as structuralism. An illustration of the double orientation in Dutch anthropology is the fact that my department recently adopted the name "Social and Cultural Anthropology."

A basic aspect of culture is that it can be used, on the one hand, in a generic singular way, as a typical characteristic of humanity as a whole, distinguishing human beings from other animals, and, on the other, as a specific plural, as when one speaks of the thousands of cultures that exist in the world and that continue to divide humanity. For quite some time, anthropologists were busy studying these different cultures, viewing them as somewhat self-enclosed and autonomous units. In fact, the village study was the privileged model, it being viewed as a mini-society representing and mirroring the larger one. Moreover, each member of such a society was thought to be a representative of the culture, just as the village was the summary of the whole society. Most probably that view was influenced by the need of colonial authorities for a type of information that facilitated their policy-making. Missionary authorities may have used the same information for their strategies.

More recently, doubt has risen with regard to the all-pervasive importance of the limits of cultures. Consequently, the question is raised as to how important these specific and autonomous cultures are in determining people's behavior. If there is a generic as well as a more specific view of culture, then the first, i.e. the human gift for meaning-making, would suggest that people use their specific culture—in the second sense—as a starting point for their own, sometimes inconsistent and contradictory, meaning-making. In doing so, they may thus produce their own version and selection of that culture, or even deviate from it, perhaps leading it into new directions. Traditions do not continue endlessly. Cultures change constantly, including their traditions, by the way people experience their lives, reproduce their culture, and live their personal and collective histories. What is more, traditions may be purposefully invented and constructed, usually to legitimate the powers that be (Hobsbawm and Ranger 1983). Something done twice may already become a tradition. Basically, the human being is a bricoleur (Lévi-Strauss 1962; see also Vroom's contribution to this book).

The move from a view of culture as closed and static to open and flexible is not only the result of growing academic insight but also a consequence of changes in world society that can hardly be overlooked. Thus colonialism, as part of Western expansion, made the world smaller to the those expanding but bigger to the subjects of this expansion, whose small worlds were opened up and subjected to a change in scale. Migration waves —some involuntary, such as that of slaves and, more recently, of political and economic refugees, others voluntary such as labor migration and emigration for demographic reasons—brought people from different cultural backgrounds into contact with one another. Christian missionaries formed a small but important transnational migration flow that spread the Christian message into the colonies, coming from the North and going to the South. After decolonization, this type of migration, though different in nature, remained, although it has found a counterpoint in a move from the South to the North, as is the case of some southern Pentecostal churches. Thus Brazilian and Ghanaian Pentecostal churches are active in the Nether-lands. Traveling has become much easier and evangelists and their organizations have grasped the chances offered by this.

Mass media has contributed to the availability of information from other cultures and, depending on the access that people have to these media, people have become more aware of the world as a cultural market. Some churches have become active in the field of mass media and are exploring the opportunities that have been created.

A consequence of the opening of the world to many of its inhabitants has been that social control has diminished and the freedom to lead one's own life has increased. Many converts have made use of the new space thus formed. Individualization is typical of Western culture and the slogan 'be an original' is one tobacco industry's summary of this development. Paradoxically, the need to be a successful individual is a social command. The expansion of Christianity has been more rapid because of individual freedom. Conversion is an individual decision. Not coincidentally, the value invested in the individual has

Christian roots. Individualism can also be seen at work in other fields of Western culture, such as personal careers, consumerism, and hedonism.

A concept that is currently fashionable, reflecting the world cultural situation, is that of globalization. Depending on the discipline of the definer, it can be characterized as an economic or political or, in my case, cultural phenomenon. The simplest way to reflect on globalization seems to be to take it as the process by which the world is experienced as one place. One would expect a world culture to be the outcome of this process, but, interestingly, global trends present themselves in local forms, to such a degree that it has been suggested to speak of "glocalization" (Robertson 1992:173). Even multinational firms depend on local marketing to discover the properties of the potential buyer. A Big Mac is not the same everywhere. Television commercials are tailor-made to match local preferences. Trying to explain this to missiologists is a waste of energy, because at an early stage they were already conscious of the need for the inculturation of the Christian transcultural message.

Though empirically observable as a local phenomenon only, globalization is a world-wide phenomenon. To an increasing number of people this means that they are increasingly more aware of how to behave in contexts other than the one in which they received their first socialization. Whether as tourists, employees, participants in international networks, development workers, refugees, or evangelists, they have to dispose of some basic knowledge of the contextual codes of behavior. Some of this knowledge is already of a global nature, such as the knowledge needed for using an airport or traveling by plane. But much of it is an adaptation of the practical knowledge that characterized the local cultures from where these people come. The international language of behavior is spoken with an accent. The linguistic metaphor is used purposely since it has been adopted to explain what happens when people move between cultures. More specifically the term "creolization" has been introduced (Drummond 1980; Hannerz 1992) as a way of referring to the process of people being fluent in more than one cultural code. Just as people are able to learn another language, using the human gift for language, in the same way people may learn another cultural language, using the gift that is referred to in the generic version of the concept of culture. But it is not simply a matter of adopting another language or cultural code; creolization also means mixing elements from different languages, usually a local language and an imported dominant one, often with colonial roots. Something similar may happen when cultural elements are mixed and new forms of culture appear. In the field of religion this happened when indigenous movements found inspiration in Christian elements. The concept of syncretism has been coined to describe the mixing of elements from different religious sources, sometimes as a descriptive term, sometimes as a pejorative concept (Greenfield and Droogers 2002).

Beside culture, another concept has recently become popular when processes of change are being described. It may even be viewed as a serious competitor. This is the concept of identity. Interestingly, a development similar to that with culture has occurred, from a rather essentialistic view to a more open and flexible interpretation. The term may indeed have the connotation of identity as a property: "this is how I am," this is my essence, my identification papers—as when somebody is apologizing for not being able to change. For some time this single unified self was even taken as a sign of mental health, of an integrated personality. More recently, the process of managing one's social roles and, accordingly, the multiplicity of selves has received more attention. This multiplicity was for some time taken as a sign of weak mental health but has been rehabilitated as the capacity to survive in very diverse contexts, even when playing contradictory roles (Lifton 1993). Moreover, the gift to adapt to change has been included in this modus of being able to live effectively with different tendencies. Since change has become an important characteristic of our era, this posture is viewed as a necessity. People constantly adapt themselves when new influences appear in their lives. A particular form of identity construction in changing circumstances has been the promotion of emancipated identity, which can also be seen as a way of provoking change. Thus racial, gender, and class emancipation can be understood as the quest for an new identity. Compared to the concept of culture, identity seems thereby to have the advantage of introducing the elements of power and political choices. Moreover, it sheds light on the role of individuals who act purposefully to reach a certain goal and thereby seek to change prevalent power relationships. In some situations Christianity has been used as a vehicle for emancipation purposes, though it must be added immediately that Christianity has often served as legitimizing the preservation of a particular identity and other interests, whether based on race, gender, or class.

In sum, whether we prefer to speak of culture or of identity, people today have opened their windows to the rest of the world, thereby often ignoring former boundaries and walls, simultaneously changing their way of life. More than ever before it has become an important question to discover the relationship in people's daily experience between the determination by their culture or identity of their socialization and the many influences with which they are bombarded from outside— including Christian intentions and projects. How do people find roads through this complex landscape? Can we get a clearer view of the current dynamics and diversity? Whereas anthropologists used to focus on the way in whcih people were determined in their behavior from within their bounded culture, today they need to pay attention to the influences from outside and how these are dealt with in a culture with perforated boundaries. One answer is to look for schema repertoires.

3   SCHEMA REPERTOIRES

To use the repertoire metaphor when discussing culture is attractive because a repertoire has three characteristics that correspond to the phenomena that were described in the preceding section. First, not all that is part of a repertoire and of culture is used or activated. Second, both repertoires and cultures are subject to change. Third, repertoires and cultures may contain contradictions and opposite tendencies. Similarly, the metaphor reflects aspects of the concept of identity that were discussed. In adapting their culture and identity people change their repertoires for behavior, thought, and emotion.

Anthropology has a sub-discipline, called cognitive anthropology, which uses elements from the interdisciplinary field of cognitive studies (e.g. Bloch 1998, Boyer 2001, D'Andrade 1994, Reyna 2002, Strauss and Quinn 1998). In this corner of anthropology the main question is how cultural knowledge is organized, especially in view of the way the human mind is thought to work. Some of the insights developed in this branch of anthropology may be helpful in elaborating the repertoire metaphor. The concept that may add to our understanding of cultural processes is 'schema'. Schemas can summarily be described as mental models or scripts for behavior, thought or emotion. Human beings have a whole repertoire of schemas that help them in finding ways of behaving, thinking, and feeling. The number of schemas is enormous—most probably in the millions. They do not exist as separate units but are connected with each other, also in a physical sense in the brain. They are connected in all kinds of ways: hierarchical, linear, in tree structures, and so on. There are very basic schemas that determine many others. They may be typical of a culture, understood in the specific sense (e.g. the schemas of shame, guilt, martyrdom, optimism, etc.). But there are also minuscule schemas that are hardly ever used because the context in which they would be useful hardly ever presents itself (e.g. if you should win the Nobel Prize). Some have a history of centuries, such as many Christian theological schemas, and others are temporary, such as those that accompanied the transition from national currency to the Euro. Language is by itself a mine of schemas, a reflection of the cultural schemas that are part of the speaker's repertoire. Exegetes and Bible translators wrestle with the meanings of schemas in biblical language and compare them to dogmatic and local cultural schemas.

If schemas exist by the millions, we must constantly use them, most often in a routine manner, as for example when we speak. One reads these words, which means that one is transforming the lines on paper into words and concepts and images. The publisher opted for a particular font that should facilitate one's reading, but there are also fancy fonts that take some time to decode, using unfamiliar schemas yet vaguely similar to well-known fonts. In a comparable manner, we routinely decipher the sounds that come from other people's mouths and turn them into a message. Misunderstanding is possible. Explorers in 19th century Africa thought they asked: What is the name of your tribe? The answer was: *Topoke*. The explorers wrote this down and thought they had registered a new tribe—not knowing that in the local language *topoke* meant: We do not understand you. If somebody speaks with a heavy accent or through a deficient sound system we have difficulty in decoding what we hear and may misunderstand. Are they calling my flight? Did they change the gate? Did she mention my name? We may become uncertain about what we think we hear or see. Suppose somebody is approaching us from afar and we think we recognize a friend. Coming closer, we suddenly see that we were mistaken. But in the meantime we very rapidly collected information—hair, beard, glasses, posture, way of walking—assembled it and drawn the conclusion: "Here comes Jerry!"

In writing this article I am also using routine schemas, making the best of my English, and respecting the schema as established by the editors, which is connected with the general academic routine of writing articles. There is an introduction with a basic question, an answer developed and finally a conclusion drawn that is a short answer to the question raised. Of course, references and bibliography must follow the schema that the editors have chosen for the book as a whole. Or, to use another example, when this book is to be offered as a Festschrift, there will be a schema for such an occasion, derived from routine schemas for similar occasions. Missiologists may develop typologies that represent schemas of and for particular cases of missions or churches. For every occasion and situation there is a schema, and when the occasion is new, an old schema is adapted or a new schema is constructed using old and new elements.

A schema can be compared to an empty form that contains a small number of more or less constant elements that are usually present but may differ according to the situation. Perhaps, along the lines of family resemblances, not all are applicable in all opportunities. For each occasion a new form must be filled in. Thus, a visit to a restaurant follows a predictable script, but each visit is different. If one is not hungry, one may skip the appetizer. It may be that, after having been used successfully for quite some time, a form is abolished, a schema is abandoned. Thus, after the Cold War various schemas became obsolete on both sides of the Iron Curtain. At the same time new ones had to be formed, such as those for the new states that emerged. And, of course, there may be some continuity: the former Soviet Communist party disappeared—but has it? The party officials lost their position—but did they?

The example also shows that a change in a basic schema has consequences for a great number of other schemas that are connected with it. This happens frequently where change occurs. Conversion to a new religion can be studied as a fundamental change of worldview schemas that sometimes has drastic consequences for the convert's way of living. The question is: Which schemas change and to what degree, how radically? It would also be interesting to see if old schemas continue but in adapted form. The emancipation movements I mentioned above also seek to provoke a fundamental change. They produce changes that are similar to conversions. The change is fundamental because so many other schemas change accordingly. Just think of what a woman's emancipation means for her partner and her nuclear family. On a different scale, one may think of what happened in South Africa to old and new schemas in the post-apartheid era.

Schemas do not change easily. Especially those that have become part of our routine prove resilient. That is why we speak a foreign language with an accent, have difficulty in driving on the left when that is not what is done in our own country, why converts nevertheless continue to show characteristics of their former religion or why African communities sing classical British hymns in a different way. It may also prove difficult to convince my readers of my argument in this article, because the readers' routine schemas call them back to what they up to now considered to be normal. Of course, our identity is largely based on the schemas that we cherish and for which we are known. Therefore we position ourselves within the whole field of alternatives. One need only think of what one decided to wear today or how one wanted to have one's hair cut the last time one visited the barber. Or, to use a less secular example, one can think of how one remains a Christian despite the secularizing tendencies in the West and how one combines science and religion in a way satisfactory to oneself.

Schema repertoires make life predictable. The routine is very helpful in that sense. Communication is facilitated. Yet misunderstanding is still possible, even among people who speak the same language and refer to the same cultural repertoire. More miscommunication may occur in situations of intercultural contact. Multicultural societies are emerging and raising debate. People may think they are using the same schemas but mean something quite different by them. Nonetheless, despite these risks, people manage to live their lives and succeed in dealing routinely with a series of different situations in the course of the day.

There is one factor that usually influences the way people make use of schema repertoires. Power is an essential part of schema praxis. Power can be defined as the capacity to influence other people's behavior. This can also be formulated as the capacity to influence other people's schema repertoire. Societies differ in the degree to which schemas are imposed. Of course, every society has laws, although there may be some difference in the rigidity with which the law is maintained. There may be a *double entendre* in the way people observe the law. As the Brazilian saying goes: "For friends everything, for enemies the law." The powers that be are interested in maintaining the schemas that keep them in their position. One way of reaching this goal is to make people internalize schemas to such a degree that they become part of routine thinking and behaving. The cultural then becomes natural. "Of course I am a nationalist, I love my country," "We certainly need a strong president," etc. Some regimes use sanctions, legal or illegal, to impose their schemas, and they may become a cause of daily worry for Amnesty International. Human rights declarations must guarantee a common schema repertoire on the ethics of politics and commerce, even in a person-to-person contact, as the imposition of schemas may be present in a tacit, unobserved way. The schemas that rule interpersonal behavior can be the result of fair negotiations, though even that process may be very subtle and almost invisible. It seems that even for negotiating our schema preferences we use schemas.

Religion is no exception to these probabilities. On the contrary, in the field of religion, power processes that rule the management of schema repertoires are very much present. Churches can even be classified in a typology according to the way in which they control schema repertoires. Some have a rather hierarchical, vertical way of guaranteeing uniformity in the way schemas are shared by the members, whereas others are more horizontal and allow for some diversity among their members and parishes. Church history, including the part that interests missiologists, contains many illustrations of this process and not all to the greater glory of Christianity.

Conversion can also be viewed as a process during which power positions influence what happens. When one person seeks to convince another of a religious view, this is a way of exercising power, at least in the sense of the above definition. The complicated play of motives may hide the power mechanisms. One need not think of the conversion of a 'rice Christian' to understand this. The other side of the coin is that precisely through their conversion people were freeing themselves from some other power mechanism that had been victimizing them. The Christian message has often had its major appeal among marginalized people. The strongest assets of Christianity are that it offers a basic schema for making the best of a situation in which power plays a role. It has the potential to invert power relations that have come to be internalized as normal and natural. True, it may be contaminated and corrupted by these same relations, but in every period of church history there have been inspired, visionary believers who have returned to the original intent of the Christian message. They often had to face sanctions used by those in power at the time to maintain their position, sometimes in close collaboration with secular leaders.

Thus church activity anywhere can be analyzed in terms of the processes that accompany the use of schema repertoires. The accumulated wisdom of twenty centuries of theology represents a large number of schemas and can be distinguished in several repertoires according to church type and hermeneutical orientation. Despite that long history, it is still in progress. Theological production, including the missiological output, thrives as never before. Being a church in a particular context of time and place brings new challenges to the formulation of schemas. Particularly in Western Europe, secularization has placed churches in a position where renewed reflection on their mission is necessary. The ecumenical movement represents another challenge. Especially when churches meet in dialogue with each other schema repertoires are compared. In the cases where churches have become institutionally unified they have had to go through a similar process, discovering new schemas that nevertheless did not sever the link to the root schemas. The role of Christianity in the present world situation demands that the familiar schema repertoires be adapted. The main actors in this process must have a strong awareness of the power mechanisms that are at work both within and outside of the churches. When dialogue with representatives of other religions occurs, similar conditions and challenges, *mutatis mutandis*, prevail.

What happens in theology and on the institutional level of the churches has its parallel in the individual believer's experience. In the course of her or his life each person is first of all socialized into a particular schema repertoire, and in a gradually more conscious way adapts and changes this set of basic models for behavior, thinking, and emotion. This may include a move to church other than that of one's parents, to a different religion or to a position outside the religious field. There is always a close connection between a person's life history, the social context in which he or she lives and the more or less dramatic nature of life's vicissitudes. What is fascinating to observe is the degree to which old schemas, despite all change, continue to influence people, perhaps in a modified form and in combination with newly acquired ones. People will seek to maintain some form of equilibrium and identity. They do so by—in either a reflected or routine manner—taking care of their personal schema repertoire. In the current situation, individuals situate themselves willy-nilly in a world becoming more and more globalized. More than ever before, people are influenced by those who have a stake in the worldview market and—unless they do not have access and are among the excluded—are constantly called to reflect on what they wish to view as their answer to the ultimate questions of life. Cultural and religious boundaries no longer shield people from the influences that this market represents. Christianity, especially—but not only—in its more assertive evangelical forms, is a strong player in this market. But other religions are there as well, especially in multicultural situations that once were the exception and are now fast becoming the rule. An interesting example is found in Hollywood films in which Buddhism, especially in its Tibetan form, plays a role.

With religions, institutions and believers operating within this new global situation, the question is what schema repertoires will become current in the world of the 21st century. One answer, widely popularized by the mass media, especially after September 11, is Huntington's (1997): a world divided in nine blocks that represent cultural and religious differences. The future of humanity is described as a succession of conflicts between these "civilizations." Huntington's scenario is based on an essentialist view of cultures. The flexibility and openness, which I mentioned as a recent development, is substituted by the autonomy and boundaries that seemed to prevail before globalization started. The impact of intercultural communication and mass media is thought to lead to a reactionary retreat to traditional positions where believers seek security in a fragmented world. The worldview market is thought to have closed down. A new power process would then rule the world. Fundamentalism is taken to be a precursor of this trend and the World Trade Center attack a first symptom of this clash of the civilizations. One hopes that another scenario will come to pass, one in which the powers that be do not opt for and are not driven in the direction of this world of nine civilizations world. In the 21st century Christianity is called to play its part in the process that will develop. Unfortunately, the optimism that lies at the base of technological innovation cannot be transferred directly to the technology of steering society and culture. Human beings are apprentice sorcerers who do not control the processes that their gift for meaning-making starts. Huntington's scenario cannot be excluded out of hand, but one hopes that people are sufficiently aware of the risks that are at stake and act accordingly. With regard to Christianity's role, one gloomy pre-vision is the rise of a Southern conservative and fundamentalist Christian majority (Jenkins 2002) that will have all the characteristics of Huntington's model, lacking the openness that anthropology's view of culture and cultures seems to suggest.

4   CONCLUSION

The basic question in this article was: what might recent developments in cultural anthropology, especially with respect to the debate on culture, mean for missiology and missiologists. We saw here that there is a tendency to move from culture as a closed unity to culture as a worldwide applicable human gift for meaning-making. This generic gift operates in a world where the cultures that were formerly understood as closed and autonomous still influence people's behavior but where at the same time a huge human potential is activated that will be needed in a globalizing intercultural world with people communicating across former boundaries. The trend may be in the direction of a complex and pluralist cultural situation, with a surprising and fascinating mix of elements from the previously closed cultures. However, the trend may also be that, under the influence of uncontrollable power mechanisms, new differences emerge and that between, on the one hand, the thousands of cultures that previously existed and, on the other, the imaginary but improbable one-world culture, a limited number of cultural clusters—e.g. Huntington's civilizations—may rise that will determine the near future of humankind. Much depends on the effect of power mechanisms and on human beings' gift for meaning-making. In the quest for a humane world, Christianity definitely has a role to play. Missiology will accordingly have to make Christians aware of the new parameters and alternatives. The cultural context is a crucial part of its frame of reference and anthropology will continue to play a role.

BIBLIOGRAPHY

Bloch, Maurice E.F. (1998). *How We Think They Think: Anthropological Approaches to Cognition, Memory, and Literacy*. Boulder, CO: Westview Press.

Boyer, Pascal. (2001). *Religion Explained: The Human Instincts that Fashion Gods, Spirits and Ancestors*. London: Heinnemann.

D'Andrade, Roy. (1995). *The Development of Cognitive Anthropology*. Cambridge: Cambridge University Press.

Drummond, Lee. (1980). "The Cultural Continuum: A Theory of Intersystems". In: *Man*, 15. No. 4. Pp. 352-374.

Greenfield, Sidney M., and André Droogers (eds.). (2001) *Reinventing Religions: Syncretism and Transformation in Africa and the Americas*. Boulder, CO: Rowman & Littlefield.

Hannerz, Ulf. (1992). *Cultural Complexity, Studies in the Social Organization of Meaning*. Oxford, New York: Oxford University Press.

Hobsbawm, E. and T. Ranger (eds.). (1983). *The Invention of Tradition*. Cambridge: Cambridge University Press.

Huntington, Samuel P. (1997). *The Clash of Civilizations and the Remaking of World Order*. London: Simon and Schuster.

Jenkins, Philip. (2002). *The Next Christendom: The Coming of Global Christianity*. Oxford: Oxford University Press.

Lévi-Strauss, Claude. (1962). *La pensée sauvage*. Paris: Plon.

Lifton, Robert Jay. (1993). *The Protean Self: Human Resilience in an Age of Fragmentation*. New York: Basic Books.

Reyna, Stephen P. (2002) *Connections: Brain, Mind and Culture in a Social Anthropology*. London/New York: Routledge.

Robertson, Roland. (1992). *Globalization: Social Theory and Global Culture*. London, etc.: SAGE.

Strauss, Claudia, and Naomi Quinn. (1997). *A Cognitive Theory of Cultural Meaning*. Cambridge: Cambridge University Press.

6   Bricolage and Fullness. On Multiple Participation

Hendrik M. Vroom

1   INTRODUCTION

"Morning has broken" came from the television. I wondered whether the BBC was broadcasting a religious program at an unusual hour, because it wasn't Sunday evening and why would television have a hymn on an Thursday night? The hymn went on: "like the first morning. Blackbird has spoken like the first bird. Praise for the singing, praise for the morning, praise for them springing fresh from the word," and I had a closer look. Some gnu's walked as quietly as only gnu's can do, a lion lay at rest, and some impala's made an image of paradise. But would that great morning have broken, really? In a glance I saw that the hymn and the pictures did not come from the British television, but from a Dutch station as an advertisement just before the eight 'o clock news. Whoever would buy that time for that hymn and those pictures of creation? Well, the World Wild Life Fund does.

It seems that the Western church lives at the dawn of a new era in which religion again is present in unexpected corners of society, sometimes in the open and fully public, sometimes also implicitly and almost hidden behind popular pictures and melodies. Religion has freed itself from the old owners, the religious elites, as our befriended cultural anthropologists usually call our church leaders. For two thousand years the churches have almost always been the authorities to dispense the Gospel, since only literate people can read scriptures, even though through all centuries stories have been told and ballads have been sung to retell the Bible, summarize the Gospel and communicate it to the common men and women. In the Middle Ages evangelists wandered through Italy and other countries, to tell the people about Jesus' love, until they died of illness or at the hands of their persecutors who tried to hinder their free religious enterprise. In our time publishing houses are free to publish religious books that people like to read, daily papers decide for themselves what they like to write, and broadcasting companies do not let themselves be lead by church committees but by what they themselves think is worthwhile. Put briefly, the modernization, globalization and pluralization of society has occasioned a broad proliferation of religious ideas and practices and the churches have lost their exclusive authority and have to share it with a great many other stakeholders on the religious market place.

Unavoidably a great many people participate in more than one tradition. They see a documentary about a Hindu mystic, attend a meeting with the Dalai Lama, read a book on an Eastern tradition, attend a church service on Christmas Eve, and are influenced by all. We will call this phenomenon "multiple participation." The usual term has become bricolage[1]: a person's beliefs are a kind of patchwork with pieces from various sources, loosely ordered in a whole. Before the term bricolage had won field, sociologists also liked to speak of "faith à la carte," like somebody composing her diner with recipes from various regions.

The expression "à la carte" is pejorative: people are not fully serious, and take what they like, but their plate is trashy and not refined. The term bricolage has a postmodern flavour. Postmoderns might ask, Why would people not combine what seems plausible to them? Perhaps I am pressing the term too much, but personally I have a slight preference for "multiple participation" because it is a descriptive term that relates to traditions which supply insights and practices, although I will use both terms. Theologians who think about the challenges for the mission of the church and viable ways of giving account of Christian hope must accept facts as they are, evaluate them and offer critical questions in order to find a responsible way to deal with this new phenomenon and help churches find a way to present themselves positively in the growing religious market place. Therefore I will try to describe the phenomenon somewhat more elaborately and formulate some of the main questions that we must consider more closely.

2   MULTIPLE PARTICIPATION

Multiple participation is the appropriation of elements from more than one religious tradition. Persons combine practices and beliefs from various traditions and let themselves be inspired by persons from differing schools. A problem lies in the term participation. It is possible that people may choose not to belong to any one tradition, yet be inspired by or convinced of other insights without taking refuge in one of the traditions. In this case people are "users" of traditions, and do not take responsibility for a group. Some may speak of "participation without belonging," although such believers can be bearers of that

---

[1] The term is from Claude Lévi-Strauss 1962, Chapter 1 (Dutch translation 1968: 29f.); he uses it in relation to mythical thinking. See Droogers, chapter 5 in this Volume.

tradition, nevertheless, if they speak about the insights that they share. It also happens quite frequently that people who belong to one of the traditions share practices and insights from other traditions.

People may share various elements of a tradition, such as symbols like a cross or a statue of the Buddha, or a picture with a clear traditional background. Another form of participation is the incorporation of certain beliefs, as, for example, human autonomy, or, on the contrary, the rejection of a traditional belief such as the after-life by a Christian or a Muslim. A third form is the use of meditational techniques, such as the use of zazen in Christian monasteries.

The stronger forms of bricolage are individual combinations of elements from various traditions. This presupposes that people do not acknowledge religious authority and have lost the idea that the beliefs and practices of a tradition form a meaningful whole. Such bricolage has some historical and contextual presuppositions, as the decline of belief in Western superiority, the acceptance of a kind of equality between several traditions, the rejection of the idea that one tradition can have the whole truth, and the freedom to make individual choices concerning religious practice.

Because church and theology have to come to terms with this new phenomenon, we should try to evaluate it. We will do that in two steps. First I will try to explain how such a configuration of beliefs and practices of various backgrounds is possible, and then I will discuss criteria that are important for the evaluation thereof. From this we may learn what challenges the church has to face when she tries to communicate the fullness of the Christian message among those seekers. However, at the outset, I will step aside for a moment in order to consider to what extent this bricolage really is a new phenomenon.

3   A NEW PHENOMENON

Although within Europe and perhaps also North America, bricolage might be a new phenomenon, it is well-known in many Asian societies. The example par excellence is Japan, which in 1984 had around 89 million Buddhists, 112 million Shintoïsts, 1,5 million Christians and 15 million people of other traditions - in a total population of about 120 million inhabitants, of whom 30% are non-believing (see, e.g., Kamstra 1988:9f.). Religious studies scholars often comment to their students about the amazing attractiveness of religious life for the Japanese people, as it baffles all Western ideas about choices in religion and the mutual exclusion of religious traditions.

For example, people in Japan like to marry according to the Christian ritual, and to be buried in the Buddhist way. They make their own bricolage, and who are we to prohibit that? However, the situation might be more complex, and perhaps it is even better to say, less complex. Many Christian marriages are celebrated in chapels build next to the hotel where the diner is served and further festivities take place. The officiating minister will be hired by the hotel and not necessarily be a member of a congregation. This is the closest resemblance to "faith à la carte" as we may think of it. The minister can be anyone who is able to read some liturgical formulas and wish bride and bridegroom the best.

Death is another milestone of life and should be marked by rituals, because we never can be sure about the other shore. Therefore people go to the experts about the chain of live-and-death and death-and-life: the Buddhist priests and monks, asking them to take care of the rituals and paying the price just as they pay the hotel for a Christian marriage. In a sense, such customs, if they are superficial indeed, may not be real cases of a bricolage in which elements from various traditions intermingle.

Such use of Buddhist and Christian rituals presupposes not being convinced of the reason the Bible gives for the death of Jesus nor believe in his resurrection, the Last Judgment and forgiveness of sins. It appears that Christian talk about love can be integrated more easily in a more or less Buddhist setting than vice versa, although many Buddhist monks will also complain about the superficial participation in their rituals. Therefore the question seems to be justified whether these popular forms of bricolage and the popularity of chapels for marriages are tokens of participation in the Christian tradition or just an acceptance of some Christian values concerning love and faithfulness.

In China, folk religions often combine elements of Taoist, Confucian, and Buddhist origins, to such an extent that in Buddhist temples Fung Zu is also venerated, and popular temples can take part in or "belong to" three traditions. So the subjects of bricolage are not only persons but institutions as well.

Another practice of intermingling traditions not usually understood to be mutually exclusive is to be found in Hindu culture. People can go to honour Nandi or Ganesha or Krishna or any of the gods and be blessed. But they will not feel that such worship is mutually exclusive because the gods are all aspects of the one divinity. Therefore, the Christian stress on the unique position of Christ is, and will, remain offensive and narrow-minded in Hindu eyes.

The examples given may help to see some of the presuppositions of at least some forms of bricolage: we do not know all about God but only some aspects; worship may focus on some of these aspects and be contextual and selective, according to the needs of the situation; no single religion exhausts all religious truth. Therefore, an important question is whether such a philosophy of religion is implied in every case of modern "faith à la carte" or bricolage.

4   TODAY'S WESTERN-EUROPEAN CHRISTIANITY

Before we go into that we better have a critical look into the present condition of Christianity in the Western-European context. Could it not be the case that the beliefs of orthodox Christians are also a blend between various worldviews? From the results of natural science we learned to reinterpret the creation story. The explanation of the Gospels has changed and in some respects has been enriched by historical-critical research that, on the other hand, has rendered a wide-spread feeling of uncertainty about the trustworthiness of the texts. Even more important, to my understanding, have been the Modern Western ideas of individuality and the autonomy of the person who as a free human being decides for himself or herself what to do and what to believe.

Such an individualistic understanding of persons has not only replaced the corporate personality and the belonging to a people in the Old Testament, but also changed the idea of being part of the body of Christ. So much so, that we may ask whether we really can understand the original meaning of this expression. The idea that God guides history and human life, has lost its plausibility for many because of the rise in acceptance of the concept of "fate" on the part of so many people in situations of war, hunger, poverty and psychological deprivation. The idea of sin has lost its comprehensive sense because of insights into human tragedy, the role of genetical factors, and circumstances that make the lives of many people a sort of "play" of many forces that make a happy life for them unlikely.

Seen in this way, beliefs take part in a constant process of change and adaption to other knowledge, insights of other worldview traditions, and new experiences. Such processes could be seen as bricolage. However, they differ in two respects. First, contextual reinterpretation of the tradition is not the same as a gathering of insights from various worldview traditions. Second, these changes presuppose a search for consistency among beliefs. Otherwise there is no point in such reinterpretation and change. This differs from a bricolage of unrelated beliefs from different backgrounds.

Let me give one more example of bricolage. Somebody believes God to be the Creator of the universe, thinks that the love of God is visible in Jesus, and practices zen meditation and learns to experience her- or himself as part of the whole of co-existing and co-arising things in which no thing has its own, independent being and that, therefore, all things are "empty" (that is, of substance or own-being). This combination of beliefs and practices is not exceptional, even if the belief that God (who has his own being) has created the world (which after creation has a certain independence of its Creator) is contradictory to the belief that all that exists is a momentary constellation of causal elements. This is a bricolage, and not a reinterpretation of traditional beliefs, which in the end, I presume, will lead to a radical reinterpretation of the idea of creation and of christology.[2]

Let us reserve the term bricolage for the putting together of contradictory beliefs and/or practices. Nevertheless, how is such a bricolage possible? Do people simply not realise that you cannot uphold two contradictory beliefs? These questions now bring us to the next section on the nature of religious beliefs.

5   A CONFIGURATION INSTEAD OF A SYSTEM

The fact that religious traditions do develop and change in exchange with other traditions and circumstances, and the rise of the phenomenon of bricolage can be understood from the nature of religions as configurations of a number of basic insights and practices. Religious doctrines are secondary phenomena that depend upon insights on a deeper level. An example of such an insight is the utter contingency of all things and their full interrelatedness in the Buddhist tradition. This is not a mere theory, but a cherished experience that is basic to all experiences that a person has.

An example from the Abrahamic traditions is the experience of the meaningfulness of life, which leads people to affirm that the world is not merely contingent but has an ultimate goal. This last way to experience reality has been related to the idea of creation, while the fundamental Buddhist experience mentioned supports the ideas of the interconnectedness of all things and their emptiness. Now all religious ideas are elaborated and explained during the course of history, and the idea of

---

[2] See Droogers' (1989) analysis of syncretism, as beliefs and practices that are contested by the religious elites and my analysis of consequences of integrating incompatible beliefs (1989).

emptiness has been elaborated in important schools as buddha-nature which implies the idea of the meaningfulness of the universe. Religious worldviews are not fully coherent theories. Christianity combines the idea of Creation with the special place of Christ, which at the one hand is related to creation (all things created by the Word) but has also a certain independence. Christian faith is rooted in impressive experiences of nature and in the impressive story about Christ, which becomes central because of its links with other deep experiences, like consciousness of failure, the not-self-evidence of the good, and the relativity of merit. Such basic beliefs form a network and not a neat systematic "system." Therefore some beliefs may become more central and other move slowly to the sidelines.

In various contexts or at differing stages of life, the belief-system of a person will vary considerably. Down through the centuries, traditions have changed; some beliefs may disappear and others be incorporated. In different cultures religious traditions have developed in different ways. Some of the beliefs will be present through the ages but their place in the configuration and their interpretation will vary considerably. Christianity will speak about creation, sin, the sovereignty of God over history, Christ and the Kingdom of God. Islam will speak about God, the Koran and the Prophet. And Buddhism will speak of the Buddha and the interconnectedness of things. But the interpretation of all these beliefs will vary from time to time and age to age. The same applies to values and virtues, and even when the list of virtues, honoured by a tradition, would not differ much through time, the way in which they are operationalized will not be the same but differ contextually.

From this we can explain the possibility of bricolage. People do not reflect systematically upon their faith. Rather, they appropriate information from many sources. So their ideas about the meaning of life, about the world, their place in society at large, and what happens after death are formed from what they think plausible. Perhaps we can express this by saying that in the past people tended to accept more a whole tradition with its doctrinal and ritual "properties" as they have been presented to them, while now many are apt to appropriate "isolated" beliefs and rituals that seem plausible or helpful to them. Beliefs can be appropriated superficially or on a deeper level. Beliefs that are foundational for a person I call "basic insights." They are being formed by impressive, emotionally loaden experiences (cf. Ridder 2002: 179, 196ff.; Vroom 1989:ch.9; 1996; 2000).

Somebody who believes in God's steering of history may loose such a belief after a series of tragic accidents, and instead accept the sheer arbitrariness of what happens. Because many people no longer acknowledge the authority of the church, they have to decide for themselves what to believe. And they will do so by a learning process in which some mere superficial beliefs that are not supported by emotionally relevant impressive experiences, fall away and other beliefs may be adopted instead. The development of personal ethic may follow analogical lines. People who are apt to sacrifice themselves but really become hurt by it, may try to become more assertive and less generous.

With the decline of authority in non-orthodox circles, the importance of theological reflection and control of faith has become less important. By consequence, the configuration of somebody's faith can be less systematic and more fragmentary than the beliefs in orthodox circles used to be. Although church-going Christians can also incorporate foreign beliefs, non-church-goers are more likely to do so and to get their own packet of insights in life and their own views as to the importance of specific values and virtues. It is clear that the old mechanisms of the plausibility structure also will do their work, and that the formation of somebody's beliefs will be influenced heavily by friends and colleagues, by what is politically and culturally correct or, on the contrary, goes against the grain.

Before we deal with criteria to evaluate such bricolage of beliefs, we should take a moment to reflect upon functional descriptions of such belief-formation. For important reasons, it has been said that people use several repertoires. And they may use the repertoire that under certain circumstances is useful for them.

So, for example, certain people may accept that things do not go as well as they would like, recognizing that other people are more successful. In this case, they may learn from one repertoire that success and money do not necessarily make people happy—and that they have to be prepared to be humble servants of others. But if these same folks become rich, they may use another repertoire and say that they are thankful and that they have done their best. Both repertoires as such are not logically contradictory, but they nevertheless differ markedly one from the other. And they are perhaps psychologically incompatible.

Traditions have a broad arsenal of possibilities that allows people to take what suits their situation. Religious pluralism has broadened this arsenal even further, giving opportunity to use more insights, wisdom, and sayings to cope with both friendly and inimical situations. However, the question remains whether such a use of religion really helps people in more difficult situations.

Let us compare ideas and practices for a moment with using a tool like a screw-driver to turn a screw. Anybody who has lots of unused screws lying around knows that a particular screw-driver does not fit every screw. And when the screw-driver does not fit the head of a screw, it is difficult to tighten it properly. We solve the problem by looking for a screw-driver that fits the screw. Or, the other way around, we choose a screw that fits the screw-driver. However, we may ask whether this is really analogous to the use of religious beliefs and practices by people to respond to problems in their lives. Do they simply look for ideas, practices and conduct that best fit their situation? There is a major difference between the screw-driver illustration and the matter of using repertoires. We cannot simply say that a better belief fits the problem better like a better screw-driver more closely fits the head of a screw. However, the idea of a belief fitting an emotionally important situation might help to understand the bricolage and the use of repertoires. Persons who have experienced a number of difficult situations that have ended disastrously may give us their belief and hope that all things work for good for them—and they may doubt that God reigns over all details of life. New beliefs in the prevalence of evil or in random chance may seem to more closely fit their experience. So I understand the use of a repertoire *not as a real* use to cope, like using a tool to fix a repair, but rather as the *decreasing plausibility* of a belief which in some cases may then be replaced by another belief. Against this background I will discuss two more questions, first criteria for evaluation of bricolage of beliefs, and second point out some practical consequences for church policy.

6   CRITERIA FOR TRUE BELIEF

In this section I will not treat the whole list of criteria that often have been discussed. Rather, I will concentrate on the criteria of depth and the guidance that religion should give. If a religious world-view and a religious life are not just tools to cope with problems (although psychologists can study religious beliefs and practices in such a way), but form a way of life that people experience to be trustworthy, then in one form or another it requires that such beliefs give good guidance and a real insight for understanding life. True religion is trustworthy because it says how to endure happy and sad experiences, helps to choose the right priorities in conflicts of duties, and tells how life is. Worldviews make truth-claims: they tell about important traits of the world and facts of life and our place under the sun. The unique role of religion is that it helps people to fit in a larger whole: you live as a creature of God amidst other people or you are an entity, fully interwoven with other entities. In such ways we are helped to get a better perspective on ourselves, life and the world. It helps to see our lives in a different light.

This does not require necessarily that a religious worldview be coherent. People can coherently share some (not all) Christian insights in the relations between husband and wife, faithfulness and equality, and relate them to the love of God for humankind and to the love of Jesus, but do not need to share further Christian beliefs. Multiple participation is partial sharing. For a funeral people can go to the Buddhist temple, think in terms of karma and rebirth, and take care of worship on the required dates when the deceased is supposed to go move on in the process of disappearance and rebirth. This participation in Buddhist rituals does not necessitate accepting fully that all things are interconnected. In practice coherence is not a requirement for people to hold certain beliefs. Consistency in a weaker sense (that some beliefs are to be held together with others so as not to contradict each other), however, is a valid criterion. Yet even in this case people have an escape in that they may feel that some beliefs are not fully sure or that the relation between ideas that seem true is not clear to us, and perhaps cannot be. In this sense people may play with logically incompatible ideas. Someone, for example, who may be unsure about the deceased person's soul going into another realm of existence, into another human being or plant or animal, may attend a cremation service to express gratitude and show piety. Given the great variety of experiences that people have, plausibility of basic insights is a much more important criterion than coherence between insights. And religious ways of life must be helpful and salutary in order to be plausible.

Religion can only be important to somebody if it helps to truly live. If we think a proposition to be true but it has no practical value, it will not be as important to us. Therefore relevance for practical life, to overcome suffering and immoral situations, and reach salvation is decisive. Because salvation has consequences for societal life, Jerald Gort has rightly stressed the importance of the striving for liberation and defended that it is a meeting point of religious traditions and a good starting point for mutual understanding and cooperation (Gort 1993). Serious religion gives guidance and shelter. It should help to face life and to make choices, and gives comfort in difficult times, and challenges us to care for others.

The question of how much guidance a bricolage of religious insights and practices gives, is not easy to answer. May Protestants burn candles?

Is such a gesture always a secular one or does it take on a religious flavour? People have a statue of the Buddha in a room of their house or they may regulate their breath when they are anxious. Does this make them Buddhists? Does it help them? Secular people may be inspired by a production of Jesus Christ Superstar. Does that make them Christian? The marginalised poor in the streets of Buenos Airos, the *fracasados*, sometimes drink small fragments of Psalm 23 in their tea, though, being mostly illiterate, they cannot read the fragment itself (Althaus-Reid 2003). How far does it help them and give them guidance?

We could say that deeper faith and deeper insights may help people to live more consistently along the lines of a tradition. Maybe more stable points of reference help us orientate ourselves better. But it could also be that a repertoire from another tradition would help us more, when our situation and culture go through considerable change. In that case, given the deep changes in our global, individualistic and schizophrenic culture, such changes could explain the phenomenon of bricolage. Isn't it schizophrenic to live an affluent life while so many people are poor? Isn't it contradictory to use natural resources and not share them more? Given the fact of a threatened planet, is it contradictory to continue to hold to the old paradigms of a Christian era: to fill the earth and subdue it? I think many people look for guidance in the new questions that they face in a complex world. So one criterion is guidance. The fullness of life—although it will never be fully realised in this world—is more important than neat theories.

The second important criterion in relation to bricolage is whether such faith gives comfort. With respect to this that we may ask: How can I trust God if I have my own beliefs? We should be conscious of the different kinds of comfort that religions grant. While in a cosmic religion salvation is found in being a part of the whole of existence, in theistic religions salvation can be found in trust upon God. When applying this criterion we should realize the differences between the three main options for viewing the cosmos as seen by cosmic, a-cosmic and theistic religions: 1) we are part of the cosmic process; or 2) we are an estranged worldly phenomenon of the divine ground of being; or 3) we are a creation of God. Based on which of these we choose, we must 1) immerse ourselves in cosmic existence; 2) return to the divine ground of being; or 3) live in peace before the face of God.

Although these ideas are incompatible, the most important point is that people be guided and comforted in a very real way. This requires a deep personal faith: trust without depth will not hold. In order to really trust God, I have to believe and to know God. To detach myself from all attachments and live fully open in this world, I have to learn to experience myself as *empty*—as a Zen master would say. Does not faith need depth in order to hold on and act wisely in turmoil, or seek justice and endure injustice in trust?

If we apply both criteria of depth and guidance we may come to some earnest conclusions. If somebody's faith has no real depth, it is doubtful whether it will help her or him to stick to what is right, loving and wise to do in difficult situations. People may just follow the majority, be silent when people are oppressed, and do no effort to help establish a better, sustainable world. So I propose to take depth and guidance as two criteria to judge the bricolage forms of religion. I think that depth presupposes regular rituals, not ad hoc beliefs, a deepening of virtues and a faith-filled and sincere life. How does such a perspective enable us to judge the concept of bricolage?

Bricolage is not necessarily superficial. On the contrary, if a Christian deepens her spiritual life by using methods from zen meditation, her beliefs may be modified, but her faith could be deepened, although not in a "dogmatic" way. However, if somebody has serious doubts about Christian faith and does not take much effort to reflect upon faith and deepen it, but 'plays' with Eastern or New Age ideas, then such beliefs will not be deep. It seems difficult to judge the depth of somebody's faith only from a theological point of view; a psychological evaluation would be needed as well.

The challenge to live a better life may also be reinforced through contact with other religious traditions. From Muslim friends people could learn how decisive faith is, from Buddhist friends that not the afterlife but this-worldly existence is decisive, from Hindu's that God really is outside human grip and theorizing. Therefore the process of learning and sometimes taking over ideas and practices does not necessarily diminish the measure of involvement nor the critical potential of a tradition. However, who just takes what her suits, will not be challenged. Depth and challenge go hand in hand.

I will conclude by making a few remarks concerning coherence and consistency. It seems that people can hold incoherent beliefs. However, if beliefs are contradictory, it is difficult to see how both can be deep convictions that really challenge people and support them. The sola gratia cannot be combined with reincarnation. Depth requires logical and psychological consistency. A conviction is neither a systematic theory nor a bundle of contradictory beliefs.

7 CONCLUSION: A CHALLENGE TO THE CHURCH

How may the churches approach the challenge of bricolage? The incraesing individualism and the decreasingly uniform patterns of faith have made pluralism a characteristic of church life. Church services that do not reflect upon the plural culture, do not convince many people any more. In church we should be conscious of the silent bricolage among ourselves. But if it is true that challenge and depth are among the main characteristics of true faith, it follows that the main task of the church is to challenge people to deepen their faith. So it does not help to just reject some insights of other traditions; the real important point is to show how deep faith does go. From the center of Christian faith: the centrality of God's love, the reconciliation and the imitation of Jesus, follows which beliefs and practices from other origins can be combined and which not. It is one thing to reject a belief, and another to deepen that belief that essentially will exclude another one. Western culture is individualistic, and people get a lot of superficial information. Therefore the challenge for the churches is to offer community and guidance to live a more meaningful life.

Church services seldom are attractive for people who have lost their link with the church. But many people feel a need to really meet with other people and reflect upon their lifes and some elements in their work or personal circumstances. From this it is understandable that all over the world Christian retreat centers are flourishing. They seem to have some things in common with monasteries and ashrams. Ministers have to learn to be more fully the spiritual guides for their parishoners—and less the historico-critically trained exegetes of an ancient text.

After the decline of the Christian culture in Western Europe, the process of the communication of the Gospel has to find new ways—and possibly re-appropriate old and partly traditional ways to initiate people into the mysteries of Christian faith, help them pray and trust, and look with new eyes to each other and themselves. The urban areas have to be approached as mission fields. Also in Western culture many churches are present, both traditional churches as well as churches from an African and Asian background. To really reach modern young people with a broad mind and openness for all sorts of religion, the church has to develop new forms next to the old ones. Bricolage is itself not necessarily the problem. But superficiality is. And people need initiation into the heart of the Gospel. Foreign elements in beliefs need not be approached in an antithetical way, but by stressing the kernel of the Gospel, so that by that light incompatible elements will be put aside and serious elements from other cultural and religious backgrounds will be baptized and integrated into Christian faith. The church must forego the temptation to just stress theological truisms and moralistic recipes, but help people instead to deepen their faith, learn to pray, to read Scripture in a non-intellectualist and personal way and so walk with God.

"Morning has broken." We seem to live at the dawn of a new era: individualistic, secularized, yet global and religiously pluralistic at the same time. Religious sects are omnipresent and people need to be almost omniscient to make the right choice as to which religious path they should follow, and many of these groups display religious pictures as beautiful as those shown by the World Life Fund campaign. Who is not reminded of a paradise without hunger and catastrophe, without disputes and rumours of war—a world "springing fresh from the Word," in which we have learned to walk with God and not to leave it to the Life Funds of our world to "praise with elation, praise every morning—God's recreation of the new day?"

BIBLIOGRAPHY

Althaus-Reid, Marcella. (2003). "The Bible of the Fracasados: Readings from the Excluded". In: Mercy Oduyoye and Hendrik M. Vroom (eds). One Gospel—Many Cultures. Amsterdam-New York: Rodopi.

Droogers, André F. (1989). "Syncretism: The Problem of Definition, the Definition of the Problem". In: Jerald D. Gort et al. (1989). Pp. 7-25.

Gort, Jerald D. et al. (eds). (1989). Dialogue and Syncretism. An Interdisciplinary Approach. Amsterdam: Rodopi and Grand Rapids: Eerdmans.

—. (1992). "Liberative Ecumenism: Gateway to the Sharing of Religious Experience Today'". In: J.D.Gort, H.M.Vroom, R.Fernhout, A.Wessels (eds.). On Sharing Religious Experience. Amsterdam: Rodopi / Grand Rapids: Eerdmans. Pp. 88-105.

Kamstra, Jacques H. (1988). De Japanse religie. Een fenomenale studie. Hilversum: Gooi en Sticht.

Lévi-Strauss, Claude (1962). La Pensée Sauvage (Translations in English and Dutch.: The Savage Mind, 1966; Het wilde denken. Amsterdam: Meulenhoff 1968).

Ridder, Ab W. (2002). Vreugde als aanzet tot geloof, Zoetermeer: Boekencentrum.

Vroom, Hendrik M. (1989). "Syncretism and Dialogue: A Philosophical Analysis". In: Jerald D. Gort et. al. (1989). Pp. 26-35.

—. (1989). Religion and the Truth. Amsterdam: Rodopi / Grand Rapids: Eerdmans.

—. (1996). "Religious Insights and Interreligious Dialogue".In: Bulletin of the Henry Martyn Institute 15. Pp. 92-105.

—. (2000). "The (Ir)rationalism of the Theistic Concept of God". In: Henri Krop, Arie L.Molendijk, Hent de Vries (eds.). *Post-theism. Reframing the Judeo-Christian Tradition*. Leuven: Peeters. Pp. 223-236.

PART II

THE CHALLENGES OF CONTEXTUALIZATION AND LIBERATION

7 Dialogue Between EATWOT and Western Theologians: A Comment on the 6th EATWOT Conference in Geneva 1983

John S. Mbiti

1 INTRODUCTION

In 1976, twenty-two theologians from Africa, Asia, Latin America and one representative of minority groups in North America founded the Ecumenical Association of Third World Theologians (EATWOT) in Dar es Salaam, Tanzania. This was a timely event in view of the fact that around that date statistics indicated a tilting of Christianity from the northern region (America, Europe and the former Soviet Union) to the South (Africa, Asia, Latin America and Oceania). In various ways the North had been responsible for this statistical shift. Christianity in the South was beginning to emerge on the world scene. Hitherto, Christians from the southern region had met one another at universities and conferences in the North. They had always been guests of the North at such conferences. But now, in 1976, theologians from the South could meet on their own soil and could determine the agenda of their meeting. They were finally "at home", standing on their own platform and having the microphone to themselves. They were actors and not observers of the occurrence. The founding of the EATWOT was an historic event with enormous implications. Such an organisation was long overdue.

By 2002, EATWOT's membership had grown to over 700 members, largely academics and church officials. Some of the founding and early members had already passed on. Persons join the Association as individuals and not as representatives of their churches or academic institutions. One of the main features of the Association is its ecumenical nature. It brings together theologians from all the families and traditions of the church. Within a relatively short time, the Association has accomplished much in organising theological conferences and consultations on regional, continental and intercontinental bases. It has published an impressive number of books, especially reports from its conferences, as well as the journal Voices from the Third World. Individual members have also made theological contributions through their own publications.[1] Few theological organisations in the world have

---

[1] See the select bibliography at the end of this essay.

achieved as much as the EATWOT has done within the first twenty-five years of its existence.

2   EARLY INTENTION FOR DIALOGUE

From its early days, it was the aim of the EATWOT to engage in dialogue with theologians of the North. Already in the meeting in Dar es Salaam in 1976 the founders had pointed out that Western theology was "inadequate and irrelevant" for the situations of the South. At its first general assembly in New Delhi in 1981, the EATWOT stated that

> for the Third World, this [traditional Western] theology has been alienated and alienating. It has not provided the motivation for opposing the evils of racism, sexism, capitalism, colonialism, and neo-colonialism. It has failed to understand our religions, indigenous cultures, and traditions, and to relate to them in a respectful way.[2]

These were strong words. With such a concern the EATWOT felt it necessity to define its relationship to Western theology. This was a kind of dialectical relationship involving both continuity and discontinuity. The Assembly in New Delhi called for dialogue with Western theologians. That call materialised at the sixth international EATWOT conference in Geneva, Switzerland on January 5-13, 1983. Some 80 theologians came together for this conference, of which 40% were from the South and 40% were women. In addition there were 20 journalists largely from Europe.

This essay examines that theological dialogue. I am not a member of the EATWOT and did not participate in this conference. I base my observations and comments on the conference report in the book edited by Virginia Fabella and Sergio Torres, *Doing Theology in a Divided World* (1985), and to a lesser extent on the book by Hans Schöpfer, *Theologie an der Basis* (1983).

3   DIALOGUE CONFERENCE IN GENEVA

In preparation for the Geneva gathering, the European participants held a conference in Woudschoten, Holland, on December 10-14, 1981, at which they formulated their concerns. The preparation followed three

---

[2] Fabella and Torres 1985:197. The quotation is from the "Final Statement", of the Fifth EATWOT conference which was its first General Assembly, in New Delhi, 17-29 August 1981.

approaches: a) An analysis of the "European reality," in order to bring out the oppressive and liberating elements; b) the role of the church; and c) the search in the European context for a new way to carry out an appropriate interpretation of the Gospel. The concerns focussed on six themes thought to be important for the situation in Europe. These were (according to Schöpfer):

- Feminists looking for the cause of opposition to women's demands, including men's fear of losing their power. Here, attention would also be upon the victims of dominant theologies such as women, Afro-Americans and the poor, those who have to wage a double fight to question traditional theology and to defend themselves. Special attention was to be given to the image of God, man and woman, sexist language in theology and liturgy; and an exposition of the relationship between sexism and racism.
- The minorities who do not feel at home in their own environment. They suffer from a culture of silence.
- Employment as a situation of crisis in Europe due to structural, personal and ideological factors. A new ethic of liberation was needed.
- Peace in connection with peace movements, militarism, production of weapons, justice, and the mutual relationship between peace and justice.
- Culture: the dominant culture today was seen as a scientific culture whose power of attraction is technology. The church has sanctified false values in the world of industry.
- Capitalism that finds itself in a major crisis affecting both the exploiter and the exploited. The characteristics of the economic system were seen to be oppression by a minority, oppression of the majority, and oppression of the Third World in such a way that the West European society flourishes only at the cost of the Third World. There is a class struggle. It was "concluded that the capitalist system cannot be improved."

The main points from the Woudschoten conference ran parallel with the points from the General Assembly of the EATWOT in New Delhi in August, 1981. The two conferences took place four months apart. The latter's themes were: poverty, exploitation, racism, the position of women, imperialism, affluence, people's struggle for social justice, theology from below, dialogue with other religions, and the role of culture in the theological task.

Two possibilities stood in the foreground of the Geneva conference: to start with the final declarations from New Delhi and Woudschoten or to work with themes that could be jointly determined beforehand. The organising committee of the EATWOT chose *Doing Theology in a Divided World* as the main theme. The aims of the conference included: 1) to examine the struggles of the poor and the oppressed against all forms of injustice in the First and Third Worlds; 2) to define the different yet interreleted forms of oppression; 3) to consider the Biblical understanding of God and Jesus Christ from the experience of liberation struggle; 4) to examine the meaning of theology in the liberation struggle; and 5) to formulate appropriate theological methods that could used by Christians in such situations (Schöpfer 1983:52ff.).

Sergio Torres, the then general secretary of the Association, expressed the point of departure of the EATWOT at the conference. "The general conclusion was that Western theology is inadequate for the Third World and irrelevant as the Christian interpretation of the gospel message for the people of underdeveloped countries. Through the years this conclusion has been confirmed" (Torres in: Fabella and Torres 1985:ix). The EATWOT theologians understood theology as "talk about God in context." This theology takes the realities of the Third World seriously and addresses the longing of the poor in their struggle for liberation. Third World theology has both continuity with Western theology in reading the same Bible and discontinuity in its interpretation, especially with reference to the West's separation of theology from practice.

As planned, the conference evolved in three phases: telling personal stories, making a social analysis, and reformulating the methodology and content of theology. Each participant told how he or she was engaged in the struggle for liberation. Some personal stories were included in the report. They came from Holland, Nicaragua, Sri Lanka, Sweden and Canada. The EATWOT has always occupied itself with social analysis. Four presentations highlighted the question of oppression and liberation. These were on South Africa by Bonganjalo Goba, economic analysis by Julio de Santa Ana, feminist perspective by Rosemary Radford Ruether and cultural perspective by Engelbert Mveng. Both Dorothee Sölle (at the time professor at Union Theological Seminary, New York) and Johann Baptist Metz (from the University of Münster, Germany) strongly criticised European theology. Sölle held that European theology was coloured by a kind of apartheid. It did not allow the theologians from the Third World to enter into it. Metz expressed the opinion that we are at the end of the Christian phase in which Europe was the centre of Christianity.

Five papers addressed the need for a "reformulation of the methodology and content of theology": James H. Cone, Georges Casalis, Samuel Rayan, Mercy Amba Oduyoye and Jim Wallis. Three participants made final assessments: "A Third World Perspective" by Tissa Balasuriya, "A First World Perspective;" by Letty M. Russell, and "An East European, Orthodox Perspective" by Ion Bria.

During the course of the conference, the women of the First and Third Worlds came together to form a strong group. They called for a theological practice that would be free of male domination and sexist language. However, the final report does not contain the exact nature of this contribution.

The reformulation of theology was one of the most important foci from Geneva. An Indian theologian, Samuel Rayan framed this in his address.

> We want theology to be a service to life at all levels — from the tiny blade of grass, to the singing bird, to the growing baby, to the heights of rigorous thought and warm friendships, to the depths of mystic joy and divine darkness. We want a theology that will be at the service of life with its many needs and spiralling possibilities as well as its transcendence and its endlessly expanding quest and onward thrust. Our theology will be at the service of those who work, suffer, and hope, those who struggle for justice and human dignity for all women and men (Rayan 1985:124).

4   AFFIRMATIONS OF THE EATWOT CONFERENCE IN GENEVA

The main content of the conference is found in the Final Statement that called for the "need for a comprehensive analysis." This is a primary emphasis in EATWOT's theological exercise.

> We have said in our past final documents that social analysis helps us to uncover the causes of oppression and enables Christians to love their neighbours through strategies of change and structural reform. Many First World theologians involved in renewal also use analysis as an essential element in their effort (item 10:182).

The Final Statement says that "the original plan called for an analysis of three major forms of oppression and their interrelatedness: racism, sexism, and classism." However, discussions at the conference also included cultural and religious elements.

On racism, the Statement points out that this

has two aspects. The first and most evident is the dehumanization and subjugation of persons because of their colour and physiognomy... But the second aspect goes beyond rational economic exploitation and takes the form of an odious ideology... Any working toward a just world order must expose and combat the ideology and institution of racism (item 13:182 f.).

In speaking about "classism, militarism, and imperialism," the Statement asserts that

the division of classes, due to economic and social differences, is a fact that exists both within and between nations, and is aggravated by racial and sexual divisions that are also turned into structures of labour exploitation. Furthermore, class analysis disregards the cultural and religious dimensions of social relations and does not account adequately for racism, sexism and their interstructural relationship with classism (item 15:183).

The Statement reflects on both capitalist and socialist systems and holds the opinion that "we are convinced that the efforts to nurture new life must confront not only the economic dimensions but also the issues of culture, anthropology, and spirituality that inform the development of institutions, structures, and technology of a new society" (item 19:84).

Asian delegates raised the matter of religious and cultural analysis. This won considerable support among the participants. "The continent [of Asia] has had a protracted history of cultures and religions that have dominated and oppressed along with a long heritage of acceptance of poverty and suffering" (items 20, 21:184f.). The African delegates highlighted their view that

what they consider to be the worst form of impoverishment is anthropological poverty. This is a serious form of oppression that despoils human beings not only of what they materially have but of everything that constitutes their being and essence. The root of this problem is the imposition on Third World people of Western anthropology that embodies a concept of human nature based on individualism, competition, and struggle for power (item 22:185).

The document maintains that "the analysis of the role of culture is a necessary step in uncovering neo-cultural domination." It sees European expansion as having resulted in cultural domination in the past; whereas today this is in the form of "the imposition of a technocratic and consumerist mentality... Thus the struggle against cultural imperialism is an intrinsic aspect of all liberation struggles" (items 23, 24:185). Concerning the oppression of women, the Statement pointed out that:

Sexism, understood as the distinct structure of mariginalization of women within the system of domination, became one of the major issues
of the conference... Several important clarifications were made.

a) Sexism is not only a women's issue; it is a men's issue as well...

b) Sexism is found in all the traditional patriarchal cultures throughout
the world which deny women their human and civil rights and divest
them of power and influence...

c) In liberal capitalism in Western Europe and North America, and
increasingly in the Third World,... industrialization and modernization have created new structures of oppression for women...

d) Feminism in the First World has often not taken seriously racism,
class exploitation, and imperialism... Feminist theology has brought
a heightened awareness of the need for a different and critical exegesis
of scriptures and a new sensitivity to symbols, rituals, and community...

e) Progressive men in both the First and Third Worlds have not taken
sexism seriously...

f) Unfortunately, the dependency and domination of women has been
legitimated by Christian theology and expressed institutionally in the
Christian churches... (items 25-31:186-187).

In addressing theological analysis, the Statement comments,

> The capitalist system is using religious language and symbols to
> legitimize its policies... Its call for peace and security can be
> understood ultimately only in terms of idolatry, or allegiance to false
> gods... Conflicts between oppressors and their victims have become
> spiritual battles... The present economic system, like an immense
> idol, like the beast of the Apocalypse (Rev. 13), covers the earth with
> its cloak of unemployment and homelessness, hunger and nakedness,
> desolation and death. It destroys other ways of life and styles of work
> which counter its own. It breeds pollution and hostility to nature...
> But in the struggles of the poor and the oppressed throughout the
> world against all forms of dehumanization, there is a sign of life and
> victory (items 32-35:187f.).

The Geneva conference also gave considerable space to what it called "a
reformulation of theology." The outcome is recorded in items 36-56 of
the Final Statement. From its very beginning, the EATWOT considered
theological methodology to be important. This came out strongly in the
discussion in Geneva.

> Because EATWOT does not have a fully developed method for doing
> theology, our exchange with First World theologians has helped us to
> clarify our own direction, while First World theologians have been
> enabled to re-examine their own emerging methodologies. In many in-

stances we found ourselves in agreement on tentative principles involving a new way that we are trying to do theology. In identifying the
principles of a different theological method, it was commonly
accepted that commitment is the first act and theology is the second...
No theology can be neutral... Because commitment is the first act,
theology is inseparably connected with the Christian community out
of which it emerges and to which it is accountable... No theological
method is adequate apart from a critical analysis of all the major
struggles of oppression... The practice of liberation is a basic element
in the life of Christians: without it, no renewed theology can be born
(items 36-43:188 f.).

This part of the dialogue was not easy. The conference admitted that:

Even though the reformulation of theological themes was a major goal
of the conference, we were unable to accomplish this task in a
systematic way. A new theological methodology and the liberation of
the theologian and of theology must lead to the reformulation of
traditional themes... Integral liberation from all structured oppression
leads to a different way of thinking about God, Jesus, and the
kingdom... In the emerging theologies there is also a new understanding of Christology. This new Christology has recovered the
practice of the historical Jesus as the model for discipleship in
Christian life (Luke 14:27; John 12:26; Colossians 2:6-7) (items
44-48: 189 f.).

The conference recognised the role of the Bible, and affirmed,

In emerging theologies there is a renewed reading of the Bible that
consists in a dialectical interaction between current reality and the
biblical story... It has become clear in recent years that there are other
sources of inspiration and revelation besides the Judeo-Christian
scriptures. The other great religious traditions are also sources of
revelation. Thus dialogue with other religious traditions is a necessity
if theology is to be relevant for our times (item 50:191).

Spirituality received a passing reference in the Statement

Many of the participants reported the resurgence of new expressions
of spirituality as a reaction to the spirituality developed in the
capitalist world, and in response to the demands of the times.
Spirituality developed under capitalism promotes aggressive individualism, acquisitiveness, hostility to the earth, ruthless competition,
hierarchical discipline, and elitism. The emerging spirituality rooted
in the person of Jesus celebrates the values of integral human
development, openness to human needs, social responsibility toward
the earth and its resources, harmonious cooperation, coordinated
participation, and asceticism (item 52:91).

The Statement devotes some paragraphs to a review of European theology:

> We were reminded that for the past 150 years, European theology has in fact been a response by European elites to the challenges of the Enlightenment to Christian faith... Our brief study of this response... pointed to the coming end of Eurocentric Christianity... First World participants themselves recognised that most theology in the First World has not been sensitive to the suffering of oppressed peoples in the Third World... But neither has it been sensitive to the plight of the poor and working classes in the First World... Recently, European theologians seeking genuine renewal are reacting against their own traditional theology (items 54-56:192).

The Statement ends in hope:

> We are aware of the incomplete and all too fragmented nature of our meeting... We look forward to future opportunities to continue what we began in Geneva. For many of us, our first dialogue between First and Third World theologians was a ray of hope in a dark and divided world (item 59:193).

5   SOME COMMENTS AND QUESTIONS

There is no doubt that the EATWOT is a fitting forum for theological inspiration, challenge and discussion. In the Southern regions of Christianity, it has reached the front line of theological creativity. It has found to hold a substantial number of issues in common, whatever regional or continental distinctions may be observed. Its ecumenical nature opens new directions to the ecumenical movement as a whole.

The EATWOT needs to continue its dialogue with theologians from the West. It is significant that the Association put this desire into action at the Geneva conference, within less than seven years after its founding. The hope for continuation of the dialogue underlined the importance of such conversation. In many ways, the North was the theological guru of EATWOT theologians. Could they now enter into dialogue with one another? That would prove to be a profound experience for both sides.

However, since the Geneva conference of 1983 the EATWOT has not organised or been involved in subsequent dialogues with the West. What could this mean? The Association has held over thirty conferences up to the end of 2001. These included Asian, African, Latin American, Women's conferences, consultations and workshops. Only one of them dealt with dialogue with the West and North: the conference in Geneva in 1983. Why has there been no repetition or follow-up of this dialogue?

Did participants and (outside) observers judge it to have been so successful that it needed no repetition? Or was it such a failure that nobody dared to organise another one? Perhaps only the EATWOT itself has the right answer.

The Geneva conference seems to have been dominated by the agenda of the theology of liberation. Indeed, that has been the main thrust of the Association, as far as reports of its conferences are concerned. At the time of its founding, the theology of liberation was stretching its network throughout the southern region of Christianity, with concentrations in Latin America, North America, Southern Africa and Asia (especially South Korea, India, and Sri Lanka). Most members of the Association would consider themselves to be liberation theologians, or at least to promote this brand of theology. The theology of liberation (in its various forms) seems to have permeated the Geneva conference to such an extent that the dialogue that took place became largely a presentation of liberation theology by the EATWOT to the theologians of the First World. The Association seemed to say that dialogue must be conducted primarily within the parameters of liberation theology.

The final statement makes this explicit.

> The doing of theology should arise out of a prior commitment on behalf of the victims of oppression who are struggling for their freedom... No theology can be neutral... Because commitment is the first act, theology is inseparably connected with the Christian community out of which it emerges and to which it is accountable... No theological method is adequate apart from a critical analysis of all the major struggles of oppression... The practice of liberation is a basic element in the life of Christians: without it, no renewed theology can be born (items 37, 38: 188f.).

I feel uncomfortable with these statements. They place theology into a kind of ghetto in which there is no freedom of movement or speech outside of liberation theology. This is not to pass judgement on liberation theology as such. It has its merits and weaknesses. But it should not be placed dogmatically at the centre of Christian theology so as to eclipse other forms of theological discourse. To make liberation theology the point of departure for doing any and all theology whatsoever is to cripple theology for all times and places. Was the First World attuned enough to liberation theology so as to engage adequately in dialogue with the EATWOT at that level?

Whereas on the part of the EATWOT the participants came largely from the top echelons of theologians in the South, those of the First

World were not necessarily the "giants." This gave a degree of imbalance from the very beginning. Why did the "giants" from the First World fail to participate in Geneva? Were they not invited? Was the agenda of the conference too restricted for them? Would they have found themselves out of place when it came to doing liberation theology there?

The issues that Geneva took up for discussion were appropriate issues affecting many people throughout the world. In some ways they were not new issues, since they were already being discussed locally and regionally in the areas of EATWOT. But it was important that the issues from the First and Third Worlds "converge," thus allowing for a measure of commonality in the dialogue between them. It was appropriate that the First World would hear the concerns of the Third World as the EATWOT saw them. But it is not clear in the report what the main issues of theology were in the First World.

The North have been giving attention to the theological task for two thousand years. It has accumulated a wealth of understanding concerning our common faith, including biblical scholarship, spirituality, art, music, pastoral care, philosophical theology, systematic theology, and hermeneutics. What happened to all this great heritage of the Church at the Geneva conference? Why did it not surface at such an important dialogue conference? There are few passing references to it. Can a dialogue between North and South concerning our common Christian faith afford to be silent on the rich heritage of two thousand years? There are precious jewels in that heritage that can be regarded as a heritage of the whole of Christianity.

Even our most common point of reference, the Bible, is missing at the Geneva conference. This is surprising if not alarming, since in the past century the Bible has become very much a book of the southern region. At the end of 2001, translations of the Bible in full or in part into different languages were as follows: Africa 641, Asia 570, Australia / New Zealand / Pacific 405, Europe 203, North America 73, Latin America and Caribbean Islands 392, and Constructed languages 3, for a total of 2,287 languages.[3] The Bible lends itself readily as a theme for dialogue between the South and the North, making use of the biblical wisdom of the North and the enthusiasm of reading the Bible in the South. It holds Christians together more firmly than anything else of Christian heritage.

---

[3] United Bible Societies Scripture Language Report 2002, from the Internet.

Likewise a dialogue around the common theme of spirituality is missing. In the course of its long history, the Church has evolved rich resources of spirituality. The North has its treasures of spirituality shaped over generations by many spiritual movements. The South also has its heritage of spirituality, shaped largely through its encounter with other religions. These have a bearing on Christian spirituality. Dialogue around this theme would be a great spiritual eye opener for both sides involving mutual enrichment.

Geneva did not give adequate consideration to the theme of christology. Our faith is built around Jesus Christ. Therefore, Christian theology falls and stands with christology. The North has accumulated many insights into christology, many of which have been exported to the South, especially through the missionary expansion. Traditional concepts of christology have been transplanted to the South, and the South has embraced the faith through these concepts. At the same time, the South is developing additional insights and rediscovering traditional concepts anew. A theological dialogue on christology between the North and the South could be an exciting endeavour, enabling both sides to share these insights: old and new, traditional and modern.

The report from Geneva and especially its Final Statement, conveys the impression of a constant critique of the North by the South: in terms of the former's theology, economics, politics, oppression, liberation, racism, sexism, etc. It is clear that a prophetic voice needed to be raised in these and other areas. Yet, in a setting of dialogue I feel uncomfortable if one side is constantly making the other side feel guilty. That does not seem to open up the atmosphere for an honest and free dialogue. The North is aware of its shortcomings, but this should not mean that the South is free of shortcomings. If each side comes with quivers full of the shortcomings of the other side, dialogue becomes artificial and inadequate for either side. A dialogue of sharing both our strengths and weaknesses, rather than one of shouting the faults of others, might create an academically beneficial atmosphere that builds an environment for further dialogue.

6   SUGGESTIONS FOR THE FUTURE

Whatever Geneva achieved or failed to achieve, its intention to carry out a theological dialogue between the North and the South is an ongoing agenda that has yet to be taken seriously in both church and academic circles. Theologians from the South know the North fairly well because many of them have studied in the North and have drawn from its scholarly treasures, ecclesiastical ties, and church traditions. But the North does not seem to know the South to the same extent. Indeed, it seems to be ignorant of southern Christianity. Perhaps through dialogue, this inadequacy could be ameliorated. Theological education in the North has yet to integrate the South in its courses. There are a few attempts, especially in missiology courses. But the South deserves more than token or peripheral courses. Theology is more than the theology of the North. The Church today has become truly global. So also theology must become truly universal: unless such a development is seen as a threat to both North and South.

Preparation for dialogue could best begin in theological institutions of both the North and the South. This calls for a fundamental re-examination and adjustment of academic content to reflect Christianity as a universal reality. A common language for dialogue would begin to evolve, drawing from the riches of the Christian faith in both North and South. How can such dialogue begin and proceed if the North does not know the South the way the South knows the North? For both, the study of theology has to be global. Otherwise it remains impoverished, provincial and inadequate for global Christianity. Theology is where the church is, and the latter has become universal, both in history and geography. Dialogue has the great potential of promoting theology in both areas. Theology is not exclusively Northern or Southern. It is global in time and space. Theological Dialogue between the North and the South of Christianity is necessary to keep us all on a road that is self-correcting and self-generating.

BIBLIOGRAPHY
(includes a short list of EATWOT and related publications)

Abraham, K.C. and Mbuy-Beya, Bernadette, (eds.). (1994). *Spirituality of the Third World*. Maryknoll: New York.

Abraham, K.C. (ed.). (1986). *Third World Theologies, Commonalities and Divergences*. Oaxtepec Mexico. 1986. Reprint: Maryknoll NY: 1990.

Appiah-Kubi, Kofi, *et al.* (eds.). (1992). *African Dilemma, a cry for life. Papers from the EATWOT West Central African Sub-Regional Conference, in Jos, Nigeria 1991*. Nigeria: The Ecumenical Association of Third World Theologians. West Central African Sub-Regional Conference.

Boff, L. & C. (1992). *Introducing Liberation Theology*. London: Turnbridge Wells.

Bonino, Miguez. (1997). Theol. im Kontext der Befreiung, Göttingen.

Bürkle, Horst (Hrsg.). (1978). *Theologische Beiträge aus Papua Neuguinea*. Erlangen.

Cadorette, C., Gibellini, R. *et al.* (1992). *Liberation Theology, An Introductory Reader.* Maryknoll NY.

Chandran, J. Russell (ed.). (1991). *Third World Theologies in Dialogue.* Bangalore.

Colaco, J.M.. (1997). *Jesus Christ in Asian Suffering and Hope.* Madras.

*Culture, Religion and Liberation: Proceedings of the EATWOT Pan African Theological Conference in Harare, Zimbabwe, 06-11 Jan.*1991. Pretoria: UNISA.

Fabella, Virginia (ed.). (1980). *Asia's Struggle for Full Humanity.* Maryknoll NY.

— and Torres, Sergio (eds.). (1983). *Irruption of the Third World.* Maryknoll NY.

—. and Torres, Sergio (eds.). (1985). *Doing Theology in a Divided World.* Maryknoll NY.

—. and Park, Sun Ai Lee (eds.). (1991). *We dare to Dream. Doing Theology as Asian Women.* Maryknoll NY.

—. and Lee, Peter K.H. and Suh, David Kwang-Sung (eds.). (1992). *Asian Christian Spirituality.* Maryknoll NY.

—. and Oduyoye, Mercy Amba (eds.). (1998). *With Passion and Compassion. Third World Women Doing Theology.* Maryknoll NY.

—. and Sugirtharajah, R.S. (eds.). (2000). *Dictionary of Third World Theologies.* Maryknoll NY.

Goldstein, Horst. (1991). *Kleines Lexikon zur Theologie der Befreiungstheologie.* Düsseldorf.

Hennelly, A.T. (1992). *Liberation Theology: A Documentary History.* Maryknoll NY.

Mananzan, Mary J. (ed.). (1996). *Women Resisting Violence. Spirituality for Life.* Maryknoll NY.

Perera, M. *et al.* (eds.). (1997). *Springs of Living Water.* Bangalore.

Schöpfer, Hans. (1979). *Theologie an der Basis.* Regensburg: Pustet.

Sugirtharajah, R.S. (ed.). (1984). *Frontiers in Asian Christian Theology.* Maryknoll NY.

Sugirtharajah, R.S. (ed.). (1991). *Voices from the Margin. Interpreting the Bible in the Third World.* London.

Torres, Sergio and Appiah-Kubi, Kofi (eds.). (1979). *African Theology en Route.* Maryknoll NY.

Torres, Sergio and Fabella, Virginia (eds.). (1987). *The Emergent Gospel. Theology from the Underside of History. Papers from the Ecumenical Dialogue of Third World Theologians, Dar es Salaam, 5-12 August 1976.* Maryknoll NY.

8 The Sweetness of Life in Madagascar: A Theological Debate

Marc Spindler

1 INTRODUCTION

Although less known than African or Latin American theology, Christian theology in Madagascar has proven its vitality and creativity for a long time. It draws from almost two centuries of Christian experience and a constituency of between six and seven million faithful. Most of these Christians belong to four traditions: the Roman Catholic Church, the United Reformed Church (known as FJKM, Church of Jesus Christ in Madagascar), the Evangelical Lutheran Church, and the Episcopal (Anglican) Church. Other denominations are active too: the Adventist Church, the Baptist Church, a number of independent churches, charismatic and revival movements, and an American Greek Orthodox mission. A very substantial theological production has emanated from Christians in Madagascar. This theological thought is little known outside Madagascar, to a large extent because most of it is written in the local language, Malagasy, not widely known outside the island. As a rule, creative Malagasy theologians are serving with the Roman Catholic Church or the Reformed Church, while some important contributions come from other quarters, including non-affiliated or secular thinkers.

It is not my intention to tell the story of various theological debates that have kept theologians in Madagascar busy during the last fifty years.[1] Rather, I want to focus on a particular subject related to the theme of the present volume, namely the theological debate on the concept of life, a theme that seems to be of paramount importance in the contemporary effort of "inculturation" of the church in Madagascar.[2] We shall discover that the concept of life that seems so attractive and evident at first sight may become a theological pitfall to be avoided unless the concept of life is qualified in the light of the Word of God. I take for

---

[1] I told part of the story in my survey (1983).

[2] In his short contribution (1995) Father Benolo, a Lazarist, makes an interesting distinction between the ontological nature of life expressed by the concept of *aina*, over against the existential predicament of a human living person expressed by the concept of *fiainana*. Both Malagasy words, however, are translated by the term of life.

granted that parallels can be found between the famous word of Jesus: "I have come that men may have life, and may have it in all its fullness" (John 10:10 NEB) on the one side, and the philosophy of life permeating Malagasy culture on the other side, but I will argue that the selection of 'life' among other concepts is a logical step that is consistent with a definite theological method. It is more than a literary device.

2   THE SEARCH FOR A STARTING POINT FOR THEOLOGY IN MADAGASCAR

The method of theology consists primarily in finding and choosing a starting point or rather a track, a runway from which the discourse on God can take off safely. I distinguish two different kinds of starting points. The first one is God's transcendent revelation in as much as it is accessible to humankind in the Word of God. This approach is cherished by the fathers of the Protestant Reformation and their modern disciples. The latest variation of the same theme is the introduction of the hermeneutical condition, meaning that God's revelation always occurs by means of human linguistic forms that must be interpreted. But the horizon of interpretation remains the Word of God. The second method takes its starting point in natural philosophy. The first theological task here is to secure a philosophical ground to build on. According to this view, theology is a two-tiered construction, following the well-known pattern of the Roman Catholic tradition on the relationship between the natural and the supernatural, nature and grace. According to my view, this pattern governs the construction of theology in Roman Catholic circles in Madagascar and applies to the debate on the concept of life as we shall see.

If my interpretation of the Roman Catholic position is correct, there is an inescapable condition for the emergence of a true inculturated theology in Madagascar: namely the satisfaction of a philosophical clause. Before starting the construction of a serious Malagasy theology, a Malagasy philosophical basis must be established. This philosophical agenda was proposed by a Malagasy Jesuit at the Jesuit Conference on Africa and Madagascar in Kinshasa, October 5th-8th, 1976, at a time when the whole discussion on inculturation gathered momentum among Jesuits and later in the Roman Catholic Church as a whole (cf. Roest-Crollius 1993 and Chanson 2001). At this meeting, Father Adolphe Razafintsalama presented a major discussion paper on "Afro-Malagasy Theological Research and Fidelity to the Church." Finding support for his views in the Decree on the Missionary Activity of the Church, *Ad*

Gentes §22, which encourages local churches to investigate theologically the "philosophy and wisdom" of the peoples, he identified the task of Malagasy theologians in the following way:

> A theology, in order to acquire scientific standing, necessarily implies a philosophical theory... the churches of East and West were, in a certain way, privileged. For, even before the proclamation of the gospel, their intellectuals had a very developed instrument of philosophical analysis inherited from Plato and Aristotle... By contrast, African and Malagasy civilizations know sapiential literature but no philosophies in the strict sense; these must be *created* [emphasis added, MS]. This will require time, talent and even some genius.[3]

Malagasy Jesuits and other religious have taken the lead in identifying stepping stones in Malagasy culture and creating a Malagasy natural philosophy. The first attempts addressed the religious ideas of ancient Malagasy culture, a method also followed by Protestants.[4] A second wave focussed on the wisdom tradition, the Malagasy way of life and way of dying. A third, still active trend is interested in worship and rituals within the so-called traditional religions. But the emergence of a creative cultural anthropology that aimed at discovering the secular common ground of Malagasy social life, and sought to avoid religious overtones as much as possible, led Roman Catholic theologians in another direction. They did not search primarily for theological points of contact in Malagasy culture, but set out to articulate the anthropological pattern which can be distilled from every day life in a Malagasy village and from old stories of the past.

Father Adolphe Razafintsalama, at the time of his contribution at the Kinshasa meeting, was himself lecturing on Malagasy anthropology and finally devoted his energy to cultural anthropology altogether.[5] He had

---

[3] Father Razafintsalama was at that time a lecturer at the Institut Supérieur de Théologie, Ambatoroka, Antananarivo (1976:90).

[4] Father Hubert Nicol, a Malagasy Jesuit, opened the row with his doctoral dissertation (1936).

[5] See his 1975, 1978, 1981, 1998 (a collection of articles). Born in 1926, Father Adolphe Razafintsalama died in 2001. His one-sided interest for Malagasy anthropology made him a rather controversial figure in the eyes of the Roman Catholic hierarchy. He apparently made a radical shift of concerns when we remember his doctoral dissertation (1962). Father Razafintsalama was at that time perfectly at home in the scholastic theology of the 13th century, when the 'birth of theology' (Y.

harsh words of criticism on current "impressionistic and superficial analyses of [Malagasy] culture", geared to an immediate but premature exploitation of Malagasy values for catechetical or pastoral ends (1998:12). This last remark opened the door to another fascinating debate about the purpose of cultural anthropology. The question was whether anthropology could pretend to be a self-sufficient, free-wheeling enterprise. But that is another story.

At any rate, the intensive investigation of Malagasy culture seeking to create a Malagasy philosophy led to the selection of two basic anthropological concepts: life (*aina*) and solidarity (*fihavanana*). These twin concepts have become the basis of a coordinated development of catechetical instruments and Roman Catholic theological debate in Madagascar today. I limit this presentation to the concept of life and some of its recent applications.

3   THE ANTHROPOLOGICAL DESCRIPTION OF LIFE IN MADAGASCAR

"Life is sweet" (*mamy ny aina*) is one of the most frequently used idiomatic expressions in Madagascar. Another form is "To live is sweet" (*mamy ny miaina*) (cf. Randriamitatsoa 1967). It is not exactly a "proverb" and I did not find it in big collections of Malagasy proverbs.[6] It expresses the love of life and in some way the precariousness of life. Life is a precious gift, a chance, a happiness given to a human being. A human is called *olombelona*, literally a living (*velona*) person (*olona*). "Life is sweet" is a word of praise and bliss, but it can be contrasted with the heroism of people risking their lives, using their lives like "lost iron" (*manao vy very ny aina*). "Life is sweet" may be used as an excuse for inaction and passivity as soon as one's life is threatened. Nobody likes to die anyway and to die for nothing must be avoided. Many proverbs

---

Congar) took place in the West. This was possibly an analogy with the situation in Madagascar.

[6] Proverbs provide an entry into "the wit and wisdom" of the Malagasy people and a precious tool in the expression of thoughts. Every speech in Madagascar must quote proverbs. The necessities of preaching induced the search for proverbs which resulted in the first collection of Malagasy proverbs published in 1871 by W.E. Cousins & J. Parrett. See also the collection of Houlder, edited by Sibree (1929). The academic study of proverbs has become a special discipline illustrated by Malagasy and foreign scholars such as Bakoly Domenichini-Ramiaramanana, Gabriele Navone, and Jean-Germain Rajoelison.

convey this attitude: "Better die tomorrow than die today," "If we are really to die, then better let it be my sister's child," "If I am to die, let my relative die; if my relative is to die let the ox die" (cf. Sibree 1929: nrs. 2099, 2100, 2101).

No doubt that life may be bitter too, but on the whole, life is valued as such. But its value is not isolated. It is interconnected with a nexus of values, enhancing them and receiving enhancement from them. In the chain of values, life is first of all connected with family values, with the precious network of siblings and relatives sharing the same life. According to Father Robert Dubois' field research, the basic experience of life takes place within the extended family (*communauté familiale*). Speaking of his child, his father, his mother, a brother, a sister or his wife, a Malagasy likes to say: *Aiko ity* (he is, or she is my life).[7] The meaning of *aina*, then, is variable. In this case study, life (*aina*) means the basic flow of energy uniting different persons of common origin, but it also means the bodily predicament attached to human beings, and it can point to the personal subject existing by means of his/her body (ibid.:52).When a brother says of his sister *aiko ity* (she is my life), he implies that both of them have the same ancestors who gave them the gift of life, actually their ancestral life which has created the whole family. This ancestral life continuing throughout the family can be traced back to the Creator God who assembles all human beings. Ultimately, all humans share one life. Humankind as a whole is a sole and unique corporate personality.[8]

Father Robert Dubois comes to the conclusion that life (*aina*) is the principle of integration of the successive generations and the source of the deep solidarity between all living human persons. Malagasy have a name for this human solidarity. It is the concept of *fihavanana*. It is difficult to translate into a western concept. Ideally it is the sign of a perfect social integration, everybody in the extended family considering everybody as a sibling, deserving appreciation and love. It is, then, a reversible concept. Nobody owns the solidarity, it is a common property and ultimately a common obligation. The step from a cultural

---

[7] Dubois 1978: 52. The word *aiko* is composed of the substantive "*aina*" and the possessive adjective "-ko"'.

[8] I borrow this expression from the famous Old Testament scholar H. Wheeler Robinson (1872-1945), although the term is not used in the cultural anthropology of Madagascar. See De Fraine 1959; this superb study in French is more easily accessible to Malagasy theologians.

anthropological description to an ethical prescription is a matter of course in the Malagasy concept.

4   LIFE IS PARTICIPATION

In a well-researched study Father Hilaire Raharilalao emphasises the intimate connection between life and human solidarity (*fihavanana*). He accepts Father Robert Dubois' conclusions (cf. Dubois 1975) and goes a step further when he affirms that acts of solidarity have the sole aim of maintaining and, if possible, increasing life in its double meaning of vital impulse and social existence. In my translation, I quote from the presentation of Raharilalao's doctoral dissertation describing an interdisciplinary study week at the Institut Supérieur de Théologie Ambatoroka, Antananarivo, 30 March-4 April 1990 (Raharilalao 1990, cf. 1991):

> How is the Malagasy able to stay within the flow of life? That is the question! Nothing is thought outside this precious *aina* which must be kept and increased in order to remain in connection with the common stem of kinship.[9] The way to participate in this life and in this human solidarity (*fihavanana*) is to hold fast to traditional rites and customs... Malagasy customs as a whole express the fundamental aspiration of human self-realisation, while human spirituality is a quest for *fihavanana*, the main factor of harmony and well-being... The Malagasy consciously believes in life... To live for the sake of life is, doubtless, the most authentic expression of Malagasy spirituality perceived through *fihavanana* as a human reality, the pre-eminent place of fecundity in which the sap of life (*aina*) circulates... *Aina* and *fihavanana* [are] the twin sources of Malagasy wisdom... Malagasy wisdom yesterday and today will always say "*mamy ny aina*" (life is sweet); this means, in the Malagasy spirituality of *fihavanana*, that in spite of the uncertainties and hazards of existence (*fiainana*), nothing is worth having except life (*aina*), and that life is pleasant anyway (Raharilalao 1990:51-52, is: 1991: 183-186).

In his dissertation, Frère Hilaire Raharilalao explains a little further the philosophical implications of the option for the concept of life in Roman Catholic theology in Madagascar. Life (*aina*) can be interpreted as the

---

[9] Reference to the Malagasy proverb "Men are like the creeping stem of the pumpkin, and if traced, are found to be one" (*Ny olombelona hoatra ny ladim-boatavo, ka raha fotorana, iray ihany*) (English translation, Houlder in: Sibree 1929: nr.11).

dynamic equivalent of the concept of Being, so dear to the Roman Catholic philosophical and theological tradition. I quote again from Raharilalao in my translation:

> Malagasy wisdom happily counterbalances the western philosophical tendency to speculate on ideas and schemes unrelated to life. To exist, is to be Olona [a human being] facing other consciences of Olona and altogether dependent upon Aina. These two conditions are necessarily related to *fihavanana* by means of which human identity takes its value. In the Malagasy philosophy of Being, personal existence serves as a function of collective existence. The Malagasy will say: I have *Havana* [siblings], therefore I am; life is the other.[10]

Although Malagasy theologians rarely use references to African religion and philosophy, I think it is obvious that many Malagasy ideas have their parallels in Africa. Life (*aina*) is similar to the 'vital strength' (force vitale) of Vincent Mulago (see his 1979). The importance of genealogy, i.e. of the ancestors as mediators of life, is also common to both Malagasy and African philosophies of life.

5   LIFE AND DEMOCRACY

The social background of the experience of life in Madagascar explains why the concept of life has met a rather surprising expansion in the field of politics, a fact that is increasingly worrying Malagasy Christians today.[11] In a paper prepared by the *Commission Malgache de Théologie*, a think- tank of the Roman Catholic Church in Madagascar consisting of all Malagasy and expatriate scholars in possession of a doctorate in theology, the search for democracy in Madagascar is linked to basic Malagasy values. Without this link, democracy is at risk of being manipulated by a small minority and will frustrate the real political expectations of the ordinary citizen. This document from December 1992 is entitled *Pour la démocratie malgache*. In a full chapter on "Democracy and Malagasy values" the document argues that "Demo-

---

[10] "J'ai des *Havana*, donc je suis; la vie c'est l'autre, les autres". Cf. Raharilalao 1991: 152.

[11] The present political crisis in Madagascar is characterised by an explicit commitment of the four great Christian churches to democracy and against dictatorship. In order to follow the role of churches in recent political developments, the best way is to read the monthly information bulletin *BEMOI [Bulletin des Eglises de Madagascar et de l'Océan Indien]*, published since 1998 in association with local journals by the Missions Etrangères de Paris, 128 rue du Bac, 75341 Paris Cedex 07.

cracy in Madagascar will have a Malagasy face, only if traditional values shape it."

What are these traditional Malagasy values? The list includes God's sovereignty, the ground in which ancestors are buried, *fihavanana* (human solidarity, almost the same as fraternity), the *fanahy* (spirit, spirituality), and finally *aina* (life). At this point a comprehensive philosophy of life is articulated. I quote a few essential passages:

> *Aina* is the primordial value. It is a reality that man cannot give to himself. It is received, whereas *fihavanana* is much more cultivated than received... To live is primarily to be; not to be an M.P., a president, or a priest; or to be a tree or a bird, but to be, quite simply, by way of an interiority prior to all these manifestations. *Aina* for the Malagasy is certainly the metaphysical experience of being in the world. Life is an invisible reality... Life is not seen, but felt, experienced in itself... Life is self-supporting; it is suffering, but at the same time pleasure and joy... The Malagasy knows that life includes joy as well as suffering; therefore he is patient. The rhythm of life cannot be forced. The transition[12] has been going on for long months. Patience was needed according to the rhythm of life... Life is invisible; it is mysterious; one doesn't know everything in advance. Good solutions. Life invents them; also in a democracy. This was not understood by those leaders who sought models outside Madagascar. Life needs time in order to create something new. Every citizen feels himself to be Fanahy (spirit) and also to be a capital of life. This is why totalitarian or absolutist ways cannot really have a hold in Madagascar.[13]

This document is revealing. It shows the effort made by Roman Catholic theologians to bridge the gap between political consciousness and cultural awareness, between urgent political commitment and unhurried philosophical reflection. Behind the scene, two groups of theologians can be recognized: scholars with a longing for philosophy working on

---

[12] "Transition" is here a political concept. It designates the period 1991-1993 when the socialist republic of Madagascar collapsed and was replaced by a new "liberal" regime. Laurent Ramambason calls it "the transition from socialism to IMF capitalism" (1999: 183-185).

[13] "Pour la démocratie malgache" was intended as a first draft of the planned pastoral letter of the Episcopal Conference of Madagascar on democracy. The actual *Lettre Pastorale sur la démocratie,* dated of 25 March 1994, contains no mention of life in the sense of a traditional Malagasy value. The right to live (from the day of conception) is well quoted, but this was not a traditional concept in Madagascar.

the project of creating an authentic Malagasy philosophy, and activists facing the tragic predicament of the nation and the urgency of a political and social reconstruction in the spirit of "Faith and Justice". Not surprisingly, activists have won. In 1994 the Episcopal Conference of Madagascar (ECM) issued quite a different letter on democracy. Again, in 1995, the ECM pastoral letter to the national elites called all of them to act responsibly and quickly in favour of the desperately needed national recovery.[14] Apparently, traditional values were no longer sufficient for the task ahead.

6   REAPPRAISAL AND CRITICISM OF THE TRADITIONAL CONCEPT OF LIFE

It is remarkable that Roman Catholic theologians in Madagascar constantly refer to life as a fundamental value, while Protestant theologians in the country hardly mention the topic in their reflection on the contextualisation of the Gospel and the "malagasization" (fanagasiana) of the church.[15] The sources of the present paper are almost entirely Roman Catholic.

Generally speaking, Protestant theologians in Madagascar are reluctant to follow the same method as their Roman Catholic colleagues. They don't see the necessary contextualisation of the Church in a revitalisation of so-called traditional models. Instead they are inclined to address the root causes of the crisis that is destroying Malagasy society and its economy. They see Madagascar in the global setting of international relations that must be reshuffled and in the lingering trauma of colonialism that inflicted and still inflicts severe handicaps on many aspects of life in the country. They seem to feel that these modern problems cannot be solved by means of old remedies. The old patterns did not prevent the island from being colonized. Protestant theologians like Richard Andriamanjato, Aubert Rabenoro, and Jean W. Rabemanahaka have been working towards the "malagasization" or the contextualisation of the Church, of worship, liturgy, and theology in their own way, without taking into account Roman Catholic attempts. Conversely,

---

[14] Lettre de la Conférence Episcopale Catholique à tous les Responsables de la Nation. 24 October 1995.

[15] Rev. Michel Fety (1921-1998) has been the main advocate of contextualisation in Malagasy theology. But for him the real context is political, not ethnographic. A survey and assessment of this theology has been written by Razafiarisoa Ratsimandresy 1985.

Roman Catholic theologians have shown little interest in local Protestant concepts, except in the field of ecumenics. Among Protestants, I see very few theologians in Madagascar discussing the theological method proposed by their Catholic colleagues in order to achieve an authentic inculturation. An exception is Michel Fety, founding dean of the Theological Faculty of the United Reformed Church in Ambatonakanga, Antananarivo. In his programme for the Faculty, he articulates the scope of a missionary theology and criticises in veiled terms a form of Roman Catholic inculturation. Fety says:

> In Africa as well as in Asia... a number of theologians, fortunately a small minority, are seeking to build their theology on the ground of ancestral socio-religious concepts, or those religious and cultural concepts peculiar to each tribe or each ethnic entity. People leaning towards syncretism try to adapt their theology to existing religious beliefs or traditional philosophies, the result being that the Church would no longer evangelize the heathen but simply make arrangements with them in order to integrate Christian theology into their ancestral religion. Indeed, in terms of public relations, this move corresponds well with the needs of the Third World, which is presently in a state of effervescence, and jealous of its cultures and operative value systems. Such positive reappraisal of ancestral religions that enhances them and puts them on a par with revealed religion, i.e. on the same level with Christian religion, is not free from severe criticism on the side of the word of God in the Bible.[16]

While this Protestant criticism is little known among them, Roman Catholic theologians in Madagascar have also recently felt the need of a reappraisal of their theological method of inculturation. Father Adolphe Razafintsalama himself, one of the main exponents of the method, came to the conclusion that traditional norms and values, that is, traditional culture, were ambiguous realities that may obliterate the

---

[16] Fety 1988:86. This paper was actually the manifesto of the new Reformed theological faculty, launched by Rev. Michel Fety in 1979. In this context, "missiology" has to be understood as a cover name of the whole theological enterprise, and not in the restricted sense of a particular discipline within the theological curriculum. More on this topic in Laurent Ramambason (1994), *Mission-Doers and Missiology. A Critical Study with Special Reference to Madagascar (1985-1993)*, Ph.D. Dissertation, University of Birmingham, July 1994 (unpublished). Ramambason quotes the words of Michel Fety as part of a paper presented at a theological consultation held in Mandriambero, Antananarivo, May 1992 ("Non au syncrétisme!"). This quotation has been left out from the published version: 1999:178-179. The translation is the author's.

Gospel they are seeking to support. Inculturation requires much more prudence than it was thought. I quote from his preface to the dissertation by Frère Hilaire Raharilalao:

> As an anthropologist, I tend to be personally impressed by the historical, differentiated record of the concept of *fihavanana* [human solidarity]. For instance, the position of *fihavanana* is different according to the epoch under scrutiny... This means that the Malagasy *fihavanana* did and does only ideally imply the internal harmony it seems to express at first sight. I mean that the *fihavanana* is never given, it must be constructed in a world permeated with tensions, with continuous reappraisals of old values in the light of the Gospel.

Razafintsalama suggested the need for reappraisal of present methods of inculturation in a paper presented to the Jesuit Conference on Africa and Madagascar, held at Bingerville, Ivory Coast, March 25-30,1998.[17]

Cultural norms, values, and ordinary customs should be analysed in their real historical development and their socio-economic context, he said. This also implies a realistic assessment of their negative as well as their positive aspects. Furthermore, this new approach takes into account the reality of the historical development of Christianity in Africa and Madagascar. The so-called traditional culture, traditional religion, and traditional philosophy are no longer directly available today. Christianity in Madagascar has a long history and a form of Christian culture emerged in the past under the independent monarchy that produced authentic Christian martyrs. Today's anthropologists and theologians miss the mark when they try to begin their task from scratch, as if Christianity never existed in their context.

Among a number of topics reviewed by Father Razafintsalama, I will summarize here his argument concerning a reappraisal of the concepts of life and solidarity, so prominent in the Roman Catholic construction of a Malagasy philosophy today. The concept of life is not the private property of Malagasy culture. It is available in every culture: traditional or modern. The Malagasy have a love for life, and believe that life is God's gift. They know that life does not begin at birth but at the time of conception. This gives the foetus a human status. However, Malagasy tradition does not recognize the right to life to certain categories of new-born babies, for example, twins or those born on an

---

[17] See, in *Afrika Yetu. S.J. Perspectives,* Razafintsalama (2001). This is the opportunity to celebrate the birth of this new bi-annual journal of African theology, published by the Jesuits in Nairobi, Kenya.

astrologically bad day. Abortion is widely accepted. This means that life is not an absolute, but is related to the social and ideological context of the group. The Malagasy concept of life, then, cannot be the touchstone of the Malagasy philosophy.

The concept of solidarity (*fihavanana*) also draws from historical developments. It may be a closed solidarity within the tribe or the clan, which implies the prohibition of intermarriage of persons with different genealogies. Thus under the monarchy, Malagasy society had no objection to the slave trade. Modern forms of solidarity may cover a complicity in wrong-doing such as corruption at the expense of other social groups or political parties. However, the *fihavanana* [solidarity and fraternity] can be extended to foreigners, and is potentially universal. Thus, it cannot function as the touchstone of Malagasy culture (ibid.:14, *passim*).

The same conclusion was also reached by another theologian, Jean-Baptiste Randrianasolo, in an article pertaining to the key concepts of Malagasy philosophy, namely *fihavanana* (solidarity), *aina* (life) and *fanahy* (spirit) (Randrianasolo 1992). I summarize the relevant development in Randianasolo's thought. Some theologians take the concept of life as point of departure of Malagasy philosophy. It is true that life is the foundation and condition of solidarity and parenthood. But is it a primary or a secondary foundation? Human beings participate in the same life as plants and animals. Life can be transmitted and perpetuates itself by transmission. However, it is extremely fragile. Life is also multiple, and not unique, because man and woman united in one life in marriage have necessarily two different vital origins. Malagasy are not the sole people with a love for life. Everybody wants to live as long as possible. And there is obviously a superior value above life when heroes and martyrs sacrifice their own life for a cause. Life cannot be the absolute foundation of existence. Instead, one should take the starting point of philosophy in the discovery and experience of the divine presence. Behind and beyond life, there is God, the absolute presence. "God is the unique root of Aina, the Inevitable who fills all existence" (ibid.:215-217).

7   CONCLUSION

To conclude, I would like to mention the contribution of Father Jean-Marie Estrade, a Lazarist missionary working in Manakara, on the East coast of Madagascar. He too has taken the concept of life very seriously and has created a community development centre precisely called *Aina*, Life. In the multiple programmes of this centre, many aspects of real life come to the fore. The experiences of the people around this centre can be found in a book that is in some way the diary of Father Estrade (his 1996a). Here we see the wide implications of the concept of life in the difficult struggle of the poor against natural calamities and man-made oppression. Father Estrade is also familiar with modern developments of the so-called Malagasy traditional religion and makes an illuminating comparative assessment of the prospects (Estrade 1996b; 1996a:1-28). In this context, the debate on the concept of life in Madagascar appears to be a practical affair that will not be solved only on the basis of philosophical and theological arguments. The debate is bound to continue.

BIBLIOGRAPHY

Benolo, François. (1995). "Propos sur l'*Aina* dans le cadre de l'inculturation". In: J.-M. Aubert (ed.). *Comment peut-on être philosophe ? Mélanges offerts au Père Louis Rasolo, S.J.* Ambatoroka, Antananarivo: Institut Supérieur de Philosophie et de Théologie. Pp. 69-75.

Chanson, Philippe. (2001). "Inculturation". In: *Dictionnaire Œcuménique de missiologie*. Paris: Cerf / Genève: Labor & Fides / Yaoundé: CLE. Pp. 165-170.

Cousins, W.E., and J. Parrett. (1871). *Malagasy Proverbs*. Antananarivo: LMS Press.

De Fraine, Jan. (1959). *Adam et son lignage. Etudes sur la notion de 'personnalité corporative' dans la Bible*. [Bruges:] Desclée de Brouwer.

Dubois, Robert. (1978). *Olombelona. Essai sur l'existence personnelle et collective à Madagascar*. Paris: L'Harmattan. Revised edition in Malagasy: (1998). *Malagasy aho*. Antananariv: Edisiona Masindahy Paoly.

—. (1975). *Aina sy Fihavanana. Approche occidentale de la manière de penser et de vivre les relations humaines*. Ampasimanjeva: Document de la Commission Épiscopale de Catéchèse et de Recherche sur les Coutumes (mimeographed, private circulation).

Estrade, J.-M. (1996a). *Aïna—La vie. Mission, culture et développement à Madagascar*. Paris: L'Harmattan.

—. (1996b). "Religion malgache et christianisme". In: *Recherches et documents* 21. Pp. 115-148.

Fety, Michel. (1988). "La place de la missiologie dans notre faculté". In: *Théologie et Culture* 1. Nr.2. Pp. 80-90.

Lettre de la Conférence Episcopale Catholique à tous les Responsables de la Nation. 24 October 1995. In: *Aspects du Christianisme à Madagascar*. Tome 6. Nr.5, janvier-mars 1996. Pp. 195-199.

Lettre Pastorale sur la démocratie, dated 25 March 1994. In: *Aspects du christianisme à Madagascar*. Tome 6. Nr.2, avril-juin 1995. Pp. 51-68.

Mulago, V. (1979). *Simbolismo religioso africano. Estudio comparativo con el sacramentalismo cristiano.* Madrid: EDICA [La Editorial Catolica]. With a comprehensive bibliography.

Nicol, Hubert (1936). *Dieu dans les croyances malgaches. Aperçu descriptif et contenu doctrinal.* Rome: Université Grégorienne (unpublished manuscript).

"Pour la démocratie malgache". (1992). *Bulletin de la Commission malgache de Théologie.* Nr.20. Pp. 1-15 (stencil, restricted circulation).

Raharilalao, Hilaire Aurélien-Marie. (1990). "La philosophie malgache du *fihavavana*". In: *Revue d'Ambatoroka ISTA* 6. Pp. 47-53 (mimeographed, private circulation).

—. (1991). *Église et Fihavanana à Madagascar. Une herméneutique malgache de la Réconciliation chrétienne selon Saint Paul 2 Cor 5, 17-21.* Fianarant-soa: Editions Ambozontany. Doctoral dissertation, presented at the Institut Catholique de l'Afrique de l'Ouest, Abidjan, Ivory Coast.

Ramambason, Laurent W. (1999). *Missiology: Its Subject-Matter and Method. A Study of Mission-Doers in Madagascar.* Frankfurt am Main: Peter Lang.

Randriamitatsoa, Jean-Baptiste. (1967). *Mamy ny miaina, mémoire de philosophie.* Ambatoroka, Antananarivo: Institut Supérieur de Théologie (unpublished paper).

Randrianasolo, J.-B. (1992). "Vers une expérience existentielle". In: *Aspects du christianisme à Madagascar.* Tome 4. Nr.5, janvier-mars. Pp. 211-217.

Razafiarisoa Ratsimandresy, Esther. (1985). *Ny andraikitry ny kristiana eo amin'ny firenena araka an'Atoa Fety Michel.* [The Christians' Responsibility in the Nation according to Michel Fety]. Mémoire de maîtrise en théologie. Antananarivo: Faculté de Théologie Protestante Ambatonakanga. (Unpublished dissertation, with a comprehensive bibliography of Michel Fety).

Razafintsalama, A. (1962). *Doctrine sur les sacrements en général selon la "Glossa" d'Alexandre de Halès.* Rome: Université Gregorienne.

—. (1975). *Anthropologie malgache.* Livre 1. Ambatoroka, Antananarivo: Institut supérieur de théologie. Vol. 2: 1978.

—. (1976). "Afro-Malagasy Theological Research and Fidelity to the Church". In: *Jesuit Response to the Challenge of Mission in Africa and Madagascar Today.* JECAM [Jesuit Conference on Africa and Madagascar], Kinshaha, 5-8 October. English Edition. Washington, D.C.: Jesuit Missions Inc. Pp. 77-94.

—. (1981). *Les Tsimahafotsy d'Ambohimanga: organisation familiale et sociale en Imerina (Madagascar).* Paris: SELAF [Société d'Études linguistiques et anthropologiques de France].

—. (1998). *Essais de théologie malgache.* Antsiranana, Madagascar: Institut Supérieur de Théologie et de Philosophie de Madagascar. (Recherches et documents. Nr.5).

—. (2001). "Les cultures d'Afrique et de Madagascar". In: *Afrika Yetu. S.J. Perspectives* 1 (August). Pp. 8-20.

Roest-Crollius, Arie. (1993). "Inculturazione". In: *Dizionario di missiologia.* Bologna: Edizioni Dehoniane. Pp. 281-286.

Sibree, James (ed.). (1929). *Ohabolana or Malagasy Proverbs. Illustrating the Wit and Wisdom of the Hova of Madagascar.* Collected, translated and arranged by J.A. Houlder. Translations into French by Henri Noyer (1929). Antananarivo: Friends Foreign Missionary Association.

Spindler, M.R. (1983). "Theological Developments in Madagascar". In: *Exchange. Bulletin of Third World Christian Literature* 12. Nr. 35, September 1983. Pp. 1-43. French: (1984). "Evolution de la théologie malgache". In: *Aspects du christianisme à Madagascar* 19. Nr.11-12, septembre-décembre 1984. Pp. 329-344.

Intra-Religious Religiosity Of Christian Africans
   And Its Significance For Christianity In Europe

Frans J. Verstraelen

1   INTRODUCTION

The title of this essay uses the term "intra-religious", referring to a
condition "on the inside" of a person or a group. It also consciously
refers to "Christian Africans" of which the sequence of words indicates
that being or becoming a Christian is always annexed to a previous
existence, in our case to "being an African". "Religiosity" in the title
refers to the religious understanding and practice of people in contrast to
"religion" understood as a system. The implications for Africa and the
world by using this terminology will, I hope, become visible during the
course of this article. To found my case I will follow a historical and
missiological approach in describing and evaluating Christian African
religiosity in three parts: 1) Pre-stages of Christian African Religiosity;
2) Christian African Religiosity; and 3) Change and Significance.

2   PRE-STAGES OF CHRISTIAN AFRICAN RELIGIOSITY

Part One refers to two religious currents, African Traditional Religion
and European Christian mission. Because each current contributed only
in part to an integrated Christian African religiosity, I have called them
"pre-stages".

2.1. Traditional African religiosity
Quite a number of scholars have researched African Traditional Religion
(ATR). They have moved knowledge beyond a declaration made by E.
Sidney Hartland, saying, "The most obscure and difficult question
connected with the religion of the Bantu is whether they have any belief
in a supreme God, a Creator, an overruling Providence" (Hartland 1909:
363). In the 1950s and 1960s non-African scholars studied ATR: Smith
(1950), Parrinder (1954), Verstraelen (1961), Damman (1963), and
Zahan (1970). From the beginning of the 1970s African scholars came
to the fore like Mbiti (1969, 1975); Adegbola (1983), Ikenga-Metuh
(1987), and Magesa (1998). I have no intention to evaluate the quality of
the products of Western and African scholars as is, for instance, done by
David Westerlund (1985). In order to put Traditional African Religion
in proper perspective, one should realize that:

• ATR is a religion and as such it has beliefs, practises (ceremonies, festivals), objects and places, values and morals, religious officials or leaders.

• ATR is part of the African heritage: through the ages religion has been the normal way of looking at the world and experiencing life itself.

• ATR, unlike Christianity and Islam, has no founder. It evolved slowly as people responded to the situations of their lives, the problems of evil and suffering, and by trying to obtain a safer and better life.

• ATR has no scriptures or holy books. It is written in the history, the hearts and experiences of the people; it is kept alive through myths, proverbs, art and symbols, names of ancestors and sacred places, music and dance.

• ATR functions more on a communal rather than an individual level. What matters are the beliefs held by the community; ceremonies are performed mainly in or by a group: the family, relatives, or the whole population of an area.[1]

There is an academic discussion whether to speak of African Religion (in the singular) or of African Religions (in the plural) (see Ikenga-Metuh 1987:5-10). The latter option is based on the understanding that ATR is ethnic, locally bound, and shows differences which depend on different locations. The former option is based on the interpretation of religious beliefs and practices in African communities that show substantial agreement and can be seen as variations of one common religious tradition. With Magesa, I opt for African Religion in the singular (Magesa 1998: 24-27). Aside from other academic questions and controversies,[2] I will concentrate on the role of religion in the lives of African people.

ATR is concerned with two main issues: to make life possible and maintain it and to solve the problems of affliction. For traditional African people the vital force or life force is central. Africans desire to live as fully as possible. Hence ATR is intimately connected with everyday life in all its expressions: food, children, cattle, setbacks, disease, and death. The whole world is experienced as a field of forces that influence life for better or for worse. An action is either good or evil

---

[1] See Mbiti 1975: chapter 2, "What is African Religion?".

[2] Like e.g. p'Bitek's criticism of Western scholarship, dealt with in Westerlund 1985: 60-63.

depending on whether it promotes or harms the vital force. In ATR people therefore try to link up with powers that dispose of the force of life. These powers are ancestors, spirits, benevolent or malevolent magical powers (witchcraft), the Supreme Being, God.

The ancestors, deceased adult relatives, continue to be part of the family. They are the "living dead," whose influence remains great. They are the caretakers of the fertility of the land and they promote the growth of crops. They are very much interested in the birth of children because in them they can be re-incarnated. The dead often appear in dreams to communicate their wishes. In sum, ancestors are supposed to restore, protect or increase the vital force of their descendants. They will do so on condition that they receive sufficient attention and respect.

Africans experience the proximity of spiritual power also in nature: storms, lightning, thunder, and the rainbow. Land in particular is considered holy and cannot be sold. Hence the struggle against European settlers who occupied the land (cf. the Mau-Mau uprising in Kenya, and land reform in Zimbabwe; see Verstraelen 1998:103-116). They further have a deep-seated belief in magic and witchcraft. All sorts of objects are utilized by traditional medicine men or women to protect against evil influences. Witchcraft is greatly feared because it is directed against the force of life of individuals and communities. Witches are in fact scapegoats for all kinds of evil within society: diseases, death, tensions caused by childlessness, quarrels and especially jealousy.

Almost all Africans believe in a Supreme Being, God. God represents the highest power as creator and cause of everything that exists. God forms the top of a pyramid, so to speak. The two sides are the ancestors and the spirits of nature, while the base consists of the magic powers. In the centre of this pyramid of powers is the human person who tries to use them to his or her advantage. Because human beings are so central to traditional African religion, crisis moments in the course of life receive special attention. They form part of the rhythmic movement of the cosmos and the drama of the seasons. They are born and they die, go up and go down, many times during their lifetime. All these moments of crisis are marked by rites directed ultimately to let life triumph. This applies particularly to occasions of birth and the transition to adulthood (Verstraelen 1981:30).

The relationship to God is a complicated one. Myths tell that the first people were created by God and were called "children of God." Because of human failings a separation took place. Yet belief in God is real, though there is no regular or organized worship of God. Only ancestors are regularly honoured through sacrifices and prayers. Though there are no temples and priests for God, they do exist for spirits of nature. God is briefly addressed from time to time by anybody, at any place and at any time. When ancestors or spirits do not grant their wishes, Africans do resort to God.

In a chapter on "The Mystique of Life in African Religion" Magesa deals with abundant life realized in ancestral community, referring to conception, birth and naming, and to initiation as confirmation of the vital force. He states:

> There is no other purpose of life but fostering life. Herein lies the mystique of life. All rites and rituals from birth to adulthood are meant to solidify this life. All of them connect human beings with other visible elements of creation and with the invisible world of God, the ancestors and the spirits (1998:109).

2.2. Christian missionary religiosity

Christianity has been in the northern part of Africa from its earliest beginnings. Between 1500 and 1800, Christianity was brought to some parts of sub-Saharan Africa, with little impact. The effective Christianisation of Africa started around the beginning of the 19th century—first by Protestants, later by a return of Catholic missionaries. These missions, begun before the scramble for Africa by European nations, obtained a relatively strong position during the colonial period (begun after 1880 and intensified in the height of imperialism around 1920). While African traditional religion had emerged out of the experiences and aspirations of the Africans themselves, the coming of Christianity into their midst was an imposition from outside.

From their point of view, the missionaries considered their activities none other than a God—given blessing for the African people. First of all, they offered to the "lost heathens" the way of salvation that opened heaven to their souls. Secondly, they brought to these "poor African creatures" a material civilization that would improve their lives on earth. They promoted a new kind of agriculture and health care based on scientific insights, and they taught all kinds of technical-practical skills. The missionaries had no doubt that their presence and work was of great spiritual and material benefit for the African people who—in European eyes—had strange superstitious beliefs and practices together with a very low standard of living. As bearers of the "one, true religion" and as representatives of a higher civilisation, missionaries felt consciously or unconsciously superior. But they hardly realized that their denominational rivalry contradicted the gospel of unity and love they were preaching.

The new religion, called Christianity, was an import that did not really disturb Africans. In religious matters, Africans are pragmatic. If one religion does not help in their problems, another is tried. In the words of a traditional Ashanti priest in Ghana, "We in Ashanti dare not worship the Sky God alone, or the Earth Goddess alone, or any one spirit. We have to protect ourselves, and use whenever we can the spirits of all things in the Sky and upon Earth" (Rattray 1923:150). Thus, when Ghanaians in the 1930s observed that their own tutelary spirits—such as the Ashanti river gods Tano and Pra—had lost power, they did not hesitate to import new cults from the north, like the medicine cult of Tigare and Blekete, considered more powerful than their own because these latter gods had been less exposed to influences of colonial intrusion.[3]

Both Catholic and Protestant missionaries regarded Christianity as the faith that had to replace the superstitious religion of the Africans. The latter tended to consider Christianity as the religious dimension of "modern life" that had entered their lives through European contact and colonization. Important for them was the power for good life and well-being that this new religion might offer. Christianity in the eyes of Africans was a new religious power to be added to the totality of existing religious powers they were already using. Missionary and African interpretations were thus diametrically opposed to one another as "replacement" versus "incorporation". On the level of modern life, Africans could find links with Christianity. But on the level of religion missionaries had a very difficult time finding links with African life, for which African traditional religion continued to provide a vital force.

Because of their replacement ideology, missionaries saw no need to get to know the nature of ATR and its role in African life. They therefore did not enter into dialogue with representatives of traditional religion and society: medicine-men (n'angas), spirit mediums, and chiefs. Missionaries tried to replace paganism with a spiritualized type of Christianity concerned with saving souls for eternity. They had forgotten (or had never learned) that Christianity was in fact a new interpretation of paganism. The first Apologetes and theologians of pre-Constantinian Christianity insisted that Christianity was consonant with paganism's deepest aspirations. For paganism raised the great problems and challenges facing humanity: health, life, justice, land, peace, and happiness. These same issues were embedded in the new

---

[3] Beckmann, quoted in: Verstraelen 1995:75-76.

values that Jesus had demonstrated and taught (cf. Acts 1:1) against meaningless observances and lifeless rules of Judaism (see Hoornaert 1989: 261-264). The Church, in the view of the Apologetes, was also not a new beginning, but a continuation and universalization of earlier forces. When meeting non-Jews (gentiles), the Apostle Paul would refer first to the gods of rain and harvest and then speak of the God of universal salvation, not only the God of Israel (see Acts 14:15-18). Jesus did not come merely to replace existing previous beliefs and practises. He came to complete and radicalize the "Old Law" of Israel. Following the example of St. Paul, the first missionary to the non-Jews (pagans), the missionaries sent to Africa should have recognized the deep longings of the African for abundant life.

Because of a rationalistic outlook that a priori condemned ATR as pure superstition, missionaries were ill-prepared to enter into a meaningful and, what would have been for them an inter-religious, dialogue. They also were not capable of dialogue because of their unqualified feeling of superiority with regard to material and technical power. In the view of the missionaries, Africans had only one choice: to accept the missionary way of religion and life wholesale or reject it completely. Admittedly, there were some attempts in Christian mission history to have a positive approach to other worldviews. Matteo Ricci, for instance, tried to demonstrate that Confucianism, far from being Christianity's rival, was a vehicle to introduce the Gospel as the Way of Life.[4] But the missionary policy of the official (R.C.) church remained one of replacement. The result was the transmission of a foreign religiosity that could not be assimilated.

Missionaries apparently had forgotten the mission history of their own countries in Europe. Their Germanic ancestors, for instance, practised a religion very similar to ATR. They too had cults for obtaining fertility and vital power. And they believed in spirits, witchcraft and magical forces (see e.g. Ellis Davidson 1981 and Parrinder 1963). The missionaries at the time did not ignore Germanic traditional religion. On its sacred places they built churches, its festivals were often transformed into feasts in honour of Christian saints. "The same Christianity that, by way of the effort of innumerable anonymous Christians had assimilated European paganism, refused a dialogue with the paganism it confronted in America, Africa, and Asia" (Hoornaert 1989:264).

---

[4] See Arnulf Camps' contribution to this Volume, chapter 13.

Yet the missionaries created—largely unintentionally—the conditions for authentic Christian African religiosity. Because they had to communicate a message, they had to use the language of the people. In this process, the missionaries—though cultural outsiders—somehow entered the local culture. They also gradually realized, mainly under pressure from outside, that they had to hand over control to local leadership (see Sanneh 1993: 152-183). The major contribution by the missionaries has been that they, often with the help of native speakers, have translated the Bible into local languages. Henceforth, Africans obtained access to the source of Christian revelation for an African interpretation that was independent from missionary mediation.

3   CHRISTIAN AFRICAN RELIGIOSITY

While in past missionary historiography the focus was almost exclusively on the work of missionaries, the new historiography,[5] developed since the 1960s, is paying due attention to the crucial contribution to evangelization made by local agents: teacher-evangelists, catechists, migrant workers, and women.[6] Yet, as long as expatriate missionaries remained in control, the kind of Christianity officially sanctioned remained the replacement-type of missionary religiosity.

A new situation within sub-Saharan Africa developed under the influence of nationalist movements that intensified after World War II with the rise of political independence during the 1960s. Concurrently, but not independently, new, positive, interpretations of Christianity developed vis-à-vis the world and other religions. These also affected the understanding and practice of Christian mission. Major centres of renewal in mission were Rome, notably with its Vatican II Council in 1962-1964, and Geneva with the World Council of Churches that, in the period of nationalism and decolonization, stimulated similar new viewpoints.[7] The biblical parameters for mission were in a way re-discovered. The Pentecost event (Acts 2, respecting each people's culture), the Council of Jerusalem (AD 49, opposing the imposition of irrelevant religious observances), and the authentic memory of Jesus

---

[5] For a summary of "new historiography": Verstraelen 2002:1-6.

[6] See Gerdien Verstraelen-Gilhuis 1982: "African and Missionary Actors" (41-72).

[7] Resp.: e.g. the "Declaration on the relationship of Christianity to non-Christian religions," in: Abbott 1966:656-674; Wind 1995.

showed love and concern for all people, with a predilection for marginalized persons and groups. These parameters became signposts for any mission undertaken in accordance with God's intention and action (*missio Dei*) by human actors who may be faithful or unfaithful to the vision (Verstraelen 1993:143-147).

The main failing of the missionaries in the colonial period (1880-1945/1960) was the practice of mission by diffusion, in which the culture of the missionaries constituted the inseparable carrier of the Christian message. Rather, authentic mission must be mission by translation. This takes place when the recipient (in our case, African) culture is considered "the true and final locus of the proclamation, so that the religion arrives without the presumption of cultural rejection" (Sanneh 1989:28-29). There is a general impression, not without some foundation, that the missionary enterprise during the colonial period was mission by diffusion. Yet we must make some important qualifications by clarifying the following statement, "If missionaries are associated with the rise of imperialism, they are equally associated with the factors that brought about its destruction" (Walls 1971:561). The missionary educational system contained impulses for freedom, development and emancipation because it was based on the natural and religious law of the basic equality of all human beings before God. Though missionaries often did not envision such, mission schools were in the end catalysts for national emancipation. Most important for the development of Christian African religiosity has been the missionary project of translating the Bible into the vernacular. Missionaries herewith created the conditions for the receptors of the message to appropriate it on their own terms.[8]

3.1 Different local stakeholders

A new political climate joined the new missiological insights flowing from access to the Bible in the vernacular and created favourable conditions for authentic Christian African religiosity to emerge. This goal was not reached overnight. Different local stakeholders, each with their own interests and approaches, were conditioned by different positions and roles in the Christian community to contribute in a variety of ways to the rise of authentic Christian African religiosity.

After independence, now mostly local church leaders were very cautious about breaking new ground. This, for two major reasons: 1)

---

[8] For a detailed analysis of mission and Bible in early Christianity and in the colonial period, see Verstraelen 1993.

They had been trained during the missionary period and had internalized previous missionary "replacement" tenets ; it was in a way ironic that in several instances expatriate missionaries became more open towards Africanizing Christian religiosity than their African superiors. 2) Though in general terms there developed in principle a positive approach to other religious traditions, it was not at all clear what that would entail in concrete terms. For instance, how were they to deal with the role of ancestors, spirits, and traditional funeral rites.[9]

Hence local church leaders tended to follow the safe way of remaining close to what they had inherited from their missionary predecessors. For instance, pastors and elders in the Presbyterian Church in Ghana continue to follow the church's Regulations, Practice and Procedure formulated by the missionary administration (Bediako 1995:67). In the Reformed Church in Zambia, the Book of Laws, Instructions and Regulations (popularly known as *Zolamulira*) was a straight translation of the missionary one, with only few minor adaptations (Verstraelen-Gilhuis 1982:237-241). Of course, the Catholic bishops had to follow Canon Law, universally prescribed for the Catholic Church, though with some practical additions in the so-called Apostolic Faculties (Mulders 1962:255-291 on mission law).

There was, however, a considerable difference in understanding Christian religiosity between African church leaders and ordinary African members. Many Africans who associated with Christianity, did so on their own terms, as will be described below. A third group that was important for Christian African religiosity were African theologians. They came to the fore in the post-missionary context with theology as a systematic, stimulating, and critical force within the development of Christian African religiosity. Their relevance depended not on ideas elaborated behind a desk (the usual locus of many Western theologians), but on sharing the lives of their co-Christians and reflecting on them from a biblical and church-historical frame of reference. The Ghanaian theologian Kwame Bediako refers to the

---

[9] For instance, though bishops from Africa and scholars of religion like Franziscus Cardinal Koenig, archbishop of Vienna, pleaded with the Council Fathers to mention explicitly also African religions, the Vatican II Council decided to do so only for the great world religions (Hinduism, Buddhism, Judaism, Christianity, and Islam), and to refer to all others in this general summary: "Other religions to be found everywhere, strive to answer the restless searching of the human heart by proposing 'ways' which consist of teaching, rules of life, and sacred ceremonies", in: Abbot 1966:662 n.9.

problem of how to arrive at a unified vision of what it meant to be Christian and African and how this affected African theologians: "The issue also forced the theologian to become in himself or herself the point of intersection of this struggle for integration through an inner dialogue which became infinitely personal and intense if it was to be authentic (Bediako 1995:256).

3.2 Different types of Christian African religiosity

We can discern among African Christians three types of Christian African religiosity: 1) as separation in a completely dual system; 2) as independent appropriation; and 3) as dialogical integration.

Christian African religiosity in a dual system

The missionaries who brought Christianity were embedded in a cultural tradition and outlook quite different from African people's worldview and culture. While their first intention was no doubt to bring the Christian message and way of life, they made in fact a greater impact with the ways, products and methods of European civilization (clinics, scientific agriculture, schools, technical skills) they brought with the Gospel. The missionaries considered their answers to be superior to African answers regarding African needs and aspirations. African culture and African religion in particular were considered to belong to the past and of no value when compared to the blessings of Christianity and Western civilisation (see Verstraelen 1975:318-319). The missionaries did not seem to realize that their Christian message was in fact a European Christian message, one that in some ways had been distorted by a rather rationalistic and spiritualised reduction of the original Jesus-based Gospel. Many Africans did indeed join missionary Christianity because they considered it "a new framework within which there could be a new rationale for the new way of life that was appearing... The Christian religion commended itself as a way of accounting for the new."[10]

Because missionary Christianity did not answer their day-to-day needs and problems, Africans continued to rely on their traditional African religion, even when they had formally accepted Christianity. As a consequence, there was a split between professing being a Christian and practising ATR. This dichotomy was more of a problem for the missionaries than for their African converts, because the former could

---

[10] Forman 1982:90f. discusses "primal religion" in the South Pacific, which is very similar to the "primal religion" of traditional Africans.

not admit anything of ATR into their understanding of Christian religiosity. Combining Christianity as a religion for modern life with ATR as a religion that answered their daily needs and aspirations was, from an African point of view, an obvious and normal way to maximally guarantee abundant life. In sum, during the missionary-controlled period there existed an intra-religious condition of two separate religions coexisting within one and the same person, a kind of internal, bifurcated religious apartheid.

Christian African religiosity through independent appropriation
The translation of the Bible into African vernaculars created a "surprise story of the modern missionary movement" (Bediako 1995:203). Because of it, Africans were enabled to make their own responses to the Christian message, independent from missionary interpretation. Having obtained access to the biblical message, Africans made a number of surprising discoveries. They found out that there were many things in the Bible that made sense to them but which were played down or omitted by the missionaries from the West. Africans noticed that the Bible took seriously important elements of their traditional religious heritage, in contrast to the indifference and more often wholesale condemnation by Western missionaries. In traditional African perspective, the Bible confirmed their acceptance of the role of dreams, the reality of spirits, demons and witchcraft, and the involvement of the dead, especially of the ancestors. In their view, the Bible demonstrated the gross ignorance and misrepresentation of these elements by expatriate missionaries (cf. Verstraelen 1998:79-101).

The correspondence between the traditional African worldview with the biblical worldview can be explained because the latter, as a reproduction of experiences and insights of the early Christian community, was written down before technical industrialisation. The Bible therefore corresponds to a social setting regarding a type of civilization and a spiritual outlook that to a large extent are analogous to the rural culture of Africa (Maquet 1967:128).

The availability of the Bible in vernacular languages has been an important stimulus for the formation of African Independent Churches (AIC).[11] The AICs emerged in the second half of the 19th century, developed after World War II and Independence, and continue to be a vital part of African Christianity. They are called "independent" because

---

[11] It is not the intention of this article to deal in detail with AICs. A helpful introduction is Daneel 1987.

under local leadership of inspiring men and women, they either separated from older mission churches or came into being through their own, independent initiatives. The AICs emerged partly out of frustration with missionary paternalism and control, but also out of an urge to express the Christian faith and worship in a dynamic way: participation by all through clapping, shouting exclamations, and dancing, while everyone receives personal attention regarding problems of health, marriage, jobs and so on. There are two main categories of AICs: the Ethiopian type with emphasis on local leadership, and the spirit/prophet type (also called Spiritual and Zion Churches) with stress on the working of the Holy Spirit. Although the African interpretation of the Bible plays an important role in belief and practices of AICs, there are a number of churches that place a greater emphasis on revelation to prophets by means of dreams, ecstacy, trance or possession. It is mostly through these events that the will of God is made known (Magesa 1998:31).

The revelations claimed by prophets or prophetesses of AICs are similar to the ones claimed by the medicine-men (*n'angas*), the specialists of ATR. The difference consists in the frame of reference. In the AICs an intra-religious process takes place in which persons with a traditional African worldview discover and recognize the validity of a biblically based Christianity as meaningful for their lives. Mainline churches and missionaries initially expressed their reservations. For instance, Bengt Sundkler, in his pioneering study *Bantu Prophets in South Africa* (1948; see also Oosthuizen 1968) called some of the Zionist Independent Churches, "syncretistic sects through which Africans are brought back to heatheism" (ibid.:297). Almost thirty years later in his *Zulu Zion and Some Swazi Zionists* (1976), Sundkler had changed his evaluation, saying, "From the point of view of those involved, Zion was not turned to the past, but to the future, and was their future".[12]

In mission circles and in missiological publications a rather positive attitude gradually developed towards AICs, not in the least because they made it clear that the churches founded by foreign missionaries were in many ways alien and largely irrelevant for Africa and its people. African Independent Churches were more and more seen as a challenge to the mission-established churches. However, the AICs are not without weak-

---

[12] Mentioned in Bediako 1995:204, where he suggests to study these two books of Sundkler in order to follow his change of interpretation.

nesses. Perhaps the main weakness is connected with their independence as they claim a new beginning, unrelated to the Christian experience throughout the ages. There is, however, room and opportunity for mutual inspiration and correction. The AICs need to become more open to the Christian tradition, being aware of belonging to a larger, catholic community of faith. The established churches can learn fellowship and relevance by putting more emphasis on being a church with, for, and by the people. Through an independent appropriation of Christianity, made possible because of a direct access to the Bible in the vernacular, members of AICs have found a way to opt for Christianity as good news for them. Among the members of AICs a kind of intra-religious osmosis has taken place between their traditional African worldview and Christianity as encountered in the Bible.

Christian African religiosity through dialogical integration
In the mission-related churches, the African element also gradually came to the fore, especially after Independence. It was commonly known that many of their members were attracted by the Independent Churches. On Sundays they attended services in the mainline churches as a kind of fashionable and respectable act; during weekdays they often went to one of the AIC meetings to satisfy their human and religious needs. In times of deep crisis they even consulted a specialist of ATR, a *n'anga*, and did the things he prescribed. African members of mainline churches, just like traditionalists and followers of AICs, were also looking for power, prosperity and protection against natural and spiritual enemies, in personal and family circumstances. To become effective in these respects required that mainline churches reorient the past missionary models of Christianity (Walls 1996:41).

The missionaries who generally had imbibed the spirit of European Enlightenment had concentrated their efforts on education and modernization in the context of their specific form of Christianity. Theirs was a rather intellectualized and materialized type of religion based on texts and expressed itself in heavy social and administrative structures. This was in sharp contrast to the traditional experience of Africans who established a more direct communication with the cosmic and interdependent reality of the world in which they participated.[13] It meant that ATR had a direct link with the powers of nature and the day-to day problems

---

[13] Maquet, "Prospective de l'Africanité" (Idem, 1967,128) refers to both Christianity and Islam "qui sont à la fois plus intellectualisées (se fondant sur des textes sacrés) et plus matérialisées (se traduisant en de lourdes structures sociales)".

and aspirations of people. It is the great merit of the African Independent Churches that they have brought the traditional worldview that grounded the old religion into allegiance with the Christian faith (according to Baëta 1962; quoted by Bediako1995:66). They thus filled the gap that existed between the missionary and African concepts of reality.

After Independence a new situation arose in the mission-related churches. First of all, the leadership was handed over to locals. In this respect the churches received at least a local face, though this did not necessarily change much in the life of the church. Yet, new forms of Christian life emerged that deviated from missionary Enlightenment reductionism and found expression in charismatic renewal movements consisting of interdenominational fellowships and renewal groups related to mainline churches. What interests us here is the traditional background and influence that occurred in the beliefs and practices of charismatic renewal groups related to and sometimes within mainline churches, especially as regards exorcism, deliverance, and healing.[14]

Charismatic renewal groups, (just like African Independent Churches), are opposed to traditional religious practices, but they oppose them on traditional terms. There is both discontinuity and continuity with ATR. On the one hand, formal parallels to traditional practices of divination and healing are given a different rationale and justification. On the other hand, the real continuities between traditional and Christian African religiosity lie in worldview and perception (Walls 1996:6). For charismatic renewal groups life is spiritual warfare, the warding off of evil (Omenyo 2002: 225-231). This is also at the centre of African traditional religion. Charismatic renewal groups believe that a person can be negatively influenced by Satan, demons and evil, including sometimes also ancestors.[15] Deliverance from this bondage of evil spirits (Satan) is achieved through prayer, the power of the Holy Spirit, and the conviction that Jesus Christ has won victory over Satan.

The official position of the mainline churches regarding Satan (the Devil) has long been either a denial of his existence or playing down his influence on people. Recently some churches are becoming aware that

---

[14] For information about the Ghanaian situation, see Omenyo 2002. This doctoral thesis deals with charismatic renewal in the RC. Church, the Presbyterian Church, the Methodist Church, the Evangelical Presbyterian Churches, and the Baptist Church.

[15] There is, however, also an attempt in some mainline churches to positively incorporate ancestors into Christian life. Cf. Triebel 2002:187-197. See also Verstraelen 1998:31ff.

in order to reach people, they have to recognize and address the issue of the existence and activities of Satan and evil spirits. "After all, religion becomes meaningful to the traditional African when it ensures personal and social well-being rather than blind obedience to ecclesiastical traditions and doctrinal orthodoxy." (Omenyo 2002:230). Since charismatic groups believe that sickness is sometimes caused by Satan and demons, deliverance and healing are their major concerns. And the most important reason why people join charismatic groups, is their search for divine or faith healing.

Some observers of traditional as well as Christian African religiosity have come to the conclusion that it is a this worldly, utilitarian type of religion. From a Western point of view it looks as if it has to do purely with earthly aspects of life here and now. However, in an African setting "the whole point about this world is that it stands at the frontier of human and spiritual activity, and the two are in constant interaction" (Walls 1996:6). This African position is surprisingly in consonance with biblical anthropology. The Bible does not see the human person in idealist terms, as an abstract entity apart from the world. It takes all of human corporeality seriously. In other words, "the spiritual nature of the human person is neither denied nor so one-sidedly absolutized to be a spiritual being and nothing more" (Schottroff 1984:4).

The traditional worldview and its religious concepts continue to form the background of charismatic renewal groups in mainline churches. But their acceptance of the Christian faith has at the same time brought deep-rooted changes to African religiosity. These changes have taken place in relation to two spheres: through a re-ordering of the African religious worldview, and through the introduction of new elements (cf. Walls 1996: 6-14).

RE-ORDERING
- God, who was already known and in principle considered to be the dominant factor, has been magnified and has become the central focus of worship.
- Spirits are usually identified with Satan and demons, but sometimes accommodated as mediating beings, like angels or other spirit servants of God.
- Ancestors: Protestant strands tend to proscribe any form of ancestral cult, while the more Catholic strands attempt to reinterpret ancestor veneration in terms of the communion of saints, though "neither of these procedures could abolish or fully replace the

religious consciousness from which ancestor cult arose."[16]

• Impersonal objects of power (witchcraft) are still very strongly believed in, but they are utterly rejected. A person who uses charms in
whatever form cannot receive healing unless he/she has destroyed
such things.

NEW ELEMENTS

• Christian African religiosity in the charismatic renewal movement
of mainline churches has not only re-ordered and transformed the
four major components of traditional religion, it has also introduced
new symbols and sources.

• God is not only magnified, but he is also identified with the God
of Israel, of the Hebrew Scriptures, and with the God and Father of
Jesus Christ.

• The Christian impact has greatly intensified the sense of the im-
mediacy of God's presence, particularly in the figure of Jesus
Christ. God is speaking directly to Christian Africans. They learn
the will of God by hearing his voice, having a vision of Christ,
finding direction through dreams or through ecstatic utterance in a
charismatic assembly. This in contrast with traditional divination in
which usually the voice of a lower spirit is heard.

• The Holy Scriptures in vernacular on the one hand reaffirm traditional African religious culture, and on the other hand, re-interpret
it in Christian terms by relating it to Christ and to the Holy Spirit.
Christian Africans make their own selection of Bible passages in
resonance with their own local conditions. For instance, the Book of
Leviticus (which is almost unintelligible for Western Christians,
except by forcing allegorical interpretations upon it) is frequently
used in the Spiritual Churches in West Africa, and considered
important also by other Christian Africans.[17] To them, issues of
ritual purity as expressed in the Holiness Code of Leviticus are
important to bring order within personal or social chaos.

• A new element in the charismatic form of Christianity is a lively
apprehension of the significance of the powers of evil and the

---

[16] Walls 1996:9. This applies in particular to funeral rites, in which the spirit of a
deceased person is brought home as (hopefully) a benevolent ancestor. For an
example studied in Zimbabwe, see Kadenge 1998.

[17] Walls 1996:13, mentions that Samuel Ajayi Crowther (1806-1891), the first African
to be made an Anglican bishop, argued that the Book of Leviticus should be among
the first books of the Bible to be translated.

demonic. These powers are organized under control of the devil, the enemy of God and of human well-being. "The dramatic opposition of good and evil forces is one of the distinctive characteristics of African Christianity" (ibid.). The life of a Christian is spiritual warfare whose outcome is victory through the power of Christ.

Christian African religiosity is African because it is rooted in a belief in spiritual and cosmic powers that influence people's lives for better or for worse. Christian African religiosity is Christian because it relies on the power of God, of Jesus Christ, and of the Holy Spirit who counteract negative powers, and who protect and enhance the life of people who follow Christ, the new source for fullness of life (John 10:10). Through members of formerly missionary churches who, because of an existential dialogue between traditional African worldview and charismatic movement, found a dynamic way of being Christian, Christian African religiosity penetrated, and was finally integrated into the mainline churches. With the coming of this dialogical integration one could rightfully speak of the end of the foreign missionary period.

4   CHANGE AND SIGNIFICANCE

Religion in Africa and African religiosity are not static. In the religious sphere changes took place in the past and are taking place now. This applies to African Traditional Religion that borrowed religious ideas and cults from other regions just as invading African conquerors usually accepted the local rituals for spirits of the land.[18] The coming of Christianity and Islam as well as European colonial control and civilization had considerable impact on the African religious scene. The peoples of Africa have been subjected to quite a number of different influences, like people of other continents. Thus religion in Africa involves not only the conventional three movements (ATR, Christianity, Islam), but also a host of other religions or religious movements.[19] Some of these have attracted a number of African devotees like, for instance, new religious movements from the Orient (India, Japan), and from the African Diaspora (Rastafaria, the Nation of Islam) (Dovlo 1998). This confirms the openness of Africans to religion. But there is also a movement in an

---

[18] This has, for instance, been the case among the Kasena (Navrongo) in Northern Ghana, according to my field research in August/September 1966. Cf. Manoukian 1951.

[19] Mbiti 1969:254-261, refers to African Judaism, Hinduism, and the Baha'i Faith. See also Platvoet 1996.

opposite direction, a development of secularism. Notwithstanding his remark on Africans as being "notoriously religious", Mbiti has noticed this (Mbiti 1969:253, 264 f., 274). Only recently has attention begun to be given to this phenomenon.

4.1 Change in the religious scene: secularism and a Christian response
The late Nigerian theologian Emefie Ikenga-Metuh stated,

> One of the impacts of Christianity and modernization on [African] traditional religion is that it has given rise to a large number of Africans who do not practise any religion. The collapse of traditional societies led also to the collapse of organised forms of traditional religion (Ikenga-Metuh 1987:272).

Not-practising religious rituals is not the same as secularism. Secularism means indifference regarding religion or even unbelief. These latter non-religious attitudes are beginning to be found in Africa today.

A systematic case-study of secularism in Africa has recently been undertaken by Aylward Shorter and Edwin Onyancha (1997:5, 14). The aim of their research has been "to discover the various ways in which secular values are at work in African society and the manner in which they erode or displace religious values, especially those of the Christian Gospel." Secularism is defined as "a world-view which, in theory and/or in practice, denies the immanence of God. Organized religion ceases to dominate or pervade society...Religion, whatever form it takes, is seen to be a mere department of the social order."

Pope John Paul II, in his exhortation *Ecclesia in Africa* delivered after the African Synod, pointed to the growing threat of secularism in Africa. "The rapid evolution of society has given rise to new challenges linked to the phenomena notably of family uprooting, urbanisation, unemployment, materialistic seductions of all kinds, a certain secularization, and an intellectual upheaval caused by the avalanche of insufficiently critical ideas spread by the media" (1995:60 n.70). Shorter and Onyancha have taken these words as the agenda for their book. Its content refers to secularism as unbelief (especially among intellectuals and élites in universities and higher educational institutions); secularism as consumer materialism among affluent Christians especially in urban Africa, leading to religious indifferentism; secularism among the urban poor; the impact of the mass media; youth disorientation; and rising secularism in the rural areas.

The authors of Secularism in Africa also examine the concept of "new evangelization" as an appropriate Christian response to secularism.

This implies a fourfold approach: social transformation and the acceptance of social responsibility by Christians; greater cooperation at all levels and between all social groupings; an internal transformation within Christianity, especially a spiritual transformation; and a better use of the means of social communication including more effective communication with young people who must be allowed to become evangelizers themselves.[20] The Church must make a fair and sober assessment of modern culture. Otherwise the Christian faith will be separated from real life. Religion has to to be open to modernity, "but surpass or transcend it." (Bertsch 1993-1994:104; quoted by Shorter / Onyancha 1997:15). Central to a fair and sober assessment is a critical evaluation of science and technology as an important human achievement but one that does not answer the question of the ultimate meaning of life.

4.2 Significance of (Christian) African Religiosity for a Proper Understanding of Religion

This section will deal with three aspects of Christian African religiosity: 1) The nature of African religion as both secular and sacred; 2) Christian African religiosity; and 3) The Significance of Christian African Christianity in Europe.

Christian African Religiosity: Secular and Sacred

Well-known and much discussed is the opening sentence in John S. Mbiti's *African Religions and Philosophy*: "Africans are notoriously religious." It apparently means that this is a well-known ("notorious"!) fact. It does, however, not necessarily mean that all Africans are religious in outlook and practice, as the discussion on secularism has shown (see 3.1). Compared with the status of religion in the West, one can still maintain that—generally speaking—Africans are "notoriously religious." But they are religious in their own way, pragmatic and practical. Religion has to protect life and guarantee abundant life. Such an understanding applies to traditional African religiosity, but has also been carried over into Christian African religiosity. The human person, in their perception of religion, is central, but he/she depends on spiritual forces for protection and growth. In their understanding and practice of religion there is a certain balanced tension between the natural (secular) and the supernatural (sacred) condition of being human.

In charismatic renewal groups and churches this tension is expressed by the term "spiritual warfare." Charismatics, in the midst of a constant

---

[20] Shorter/Onyancha 1997:8 (a summary of chapter 9, 130-144).

threat of all kinds of evil, are primarily pre-occupied with obtaining "spiritual power," for themselves, but they also want to impart it to their respective churches through "spiritual renewal." A real danger exist that being so obsessed with the reality of demonic activity, that every misfortune is attributed to the negative influence of the Devil (Satan). Yet, charismatics are becoming aware that for obtaining "abundant life" they have not merely to depend on spiritual forces (God, Christ, and the Holy Spirit) and to wage a "spiritual war" against the Devil, there is in addition a "natural" realm in which humans have to exercise responsibility (Omenyo 2002:258). In post-missionary Christian African religiosity one can discern a threefold intra-religious dialogue between traditional, charismatic and mainline church elements, which result in a transformation of religion and Christianity, that keeps both the secular (natural) and the sacred (supernatural) in a balanced tension.

Christian hope in Africa's chaos and suffering

May we expect any contribution to the world from Africans while their continent is in chaos, characterized by many as a lost continent?[21] Is it not sheer naivety or even hypocrisy for Christian Africans to claim that their religiosity aims at "abundant life" or "wholeness of life" while their context is one of continuing violence, suffering, and human degradation? We should realize that the majority of African people are victims of exploitation, strife and violence. The main culprits causing this sad situation are a small group of politicians and businessmen who often associate themselves with and are at the same time being used by outside forces, and by a power-hungry and corrupt leadership surrounded by a gangster group of cronies.[22]

From a Christian perspective, it is precisely in the context of massive suffering that "wholeness of life" can become meaningful. There is a Christian tradition that sees "the dawning of hope precisely in hopelessness as the hall mark of God's redemptive movement... We come to see that hopelessness and abandonnement are the privileged places of encounter with God's creative power."[23] African people find

---

[21] For a distressing survey see Ayittey 1999.

[22] See ibid.: chapter 5: "The Vampire State", chapter 8: "How the West compounded Africa's crisis" but also chapter 9, "Alternative solutions to Africa's crisis.

[23] Langerak 1992:458. Cf. Jeremiah's vision of the "two baskets" containing good and bad figs: the good, excellent figs are destined for the exiles in the land of the Chaldaeans. Yahwe says, "My eyes will watch over them for their good, to bring them back to this land" (Jer. 24).

confirmation of this biblical Christian tradition in their own tradition, in which religion relates to all aspects of life, both joyful and sad. It is religion that gives cohesion to their lives. Religion seeks to bring wholeness. The Christian tradition has added the Cross as a powerful symbol of endurance in life's adversities. As such, it transcends traditional African religiosity. The cross must be preached. The problem is what kind of cross? How is one to interpret the Gospel of a crucified God? Jesus on the Cross forms part of the Christian message not only as a sign of a saving love or a source of spiritual consolation. It is also a sign of faithfulness to a cause. This message is appropriate especially for the lowly and the marginalized (cf. 1 Cor. 1:17-31). It is not a question of overcoming the Cross but of deriving from the same Cross the energy for shouldering the task imposed by one's own and other people's liberation.[24] According to the Tanzanian theologian Magesa, "A conception of Christian discipleship reduced to common sense, in which there is no room for the "foolishness of the Cross"is a satanic triumph." This is not an invitation to passivity or an escape from reality. Magesa links defeat and struggle for justice with the Christ of the Cross who inspires Africans to accept the risk involved in the struggle to transform the world in which life will triumph (Magesa 1974:282). Besides reliance on religious support for endurance in times of adversity (Christian) Africans show resilience and courage in fighting for survival and in seeking abundant life (Verstraelen 1996:259-260).

Significance of Christian African religiosity for Christians in Europe
A major fact in contemporary Christian history is the shift of the centre of gravity of Christianity from the North (Europe and North America) to the South (especially Latin America and Africa). Christianity has become a true part of Africa because it is firmly rooted in African soil through a dynamic interaction with African cultural and religions traditions. Because of its numbers, but more so because of its interpretation and implementation, "African Christianity is the likely *representative* Christianity of the twenty-first century" (Walls 1995:xi-xii). In other words, Christianity has become a non-Western religion.

In contrast, the West and Europe in particular, that initiated Christianity in sub-Saharan Africa is moving away from the Christian faith because of widespread secularism. The Christian faith has, to a great extent, been replaced by "a popular myth of science as the ultimate theory of everything, a conviction that the only truth are scientific truths,

---

[24] Verstraelen 1977:75-85, referring e.g. to Galilea 1975, 43.

reality as accessible to observation and experiment."[25] An important part of this myth is the belief in unlimited progress. The technological advances since the industrial revolution have convinced many people that secularism, a worldview without religion, is the final condition of the human race. In this view, religion belongs to the childhood of humanity, to naive and credulous people. The Enlightenment has had, and still has, profound impact on Western society, including Western Christianity and theological reflection[26]. Its influence has been positive in that it unmasked superstition, but negative in as far as it undermined religion by deifying reason.

Today this secularist worldview is shaken by the ecological crisis and by the weakening or even possible collapse of world economy that undergirds the high standard of living in Europe and North America. Moreover, the experience of two devastating World Wars (initiated by "enlightened" European nations); the contemporary menace to national and personal security by terrorism (partly stemming from an unjust world order); and the continuing nuclear threat with the potential to completely annihilate the world have demonstrated the limits of reason and progress. The Cameroonian theologian Jean Marc Ela has observed, "At the present the West is doubting itself. It has discovered that it is not absolute. To be able to rise above its own contradictions, it must have the courage to *drink from other sources*"(Ela 1981: 3, italics added). The "other sources" Ela refers to are the experiences of Christian African religiosity and its dynamic relationship to real life.

However, persons will only "drink" when they are thirsty. It seems that a new thirst is beginning to appear in the West. This new thirst includes a growing interest in religion as something that goes beyond reason. Many Europeans are disillusioned with science and technology that rather than promoting progress has furthered dehumanisation. People are searching for doors to the interior, psychic and spiritual realms of human existence. This is a revolution in consciousness

---

[25] Shorter/Onyancha 1997:15. For this and the next paragraph see: ibid., "Some Popular Assumptions Concerning Secularism", 16-19.

[26] See entry the "Enlightenment" (in F.L. Cross and E.A. Livingstone 1990: 458-459) which states that "the movement embraced a wide spectrum of views and aims", such as defence of the victims of religious persecution (Voltaire), attempts to improve the legal practice in Italy, and the economy in Spain. The majority of the Enlightenment thinkers were probably deists, though the movement as a whole was undoubtedly hostile to orthodox Christianity.

involving a popular awareness that "there is more between heaven and earth than rational thinking can fathom." This has created a new search for the deeper meaning and value of human life (see Verstraelen 1996: 197-200). Westerners who have abandoned the practice of organized (church) Christianity are now often reverting to cosmic religion in a non-Christian form as, for instance, in the case of the New Age movement. Some feel attracted by cults from Asia, others create their own forms that correspond to their spiritual longings. Practising Christians, church leaders in particular, seem not to be aware of the obstacles that prevent secularized people searching for deeper meaning to find it in the type of Christianity they see or have been acquainted with. It is here that Christian African religiosity can make a contribution.

Christian African religiosity has gone through a process that could indicate how European Christianity could become again a dynamic, inspiring religious reality. During its foreign missionary period, Christian African religiosity encountered a type of Christianity that did not respond to the real needs and deeper longings of African people. Only through linking the Christian faith with their own religious traditions, first by the African Independent Churches and later by the charismatic renewal movement in the established churches, could Africans make Christianity a vital part of their lives. Christian Africans, confirmed in their endeavour by having access to the Bible in the vernacular, were able to go beyond a tele-guided, intellectualized, overly-spiritualized and unappealing type of Christianity imposed upon them from the West and North. The day has come when Christian African religiosity will contribute to new understandings of faith in Africa and in Europe and North America as well.

BIBLIOGRAPHY

Abbott, Walter (ed.). (1966). *Documents of Vatican II*. New York: Guild Press.
Adegbola, E.A. (1983). *Traditional Religion in West Africa*. Ibadan: Daystar Press.
Ayittey, George B.N. (1999). *Africa in Chaos*. London: Macmillan Press Ltd.
Baëta, C.G. (1962). *Prophetism in Ghana: A Study of Some Spiritual Churches*. London: SCM Press
Beckmann, D.M. (1975). *Eden Revival: Spiritual Churches in Ghana*. St. Louis.
Bediako, Kwame. (1995). *Christianity in Africa. The Renewal of a Non-Western Religion*. Edinburgh/Maryknoll: Edinburgh University Press/Orbis Books.
Bertsch, Ludwig. (1993-1994). "Inculturation in Europe's social situation: an Introduction". In: *Yearbook of Contextual Theologies*. Aachen: Missio Institute.

Cross, F.L., and E.A. Livingstone. (1990). "Enlightenment". In: *The Oxford Dictionary of the Christian Church*. Oxford: University Press. Pp. 458-459.

Dammann, Ernst. (1963). *Die Religionen Afrikas*. Stuttgart: W.Kohlhammer Verlag.

Daneel, M.L. (1987). *Quest for belonging—Introduction to a study of African Independent Churches*. Gweru: Mambo Press.

"Declaration on the relationship of Christianity to non-Christian religions". (1966). In: Walter Abbott (ed.). *The Documents of Vatican II*. New York: Guild Press. Pp. 656-674.

Dovlo, Elom. (1998). "The Church in Africa and Religious Pluralism". In: *Exchange* 27-1. Pp. 52-69.

Ela, Jean Marc. (1981). "De l'assistance à la libération. Les tâches actuelles de l'Église en milieu Africain". In: *Foi et Développement*. Nrs. 83-84.

Ellis Davidson, H.R. (1981). *Gods and Myths of Northern Europe*. Harmondsworth: Penguin Books.

Forman, Charles W. (1982). *The Island Churches of the South Pacific. Emergence in the Twentieth Century*. Maryknoll, NY: Orbis Books.

Galilea, Segundo. (1975). *La predicación de la Cruz*. Collección Iglesia Nueva 18. Bogotá, Colombia.

Hartland, E. Sidney. (1909). "Bantu and South Africa". In: *Encyclopaedia of Religion and Ethics*. Edinburgh: T&T Clark.

Hoornaert, Edward. (1989). "Christianity and Paganism". In: Idem. *The Memory of the Christian People*. Turnbridge Wells: Burns & Oates. Pp. 261-264.

Ikengah-Metuh, Emefie. (1987). *Comparative Studies of African Traditional Religions*. Enugu.

John Paul II. (1995). *Ecclesia in Africa*. Nairobi: Paulines Publications.

Kadenge, Levee T.C. (1998). *Death and Mourning among the Zezuru. The Attitude and Response of the Methodist Church in Zimbabwe. Theological and Pastoral Implication for Christian Ministry*. University of Zimbabwe. Ph.D.thesis. (manuscript).

Langerak, Ana. (1992). "Healing, Releasing, Proclaiming in a Cruciform World". In: *International Review of Mission* 81. No. 323. Pp. 447-463.

Magesa, Lawrence. (1974). "Return to the World. Towards a 'Theocentric Existentialism' in Africa". In: *AFER* XVI-3. Pp. 277-284.

Magesa, Laurenti. (1998). *African Religion: The Moral Traditions of Abundant Life*. Nairobi: Paulines Publications Africa.

Manoukian, M. (1951). *Tribes of the Northern Territories of the Gold Coast*. (Ethnographic Survey of Africa. Western Africa V). London.

Maquet, Jacques. (1967). *Africanité traditionnelle et moderne*. Paris: Présence Africaine.

Mbiti, John S. (1969). *African Religions and Philosophy*. London: Heinemann.

—. (1975). *Introduction to African Religion*. London: Heinemann.

Mulders, Alphons. (1962). *Missiologisch Bestek. Inleiding tot de katholieke missiewetenschap*. Hilversum/Antwerpen: Uitgeverij Paul Brand N.V.

Omenyo, Cephas Nahr (2002). *Pentecost ouside Pentecostalism. A Study of the Development of Charismatic Renewal in the Mainline Churches in Ghana.* Utrecht University. Ph.D.thesis (manuscript).

Oosthuizen, G.C. (1968). *Post-Christianity in Africa. A Theological and Anthropological Study.* London: C. Hurst and Co.

Parrinder, Geoffrey. (1954). *African Traditional Religion.* Harmondsworth: Penguin Books.

—. (1963). *Witchcraft: European and African.* London: Faber and Faber.

Platvoet, Jan. (1996). "The religions of Africa in their historical order". In: Jan Platvoet, James Cox and Jacob Olupona (eds.). *The Study of Religions in Africa. Past, Present and Prospects.* Cambridge: Roots and Branches. Pp. 46-102.

Rattray, R.S. (1923). *Ashanti.* London.

Sanneh, Lamin. (1989). *Translating the Message: The Missionary Impact on Culture.* Maryknoll: Orbis Books.

—. (1993). "Religious Insiders and Cultural Outsiders or Religious Insiders and Cultural Insiders? The Intercultural Critique". In: Idem, *Encountering the West. Christianity and the Global Cultural Process: The African Dimension.* Maryknoll: Orbis Books.

Schottroff, Willy. (1984). "Introduction". In: Willy Schottroff and Wolfgang Stegemann. *God of the Lowly. Socio-Historical Interpretations of the Bible.* Maryknoll N.Y.: Orbis Books.

Shorter, Aylward, and Edwin Onyancha. (1997). *Secularism in Africa. A Case Study: Nairobi City.* Nairobi: Paulines Publications.

Smith, Edwin W. (ed.). (1950). *African Ideas of God. A Symposium.* London: Edinburgh House Press.

Sundkler, Bengt. (1948). *Bantu Prophets in South Africa.* London: Oxford University Press.

—. (1976). *Zulu Zion and Some Swazi Zionists.* London: Oxford University Press.

Triebel, Johannes. (2002). "Living Together with Ancestors: Ancestor Veneration in Africa as a Challenge for Missiology". In: *Missiology. An International Review.* 33-2. Pp. 187-197.

Verstraelen, Frans J. (1961). *Het religieuze erfdeel der Baluba en enige andere volken in Zuid-Oost Kongo. Een ethnologische studie over het Hoogste Wezen in Katanga en Oost-Kasay.* Rome: Pontificia Università Gregoriana. Ph.D.thesis. Partly published as "La conscience morale des Baluba et de quelques autres peuplades dans le Sud-Est du Congo". In: *Anthropos* 59 (1964). Pp. 361-399.

—. (1975). "The Church and African Culture". In: Idem. *An African Church in Transition from Missionary Dependence to Mutuality in Mission. A Case-Study on the Roman-Catholic Church in Zambia.* Leiden: IIMO. Pp. 318-337.

—. (1977). "Spirituality and Struggle for Fullness of Life: Interreligious Stimuli and Secular Challenges". In: *Exchange. Bulletin of Third World Christian*

Literature 18. Pp. 75-85.

—. (1981). "Afrika en zijn godsdiensten". In: C.Braun (ed.), *Wat geen oog heeft gezien*. Hilversum/Amersfoort: KRO/De Horstink. Pp. 24-42.

—. (1993). "Mission and Bible in Historical and Missiological Perspective". In: I. Mukonyora *et al. 'Rewriting' the Bible: the Real Issues. Perspectives from within Biblical and Religious Studies in Zimbabwe*. Gweru: Mambo Press. Pp. 141-167.

—. (1995). "Ghana, West Africa: Between Traditional and Modern". In: Idem (ed.). *Missiology: an Ecumenical Introduction*. Grand Rapids: Eerdmans. Pp. 65-87.

—. (1996). *Christianity in a New Key. New Voices and Vistas through Intercontinental Communication*. Gweru: Mambo Press.

—. (1998). *Zimbabwean Realities and Christian Responses. Contemporary Aspects of Christianity in Zimbabwe*. Gweru: Mambo Press.

—. (2002). *History of Christianity in Africa in the Context of African History. A Comparative Assessment of Four Recent Historiographical Contributions*. Gweru: Mambo Press.

Verstraelen-Gilhuis, Gerdien. (1982). *From Dutch Mission Church to Reformed Church in Zambia*. Franeker: Wever.

Walls, Andrew F. (1995). "Foreword". In: Bediako 1995.

—. (1971). "Outposts of Empire". In: Tim Dowley (ed.). *The History of Christianity*. Tring: Lion Publishing Co. Pp. 546-556, 561-568.

—. (1996). "Introduction. African Christianity in the History of Religions". In: Christopher Fyfe and Andrew Walls (eds.). *Christianity in Africa in the the 1990s*. Edinburgh: Centre of African Studies. Pp. 1-16.

Westerlund, David. (1985). *African Religion in African Scholarship: A Preliminary Study of the Religious and Political Background*. Stockholm: Almqvist & Wiksell International.

Wind, Anne. (1995). "(Protestant) mission perspectives from 1920 to 1963: the theology of mission and mission strategies". In: Verstraelen 1995: 248-252.

Zahan, Dominique. (1970). *Religion, Spiritualié et Pensée Africaines*. Paris: Payot.

10 The Effect of Liberation on the Missionary Calling of the Churches in Hungary and Central and Eastern Europe

Anne-Marie Kool

1 LIBERATION AND FREEDOM IN THE HUNGARIAN CONTEXT

The Eastern Block countries most likely have in common the experience that "no word has taken on so bad a reputation as [liberation]" (Szûcs 1996:282). In an insightful article on "Freedom and Theology in a Hungarian Context," Ferenc Szûcs refers to the years following 1948 when the Communist party took power. He reminds us that "freedom" and "liberty" have been dominant words in Hungarian literature and culture. The geographical location of Hungary on the borderline of East and West as well as the situation of being "squeezed" in between "two pagans"—according to a contemporary slogan: the Turks and Haps-burgs—created a situation in which "freedom has never been merely a philosophical concept" (Szûcs 1996:274). Hungarian (as well as Central and Eastern European) history was regularly marked by the struggle for freedom.

Szûcs emphasizes that following the "liberation" in 1945, especially from 1948 onwards, the word "freedom" was seriously discredited. It was a time of open terrorism against democratic organizations, parties and churches, started by the notorious secret police. He states: "This was the time in which workers and clerks had to greet each other with the word "liberty", when hotels and bridges were named "freedom", and April 4th had to be celebrated as the day of liberation" (Szûcs 1996:282).

The revolution of 1956 is another clear landmark in a series of struggles for freedom, leaving a general sense of despair and disap-pointment. According to Szûcs the real danger in the three decades that followed came from "the more refined methods of tearing people away from their roots and turning the churches into intellectual ghetto[es]" (Szûcs 1996:284; cf. Bogárdi 1995).

Following the historical changes of 1989, liberation and freedom gained new connotations. For many, especially those observing the events from "outside," *die Wende* was a point in the history of liberation in a socio-political sense. Those "inside" knew better: a process that had been going on for a long time had gradually offered wider possibilities for intellectual, cultural and economic forms of expression.

The question is what the effect of this historic process of liberation had on the churches. How did it influence the missionary calling of the churches in Hungary and Central and Eastern Europe? Szûcs reminds us that if we wish to make the biblical and theological concept of liberation relevant to contemporary society we have to take seriously not only its horizontal but also its vertical soteriological dimension. "Historic changes are not the equivalent of the freedom which the Bible speaks of" (Szûcs 1996:285).

2   MISSION AS LIBERATION

Over the last three decades liberation has been high on the agenda of ecumenical missiology. After the Second Vatican Council (1962-1965) discussions on the meaning of liberation shifted from a "narrower" understanding, focusing on the eternal destiny of a person, to a "broader" understanding related to the socio-political context, under the influence of Latin American Roman Catholic circles.

An important biblical motif in this shift was the (re)discovery of the (often neglected) earthly dimension of the Kingdom of God, Jesus' announcement that he had come to preach to the poor, to proclaim release to the prisoners, and to release the oppressed (Luke 4:18-20). This motif was considered to be the New Testament parallel to the Exodus event by which God freed Israel from slavery. The resulting focus is often more on a horizontal understanding (liberation among people from oppressed structures) rather than on a vertical one (relation of people with God).

For the Dutch Reformed theologian Abraham Van der Beek the essence of the meaning of liberation is found in the vertical dimension: "in Christ" or "with Christ" (Van der Beek 1996:13). Freedom in the New Testament is always understood as "freedom in Christ." "Not for a single moment can the sight of the relation with Him be lost .... This relationship with Christ is our life." It is a personal relationship. "Through his Spirit Christ dwells in us, and we are related to Him. Nothing can separate us from his love" (Van der Beek 1996:13).

Van der Beek calls attention to the fact that life in freedom has to do with "making everything subservient to Christ," which is possible because Christ is our "highest good and deepest being." In the debate on freedom in 1 Corinthians we observe that the final criterion is whether or not giving something up has a missionary connotation: "whether you can win somebody for Christ" (1 Corinthians 9:20f.), whether one helps the other to live the life of freedom as oneself does (Van der Beek 1996:19). He reminds us that Christian theology is "basically" always theology of liberation, but it never can become a program because then it turns into a new law (Van der Beek 1996:20). He states: "then political, social and economic freedom becomes an aim in itself and not a consequence of a more profound inner freedom" (Van der Beek 1996:20). He presents the deepest question related to liberation and mission very profoundly: "how we learn to live the freedom of Christ and how to find words to propagate this ... how we can make the fundamental freedom in Christ subservient to others ... and how can we deploy this freedom against all forms of slavery and oppression?" (Van der Beek 1996:24).

In this paper I will focus on this double connotation of the concept of liberation as it relates to the missionary calling of the churches in Hungary and Central and Eastern Europe, but I will concentrate especially on the historical process as it has taken place over the last decade or so. The scope of this presentation does not allow for an elaborate treatment of the topic. Instead I will select some of the most significant issues and trends.

2   VARYING REACTIONS TO THE "LIBERATION"

The "liberation" following the political events of 1989 struck the churches of Central and Eastern Europe by surprise. Many felt ill-prepared or not prepared at all. The Roman Catholic sociologist of religion Miklós Tomka refers in his research, *Aufbruch 1998*, focusing on Central Eastern Europe, to three possible options for the churches following the "changes'. Apart from the possibility of returning to the situation that existed before the Communist period—out of a kind of nostalgia—the opportunity arose to make use of the experiences of the churches in the West, since they had already undergone the process of learning to live in a free, pluralistic society. Quoting Peter L. Berger, who stated that "Western Europe is an ecclesiastical catastrophe area," Tomka rightly asks the question whether "this is useful" (Tomka and Zulehner 1999: 9). The third option is that the churches draw lessons from the period of Commumism, but for that a profound evaluation of that period would be needed.

The extensive research project *Aufbruch 1998, Gott nach dem Kommunizmus* seeks to offer help in this area. Although the main focus is on the Roman Catholic Church, it still provides many lessons for other denominations—all the more so since for a long time religiosity and belonging to a church or denomination were not analogous. Researchers were faced with the important dilemma of whether "the Churches of Central-East Europe have not too fast put up the old structures, instead of searching for specific ways in the radically new circumstances." After decades of "living in a ghetto," it is of great significance that the churches of Central and Eastern Europe not only orient themselves toward the West but also toward each other and to look for new models in their own countries (Tomka, quoted in Midling 2001: 1f.).

2.1 Roman Catholic Reaction

The Roman Catholic László Lukács summarizes the great expectation of Hungarian society toward the Church, which was seen as the "great Unknown, as a Utopia, as a beautiful Illusion .... The Communists were to be blamed for all mistakes and failures, and the church was expected to find a cure for the country's social illnesses" (Lukács 1991:60). Especially in the area of education the expectations vis-à-vis the churches ran high. Many thought that Christian schools and education would "immediately" create a more disciplined, diligent, honest population. This also held for the area of welfare. The hope was that restoration of the religious orders would create a better, more humane and effective health service, and solve all social diseases.

Thus it was indeed an immense challenge, a *kairos* for the church, but the church was unable to rally to these challenges. The Church was unprepared for the new situation. Not only was there a shortage of personnel, there were also too few teachers to teach in the church schools, barely enough nuns to work in the hospitals, and too few teachers to give religious instruction to children.

The reaction of James A. Scherer, an American Lutheran missiologist, and the German Joachim Wietzke, however, is striking in that in their opinion the Roman Catholic Church was relatively well prepared.[1] Scherer refers to the Declaration *Ut Testes Simus Christi Qui Nos Liberavit* (That We May Be Christ's Witnesses, Who Has Liberated Us) of the First Special Assembly of the Synod of Bishops for Europe, held in 1991. The purpose of Pope John Paul II calling this synod was to work out a strategy for Europe and for the church (Scherer 1992:112).

This Vatican Declaration pointed to the deeper causes of the fall of Communism: ethical, anthropological and spiritual. The "great anthropological mistake" of Marxism was that the human person was reduced to merely material and economic dimensions. But the damaging effects of this false and reductive anthropology remain in people's hearts, even after the changes. The way people think and act has not changed; they continue to live "merely for the satisfaction of immediate

---

[1] Scherer 1992: 112; Wietze 1994: 54; cf. Michel 1991.

desires and the acquisition of economic security" (Scherer 1992:112). The Declaration set forth principles and suggestions for constructing a new Europe.

2.2 Protestant Reaction

In an attempt to encourage partnership among the 200 evangelical mission organizations working in the region, the Lausanne Committee for World Evangelization convened in a summit conference in 1991 in Budapest on "Evangelization in Post-Marxist Contexts" (Lausanne Committee 1991; in Scherer 1992:112ff.). A six-point strategy for mission groups working in Eastern Europe and the former USSR was outlined with the purpose of discouraging "free-lance entrepreneurial approaches": 1) enabling churches and mission organizations in Eastern countries to undertake the own evangelization of their own people themselves; 2) modelling and encouraging cooperation in the work of evangelization; 3) going where Christ is not named or known; 4) involvement that had the long-term aim of producing lasting fruit; 5) working only from an adequate understanding of the people and their contexts; 6) working with complete ethical and financial integrity.

Scherer rightly emphasized that the focus of the statement was on "enabling local churches to do their own mission work, rather than doing the work for them" (Scherer 1992:114). As far as I know, the statement was only published in German (Houston 1992a,b). The fact that some mission agencies do adhere to these principles is encouraging. Others seem to favor other values. If these principles were to be practised more I am convinced it would reduce the tensions among the various groups and also promote partnership and cooperation between historical Protestant churches and evangelical groups.

3   NEW CHALLENGES

A host of new challenges and questions related to the missionary calling of the churches occurred as a result of liberation. During the first years especially the emphasis was on local mission—mission to the numerous nominal members of the churches. Gradually, initiatives were undertaken to establish or re-establish foreign mission work. Mission work was often equalled to re-establishing a system of Christian education, once again looking to models of the past. Others concentrated on addressing current needs, e.g. among drug and alcohol addicts.

In this brief treatment I would like to focus on two issues. One is a rather sensitive area, that of ministry to the minorities, especially to the Roma. It is an issue that is probably one of the most difficult missiological questions in Central and Eastern Europe. Throughout Europe it is probably an issue to which the churches pay hardly any attention. The second issue concerns "believing without belonging", the growing number of religious people who believe "in their own way" without wanting to commit themselves to a church.

3.1 "Hidden" Church Members

The February 2000 census brought to light a very interesting phenomenon. Whereas the religious demography for Hungary was usually such that 21% of the Hungarians were members of the Reformed Church, 68% of the Roman Catholic and 4% of the Lutheran, the 2000 census showed that 16% were Reformed, 59% Roman Catholic and 3% Lutheran. Generally accepted statistics point to the fact that 12 to 13% attend church more or less regularly. In the case of the Reformed Church that would mean 208,000 people. A 1996 law permits citizens to donate 1% of their income tax to a church of their choice and an additional 1% to a non-profit agency of their choice. In the year 2000 about 116,000 chose to donate 1% of their income tax to the Reformed Church.[2]

Therefore István Szabó, the recently elected Bishop of the Reformed Church in Hungary, states in his new program that in this census the Church has in fact "received invitations" from more than one million people (or probably even more) who consider themselves Reformed. The Christian tradition of Europe is no longer present in the culture as a lively faith, but the Christian roots of the culture could indeed serve as a connecting point.

3.2 Roma Ministry

In 1985 The Reformed Church in Hungary established a special ministry among the gypsies. But its leader, Dr. Antal Hadházy, also set a goal to "change the perspective of the majority society" ("*A többségi társadalom tagjai szemléletének megváltoztatása*"), so that living together with the Roma would be more in harmony with the facts and more fruitful. It was in this latter area that he faced the greatest difficulty: the prejudices of the social majority.[3]

Although the number of publications with regard to the missionary calling of the church has significantly increased over the last decade, the

---

[2] The top three churches for the year 2000 and the number of individuals who chose to donate 1 percent of their tax to that church are as follows: Catholic Church, 357,163; Reformed, 116,073; Lutheran Church, 33,217. www.state.gov/g/drl/rls/irf/2002/13934.htm

[3] Cf. www.partnershungary.hu/konferencia4.htm.

area of Roma ministry has been hardly touched upon (Szûcs 2000:41; Kovács 2000:95). Finding out what is happening in the local churches would be an important research area—if only to gain knowledge from the experiences of others (cf. Doncsev 2000:28ff).

Ferenc Szucs is one of the few who emphasizes that the effect of liberation on the missionary calling of the churches should include the Roma mission and considers that fact that bishop Gusztáv Bölcskei officially announced that the church will participate in finding a solution for the Roma question in Hungarian society to be of great importance. Reflection on a number of tasks will be required as well as establishing new mission departments. Preparation for change and taking points of view relating to inculturation into consideration are also necessary because "the Hungarian Reformed tradition has the least direct connecting point to the culture and mentality of the Roma" (Szûcs 2000). At best, this process will "arouse the still water of the people's church." Szûcs adds that this is probably the greatest mission challenge of the 21st century in such an area, which without involvement of the churches "ticks as a social bomb over our heads with unpredictable consequences." It is a good opportunity to test "how the integrating power of the Gospel is able to exert an influence on a similarly difficult integration process in the 21st century" (Szûcs 2000).

3.3 Influx from Missionaries from Abroad:
Central and Eastern Europe as New Mission Field
Since the 1989 changes in Central and Eastern Europe a massive "invasion" of evangelical missionaries has taken place. By far the majority have come with no background knowledge of the culture or language and with the attitude that they "need to bring Jesus" to Central and Eastern Europe (Volf 1996b: 28). But for centuries millions of people have worshipped Jesus Christ in Central and Eastern Europe. Miroslav Volf reminds us that what is needed is "to wash the face of Jesus ... dirtied not only by Communist propaganda, but also by so many compromises of our churches" (Volf 1996b: 28).

Davor Peterlin observes that Western Christians often operate with the false assumption that "the period of Communist rule in the former Eastern European countries has totally annihilated Christian witness," and they think that what is needed is "not only sporadic church-planting, but the actual creation of Christian culture ex nihilo." Peterlin states that the contrary is true: "the countries in question are today at least as Christian as most Western countries, if indeed not more Christian" (Peterlin 1995:167).

In 1994 a consultation convened in Oradea, Romania, focusing on the issue of Theological Education and Leadership Development in Post-Communist Europe, pointing to the "special Kairos times," a time of "unprecedented opportunities for the Gospel of Jesus Christ," and to the complexities faced in equipping new leaders. One of these complexities is "the flood of well meant, but sometimes misguided, wasteful, and inappropriate efforts from foreign agencies" (The Oradea Declaration 1994, art. 3).

4   OLD "BONDAGES"

The 1989 changes in Central and Eastern Europe required major adjustments politically and economically as well as anthropologically. A new way of thinking and a new approach to life had to be faced: "The new did not simply replace the old. A significant residue of the Communist past remains as a great shadow. A shadow of the past" (Kusnierik and Eieel 1997:1; also Kuzmic 1996).

4.1 Lack of Carrying Responsibility

Marsh Moyle, editor of some excellent research papers on the impact of Communism on church and society, says that he asked several friends what they considered to be the most significant effects of Communism on the life of church and society. Although it was a diverse group of people, they agreed on one thing: the most significant shadow cast by the Communist past on the present is a lack of responsibility.

> Who is responsible for my well-being? Who is responsible for the education of my children? Who is responsible for the environment I live in? Answer: The state and its institutions. Because I can do nothing! I am an insignificant small wheel in a big machine. And politics, education, economics, etc. are not my business anyway. (Moyle 1999: 18)

While many did not learn to bear responsibility, it is interesting that many pastors often adopted an attitude of over-responsibility for their parishioners, in the sense of being responsible for their personal decisions, their relationships, the quality of their family lives, etc. They took on a kind of a Christian "guru" role, without whom no major decisions could be taken (Moyle 1999:18).

4.2 Divide et Impera

Another shadow of the past is the lack of unity among the churches. An effective policy of the Communist governments was purposely to create mistrust and divisions between denominations and within the Christian congregations by spreading rumors and creating fear. One never knew who was spying to inform the government of one's activities.

As a result, Christianity in Central and Eastern Europe suffers from many divisions. It still has a long way to go toward restoring relationships in a process of reconciliation. Important steps were taken by Miroslav Volf when he introduced the categories "exclusion" and "embrace" to overcome the problem of otherness, providing the churches with the theological tools to begin this process (Volf 1996). The many divisions are reinforced by the countless independent mission initiatives imported from the West following the changes.

4.3 Private and Public

A third shadow of the past is the dichotomy between the private and public realms. At times during the Communist period rigorous pressure was applied to keep faith and religion in the private sphere. The result was a ghetto mentality. Churches were not allowed to be "relevant," to address the context and were portrayed as outmoded, only for "old ladies with scarves."

This dichotomy was strengthened by 19th century pietism, with its narrow view of spirituality as a personal, existential and emotional relationship with God, which had a strong influence in Eastern Europe. One consequence is that the majority of Christians still live in two separate worlds (Kusnierik and Eieel 1997:23). I sometimes wonder whether this "restricted" theology is not also strengthened by the influx of missionaries from the Anglo-Saxon part of the world with their theological baggage of a strict, separate view of the role of the church in society.

It is this same theology that is critiqued by the younger generation. A strong tendency toward the integration of the Christian faith into all areas of life, based on a larger view of God and his Kingdom, can be detected. Such a view strengthens the credibility of Christianity (Kusnierik and Moyle 1999: 33). The Slovakian researcher Juraj Kusnierik observes that deep theological reflection on issues of church and society is still missing: "we have no time to stop and think," but "we should pause and give it priority;" "the transformation of the mind is more profound and takes more time than the transformation of society" (Kusnierik and Moyle 1999: 33).

5   THE EFFECT OF LIBERATION

5.1 Proselytism

In this section I will focus on one of the major challenges we face in the church in Eastern Europe. It is part of my everyday experience: proselytism and mission.

A decade has passed since the massive influx of missionaries began. It is time to pause and ask whether their help has been adequate, whether the historical churches and the "expatriate contingent" could work together more effectively in, for instance, an area of need that also relates to my personal experience and work: that of relevant, biblical and contextual theological education and leadership development. There is a great need in Central and Eastern European churches for well-equipped leaders able to deal with the burning issues we face, such as the churches' response to nationalism and ethnicity, the revitalization of the churches with regard to local and global mission, how to communicate the Gospel in a relevant way to the secularized de-churched (nominal) and un-churched people of the former Communist countries, and how to move toward reconciliation between church and society.

The German missiologist Joachim Wietze observed in 1994 that the proselytism debate was back on the ecumenical agenda for Eastern Europe and Central Asia (Wietze 1994:63). Not much has changed since 1994. John Witte recently stated that "a new war for souls has … broken out in these regions—a fight to reclaim the traditional cultural and moral souls of these new societies and a fight to retain adherents and adherence to the indigenous faiths" (Witte 1999:3). The large number of articles published on this matter shows that proselytism is an important issue on the missiological agenda of Central and Eastern Europe. The scope of this presentation does not allow for an elaborate treatment of the issue.

Tamás Földesi traces the problem of proselytism back to a difference in opinion as to what the target group of missionary activity is. One of the most sensitive issues is whether mission should target "those who belong only formally to their respective churches" (Witte 1999:136). It is this proselytism within the Protestant churches that causes the most confusion in our Hungarian context. I agree with Miroslav Volf that differences in theology play a secondary role. "For the most part, the problem of proselytism is an issue of personal power, cultural taste, generational difference, and financial independence" (Volf 1996:27). So on both "sides" one can find Christians of Reformed or evangelical beliefs.

Paul Mojzes points to the fact that missionaries often do not understand the background of the negative reactions to their often well-intentioned activities. Most of the countries in Eastern Europe are still in the nation-building stage, focussing on national unification. Religion plays an important role in affirming this collective identity, often in the form of the dominant historical religion which was marginalized for so long. Because missionaries belong to heterodox (interdenominational) religious communities, either from abroad or from the country itself, they are considered "obstacles in the process toward maximal homogenization," and for that reason their activities give rise to great resistance from both national political and traditional religious leaders (Mojzes 1999: 35).

5.2 Widespread Division

Need for Social Reconciliation

The Croatian theologian Miroslav Volf, professor in systematic theology at Yale Divinity School, concludes on the basis of his experiences in Central Europe that there is a "disturbing absence of attempts to relate the core theological beliefs about reconciliation to the shape of the church's social responsibility" (Volf 1999:22). He refers to the fact that social issues have been isolated from the message of reconciliation. This pietistic, socially conservative evangelical reductionism leads to a situation such that "reconciliation has a theological and personal meaning, but no wider social meaning" (Volf 1999:24). In other words, the doctrine of reconciliation is reduced to the "reconciliation of the soul with God." People are seen as sinners before God, called to repent and receive forgiveness and new life in Christ.

Volf continues that "the fateful move comes" when this core belief is linked to "an almost exclusive emphasis on private morality conceived of as the ethical consequence of the reconciliation of a person with God and with a thoroughly a-political stance based on the persuasion that the church and the state have distinct spheres of authority" (Volf 1999 23). The fateful move has to do with separating private and public life, with reconciliation in Christ belonging to one world only, the private realm and not the public one.

Volf concludes that this situation results in churches having no re-sources in situations of conflict (Volf 1999:25). They find it difficult to help foster reconciliation. Thus a need for exploring the social meaning of reconciliation is evident. Speaking primarily from his experiences of conflict in the Balkans, and the purposeful policy of *divide et impera* during the Communist era, Volf emphasizes that the future of whole world depends on how we deal with ethnic, religious and gender otherness.

Partnership and Cooperation

A radical refocusing is needed in independent church planting efforts toward partnering with local churches while working toward their revitalization. One of the principles of partnership of the Anglican Communion is that "the local church in each place is primarily responsible for mission in that place, although as part of the universal church it also has gifts to offer and advice and resources to receive."[4] Partnering is a synonym for enabling.

An important prerequisite for partnering is accepting the notion that we all know partially: there is no church that possesses the full truth. Rather, the perspective of other churches enriches our understanding of Christ or, in Paul's words while praying for the Ephesians, that they "may have power, together with all the saints, to grasp how wide and long and high and deep is the love of Christ" (Ephesians 3:17f.).

Duncan Hanson states that the Presbyterian Church in the USA is purposefully not engaged in planting new congregations of its own tradition in the former Soviet Union, although there is a call to support local efforts of the Orthodox, Lutheran and Baptist churches "in planting culturally and linguistic relevant churches among the indigenous peoples who are their neighbours" (Hanson 2000:9). Emphasis is placed on partnering with the local churches in order "not to divide the church where it already exists but rather to support the church in that place" (Hanson 2000:10).

Davorin Peterlin argues that foreign missionary agencies should link up with a recognized indigenous Christian group, whether it be a denomination or a local church.

> [However,] there are still too many of those who do not adhere to this policy. Instead they send their lone ranger missionaries or teams, which then fight with other lone rangers over territory and vigorously protect their turf. We can observe this evangelical Christian conquest of the Wild West in Eastern Europe. (Peterlin 1995: 167)

6   FINAL OBSERVATIONS

The process of liberation in the last decade has greatly influenced the missionary calling of the churches in Hungary and Central and Eastern

---

[4] These four principles were agreed upon at a meeting of the Anglican Consultative Council held in Dublin in 1973. The first three are: "(1) There is one mission in all the world. (2) It is shared by the world-wide Christian community. (3) It involves a process of giving and receiving in which all have gifts to offer and needs to be met."

Europe. New opportunities have arisen. At the same time old "bondages" have resurfaced, and new "bondages" have occurred, often hindering the church from living out the full liberation and freedom in Christ.

The modern idols of our contemporary culture increasingly encapsulate not only our European societies but our churches as well. In such a context in transition the question arises as to how the Gospel relates to "our culture'. J.E. Lesslie Newbigin calls us to reflect on "Gospel and Our Culture issues" as a basis for a missionary praxis that is biblical, contextual and relevant. This reflection can only be undertaken as part of the worldwide body of Christ, in a process of mutual learning from one another, encouraging one another to dare to confront contemporary culture, and challenging one another to live as a witnessing community in today's society. Liberation is still partial.

At the same time a spiritual hunger and thirst can be observed. Large crowds still search for bread and water, living bread and living water in the churches of Central and Eastern Europe. But what to give them? In the words of Abraham van der Beek, the main questions should be "how to live the freedom of Christ and how to find words to propagate this" (Van de Beek 1996:24). The disciples suggested to Jesus: "Send the crowds away, so that they can go to the villages and buy themselves some food." But Jesus replied: "They do not need to go away. You give them something to eat" (Matthew 14:15f.).

To "live the freedom of Christ" and to "find words to propagate" —personally and corporately—is not possible without a renewal in relevant preaching and teaching, a renewal in visionary, servant-based leadership, and a biblical spirituality that corrects activism.

BIBLIOGRAPHY

Bogárdi Szabó, István. (1995). *Egyházvezetés és teológia a magyarországi református egyházban 1948 És 1989. Között.* Debrecen: Ethnica.
Doncsev, Toso (ed.). (2000). *Measures Taken by the State to Promote the Social Integration of Roma Living in Hungary.* Budapest: Nemz. es etnikai kisebbsági hivatal.
Hanson, Duncan. (2000). "Denominational Perspective on Ministry in Eastern Europe." In: *Religion in Eastern Europe* 20, No. 3. Pp. 8-17.
Houston, Tom. (1992a). "Zur Arbeit in Osteuropa Und in der UdSSR—Teil 1." *Evangelikale Missiologie* 1: 78-79.
))). (1992b). "Zur Arbeit in Osteuropa Und in der UdSSR—Teil 2." *Evangelikale Missiologie* 2: 30-31.
Kovács, Sándor. (2000). "Cigánymisszió a Kárpátalján." *Confessio* 24 (3): 95-

97.

Kusnierik, Juraj, and Milan Eieel. (1997). *Shadows of the Past: The Impact of Communism on the Way People Think in Post-Communist Society.* Sen Research Papers. Marsh Moyle (ed.). Bratislava: SEN.

Kusnierik, Juraj, and Marsh Moyle. (1999). *Trends—Ten Years On. A SEN Study Paper Describing Major Trends in Central European Church and Society 10 Years after the Fall of Communism.* SEN Research Paper, 50 pages ed. SEN Research Papers, Vol. 2000. Bratislava: SEN.

Kuzmic, Peter. (1996). "The Communist Impact on the Church." *Evangelical Review of Theology* 20: 60-76.

Lukács, László. (1991). "Opportunities for the Church in the 'Quiet Revolution' in Hungary." *Religion in Communist Lands* 19 (1): 58-65.

Michel, Patrick. (1991). *Politics and Religion in Eastern Europe: Catholicism in Hungary, Poland and Czechoslovakia.* Cambridge: Polity Press.

Midling, Andrea. (2001). "Szociológiai kutatás Kelet-Közép-Európa Egyházairól. Lezárult az Aufbruch-Program." *Új Ember* (Nov.5): 1f.

Mojzes, Paul. (1999). "Religious Topography of Eastern Europe." *Journal of Ecumenical Studies* 36 (1/2): 7.

Moyle, Marsh. (1994). "Shadows of the Past: The Lingering Effects of the Communist Mindset in the Church and Society." *Transformation* 16 (1): 17-20.

Peterlin, Davorin. (1995). "The Wrong Kind of Missionary. A Semi-Autobiographic Outcry." *Mission Studies* 12 (2): 164-74.

Scherer, James A. (1992). "Revolution in the East and Its Missionary Implications for Christians in the West." *Dialog* 31 (2): 110-15.

Szûcs, Ferenc. (1996). "Freedom and Theology in a Hungarian Context." In: A. van Egmond and D. van Keulen (eds). *Freedom.* Baarn: Callenbach. Pp. 273-85.

—. (2000). "Az elmült tiz év teológiai értékelése." *Théma* II (4): 36-42.

The Lausanne Committee for World Evangelization. (1991). "Budapest Summit Statement to Those Working in Eastern Europe and Ussr.". Paper presented at the Evangelization in Post Marxist Context. A Summit for Christian Leaders, Budapest, Hungary, 1-7 September 1991.

"The Oradea Declaration." (1994). Final Document of Equipping for the Future. Consultation on Theological Education and Leadership Development in Post-Communist Europe, Oradea, 1994. Oradea: World Evangelical Fellowship and Overseas Council International for Theological Education and Mission.

Tomka, Miklós, and Paul M. Zulehner. (1999). *Religion in den Reformländer Öst(Mittel)Europas. Gott nach dem Kommunismus.* Ostfildern: Swaben-Verlag.

Van der Beek, Abraham. (1996). "A Life in Freedom." In: A. van Egmond and D. van Keulen (eds). *Freedom*. Baarn: Callenbach. Pp. 11-24.

Volf, Miroslav. (1996a). *Exclusion and Embrace: A Theological Exploration of Identity, Otherness, and Reconciliation*. Nashville: Abingdon Press.

——. (1996b). "Fishing in the Neighbor's Pond: "Mission and Proselytism in Eastern Europe'." *International Bulletin of Missionary Research* 20: 26-31.

——. (1999). "The Social Meaning of Reconciliation." *Transformation* 16 (1): 7-12.

——. (2001). *Ölelés és kirekesztés theológiai viszgálodás az azonosság, a másság ös a kiengesztelod's tárgykörében*. Transl. by Pásztor Péter. Budapest: Harmat.

Wietze, Joachim. (1994). "Christian Witness in Eastern Europe and Central Asia." *Mission Studies* XI (1): 43-75.

Witte, John. (1999). "Introduction: Pluralism, Proselytism, and Nationalism in Eastern Europe." *Journal of Ecumenical Studies* 36 (1-2):1-6.

PART III

CHALLENGE OF RELIGIOUS FREEDOM

11 Religious Freedom and Christian Mission

Jan van Butselaar

1 INTRODUCTION

For a long time there has been little or no talk in the West about the state of religious freedom in the world. Those who were concerned about these matters and were urging their respective government to step up their efforts for the defence of religious freedom in specific situations, were often seen as diehard religionists that could not be taken serious. Furthermore, these protesters were seen to become active only when people belonging to their own religious group had their religious rights curtailed, or worse. So, public opinion in the West generally, and western governments especially, often closed their eyes and closed their ears when they were called upon to defend religious freedom in the world. When they did, it was normally not because that freedom as such was being violated, but because other fundamental human rights were also at stake. The intervention was then formally based on cases of unlawful imprisonment, torture, or violation of women's rights, to give a few examples.

2 THE TWENTIETH CENTURY

That attitude in the West over against religious freedom did not come out of the blue, although originally, there did not seem to be much of a problem. When in 1948 the *Declaration of Human Rights* was formulated and accepted, freedom of religion and belief was an integral part of it and was not disputed by western member states of the United Nations.[1] Religion, Christian religion, was still an important feature of society in many European countries and its practice much respected. Furthermore, the ideal of freedom in every sphere of life was strong in the wake of the horrors of the second world war. Nobody would think to exclude religion from that precondition of human life.

Shortly afterwards though, the attitude to religion in western culture changed dramatically, especially in western Europe. Many countries in this part of the world were organized on the principle of the separation between church and state. Even in countries where there was (still) a state church, as in Great Britain and in most Scandinavian countries,

---

[1] For a study on the function of this *Declaration* see Falconer 1980.

church-leaders in fact had little or nothing to say in matters of government, although their moral influence was still great.[2] When a church gathering expressed itself publicly on a matter of national concern, the advice was often taken seriously in society at large. That respect, an intrinsic recognition of the importance of the role of the church in western society, changed in the second half of the last century in a process that became known as secularization. It is not the place here to describe or to analyse this process. Others have done that and are still trying to do it (see Hoedemaker 1998:1-10). Fact is, that the role of the church in society declined quickly, engagement in church life dwindled, accusations of guilty behaviour of the church (and its mission!) in various situations became the daily bread of the media. Religion seemed to be a dying phenomenon.

A famous Dutch entertainer prophesied in those days that the safari park where the last existing Christians could be viewed, would shortly be opening its gates...[3] In this line of thinking, interest in freedom of religion as a fundamental human right almost ceased. When a claim was made to act against violations of religious freedom in foreign lands, the past mistakes of (Christian) religion were cited, the divisive and sometimes even violent character of the phenomenon "religion" was once more brought to the fore and possible action refused. The final argument was always: haven't we got a separation between church and state? What could possibly be the role of a (secular) government in religious affairs?[4]

This attitude over against the defence of religious freedom in the world could not only be seen outside the church but also within Christian circles. Feelings of guilt about a history of confrontation with other religions (the crusades!), feelings of uncertainty about the role of mission (should the world still be converted?), feelings of "academic honesty" (do not the Christians in country X do the same mischief as the Muslims in country Y? So what can we say?) ensured that in church and mission the theme of religious freedom could hardly come to the fore. Only in evangelical circles, where the missionary zeal was strong as before, calls could be heard for the protection of persecuted Christians,

---

[2] See for Great Britain: Fisher 2000:82-90.

[3] The name was Wim Kan, a national figure in the Netherlands in those days.

[4] In the midst of the eighties, I still had to argue with members of the Dutch parliament who where thinking along these lines in a meeting organized by Pax Christi on the violation of religious freedom in Sudan.

especially in the then communist Eastern Europe. But these evangelicals were not taken seriously at the time by the mainline churches and were sometimes even seen as religious fanatics.[5] So in general, freedom of religion or belief was not an issue in the western world. It was better if you stayed away from it…

In other parts of the world, the situation was quite different. In fact, religion played an important role in government policy, one way or the other. As mentioned above, the place of religion in the communist countries of those days was rather complicated. According to the ruling ideology, religion was an impossible possibility, but as long as it existed it should at least be kept in line with communist principles and communist politics.

In the newly independent countries in sub-Saharan Africa, there was a relative freedom of religion—although church leaders were not supposed to be critical about issues such as nation-building (see Van Butselaar 2001:6f.). In the Muslim world, the situation was again different, not least considering the diverse countries. Other religions of the "book" (Judaism, Christianity) were tolerated, but their adherents sometimes had a difficult life in Muslim society.

Later on, when fundamentalism became an important force in some Muslim societies, freedom of religion and certainly freedom to change religious affiliation came under heavy attack. Governments had to reckon with the pressure that came from those circles. Free proclamation of religious messages was also endangered in several countries. In Saudi Arabia, evangelists risked capital punishment for such actions. In countries where Hinduism or Buddhism were the major religion, freedom of religion seemed generally to be respected. But also there, certain regions of countries became closed for religious proclamation other than that of the majority group. Converts to another religion risked prison or worse.

In general, it was clear that in the second half of the 20th century, there was a deep cleft in the appreciation of religion between the West and the rest of the world. Where the West (especially Europe, the communist East included) considered religion a dying phenomenon, but possibly dangerous for peace and harmony in society, in other parts of the world religion was recognized as an important characteristic of human life. But there, in many cases freedom of religion meant in fact freedom of religion for the majority.

---

[5] A famous case that caused much discussion was the one of Richard Wurmbrand in Rumania, see his 1967.

3   A NEW CENTURY

The negative image of the role of religion and the disinterest in the defence of religious freedom in the West changed unexpectedly at the end of the last century. All of a sudden, fundamentalist movements sprang up within different religions, some full of verbal violence, some even using physical violence. All of a sudden, religion was back as a subject of public discussion: what is the role of religion? Remarkably, not only the negative and dangerous aspects of religion and religious practice came to the fore, as in previous years. Other important questions were asked in the secularized western society: had they been mistaken? Was religion actually not dying? Was it even so alive and kicking, that it could motivate people into action, even violent action? Was religion more important than previously thought? Statistics indicated that about 92% of the world population was religiously "affiliated". That created a new attitude over against religion.

In the West, governments suddenly remembered how freedom of religion was part of fundamental human rights. In several countries, actions for the defence of religious freedom were taken more serious than ever before. In the United States of America, a special Commission on International Religious Freedom was created to watch the state of this freedom in the world. The commission was even funded by the government, although the members came from different walks of life and were not government officials.

In the Netherlands, the (Protestant) Netherlands Missionary Council and the (Catholic) Commission Justitia et Pax received private and government funding to start a project to study the convictions on religious freedom in different religions. At a congress in The Hague, where the then Dutch minister of Foreign Affairs Jozias van Aartsen gave an important lecture on the issue, it was decided to create a *Platform on Freedom of Religion and Belief.*[6] That came into being in May 2002. Ba'hai, Christians, Hindu's, Jews and Muslims took part in the deliberations from the beginning. In a short period of time, advice was given to the Dutch government on the situation of religious freedom in Afghanistan and Macedonia.[7]

So a new interest was created for freedom of religion and belief in the western world. But that did not mean, of course, that the mistrust over against religion had fully disappeared. That is already clearly im-

---

[6] "Toespraak minister J. van Aartsen". In: I. van der Sluijs 2001:5-7.

[7] The text of these interventions can be found on: www.zendingsraad.nl

plied in the title of the official of the United Nations with responsibility for this matter: Special Rapporteur on the Elimination of All Forms of Intolerance and of Discrimination Based on Religion or Belief.[8]

Moreover, the whole process of secularization was not undone by this new development. In fact, the new interest for religious freedom was clearly put within the parameters of (post)modern western culture, where not God, but the human being and his or her longings are given a central place. The basis of the new concern was the principle that every human being has the right to express and live his or her religious convictions, as long as he or she also respects the other fundamental human rights as well as the laws of the country he or she is living in. So the defence of the freedom of religion has to do with the defence of the freedom of the individual, not with the search for truth. It is clear that in such a climate the word dialogue is more easily accepted than the word mission. The unspoken expectation of the new attitude was that more freedom of religion will lead to more understanding, mutual acceptance and peaceful co-habitation. Some even came to the conclusion that (Christian) mission is equal to abuse of freedom of religion and should be excluded. In the seminar on freedom of religion or belief organized by the Conference on Security and Co-operation in Europe (OSCE) in The Hague in June 2001, Manfred Nowak, an expert in these matters, declared under the heading "Freedom of religion or belief: proselytism":

> Since religions unfortunately have an inherent tendency to interfere with the religious freedom of others, States quite often feel the need to interfere with the freedom to manifest one's religion in order to protect the freedom of religion or belief of others (ibid.:65).

It is clear that he was referring to mission and doing so in a negative sense. In the debate during the seminar, Nowak expressed himself even more clearly on this topic. According to this thinking, mission is considered to be a barrier to the practice of freedom of religion.

The same was heard from an important Jewish religious leader in the Netherlands during preliminary discussions on the guidelines for religious freedom as proposed to the aforementioned congress in Holland in December 2000 (Naber 2000:207-213). He suggested that a prohibition of mission and a formal declaration of Christians to refrain from such activities, would greatly enhance religious freedom in the

---

[8] As is the title of the *Declaration* of 1981, see Seminar on the Freedom of Religion and Belief in the OSCE Region 2001:113.

world.[9] Such criticism can also be heard within the Christian church. Several Christians engaged in the defence of religious freedom are anxious to prove to their colleagues that they fiercely oppose any effort to use the newly gained religious freedom to start evangelism campaigns. It seems that many suffer from a "Clovis-complex", identifying missionary action with coercion, oppression or violence although, even in the case of Clovis, this association does not seem justified... (Ewig /Schäferdiek 1978:119ff). But through all this, the question is clearly stated: is (Christian) mission incompatible with religious freedom? As Nowak rightly suggests, not only Christians are engaged in missionary activities. Most other religions, in an organized or in a more spontaneous way, are "proselytizing," if not for the truth of their religious convictions, then at least for their moral ideas. Here, where we are honouring the life and work of an eminent Christian missiologist, we will especially consider the relation between religious freedom and Christian mission.

4   THE ATTITUDE OF THE CHRISTIAN CHURCH CONCERNING RELIGIOUS FREEDOM

A good approach to the question can be to look first to the attitude of the Christian church over against religious freedom. If we limit ourselves to modern times, some important witnesses come to the fore. In the European context, the Swiss theologian Alexandre Vinet (1797-1847), the "father" of the Free Church of the Canton of Vaud, had to fight for religious freedom for his church over against the state that did not allow this right to its citizens (Van Butselaar 1984:18ff.). In his *Mémoire en faveur de la liberté des cultes* he argues for a total and individual religious freedom, concerning the "forum internum" as well as the "forum externum", to use some modern terms.[10] Verkuyl, in his almost forgotten doctoral thesis, criticizes the almost boundless individualism in Vinet's theology and his lack of vision of the kingdom of God, but much values his basic idea of religious freedom (Verkuyl 1948:206ff.). In those days, that is the days of Vinet, this religious freedom was not at

---

[9] It was quickly explained to him that countries that are curtailing missionary activities and thus religious freedom, are the same that also show little respect for other fundamental human rights... See also below.

[10] This Mémoire has been presented by Vinet to the Société de la Morale chrétienne in Paris, 1825; see Vermeulen 2000:19-22.

all generally accepted or applied in western culture, not by Protestants and certainly not in Catholic circles (Koshy 1992:86ff.). So the insights of Vinet were at least revolutionary for many Christians of his days.

In the missionary movement, the interest for and the defense of religious freedom has been present from the beginning. In all international treaties of the 19th century that marked the colonial division of the world, it was made sure that the right to religious freedom got a solid place. In the famous Berlin treaty (1885) and the treaty against slavery inspired by Cardinal de Lavigerie and concluded in Brussels (1890), religious freedom is fully guaranteed in the colonial regions.[11] This can of course be interpreted as no more than assuring the freedom of Christian missionary action with little concern for this right in a more general and universal way. But it should be borne in mind, that the respect of this freedom was not directed against attitudes encountered in other religions that could hamper the course of Christian mission, but far more against European colonial masters who considered missionaries, often defending the rights of local people, as a nuisance that should be restrained as much as possible.

This interest for religious freedom in missionary circles was continued at the great international missionary conferences of the 20th century. The ongoing debate in Edinburgh, Jerusalem and Tambaram resulted finally in a publication by M.S. Bates, *Religious Liberty: an Inquiry* (1945). From there, it filtered through in the meetings of the young World Council of Churches (WCC), although the International Missionary Council (IMC) was not yet part of it. At the second general assembly of the WCC in Evanston (1954), a resolution on religious liberty was adopted, that was thoroughly prepared in several meetings (Wind 1984:passim). In the end, the work on religious freedom got a fixed place in the ecumenical structure of the WCC: the Churches' Commission on International Affairs (CCIA) was to monitor the developments in this respect in the world.

In his book, former CCIA director Ninan Koshy gives a very well documented overview of what the Christian church in general and the WCC especially has done to further religious freedom in the world. And although he seems from time to time to be somewhat critical of the Christian efforts to defend this human right and more enamoured with the attitude of the Hindu community in this respect, his book is a proof

---

[11] *British and Foreign State Papers*. LXXXII. Art.X: 320; C. Parry (ed.). *The Consolidated Treaty Series*, CLXXV (1891). Art.X, New York 1978:203.

of the fact that in modern times, church and mission have clearly defended religious freedom—not only their own, but also the right to that freedom for others. In Catholic circles, where religious freedom was not accepted everywhere in the same way, things also changed. The second Vatican council has worked miracles in this respect. It accepted a *Declaration on Religious Freedom* (1965) and although the discussions around this document were sometimes painful, in the end the whole church committed itself to the cause of this fundamental human right (Déclaration 1967; see Berkouwer 1968:35ff.).

In conclusion, it can be said that in modern times, the Christian church has generally been favorable towards religious freedom, not just in order to further the cause of its own mission, but also as the expression of the Christian conviction that every person should have full freedom to serve God or to search God's presence in his or her life. Or, as Jongeneel put it, "...Christians and churches on six continents have the moral obligation to recognize and to respect the freedom of other religions or beliefs. At the same time... they can demand to exercise their own missionary freedom/ Missionsfreiheit..." (Jongeneel 1991:158). So a first finding concerning the relationship between (Christian) mission and religious freedom is that, from a Christian and missionary point of view, freedom of religion or belief is an undeniable right of every human being.

5   CHRISTIAN MISSION AND RELIGIOUS FREEDOM

Obviously, the affirmation I just made above is not always trusted or at least is not always recognized as an inherent quality of Christian missionary work. There is a lot of mistrust in the air, once the word mission is quoted. In the Christian church in the West, during the decolonizing period (mid-20th century), the word was linked with the colonialism of days gone by, with oppression and exploitation. For many it was a sheer miracle that the Christian church in Africa and Asia survived the decolonization. That opinion was another expression of the above mentioned Clovis-complex. It seems that the church dearly needs a theological psychiatrist to deliver many a Christian from that frustration!

In Orthodox circles the word mission caused deep emotion, even anger sometimes. Mission was the expression of (Protestant) inroads into what was held to be Orthodox territory. Mission was seen as the cause of division and hatred in traditional Orthodox countries. The Orthodox opposition against missionary action centered foremost on the "sin" of proselytism or, in popular language, sheep stealing: convincing someone who belongs to another church to join a new church, considered more holy or more effective than the old one. In the ecumenical movement, this inner-Christian proselytism has always been clearly condemned.[12] But the suspicion in Orthodox circles remained, not only over against Protestant mission but especially against Catholic mission. The uniate churches in Eastern Europe and the Middle East were living reminders of what division could result from such missionary endeavours.

Although the complaints of the Orthodox about proselytism in mission certainly were justified, it should be noted at the same time that the Orthodox commitment to religious freedom in their own realm was often not very convincing. The general interpretation of that human right was the so called "Sippendenken", which is widespread in regions as the Middle East. It meant that everybody should be able to enjoy religious freedom as long as they stayed within the religious community of their birth. That was considered the best guarantee for harmony and peace, and in that sense, of religious freedom for everybody. It has been the great merit of people like Anastasios, Bria and Lemopoulos that ideas about mission are changing today in Orthodox circles.[13]

6   PEOPLE OF OTHER RELIGIONS AND RELIGIOUS FREEDOM

The attitude of people of other religions, that is other than Christian religion, over against (Christian) mission, is quite another topic. It has been mentioned above, that mission as such is not a Christian exclusive.[14] All religions are missionary in their inner core, since all religions have a claim on truth- and wouldn't you love to share the truth you have found with others who could largely and existentially benefit from it? Muslims have organized missionary movements, Hindus have their centers where those who want to learn more about Hinduism can be received. Normally, their actions are not linked with the idea of violation

---

[12] Among the many documents and declarations of the WCC on this topic, see Towards Common Witness.

[13] Anastasios was moderator of WCC's Commission of World Mission and Evangelism during the San Antonio World Mission Conference (1989), where he held powerful speeches on mission, see Wilson 1990:100ff., cf. Bria 1986; Lemopoulos 1989.

[14] The way Christian mission is organized (or at least was organized) is often special to Christianity compared to models employed in other religions.

of religious freedom. Christian mission is. That has probably to do with the relative success of Christian mission in many parts of the world. Two hundred years ago, the Christian church was (largely) a western church. Today, the western church is quickly becoming a minority in the world church, as Andrew Walls has explained (Walls 1996). That of course can give the wrong impression that this "gain" was obtained in unjust ways, that not enough respect has been shown towards the religious convictions of others. So, in a somewhat simplistic way, Christian mission often was characterized as violation of religious freedom. Conversion then became the proof of religious oppression.

7   MISSIOLOGICAL IMPLICATIONS

Would that mean that our question, whether Christian mission is incompatible with freedom of religion or belief, should get an affirmative response? That would certainly please some who like to have easy answers when words such as "religion," "ethics," "church" or "mission" are invoked. Today in the West, these people do the same when the word "Islam" comes to the fore. A Dutch politician was considered offensive by many in condemning Islam during the election campaign in the Netherlands in 2002.[15]

The real answer to the question whether Christian mission is a threat to religious freedom or not, seems to be more complicated, more facetted than just some one-liner. It seems that two words in fact play a decisive role in helping to distinguish between missionary action that hampers religious freedom and a Christian mission that acts as a proof of that same freedom: the words *conversion* and *coercion*.

First, *conversion*, that is the change of an individual's religious convictions because that individual has exercised free will in taking his or her own decision. In the declarations of the United Nations on freedom of religion or belief it is clearly stated that every person has this right of conversion. The *Universal Declaration of Human Rights* (1948) says:

> Every person has the right to freedom of thought, conscience and religion. This right includes freedom to change his religion or belief, and freedom, either alone or in community with others and in public or private, to manifest his religion or belief in teaching, practice, worship and observance (art. 18, quoted in *Seminar...*:110).

Similar wording is used in the *Charter of Fundamental Rights of the*

---

[15] Prof. Pim Fortuyn, who, sadly, was murdered on May, 2002.

European Union (art.10, ibid.:118). And although the *Declaration on the Elimination of All Forms of Intolerance and Discrimination based on Religion or Belief* (1981) is less explicit in this respect (it uses "choice" instead of "right to change", art.1, ibid.:114), it cannot be read outside the framework of the Declaration of 1948. There too, conversion, as the relevant religious technical term, is fully admitted. When the Universal Declaration was discussed in the United Nations before its acceptance, the Muslim countries voted in favour of the full article on religious freedom.

There were some reservations, as some representatives argued that the right to change one's religion or belief is in contradiction with the precepts of Islam. But the Pakistani representative took another position:

> Islam is a missionary religion. It claims the right and the freedom to persuade any man to change his faith and accept Islam. Surely and obviously it must equally yield to other faiths the free right of conversion. It would be most unreasonable to claim for oneself the right to conversion and to deny it to others (quoted by Eltayeb 2000: 103).

Specific Muslim declarations on human rights that were formulated after the Universal Declaration, seem to regress on this fundamental aspect of freedom of religion (ibid.:106ff.). But for relations between Muslim countries and non-Muslim countries,[16] the clear formulations of the *Universal Declaration of Human Rights* remain the norm for the definition of religious freedom.

That makes conversion, and the call to conversion an absolutely acceptable phenomenon, not only for Muslim mission, but also for Christian mission and for others. That does not mean that conversion is readily accepted. It is hard for a religious community to see one or more of its adepts leave the flock and by that, intrinsically denying the faith truth of the group. That creates sadness, irritation, or even hatred. In some cultures, it is experienced as a breach in family loyalty and as such not permitted. Many a convert has died at the hands of his or her own family. But more important than these (violent) emotions is the freedom of the individual to express himself or herself religiously or non-religiously in the way that he or she seems fit. Denying the freedom of

---

[16] I use the terms "Christian countries", "Muslim countries", "Orthodox countries", etc., with great reluctance. In fact, they are not adequate. Not geographic territories have faith convictions, but the people that live therein. These terms can therefore not be used to limit religious freedom.

change means at the same time denying the freedom of growth, of insight, of independence. The right to conversion therefore highlights the difference between the right to religious freedom and a state of religious slavery. It is in fact the proof for the proper functioning of this fundamental human right.

Secondly, we must consider the matter of *coercion*. To consider religious freedom as a fundamental human right is quite different from the role that coercion seems to have played at certain moments to make someone change his or her religious allegiance. Before studying this, a note of warning should however be sounded. Not all missionary activity that stands accused of coercion is in fact a case of such malpractice. Many an accusation of coercion does not come from an actual and factual wrong missionary practice, but stems from feelings of irritation and incomprehension that often exist in a religious community when one or more of its members change their faith commitment. The reaction often is: "Since you enjoy the knowledge of truth, the presence of God even, in your community, how can you change your commitment? There must be other motives active than just religious convictions." These type of accusations are rather difficult to deny by the receiving group. It quickly sounds as an *oratio pro domo* and not as an *oratio pro libertate*.

In Christian circles, in the church, accusations of coercion are quickly connected with the "Clovis-complex" quoted above and seem to put Christian mission in a bad light. Having said that, it has to be admitted that sometimes there has been coercion in missionary activities. Two forms of coercion have to be distinguished. The first is willful coercion, that is, to try by means of gifts of privileges to gain the religious loyalty of a person. It should be clear that under all circumstances, such a practice is against true freedom of religion and therefore to be condemned. This coercion can have rather rude forms (you only get food if you convert to my group) or more subtle ones (I have difficulty to recommend you for this job as long as you are not...). Both are against all true humane behaviour. Certainly in situations of poverty, missions and missionary personnel of all religious convictions should be careful not to exploit the needs of people, not even giving the impression that they are doing so.

The other form of coercion is a subconscious, unwillful one and as such far more difficult to deal with. When a religiously inspired group comes with food and clothing to a refugee camp, "automatically" their image and reputation will improve in the eyes of the people, even if they don't say a word about their convictions: is that coercion? When a beautiful religious building is erected in a poor neighbourhood, it attracts the attention of all and gives the impression that those who belong there, are well protected in many ways: is that coercion? When a missionary campaign can work with modern educational material, or modern (and loud!) communication gadgets, people, youth is attracted and comes in masses: is that coercion?

When a religious leader is coming to a country where his or her followers are a small minority, and there he or she shows pomp and ceremony that impresses and attracts people: is that coercion? It is sure that for some, these missionary methods are one step too far. It is clear also that these methods are not only to be found in Christian mission, but also in actions of other groups, religious and non-religious. The missionary fervour of secular western culture to urge people to adhere to a "politically correct" set of opinions and behaviour, a complex promoted by all possible means including the judicial system, is a clear example thereof.[17] New Europeans feel the coercion of western society.

8   CONCLUSION

In conclusion, it could be said that willful coercion is an abuse of religious freedom and has to be rejected under all circumstances. Unwilful coercion should be prevented as much as possible, in order to exclude the creation of a wrong image of what freedom of religion and the right to change his or her religion or belief really means for the life and happiness of a person.

Religious freedom and Christian mission: the two are not so much opposed to each other as is often thought, but rather intimately linked. The freedom of mission, Christian mission, is not an infringement of the freedom of religion, but rather the proof of its proper functioning. It is clear that those countries that forbid missionary activities, sometimes even on penalty of death, are at the same time the countries where other fundamental rights of the people are equally violated.

Governments should shy away from limiting religious freedom and the right of conversion, in order not to give the impression that they do not take the freedom of their citizens seriously. Governments should recognize that they cannot decide for their citizens how their relation to

---

[17] In the Netherlands, a Muslim religious leader was indicted for condemning homosexuality in terms considered offensive. His acquittal in court (April 2002) met with little understanding in some circles. Critique on the freedom of religion became vehement: this right should be subjected to the "general" (i.e. politically correct) feelings of society at large.

God, to the ultimate, should be. For the Christian church and its mission, it is very important to continue to defend full freedom of religion for all religious groups, including for itself. It should not let a Clovis-complex of guilt feelings cause it to refrain from defending anyone who is suffering from a lack of religious freedom, Christian or non-Christian. The church and its mission should, above all, let shine through all its methods that the heart of the Christian message is God's mercy with humankind. That in Jesus He wants to restore true freedom for all men and women in this world (Verkuyl 1948:238ff.).

BIBLIOGRAPHY

Bates, M.S. (1945) *Religious Liberty: an Inquiry*. New York: IMC.

Berkouwer, G.C. (1968). *Nabetrachting op het Concilie*. Kampen: Kok.

Bria (ed.), I. (1986). *Go forth in Peace. Orthodox Perspectives on Mission*. WCC. Mission Series. No.7. Geneva: WCC.

"Déclaration sur la liberté religieuse *Dignitatis Humanae*". (1967). In: *Concile oecuménique. Vatican II. Constitutions, Décrets, Déclarations, Messages*. Paris: Centurion.

Eltayeb, M. (2000). "Religion and State in Islamic Perspective". In: J.M.M. Naber (ed.). (2000). Pp. 100-118.

Ewig, E. and K. Schäferdiek. (1978). "Christliche Expansion im Merowinger-reich". In: K. Schäferdiek (Her.). *Kirchengeschichte als Missions-geschichte. II. Die Kirche des früheren Mittelalters*. Erster Halbband. München: Chr. Kaiser Verlag.

Falconer, A. D. (ed.). (1980). *Understanding Human Rights: An Interdisci-plinary and Interfaith Study*. Dublin: Irish School of Ecumenics.

Fisher, E. (2000). "Freedom of religion: a view from within the Church of England". In: J.M.M. Naber (ed.). (2000). Pp. 82-90.

Hoedemaker, B. (1998). *Secularization and Mission. A Theological Essay*. (Christian Mission and Modern Culture Series). Harrisburg PA.: Trinity Press.

Jongeneel, J.A.B. (1991). *Missiologie. II. Missionaire theologie*. 's-Gravenha-ge: Boekencentrum.

Koshy, N. (1992). *Religious Freedom in a Changing World*. (Risk Book Series No. 54). Geneva: WCC.

Lemopoulos (ed.), G. (1998). *Your Will Be Done. Orthodoxy in Mission*. Gene-va: WCC.

Naber, J.M.M. (ed.). (2000). *Freedom of religion: a precious human right*. Assen: Van Gorcum.

Parry (ed.), C. (1978). *The Consolidated Treaty Series*. CLXXV (1891). New York.

Seminar on the Freedom of Religion and Belief in the OSCE Region: Challenges to Law and Practice (The Hague 26 June 2001). (2001). The

Hague: Ministry of Foreign Affairs.

Towards Common Witness. A call to Adopt Responsible Relationships in Mission and to Renounce Proselytism. (1997). Geneva: WCC.

Van Aartsen, J. (2001). "Toespraak minister J. van Aartsen". In: I. van der Sluijs *et al.* (eds.). *Godsdienstvrijheid, een kostbaar mensenrecht.* Verslag van een conferentie. Den Haag: BBO. Pp. 5-7.

Van Butselaar, G.J. (1984). *Africains, missionnaires et colonialistes. Les origines de l'Eglise Presbytérienne du Mozambique (Mission Suisse), 1880-1896.* (Studies on Religion in Africa, V). Leiden: Brill.

—. (2001). *Church and Peace in Africa. The Role of the Churches in the Peace Process.* Assen: Van Gorcum.

Verkuyl,J. (1948). *Enkele aspecten van het probleem der godsdienstvrijheid in Azië.* Kampen: Kok.

Vermeulen, B. P. (2000). "Freedom of religion in Western Europe: Past and Present". In: J.M.M. Naber (ed.). (2000). Pp. 19-27.

Walls, A.F. (1996). *The Missionary Movement in Christian History: Studies in Transmission.* Maryknoll NY.

Wilson, F.R. (ed.). (1990). *The San Antonio Report. Your Will Be Done. Mission in Christ's Way.* Geneva: WCC.

Wind, A. (1984). *Zending en oecumene in de twintigste eeuw. Handboek over de geschiedenis van zending en oecumene aan de hand van de grote conferenties en assemblées. I. Van Edinburgh 1910 tot en met Evanston 1954.* Kampen: Kok.

Wurmbrand, Richard. (1967). *Tortured for Christ's today martyr church.* London: Hodder and Stoughton.

12 Apostasy

Jan A.B. Jongeneel

1 INTRODUCTION

Apostasy, or standing away (i.e. relinquishing of one religion for another), occurs in nearly all religions and worldviews/ideologies. There is a lot of traffic between religions and worldviews/ideologies. Some people deliberately repudiate and abandon their non-Christian faiths and become Christians. Others renounce and abandon their Christian faith and become non-Christians. Islam may be the religion which takes apostasy most seriously.

Since the New Testament, apostasy is a major theological and missiological problem for Christianity. But it is not always recognized as such. For instance, Karl Barth, Emil Brunner, and Paul Tillich wrote dogmatic/ systematic theologies which did not pay attention to the issue of apostasy. Missiological handbooks such as *Transforming Mission* by David Bosch have also passed over this sensitive topic. Even today, many Christian theologians and missiologists regard the issue of apostasy merely as a matter of church law rather than a topic in the field of both systematic and missionary theology.

There are several kinds of apostasy. To mention one main distinction, apostasy from the Christian faith needs to be distinguished from both apostasy from ecclesiastical obedience and apostasy from religious professions and holy orders. This article concerns only the first kind of apostasy: relinquishing the Christian faith for a non-Christian religion or worldview/ideology.

This chapter can only deal with a few aspects of the above-mentioned topic. In this chapter I begin with an explanation of some aspects of apostasy in mission and church history. Thereafter, I deal with the two main streams of standing away from the Christian faith: the relinquishing of the Christian faith for Islam (since Muhammad), and the relinquishing of it for secularism (since the Enlightenment).

2 CHURCH AND MISSION HISTORY

Before the birth of Christianity, apostasy had already occurred time and time again. For example, Antiochus Epiphanes already tried to turn the Jews away from their religion by forcing them to sacrifice to idols (1 Macc. 2:15).

The New Testament mentions Jews who accused Paul of apostasy

(Acts 21:21). It also stated that persons such as Judas Ischariot, Demas, Hymenaeus and Alexander had repudiated the Christian faith (1 Tim. 1: 20; 2 Tim. 4:10). Such disappointing events have far-reaching consequences (Heb. 3:12; 6:5-8; 10:26). At the end of time, the Antichrist will appear and his arrival will be preceded by a huge apostasy of people who had been known as Christians (2 Thess. 2:3; cf. 1 Tim. 4:1; Heb. 3:12).

The Early Church experienced severe persecution by the Roman emperors. Some Christians of that era were strong enough in their faith to resist the governmental pressure of doing homage before the bust of the pagan Emperor-god. But others were not. Consequently, the Early Church had to cope with the reality of apostasy and its occurrence on a large scale. The Early Church distinguished between various kinds of apostates:

- sacrificati   people who gave in to sacrificing to idols;
- traditores   people who handed over the sacred books to the persecutors;
- thurificati   people who acquiesced in burning incense before the images of the false gods or the emperor;
- libellatici   people who obtained false certificates testifying that they had taken part in the worship of idols; and
- acta facientes   people who contrived to be mentioned in the public records as having renounced their faith.

The most famous apostate of the Early Church was Emperor Julian "the Apostate" (361-363), a nephew of his predecessor Emperor Constantine the Great. He is a good example of free, as compared to forced, apostasy. In the course of the centuries, the Church developed its own canon law with severe penalties for apostasy. Alexis Kniazeff (1991:39) referred to various penalties that differed for clergy and laity.

Clergy who have apostatized because of human fear were repudiated by the church. Clergy who disowned their clerical status as such lost it; if they repented, they were received back as laity. Those who had apostatized and had forced others to do so were excommunicated for ten years if they were of the laity. According to Basil the Great's canon 73, those who had repented after apostatizing had to remain among the penitents ("mourners") for the rest of their lives and were re-admitted to communion only just before their death. Later apostates were punished by the confiscation of their property, exile and sometimes death. In England, for instance, apostasy was formally punished by civil penalties. In 1222, a Christian deacon who became a Jew in order to marry a Jewess is reported to have been burned at the stake at Oxford. And in 1314, the Knight's Templars were accused of apostasy to Islam and experienced a downfall because of this accusation.

The period after the Middle Ages did not put an end to the apostasy problems. On the contrary, they were discussed and reformulated in new texts and in new contexts. For instance, the canons and decrees of the Council of Trent (1545-1563) accommodated the apostasy laws to the post-Reformation situation. And the discovery of new continents by Columbus, Vasco da Gama, and Magellan raised new questions outside the Western world. In this way apostasy became a global issue. The best novel of the Japanese Shusaku Endo, *Silence* (1966), has emphatically dealt with apostasy in the context of the Christianization of Japan. It refers to the relentless persecution of Roman Catholic missionaries and Japanese Christians in the early 16th century. A young Portuguese missionary who was a member of the Jesuit order is said to have apostatized, whereas several simple Japanese Christians of that time are sketched as having refused to tread on the picture of Mary and her son Jesus and consequently were put to death.

3   RELINQUISHING CHRISTIANITY FOR ISLAM

The Yale mission historian Kenneth S. Latourette sketched the rise and spread of Islam as the first great loss of territory in church and mission history. He wrote, "Islam won from Christianity a larger portion of the latter's adherents and territory than any other rival ever has succeeded in doing" (1971: II, 286). In the course of the centuries, many more Christians have indeed become Muslims than the other way around. Further, it needs to be stated that there have been more muslim converts to Christianity who returned to Islam than the other way around. Such converts were not able to cope with their excommunication and the constant muslim pressure from their family members who remained faithful to Islam. Islam—not Christianity—usually makes a big case out of each apostasy. This fact is, of course, rooted in the nature of Islam as a religion that is based much more on law than Christianity is.

Apostasy, or *ridda*, is dealt with by both the Qur'an and the tradition. The Qur'an (3:86-91; cf. 2:217; 4:137; 5:59; 9:66; 16:104-111) calls for severe punishments to be afflicted on apostates (in life after death). The hadith has forbidden the turning away from Islam under penalty of death (crucifixion or otherwise). This heavy penalty in life before death is either immediately imposed on the apostate or after a period of repentance (some sources propose a period of 20 nights, others a period of merely three days). Fikh states that the death penalty can only be imposed on adults. Scholars differ whether adult women can be sentenced to death (Wensinck - Kramers 1941:545). This abhorrent punishment was not only practised in the "dark" Middle Ages but is still used in some Islamic states (especially in Saudi Arabia). In Egypt (Attalah 2002), however, Islamic scholars have pointed out that the sharia does not clarify the length of the period of repentance. Therefore, the Committee of Ethics and Philosophy of Al Azhar's Islamic Studies Unit has rethought this issue and proposed to enlarge the period of repentance: apostates may use the rest of their lives for repentance. This proposal implies that the Committee involved recommends putting an end to the practise of death penalties. However, this Committee has added that its recommendation needs the approval by the People's Assembly. Only thereafter can it become law in Egypt. But this proposal has not yet been presented for discussion in parliament.

Although this proposal of the Al Azhar's Committee of Ethics and Philosophy is to be welcomed, it does not actually solve the problem because the proposal does not intend to abrogate the death penalty as such. Psychologically, the situation can even become worse. For the rest of their lives, apostates in prison could be placed under constant pressure to repent. This is not at all a theoretical option. The case of René Camahort (2002) who because of his Christian faith experienced punishment in a Saudi Arabian prison makes clear not only that prisoners in that country are not allowed to have and read their personal Bible; but it clarifies also that the whole regime is structured to favour those prisoners who are willing to abandon their Christian (or other) faith over against those people who are not willing to apostatize. This immense psychological pressure resulting in the conversion of high numbers of prisoners to Islam is as abhorrent as the death penalty itself. It violates the Universal Declaration of Human Rights and other United Nations' moral and juridical standards. Moreover, it denies the identity of Filippinos, Koreans, Africans and others as human beings. Because of their need for oil, Western governments are silent.

In the Twentieth Century, Islam has become a global religion. It is the task of missionary and systematic theologians on six continents to cope more seriously than in the past with the various aspects of relinquishing Christianity for Islam. This topic cannot be subordinated to being merely an issue for mission and/or dialogue. In order to give the issue adequate attention, Western theologians and missiologists need the help of local lawyers and the assistance of the leaders of the Coptic and

Syrian Orthodox Churches who for ages have wrestled with the apostasy issue in connection with Islam.

4   RELINQUISHING CHRISTIANITY FOR SECULARISM

A number of recent articles and books have been written about the secularization process and secularism as ideology. Many of these studies have pointed to the huge numbers of Westerners who have left the church (the second great loss in mission and church history). However, we must acknowledge that there is more at stake than statistics and the survival of the church as an institution. Since the Enlightenment (Jongeneel 1971), people have abandoned and still are abandoning the Christian faith. The decisions of these people on their church membership can be regarded as outward consequences of more fundamental inward decisions concerning their adherence to the Christian faith. In other words, the discussion on secularization/secularism must not focus only on the church as a body but also on the Christian faith as a personal view and commitment. As is said by the Lutheran missiologist James A. Scherer,

> The Christian West in our day, in contrast to the spiritual climate of a century earlier, appears to have been gripped by a loss of nerve which may conceal an even more serious loss of faith: some would even speak of massive "apostasy" (1987:35).

As in the case of Islam as a post-Christian religion, so in the case of secularism as a post-Christian worldview/ideology, Christianity is the losing partner. Many more Christians have become secular than secular people have become Christian. Moreover, many Christians are inclined to regard the secularization process (as compared to the islamization process) as irreversible and, consequently, to accept the trend towards secularism as inevitable. But such a blind acceptance contradicts the message of the New Testament that regards Jesus Christ as the divine agent who cannot be resisted.

The relinquishing of Christianity for secularism is usually not discussed under the heading of "apostasy". This would change if we accept the fact that the turning away from the church in the West is preceded by a turning away from the Christian faith. When we speak about "secularization / secularism," "declining church membership" and the like, we make concrete issues more or less abstract. But when we use the term "apostasy" to clarify the religious situation in the West since the Enlightenment, we take the personal dimension into account. Persons make faith decisions and thereafter membership decisions. In other words, apostasy is primarily not a matter of church law and statistics, but a matter of Christian faith and personal commitment. It is a matter of relationships and loyalties. At the deepest level, the basic loyalty to the triune God is at stake. Christians who turn away from Christianity to either Islam or secularism trample on Jesus Christ as the Lord and Saviour of humanity. The church needs to be more sensitive and prioritize apostates as people over against apostasy as an abstract or impersonal idea.

5   CONCLUSION

Apostasy is an issue that comes to the fore in the traffic between various religions and worldviews/ideologies. Some Christians abandon Christianity; and, on the other hand, some non-Christians adopt the Christian faith. An important question we must continue to explore is why Christianity was and still is very successful in attracting adherents of traditional religions but has apparently failed in its encounter with Islam and secularism.

There are both similarities and differences between relinquishing Christianity for Islam and relinquishing Christianity for secularism. In both cases, apostasy is a conversion to post-Christianity. The main difference between adopting Islam and adopting secularism is that the former is shaped by much more compulsion and violence than the latter. An exception to this rule is, of course, communism. Thousands of Christians in Russia and China were forced by Stalin and Mao to abandon their deepest convictions and feelings regarding the fullness of life.

Finally, apostasy is not only a personal problem (individuals changing their religion/worldview/ideology) and a communal problem (the relinquishing of a religious/secular community). It is also an eschatological issue. As stated above, the New Testament has testified that there will be a huge apostasy at the end of time. Evangelical Christians are much more eager than ecumenical Christians to take this testimony seriously and to question whether the contemporary apostasy in Western societies is a sign that we are facing the end of time. Ecumenicals in the World Alliance of Reformed Churches and in other bodies, however, point to another phenomenon. Apostasy as a sign of the end of time cannot be observed in the non-Western world where today, for the first time in mission and church history, large numbers of people are becoming Christian and are inviting their non-Christian relatives and neighbours to apostatize and to adopt faith in Jesus Christ as humanity's Saviour and Lord. Nevertheless, fullness of life for all will indeed be achieved only at the end of time when apostasy will lose its relevance. The new heaven and the new earth will once and for all be free of all kinds of contemporary religious and secular standing away because then all human beings will stand before God Almighty in God's full glory.

BIBLIOGRAPHY

Attalah, L. (2002). "No more death". In: *Cairo News* (29 August - 4 September). P. 11.

Camahort, R. (2002). *Brieven uit een Arabische gevangenis*. Ermelo.

Endo, S. (1982). *Silence*. Tokyo etc. First edition in Japanese: 1966.

Jongeneel, Jan A.B. (1971). *Het redelijke geloof in Jezus Christus: Een studie over de wijsbegeerte van de Verlichting*. Wageningen.

Kniazeff, A. (1991). "Apostasy". In: N. Lossky et al., *Dictionary of the ecumenical movement*. Geneva - Grand Rapids. Pp. 39-40.

Latourette, K.S. (1971). *A history of the expansion of Christianity*. Exeter. 7 vols.

Scherer, J.A. (1987). *Gospel, church, and kingdom: comparative studies in world mission theology*. Minneapolis.

Wensinck, A.J. and J.H. Kramers (eds.). (1941). *Handwörterbuch des Islam*. Leiden.

PART IV

THE CHALLENGE OF RECONCILIATION

13 Reconciliation and Forgiveness in Twenty-First Century Mission

Robert J. Schreiter

1 INTRODUCTION

If one had asked in 1985 what role reconciliation and forgiveness might play in the theology and practice of mission, one would likely have been met with a look of incomprehension. Next to no literature existed on the subject, and there was no discussion on either of these two topics. But by the beginning of the twenty-first century, a mere fifteen years later, both reconciliation and forgiveness would be very much in the centre of missiological discussion.

What had changed within a decade and a half to make such a decisive difference? One can note a number of factors that have contributed to this shift. Most important was the end of authoritarian regimes in many parts of the world, and the need both to account for the wrongdoing in the past and to reconstruct society in a manner which would create a better future. This first surfaced in Latin America, as the national security states came to an end, and some form of democracy returned. It was accelerated by the collapse of Communist ideology in the Soviet Union and its satellite states in Europe in the early 1990s. The end of apartheid in South Africa marked the culmination of this trend. In many of these instances, formal attempts were made to come to terms with the past through Truth and Reconciliation Commissions and other projects of recovery of memory.

A second factor contributing to the interest in reconciliation and forgiveness was the number of intrastate wars that occurred after the end of the bipolar world order in 1989. These were instances where issues of identity and ethnicity had fuelled conflict within the boundaries of countries. To be sure, other causal factors for the wars could be cited, such as the artificial nature of the composition of the nation-states, as well as hunger for power or access to natural resources. But attention focused especially on identity and ethnicity. As these conflicts reached a state of truce or came to an end, a delicate process of memory of the past and reconstruction for the sake of the future had to be undertaken.

Yet a third factor in the rising interest in reconciliation and forgiveness began in 1992, with the United Nations' Year of Indigenous People. The date coincided with the five hundredth anniversary of the landing of Columbus in the western hemisphere. Starting with that year, many peoples, especially in the Americas, took the opportunity to reassert their human dignity and the right to the land which had been taken away from them by the European invaders. These sentiments continued throughout the ensuing decade, culminating especially in the assertions made by the Aboriginal peoples of Australia, as the centenary of that country neared in 2001. Here was a longer-term issue of coming to terms with the past, and living a different way in the future.

All three of these factors have combined to bring issues of reconciliation and forgiveness to the forefront in missiological thought. Part of this grows out of a practical consideration: what role might the Church play in this process of reconciliation and rebuilding the future? In many instances, especially when Christians constitute a majority or major sector of the population, countries have turned to the churches to contribute to making this delicate process come about. The assumption is that the churches occupy some higher moral ground that can serve as a site to arbitrate the often bitter recriminations between previously warring sides. The respect which both sides accord to Christianity can provide a vehicle for coming to terms with the past and, perhaps more importantly, moving along a path to a different kind of future.

But there is also a theological consideration: reconciliation and forgiveness are both profound theological concepts, replete with a wealth of meanings that touch the very heart of the Christian message of what God has done for us in Jesus Christ. When these terms become so prominent in discourse that is not specifically religious, the Christian—and the missiologist—necessarily wants to see what connection there might be. More importantly, one wants to see what contribution a Christian teaching on reconciliation and forgiveness might offer to the wider world, and in so doing, witness to God's work in the world.

One might add also that, because of the fact that these situations of national reconciliation and forgiveness must take place in many instances in an interreligious setting, a clear profiling of the Christian contribution becomes important for interreligious dialogue and cooperation. All the great religious traditions have peace as a central value. But the understandings of reconciliation and the possibility of forgiveness vary within these traditions, especially as to how these might be achieved. The importance of the Christian contribution is forcing missiologists to have a clearer sense of these two key theological concepts as they enter into dialogue and cooperation with Muslims, Hindus, and Buddhists.

This chapter focuses on creating a clearer profile of the Christian understanding of reconciliation and forgiveness as these contribute to peace-making and the reconstruction of society in the twenty-first century. It will close with some reflections on a missiology based on these two concepts.

2   RECONCILIATION

The term "reconciliation" has become central to the discourse of rebuilding societies that have been torn by conflict. If one tries to survey the different uses of the word and make some guess as to its meaning based on the contexts in which it appears, it quickly becomes clear that, from a semantic point of view, there are no clear boundaries to the concept. For some, reconciliation means the cessation of overt conflict, as people try again to live together. For others, it means attaining the conditions of a peace upon which a new society can be built. To others it refers to some undefined future state beyond conflict. And for still others, it is defined mainly by achieving a justice which rights the wrongs of the past.

It is worthwhile to distinguish between personal and social forms of reconciliation. In personal reconciliation, from a Christian point of view, God restores the humanity of the victim, making of the victim a "new creation" (cf. 2 Cor 5:17). The humanity that has been wrested from the individual is restored by God, allowing the individual to contemplate the possibility of forgiveness. There are countless stories of such individual reconciliation recorded in the testimonies of victims during hearings of Truth and Reconciliation Commissions.[1] In these instances, often simple, uneducated people of deep personal faith have come to terms with the horrors of the past and have been able to forgive the perpetrators of those deeds. It is typically a profound experience of God touching their lives that leads them to a new place.

Social reconciliation builds in a way on individual reconciliation. That is to say, social reconciliation is not likely to succeed if there is not a cadre of persons who have experienced personal reconciliation. The reason for that is the need to have a more ample vision of the future, a vision that is more than an extrapolation of the present. Those who have experienced individual reconciliation have experienced the graciousness of God, lifting them out of the desolation of being defined by the evil deeds of the past. They can provide insight into the new possibilities which may be presenting themselves.

---

[1] See in this Volume the contribution of Piet Meiring. For a discussion of the relation of Truth and Reconciliation Commissions to the theological understanding of reconciliation, see Schreiter 2002:227-240.

Social reconciliation is best seen as a process rather than an end result. It is a process by which a moral reconstruction of society takes place in such a way that the past cannot be repeated. The emphasis here is on moral reconstruction, that is, the conditions for the wrongdoing of the past are eliminated or contained. It should be noted that emphasis on the moral dimension does not restrict the reconstruction to elucidating moral principles. It would involve the eradication of social structures which breed injustice as well as the punishment of wrongdoers as a warning to would-be wrongdoers in the future.

Why the emphasis on reconciliation as a process rather than reconciliation as an end state of peace? The concrete experience is teaching this in a number of ways. First of all, it is much more difficult to organize positive emotions than negative ones. This is a lesson recurring over and over again in the world today. Put simply: it is easier to organize resistance to an acknowledged evil than to gain consensus about how to rebuild society after an evil is past (see Bock 2001:37-46). Groups can join a resistance movement for very different reasons. They need not share ideologies; they only have to agree on the need to resist and to eradicate the evil acknowledged. Once the evil is gone, whatever solidarity was achieved tends to fall apart as each group comes forward with its own agenda for the future. By placing emphasis on the process of reconstruction, of steps which need to be taken to rebuilding a more just society, there are better possibilities of continued collaboration, at least in the shorter term. To be sure, some vision of the future needs to be present, at least implicitly. But emphasis on the larger vision can paralyze what little constructive action may be able to be taken.

Second, most post-conflict societies have limited resources with which to rebuild. Quite often the financial resources are not there for education, health, and compensation for the victims or their survivors. In some instances, the cessation of violence may be a precarious one. The armed forces, who may have been implicated in the wrongdoing, are still in place. And perhaps most importantly, there is no adequate level of trust upon which to build—either individuals who can be trusted to lead, or social institutions that can support debate in a peaceful manner (so-called "civil society"). To articulate a vision that is completely beyond the means of a society can lead to frustration, anger, and even a return to violence. Reconciliation is, therefore, about a process of reconstruction, taken step by step. It is not about building up expectations that may have no chance of being met.

Third, reconciliation is not really an end state, because it has no clear ending. There are things which any work of reconciliation cannot touch (at least in this life, as a Christian might say). We cannot bring justice to the dead. We cannot restore the innocence of children or the creative years of young adults. There is no point upon which a society can agree that reconciliation has indeed been achieved. Acts of punitive justice or the compensation of victims, while necessary, are symbolic gestures. The justice extended to the victims cannot completely cover the wrongdoing of the past.

For these reasons, social reconciliation is best seen as a process of moral reconstruction, whereby steps are taken, within the means available at the time, to create the conditions for a future different from the past. This will entail telling the truth about the wrongdoing of the past as best as one is able. It will be about helping the victims and their survivors cope in a post-conflict world. And it will involve taking steps to create a different moral fabric for society. Grand visions should not be disdained, however. They can impart energy to the process. But it is dangerous to allow them to be too much at the center of things, since they can divert people from the immediate work to be done.

What does a Christian understanding of reconciliation contribute to these reflections? Christians believe that reconciliation is first and foremost the work of God. Reconciliation is not something we achieve on our own. Undoing the horrendous character of the past, even though that past is a result of our own action, is something that we cannot do ourselves to a sufficient degree. This idea comes directly from the Christian experience of sin and salvation. We cannot pull ourselves out of our sinfulness. It takes the justifying grace of God to reconcile us to God. This is the meaning of reconciliation as it is articulated in Paul's Letter to the Romans. It is worked out further on a personal level in 2 Corinthians 5 and Ephesians 2. It is celebrated in the hymns that open the letters to the Ephesians and to the Colossians. Rather than our articulation of a grand vision of the end state of reconciliation, we entrust that to God, and it is in God's work that we commend our hope. This allows us to concentrate on moral reconstruction without losing hope, trusting that God will reveal to us a future far greater than we ourselves can imagine.

3   FORGIVENESS

If reconciliation is a difficult term to define—let alone implement in action—forgiveness shares much of the same challenge. Forgiveness is deemed the sine qua non condition for reconciliation. Without forgiveness there can be no reconciliation. In this view, forgiveness presumes apology on the part of the wrongdoer. But if there is no acknowledgment of wrongdoing on the part of the perpetrator, if there is no repentance accompanying the apology, then forgiveness is not possible. Moreover, some believe that certain crimes are unforgivable even if there is apology and repentance.

A host of assumptions swirl around the notion of forgiveness. There are assumptions about how the burden of power shifts from the perpetrator to the victim in the act of forgiveness. There are assumptions about what conditions must be met before forgiveness is possible. There are also questions as to what forgiveness is, as well as about how one regards the past once forgiveness has taken place.

But working through the assumptions about forgiveness is only part of the task. There also needs to be a realism about whether and how often these putative conditions for forgiveness are actually met and, if not, what the consequences may then be for the victims. For example, what if the perpetrator does not repent and apologize—which may be the case more often than not? The perpetrator may feel that there is nothing for which to apologize. The perpetrator may be absent or dead, and therefore incapable of apology. In some collective cultures, apology is deemed a sign of weakness, so apology rarely happens. Victims can have constructed their identity so completely based on their victimhood that they are incapable of accepting an apology and forgiving, even if it is proferred.

As in the case of reconciliation, it may be helpful to distinguish between individual and social forgiveness. Recent years have seen an explosion in Western psychology of what has come to be known as "forgiveness studies."[2] A certain consensus is emerging about the meaning of individual forgiveness in individualist societies. It might be stated thus: forgiveness is about a victim's coming free from the past in such a way that the victim is no longer psychologically bound and defined by that past (be it a deed or a perpetrator). Forgiving, then, does not mean forgetting the past deed or event; nor does it mean condoning what has happened. Nor does it entail developing a close or loving relationship with the perpetrator. It means that the victim is no longer held hostage to the past. Forgiveness does not preclude punishment for wrongdoing. It means that the victim has been able to choose freely to change his or her relationship with the past. It does not require the repentance of the wrongdoer, although that is desirable. It does not even insist upon the wrongdoer wanting to be forgiven. It is, rather, an act of autonomy on

---

[2] For one especially good anthology, see Enright and North 1998.

the part of a victim who, until the act of forgiveness, had been bound to that past event. Forgiving is not forgetting, as the popular adage would have it; it is, rather, remembering in a different way.

As in the case of reconciliation, so also social forgiveness is not the same as individual forgiveness, although the two are related. Social forgiveness is about the moral reconstruction of society, as is social reconciliation. It is about a change in relationship to the past, but also to the wrongdoer.[3] It involves some form of ritual of apology in order to be complete. It is not so much about forgetting the past as it is using the traumatic events of the past to construct a different kind of future.

Social forgiveness entails creating a different relationship between erstwhile enemies for the sake of a different kind of future. This different relationship requires the participation, in some manner, of both parties. It involves some kind of ritual exchange to mark both an acknowledgment of the past, and a sign of a different future. Social forgiveness cannot erase the past, to be sure. But the ritual exchange marks a certain coming free from it.

The ritual exchange regarding the past may involve ceding territory, paying for war damages, or punishing the principal wrongdoers in tribunals. This exchange re-involves both sides with each other, but in a different way. It is done under the controlled circumstances of ritual—be that of a legal tribunal, a treaty, or an agreement to pay for damages. This re-involvement brings the parties back into real contact with one another, rather than allowing them each to reconstruct the other in their minds.

A ritual exchange about the future points to a new and ongoing relationship. Its purpose is both to underscore that move away from the old and, like the ritual exchange about the past, create an ongoing and defined relationship intended to be the future. An example of the latter was the agreement reached between France and Germany after the Second World War that the secondary school pupils in each country would give priority to learning the language of the other country. (Unfortunately, this is now breaking down under the hegemonic power of English.) This was both symbolic of breaking down a potential barrier of difference (i.e., difference in language), but also made communication between the next generation in both countries more likely.

---

[3] For a more extensive study of social forgiveness, see Schriver 1995. What I present here diverges somewhat from Schriver.

Social forgiveness, then, is stylized behaviour, intended to mark both the past and the future. It does not require that the two parties like each other, but it does require that they do not seek opportunities to harm each other. The defined nature of the exchange does not entail, therefore, an unlimited number of contacts. But it does involve contacts that are real and enduring.

The early Christians, following Jewish tradition, believed that only God could forgive sin. All sin, even that committed against fellow human beings, is also a sin against God. Christians believe that, through the ministry—and especially the death and resurrection—of Jesus, that capacity to forgive sins has been entrusted to Jesus' followers. Forgiveness is our participation in the graciousness of God's mercy, of sharing in some fashion in the limitless vision of God, who sees the sin as well as the sinner. The forgiveness of sin, central to Jesus' own preaching, has to be central to the identity of any articulation of Christian faith and discipleship.

This understanding of forgiveness from a Christian point of view is especially helpful in both individual and social forms of forgiveness in the world today. Psychologists say that a key to the process of individual forgiveness is the capacity of the victim to see the wrongdoer from a different perspective. Translated into theological terms, victims become capable of seeing the wrongdoer from God's perspective, albeit in limited fashion. We become able to forgive because we participate in God's forgiving action. Looking at social forgiveness as a series of ritual exchanges about the past and the future is reminiscent of the *bonum commercium* whereby God, through the Incarnation, takes up sinful humanity and restores it to its intended glory. Thus, the question whether forgiveness is possible is answered with the response: yes, forgiveness is possible, but it is difficult and needs—from a Christian point of view—God's help.

4   RECONCILIATION AND FORGIVENESS IN TWENTY-FIRST CENTURY
     MISSION

Events in the world at the turn of the twenty-first century have pushed reconciliation and forgiveness into the forefront of people's awareness. Relief agencies that once worried principally about food supply lines and containing cholera are now interested in training their staff in conflict resolution and reconciliation practices. With the many situations of conflict around the world, there has developed what appears to be an abiding sense that, somehow, people need to get beyond the past without negating it and need to build a future that does not repeat the past. That feeds the interest in reconciliation and forgiveness.

David Bosch, in his classic work on mission, helped us all see that different paradigms of mission have grown up throughout history (Bosch 1991). There is often a certain congruence with other movements at the time. I have suggested elsewhere that those thinking about mission today have experienced two such paradigms. The first was mission as expansion, which coincided with European expansion over the past five hundred years.[4] It was during this period that Matt 28:20 came to be associated with the missionary task in a special way. That idea of mission as expansion continues today, but now has been working since the 1960s alongside another paradigm for mission, namely, mission as accompaniment. Here Luke 4:14-19 and perhaps also Luke 24:14-35 have provided the motivation. Mission as accompaniment grew especially as missionaries walked with the newly emerging independent countries after European colonialism, and in solidarity with the poor and oppressed in Latin America. It produced important missionary forms such as dialogue, inculturation, and liberation.

Might not the work of reconciliation and forgiveness provide the most powerful vehicle for hearing God's Good News for the world today? The experience of turn-around in one's life when one experiences reconciliation; or the capacity to have a new future through the act of forgiveness may provide a deep personal experience of God's action in the world and for the world through Jesus Christ. Christ is making peace in the world through the blood of his cross (Col. 1:20). The motivation for mission as reconciliation and forgiveness might be found in Ephesians 2:12-19, where those who were strangers, aliens, or at enmity with one another are brought to together: the wall of division is broken down, and all become citizens in the household of God. In an age when globalization alienates and marginalizes so much of the world's population, this passage promises inclusion. Where enmity has been the rule of the day, reconciliation is sought.

The two earlier paradigms of expansion and accompaniment are still very much with us, but mission as reconciliation and forgiveness has something compelling about it, given the circumstances of the world. Within the wider discussion as to what reconciliation and forgiveness might mean, Christians can bring a specific contribution which arises not out of the periphery of their faith, but from its very center: the story

---

[4] For more on this idea, see Schreiter 1997:122-127.

of God reconciling all things in Christ, of the preaching by Jesus of Nazareth regarding the forgiveness of sins. Those who experience reconciliation and forgiveness in turn become stirring witnesses to what God can do in the world. They may point us all toward a world of justice and peace.

Interreligious dialogue and liberation have been key themes of Jerald Gort's missiological work. Both of these come back to play in the discussion of reconciliation and forgiveness. As has already been mentioned, interreligious dialogue is key to reconciliation and forgiveness in those multi-religious situations where conflict has taken place. The relation between reconciliation and dialogue is more complex, especially since theological conservatives tried to replace concepts of liberation with reconciliation in Latin America in the 1980s. Moreover in some countries, such as Argentina, "reconciliation" meant forgetting about the injustices done in the past, especially during the "dirty war" of the 1970s. Reconciliation cannot be seen as an alternative to justice. Justice is a constitutive part of any reconciliation process. This points to reconciliation as a possible paradigm for mission. Thus, it is important to keep in mind how terms like reconciliation have been used—and misused—in local contexts. Especially to be kept in mind is that what is being sought is to overcome conflict and injustice for the sake of a better future and that the biblical meaning of reconciliation must be maintained in its integrity. How language is used will be crucial if God's mission is to be carried out.

BIBLIOGRAPHY

Bock, J.G. (2001). *Sharpening Conflict Management. Religious Leadership and the Two-Edged Sword*. Westport, CT: Praeger.
Bosch, D.J. (1991). *Transforming Mission: Paradigms Shifts in the Theology of Mission*. Maryknoll, NY: Orbis Books.
Enright, R.D., and North, J. (eds.).)1998). *Exploring Forgiveness*. Madison, WI: University of Wisconsin Press.
Schreiter, Robert J. (1997). *The New Catholicity. Theology between the Global and the Local*. Maryknoll, NY: Orbis Books.
—. (2002). "Wahrheitskommissionen im Spannungsfeld zwischen Wahrheit, Gerechtigkeit und Versöhnung'. In: G. Beestermöller (ed.). *Politik der Versöhnung*, Barsbüttel: Institut für Theologie und Frieden. Pp. 227-240.
Schriver, D.W. (1995). *An Ethic for Enemies. Forgiveness in Politics*. New York: Oxford University Press.

14 Reconciliation in South Africa: Women's Voices at the Truth and Reconciliation Commission

Piet Meiring

1 INTRODUCTION: WOMEN'S DAY 2002

The crowds gathered in the Eastern Cape town of Hankey. Politicians flew in from Cape Town and Pretoria, to mingle with men and women in traditional dress, with local celebrities and with schoolchildren waving flags in the Hankey Stadium. It was August 9, 2002, National Women's Day in South Africa. A special ceremony was planned for the day. Saartjie (Sarah) Baartman, a Khoi-San woman, had been taken to Europe nearly 200 years earlier to be paraded in cities and towns like a circus animal. After her death, her body had been dissected and placed in a Paris museum to be viewed by generations of visitors. Eventually her body was brought back to her homeland and to her people. In August 2002 she was to be buried according to the customs of the Khoi-San people. South African president Thabo Mbeki's address was televised across the nation:

> Sarah Baartman should never have been transported to Europe. She should never have been robbed of her name…, never have been stripped of her Khoi-San and African identity and paraded in Europe as a savage monstrosity. It was not the abused human being who was monstrous but those who abused her. Baartman's burial place will become a national heritage site, a reminder to future generations that women should never again be abused in South Africa.[1]

That women are still abused in South Africa was emphasized at a huge gathering of women and men on the same day, in the capital city of Pretoria. "There are still instances where women who have fought hard for their own liberation and that of their fellow men are abused and mistreated," ANC Women's League treasurer Betha Gxowa told thousands who gathered at the Union Buildings. "The apartheid government sought to rob the black people of their human dignity. They were no different from the British who mocked and ridiculed our sister Sarah Baartman many years ago" (ibid.:2).

---

[1] *Pretoria News*, 10 Aug 2002, 1.

"On Women's Day it behoves us all," Gauteng Premier Sam Shilo-wa added, to remember the past and present victims of abuse, especially the thousands of women, old and young, who during the apartheid years (1948-1994) suffered discrimination, abuse, and torture, at the hands of their fellow South Africans. "Listen to the stories of the women! Let them speak!" one speaker after the other charged the audience.

This chapter invites the reader to listen to the women who suffered under apartheid, to feel their frustration and pain, and to share in their accounts of forgiveness and reconciliation. It is important to listen, because without listening there can be no proper understanding. "If you cannot understand my story", the South African author Ellen Kutzwayo emphasized,

> you do not accept me as your neighbour. I am an African woman. I've tried to share my soul, my way of seeing things, the way I understand life. I hope you understand... Africa is a place of story-telling. We need more stories, never mind how painful the exercise might be. This is how we learn to love one another. Stories help us to understand, to forgive and to see things through someone else's eyes (Botman 1996:138).

All the accounts in the pages to follow were captured at hearings of the South African Truth and Reconciliation Commission (TRC). It was in many instances very difficult—even traumatic—for the women to appe-ar before the TRC, to tell their stories. Listening to the narratives of the women were, in the words of Kutzwayo a "strained, albeit necessary" exercise. It was "necessary to spring the trap that has prevented people from telling their stories and thus prevented them from being under-stood."

2   THE SOUTH AFRICAN TRUTH AND RECONCILIATION COMMISSION (TRC)

The Truth and Reconciliation Commission was established by an act of the South African Parliament with a fourfold mandate:
- To establish as complete a picture as possible of South Africa's apartheid past (1960-1994) and to analyse the causes, nature and ex-tent of suffering of human rights violations between 1960 and 1994.
- To facilitate the granting of amnesty for perpetrators of grave hu-man rights violations during these years.
- To establish and make known the whereabouts of the victims, res-toring their human and civil dignity by granting them the opportu-

nity to relate their own accounts of the violations they suffered and recommend reparation measures in this respect.

• To compile a report on the findings of the TRC, with recommendations of measures to prevent future violations of human rights in the country.

During the two and a half years of its existence (1996-1998) the TRC conducted 140 public human rights violation hearings. Some 21,400 victims submitted their statements. The names of 27,000 victims were recorded (*TRC Report*: II,2:1-33). In addition, 7,048 perpetrators applied for amnesty, many of them appearing before public hearings to explain their applications.

Much has been written about the process of reconciliation, in the wake of the TRC. Was reconciliation achieved? Some persons like Nelson Mandela and Desmond Tutu were positive in their judgment, arguing that the work of the TRC indeed helped prepare the table for reconciliation in South Africa (Meiring 1998:367). Others were doubtful. Ex-president FW de Klerk thought the TRC to be "totally one-sided", stating that the TRC was "doing great damage to the cause of national reconciliation."[2] The TRC itself acknowledged its concern:

> A common criticism of the Commission is that it has been strong on truth, but has made little or no contribution to reconciliation... History will judge whether or not this particular criticism is accurate. It is, nevertheless, worth making two points in this regard. The first is that, while the truth may not always lead to reconciliation, there can be no genuine, lasting reconciliation without the truth... Secondly, it is readily conceded that it is not possible for one commission, with a limited life span and resources, on its own to achieve reconciliation against the backdrop of decades of oppression, conflict and deep divisions (*TRC Report*: V,306).

It may well be true that the drafters of the TRC Acta—as well as many of us involved in the process—were naive in thinking that reconciliation will come easily, that once Truth was invited through the front door of the house, reconciliation would slip in through the side door. Reconciliation, we came to realize, is a very fragile flower. Also, reconciliation does not come cheap. Reconciliation does happen, but the road is rocky, full of dangers and disappointments. But it is also full of surprises. "It never ceases to astonish me," TRC Chairperson Desmond Tutu com-

---

[2] Meiring 1998:369; see also Jefferey 1999:6; Roodt 2000: 27ff; Le Roux 1998: 120ff.

mented, "the magnanimity of many victims who suffered the most hei-
nous of violations, yet who reach out to embrace their tormentors with
joy, willing to forgive, wanting to reconcile." The following narratives
come from the files that I as a member of the TRC kept during the hearings.

A few months into the life of the TRC, it was noted, to the surprise
of many, that more statements on human rights violations were made by
women (54.8% of the total, versus 45.2% of men). Equally surprising
was the fact that the majority of the women's statements pertained not to
their own suffering but to that of a beloved one: a husband, a father, or
a child. Did that mean that, while more statements came from women,
they did not suffer as much as the men? Apparently not. "I don't think
there were more victims among the men than among the women," TRC
Commissioner Yasmin Sooka said.

> The explanation must be more deep seated. I think there are many
> women who suffered hugely...but they are not prepared to talk about
> it. It was too terrible, too traumatic! How can one expect them to
> shout from the rooftops the most intimate things that happened to
> them, the greatest humiliation they had to endure?" (Meiring
> 1998:190).

Special care was taken to encourage women at the hearings to include
their own experiences in their statements (*TRC Report*:IV,283). To make
it easier for women who were too embarrassed or reluctant to testify in
public, three special Women's Hearings were organized: in Cape Town,
Durban, and Johannesburg. In Cape Town the hearing took place behind
closed doors. Only women were invited to attend. Only women led the
evidence, or sat in public gallery. In Johannesburg it was decided that
while women only would chair the meeting, men would nevertheless be
invited to sit in. They had to come, Commissioner Hlengiwe Mkhize,
who chaired the hearing, insisted. It would do them good to listen to the
stories of the women, to listen to what they had to endure and how they
managed to survive, she argued. It would also mean a great deal to the
women, to know that there were men who interested themselves in their
plight (Meiring 1998:191).

The narratives below come from the special Women's Hearings, as
well as from other sessions of the TRC's Human Rights Violations
Committee and the Amnesty Committee, recorded in different parts of
the country.

3   THE SHOCKING ACCOUNTS OF PHYSICAL ABUSE

Although a number of women reported attempts made against their lives (5% of the total), the vast majority told stories of severe ill treatment (85%) and torture (9%). The accounts of Thandi Shezi and Rita Mazibuko are typical of the physical abuse women had to suffer at the hands of the security police, as well as, in some cases, in camps of the ANC and PAC.

At the Johannesburg Women's Hearing Thandi Shezi recounted her experiences in the police cells:

> When they raped me I was already torn and injured through electric shocks. The pain was deep inside me. I could not tell anybody. My mother is in the audience today. She is hearing it for the first time... I am frigid... If I enter into a relationship with a man I get frightened. I have not told anybody a single word. I don't want their sympathy. I don't want the people to give me all kinds of names (Meiring 1998:191).

After her Rita Mazibuko then took the stand. Her tale created a storm in the ranks of the ANC.

> She told the audience that she had undergone military training in Angola and Mozambique before being sent to Swaziland. There she was responsible for working out the routes ANC cadres had to take. At one point, nine of them were caught, and Rita was suspected of being a spy. She was detained in Tanzania and Zambia. For an interminable six months, she said, she had been kept in a hole in the ground. When she refused to have sex with her jailers, they tortured her in various brutal ways, also raping her repeatedly (ibid.:191).

Sometimes it was young girls who bore the brunt of the violence. At the Children's Hearing the following was reported:

> Nomande Ntabeni was 16 years old when she, in Soweto in 1976, had been shot in the stomach. A high school girl, her name was not revealed, was forced to take off her blouse. Electric wires were connected to her breasts. She was shocked several times and had to be admitted to hospital. Her breasts had been badly swollen. The scars were still visible (ibid.:146).

4   TALES OF PSYCHOLOGICAL ABUSE

While many were able to cope with physical abuse, the psychological pressure often became unbearable. Both Ms. Narkedien and Ms. Middelton testified at the Prisons' Hearing in the Old Fort in Johannesburg.

Zarah Narkedien had to live in an isolation cell in the basement of the prison for seven months. She remembered:

> That was very, very painful. I don't even want to describe what it did to me psychologically. I'll write it down one day but I could never tell you. But it did teach me something, and that is that no human being can live alone for more than I think even one month... because there's nothing you can do to survive by yourself every single day... The cells had high walls... As the months went by, I felt that I was going deeper and deeper into the ground... I became so affected psychologically, that I used to feel that all these cells were coffins... it was as if I was alive and all these people were dead... I've been out of prison now for more than seven years but I haven't recovered. And I never will...They tortured me for seven days and the only thing that really made me break in the end was when they threatened to go back to my house and kidnap my four-year-old nephew Christopher, to bring him to the thirteenth floor and drop him out of the window... At that point I really felt I was at my weakest. I felt I could risk my life and I could let my body just be handed over to these men to do what they liked. But I couldn't hand over someone else's body... So at that point I fully co-operated (ibid.:176f.).

Jane Middleton also spent time in solitary confinement:

> Should solitary confinement be regarded as severe ill treatment? The prison authorities themselves know its ill-treatment, that's why they use it as a punishment. I can't describe its effects on you very well, because you do go slightly crazy, and it's very difficult to describe your own craziness... I think Colonel Fred van Niekerk of the Special Branch once told the court that prisoners started showing evidence of disorientation within three days (ibid.:176f.).

Murthie Naidoo had a similar experience: "I was kept in solitary confinement for four months under the 180-day law. It is the worst kind of torture that can be inflicted on a human being. It is far worse than any physical torture" (ibid.:177). The suffering of mothers and wives who had to stand by and watch their loved ones being taken away was equally painful. On 28 October Mrs. Hawa Timol received news from the police that her son Ahmed had committed suicide by jumping from the tenth floor of the Police Head Office, John Vorster Square. This had been on the fifth day of his detention.

> During the week before the news of Ahmed's death reached the Timol family, they had often been visited by the police. They, as well as their neighbours, had been intimidated in many ways. Their questions about Ahmed and his brother had been ignored. 'I was so frightened

that I even said to one of the policemen that perhaps he should go home and speak to his wife to find out what it is like to bring up a child
and not know the whereabouts of that child! I remember saying to this
policeman, "If my body had a zipper, you could unzip me and see how
I ache inside.'"

Her voice breaking at times, Auntie Hawa continued: 'On the
Wednesday evening, my husband and son had gone to the mosque for
evening prayers. During this time three policemen... entered my house. One of them pushed me into a seat and then proceeded to tell me
that my son Ahmed had tried to escape by jumping from the tenth
floor of John Vorster Square and that I was to tell my husband that his
body was laying in the Hillbrow Government Mortuary... I was crying and screaming so much that the neighbours thought I was being
arrested!'

On the Friday of the funeral as is customary in Islamic tradition,
Ahmed's body was brought to the house after it had been washed and
bathed at the mosque. After the body had been returned, wanted to see
her son's face, which was covered, friends and relatives tried to prevent her. 'But I insisted that I wanted to see my son for the last time.
Nothing could have prepared me for what I saw. His face was disfigu-
red and one of his eyes appeared to have come out of the socket. There were bruises and marks on his face and other people who also saw
the rest of his body remarked on all the injuries that they had seen. His
nails had been ripped out and the coffin was smeared with blood.'

Ahmed's brother, Mohammed, who was released months after
the events, came to support his mother: 'She has been living through
the death of Ahmed every day for 25 years' (ibid.:33f.).

5   INSTANCES OF GRACE AND FLASHES OF HUMANITY IN PRISON

During the victims' hearings, the painful testimonies of women who
were treated harshly by their tormentors, were from time to time inter-
rupted with accounts of grace, of experiences of humanity that lightened
the darkness of prison. Deborah Mathsobe told the audience at the Johannesburg Women's Hearing of what happened to her, first in the Old
Fort in Johannesburg, and later in Phoenix, near Durban:

> By Tuesday they began hitting me and choking me with a wet towel.
> I fainted. When I came to I was lying on the ground, wet through.
> They must have thrown water over me. Roy Otto (a warden) threw a
> packet of sanitary towels at me. In the bathroom I found out that I was
> menstruating. I wondered how he knew... The cell was crawling with
> lice. The blankets were dirty and smelled of urine. I did not know
> where I was. I shouted and shouted again. I got severe asthma attacks.
> Yet I was fortunate. An Afrikaner came up to me. His name was Tal-

jaard and I'll never forget him. He said that he had at first thought that
I was crazy. I told him that I was a political prisoner. He listened to
me and then smuggled in an asthma pump and some pills, and helped
me hide them behind the toilet. Every day Roy Otto would walk into
the cell and say, 'We don't need to kill you. The asthma will kill you
anyway!' But the asthma did not - thanks to Taljaard (ibid.:191f.).

Ms Matshoba was later locked up in the Middelburg prison. Her experience there sheds light on the extraordinary relationship that sometimes
developed between prisoners and wardens.

> There were two wardens, Kara Botha and Maryna Harmse. They were
> supposed to be the meanest of the mean, but even they flinched when
> they unlocked my cell in the morning. I could walk around where I
> wanted to. One day, when I was walking around in the courtyard ta-
> king my exercise, I saw Maryna talking to her boyfriend at the gate.
> She was in tears. When she unlocked my cell door that afternoon, her
> eyes were red from crying. I asked her, 'Why are you crying?' 'None
> of your business", she replied, 'Leave me alone!' I told her that I
> would not leave the cell until she told me. 'I heard your friend say that
> he was on his way to Katima Mulilo, and that you would not see him
> for a long time. Against whom will he be fighting there? You see, we
> are in the same boat. He is going to die on the border—and it will be
> my brothers and sisters who are going to kill him. Maryna, why do
> you allow it?' She began crying and opened her heart to me. We be-
> gan talking... (ibid.:193).

6   THOSE WILLING TO FORGIVE

Much has been written about the possibility of forgiveness. Desmond
Tutu's book on his TRC experience aptly carries the title: *No Future
Without Forgiveness*. In the book Tutu discusses at length the biblical
injunction to forgive, as well as the spiritual and psychological processes
involved. The stories of the women, however, throw their own special
light on the issue of forgiveness, on the possibility of forgiving one's
tormentors, and of the difficulty of doing so.

In the USA as well as in South Africa the story of Amy Biehl attracted a lot of attention. Amy was the bright young Fulbright scholar from
Newport Beach. California, who volunteered to help with development
and voter education programmes in Cape Town. On 25 August 1993,
after work, she drove a few of her black teammates home to Gugulethu,
outside Cape Town. A stone-throwing mob pulled Amy from the car,
shouting the infamous anti-white slogan: "One settler, one bullet." She
was beaten with bricks and stabbed to death. Amy's parents came from

their home town to attend the amnesty hearing of the perpetrators of their daughter's death (8-9 July 1997).

> For the Biehls the events of the first day were traumatic. 'I must confess, it was very difficult,' Mrs Biehl told the reporters at the door. But when the couple addressed the press formally the next day, they declared that they would not oppose the amnesty application. The Biehls had continued to be involved in South Africa as Amy's parents and also as the representatives of the Amy Biehl Foundation. Various projects, particularly a training project for nurses working in the townships and squatter areas, were already on the agenda. 'I don't think I have anything to forgive,' Linda Biehl said. 'I never truly felt hatred. Our family never really felt anger or hatred, only incredible sadness.'
>
> They attended the hearing, Peter Biehl said, because they wanted to know exactly what happened. 'I could imagine that the four young men were terrified during the hearing and that they would be careful about what they said. But I made a point of looking them in the eye when reading them an excerpt from a poem by Victoria West during the hearing.' Amy had quoted the poem in a letter she had sent to a Cape Town newspaper:
>
> *They told their story to their children*
> *They taught their vows to their children:*
> *That we shall never do to them*
> *What they did to us.*
>
> 'We have the greatest respect for the TRC and the entire process of reconciliation,' Peter Biehl concluded. 'We therefore do not oppose the amnesty application... But in reality it is South Africa that needs to forgive its own people, based on the tradition of *ubuntu* and the other principles of human dignity. My wife and I came to South Africa, just like Amy did, in a spirit of friendship.'
>
> That the people of Cape Town greatly appreciated the Biehl's attitude became obvious soon afterward. On the front page of the Afrikaans newspaper, *Die Burger*, appeared a photograph of the Biehl couple being handed a painting by Tyron Appollus, a Cape Town artist. Bearing the title *A Plea for Peace*, Appollus had painted it on the very day Amy Biehl had been murdered.

To forgive is not easy. Marina de Lange (Geldenhuys) was a victim of a bomb placed by MK cadres near the entrance to the Air Force Headquarters in Church Street, Pretoria. Nineteen passers-by died, 217 were injured, some maimed for life. Fifteen years later she stood before the TRC, telling her story:

> She had wanted to become a beautician. But in one dreadful moment everything changed. When she came to her senses later in hospital she

found that her hands had been seriously injured and one of her legs was permanently damaged. She had to undergo a number of skin transplants. She still has shrapnel that could not be removed lodged in her body. Marina also testified at the first TRC session in Johannesburg two years earlier. At that stage she did have some understanding for the suffering of her black fellow-South Africans. But now, to meet face to face, the man who had been responsible for all her grief and to forgive was not so simple. Marina frankly admitted that she still could 'not make peace with the cowardly deeds' (ibid.:340).

7   JUSTICE AND REPARATION

Since the inception of the TRC, a serious debate has taken place in South Africa on the relationship between justice and reconciliation (Villa-Vicencio 2000:42ff., 60ff., 77ff., 174ff.). It is often said that the two issues are two sides of the same coin. For reconciliation to happen, there has to be as sense that justice is part and parcel of the process. Lasting reconciliation can only flourish in a society where justice is seen to be done. This brings a number of issues to the fore like government reparation for the victims that balances the granting of amnesty to perpetrators, addressing poverty and unemployment, dealing with matters of restitution, tackling the very sensitive land issue. But justice and restitution are also the responsibility of the individual, of the perpetrators as well as those who profited from the unfair system of apartheid. While the TRC Act did not require of amnesty-seekers to say that they were sorry to ask for forgiveness, or to contribute to reparation and restitution, from time to time that did happen. A telling example is that of Brian Mitchell who had to face the women of the Trust Feeds Community.

> When Brian Mitchell walked into the Trust Feeds School Hall, an audience of three hundred awaited him. One song after the other followed before it was the ex-policeman's turn to speak. 'I understand that it is not easy to forgive,' Mitchell, his mouth twitching nervously, started. 'But I would still ask you to forgive me for everything that happened.'
>
> There was a great deal to forgive. Just more than eight years earlier, three policemen, of whom Mitchell was one, attacked a house in Trust Feeds. They were under the impression that a group of United Democratic Front officials closely connected to the ANC were in the house. They were wrong. The house was filled with men, women and children holding a vigil the night for a funeral. When the policemen drove off, eleven bodies were lying on the floor, together with a great number of wounded.

Brian Mitchell was arrested in 1992 and sentenced to death on eleven charges of murder. When the death penalty was abolished in 1994, the sentence was changed to 30 years' imprisonment. The Trust Feeds community was bitterly opposed to Mitchell's amnesty application. The Amnesty Committee's finding that his action was politically inspired and was part of a campaign against the ANC stuck in the throats of the families of the victims. Mitchell's first attempts to meet people from Trust Feeds were firmly turned down. They did not want to have anything to do with him. When the gathering was eventually arranged, it was clear that there were many people who were not willing to forgive the policeman.

'I lost my husband on that terrible day in December 1988,' Mavis Madondo called out in tears. 'Now I have to struggle on my own with my children. I cannot send them to school. How can you help us?' An elderly woman, on crutches as a result of the wounds that she had sustained that night, stood next to Mavis. Mothers in the halls comforted the two crying women and led them back to their seats.

While song after song was sung and several inhabitants of the town came forward to speak, Brian Mitchell sat alone in the front of the hall. Finally he rose and, using a loudspeaker, he addressed the audience.

Simply, humbly, Mitchell thanked the Trust Feeds community that they were willing to meet him. He related how he, for a long time, had tried to create such an opportunity be means of intermediaries, church groups and other institutions. He explained how he had become involved in various projects aimed at advancing the economic development of the town. He proceeded in telling how he had lost his job when colleagues heard about his dark past, and how difficult it had become to maintain his own family.

After Mitchell had finished talking, many questions followed. It was clear that everybody was not satisfied. But the majority in the hall were willing to extend an olive branch to the ex-policeman.

Jabulisiwe Ngubane who had lost her mother and several children in the attack told journalists that it was her faith in God, the God who constantly forgives our sins, that made it possible for her to reach out to Brian Mitchell: 'It is not easy to forgive, but because he stepped forward to ask forgiveness, I have no choice. I must forgive him…' (ibid.:121ff.).

8   HEALING

Tears flowed freely during the TRC hearings. Often those were tears of catharsis and healing. Allow me to quote two examples. From a black mother during the East London Hearing:

'Was everything worth it?' I asked myself when, after one of the morning sessions, I walked out of the room. Then I heard one of the Xhosa women—one of the unknown, practically forgotten witnesses—speak in the hall. Her words not only moved the archbishop to tears, but left every one of us with a lump in the throat. With effort she spoke of how years ago, she had sent her fourteen-year-old son to the shop to buy bread. There was unrest in the township and somewhere along the way it must have happened that the boy landed in the cross-fire. For some reason, the Security Police arrested the wounded child and subjected him to brutal torture. Two days later, the mother, panic-stricken, fumbling about to find out what had happened to her son, saw on her neighbours' television set during the eight o' clock news, the boy being pulled down from a bakkie (open vehicle) by his ankles and dragged across the tarmac.

It was difficult for the old mother to relate how the police eventually gave her an address where she could find her son. When she arrived there, it was the mortuary. With her own hands she had to prepare her son's body for the funeral, with the bullet wounds, a gaping wound on the back of his head, the burn marks where he was tortured.

My lunch in my hand, I encountered the woman in the midst of a small group of victims.

'Madam, please tell me,' I asked, 'you have come such a long way, over so many years, with your story. Yesterday you had to travel such a long distance to come here. All of us saw how difficult it was for you to tell the story of your son in front of all the people. Please tell me: was it worth it?'

With tears on her cheeks, she raised her head and her smile was like the dawn breaking:

Oh yes, Sir, absolutely! It was difficult to talk about all these things. But tonight, for the first time in sixteen years, I think I will be able to sleep through the night. Maybe tonight I will sleep soundly without having nightmares! (ibid.:25).

Lesley Morgan, a white lay leader in the Presbyterian Church, was deeply affected when she attended the Soweto Hearing. At a subsequent meeting in Central Johannesburg, she poured her heart out:

I am 47 years old. I am a middle-aged, middle class South African housewife, an elder in my congregation, a wife, a mother, a nursing sister… I grew up with all the advantages and opportunities afforded me because I was white. I was oblivious of the fact that there were so many people around me who were not as privileged as I was; not because I was unfeeling, but because I was unaware. I became aware by the time I reached high school and can remember heated discussions in classrooms...

When I was in my twenties, I had many friends at university that included young people who were arrested and harassed by security policemen. It filled me with anger, but also with helplessness... By the late 70's and early 80's I was married, with a young family. Although I was fully aware of the dreadful things that were happening all around me, fear paralysed me. I was no activist. I was afraid of being arrested, afraid of being detained without trial, afraid of being tortured or killed. I do not even have the excuse of not knowing. I was well aware of what was happening. I read the Black Sash publications and knew the terrible consequences of the apartheid laws... God forgive me, I did nothing to speak out against these obscene laws.

The TRC hearings on gross human rights violations have devastated me! I have watched them on television and read about them in the press and in magazines and they have made me weep with anger and horror. There is a strong feeling of denial... I don't want to believe those things... There is a sense of complicity, a terrible feeling of failure. I remember a quotation I read many years ago. It disturbed me then, it haunts me now: 'It is sufficient for evil to prosper that good men do nothing...'

I started talking about it in my community and discussing it with my friends. I started asking myself why I had not attended the TRC Hearings. I know it is causing great pain in the black community. I cannot imagine how it must feel to bear your pain and suffering so openly and publicly. I can imagine what it must feel like to stretch out your hand in an attempt to forgive and reconcile and have no-one there to grasp it...It is not denial that keeps me away, it is a deep and overwhelming sense of shame... I find it almost impossible to look you in the face...

If you had asked me a week ago about my faith, I would have said to you that I was of strong faith, that I believe in God as Creator,... in Jesus Christ as my Saviour... That because of my faith, I have tried to do the best I can, that I have treated all people as human beings, that I have tried to follow the teachings of the Scriptures... I have always loved God with all my heart... I have not always been successful with loving one another...

I am of the Reformed tradition. We are not given to Pentecostal or Charismatic experiences. On Wednesday, I was driving to a conference on the eradication of poverty... For the first time in my life I truly heard the voice of Christ. In all the years I ignored the cries of the oppressed... In my fear and concern for my own safety, like Peter before me, I denied my Lord. Like Peter, the realization of that denial has filled me with unbearable sorrow. The realization that my faith is so small, so selfish, so empty, has broken me... I profess to be a follo-

wer of Christ, but have been unwilling to go where He has led me...
It would be so much easier to blame apartheid for all of it. The truth
is, I made my own choices... I will not run away from what is happening...

Finally, I need to say one last thing... the hardest part... It is so
hopelessly inadequate to make right what has happened, so puny in
the face of such suffering and I am overwhelmed at my temerity in
even offering it, but it is all I have to give—I am sorry!

After Lesley had finished speaking, there was a moment of total
silence. Then applause broke out. Somebody intoned a song. Women
from Soweto and Alexandra, from everywhere, stepped forward to
embrace the white, English-speaking, middle-aged housewife from the
northern suburbs and to ensure her that her plea, her apology, had
been accepted (ibid.: 55f.).

9   RECONCILIATION IS COSTLY, BUT IT PREVAILS

One of the most stirring examples of the cost of reconciliation as well as
the reality of the experience came from King William's Town. Beth Savage told the story of the annual Christmas party that she and her friends
attended at the local golf club on 28 November 1992.

They had been chatting cheerfully, Beth Savage related, when she
became aware of something that sounded like firecrackers. When she
swung around to look what was happening, she saw that a man wea-
ring a balaclava on his head, with an AK47 in his hand, was shooting
at her and her friends. Hand-grenades were thrown. Before she blac-
ked out, she saw her friends falling around her. Beth was taken to a
hospital in Bloemfontein by helicopter, where she remained in the
intensive care unit for a month. Open-heart surgery followed. She also
had a large part of her intestines removed. So much shrapnel remains
in her body that (in her own words) 'all the bells ring when I go
through the airport!'

Beth's life, as well as that of the members of her family, would
never be the same. Her husband and children still struggle to cope
with the trauma. Her father, who had been against apartheid all his
life, sat by her bedside for days. Over and over he muttered through
his tears, 'I can't believe what has happened!' He went into a deep
depression. Six months before Beth would testify in East London, her
father, a broken man, died. Two months later her mother passed away.

And still, Beth testified, not everything was bad. What had happened to her had wonderfully enriched her. It had made her grow. 'It
has given me the ability to relate to other people who may be going
through trauma.' When one of the TRC members asked Beth Savage
how she now felt about the perpetrators, she answered quietly, 'It is a

difficult question. But truthfully, my honest feeling is: "There, but for the grace of God, go I." I do not know how I would have reacted, if I were one of (the freedom fighters). It is all I can say. I think it is marvelous that we can have a Truth Commission. To be able to get everything off your chest brings healing... I hope that everybody will experience this healing. You know, there are people present here who wrestle with many more problems than I do.'

When questioned further, about what the TRC could do for her, Beth's reaction was, 'I have often said this: what I really want, is to meet the man who threw the hand-grenade. I would want to do it in a spirit of forgiveness, in the hope that he, for whatever reason, will also forgive me...'

Archbishop Tutu was greatly moved: 'Thank you very much! All I can say is, what a wonderful country this is! We really have extraordinary people. Yesterday I declared that I was proud to be black, for the way in which black people have endured the hardships they encountered. And now we have another such example. A white example! I think this predicts a wonderful future for our country. We thank you for the attitude of forgiveness that you have shown and pray that everybody who hears you, and sees you, will say, "We have indeed an astonishing country, with extraordinary people, of all races"' (ibid.:26f.).

10 CONCLUSION

These, then, are the stories of the South African women. Many more could have been added. Indeed, more may be added from the recent past, because after 1994—when the New South Africa came into being—violations against women did not stop. The words spoken on Women's Day by President Thabo Mbeki and Gauteng Premier Sam Shilowa, quoted in the opening paragraphs of this chapter attest to that. Reconciliation in all spheres of society is still in contention. It is as difficult to attain as ever. Yet there is hope!

On the day the TRC Report was handed to the South African nation (29 October 1998), Archbishop Desmond Tutu took the podium: "We have been wounded but we are being healed. It is possible even with our past of suffering, anguish, alienation and violence to become one people, reconciled, healed, caring, compassionate, and ready to share as we put our past behind us to stride into the glorious future God holds before us as the Rainbow People of God" (ibid.:379).

Of course he did not speak only of women. But his remarks were especially true of women. The women of the TRC have already said that!

BIBLIOGRAPHY

Boraine, Alex. (2000). *A Country Unmasked: Inside South Africa's Truth and Reconciliation Commission.* Oxford: OUP.

Botman, H Russel (ed). (1996). *To Remember and to Heal.* Cape Town: Human and Rousseau.

Jeffery, Anthea. (1999). *The Truth about the Truth Commission.* Johannesburg: S A Institute of Race Relations.

Le Roux, Jurie. (1998) "Verlos ons van die waarheid ". In: *Fragmente.* Number 2, June.

Meiring, Piet. (1998). *A Chronicle of the Truth Commission.* Vanderbijlpark: Carpe Diem.

Roodt, Dan. (2000). *Om die waarheidskommissie te vergeet,* Dainfern: Praag.

Truth and Reconciliation Commission of South Africa. (1998). *Report,* Vols. 1-5. Cape Town: TRC.

Tutu, Desmond. (2000). *No Future Without Forgiveness.* London: Rider.

Van Vugt, W.E. (ed). (2000). *Race and Reconciliation in South Africa.* Oxford: Lexington Books.

Villa-Vicencio, Charles (ed.). (2000). *Looking Back, Reaching Forward.* Cape Town:UCT/London: Zed Books.

PART V

THE CHALLENGE OF INTERRELIGIOUS DIALOGUE

15 Do the Three Jesuits, Jerome Xavier, Matteo Ricci and Roberto de Nobili, Still Have a Say in our Missiology?

Arnulf Camps OFM

1 INTRODUCTION

Two years ago I wrote a contribution on the Jesuit Epoch in Asia (1549-1773) (Camps, 2000a). Many members of the Society of Jesus, active in China, Japan, India, Tibet, Indonesia, The Philippines, Malaysia, Sri Lanka and Vietnam, brought Christianity closer to the realities of Asian cultures and religions. Some of them may be mentioned here: Francis Xavier, Jerome Xavier, Antonio Monserrate, Heinrich Roth, Ippolito Desideri, Michele Ruggieri, Matteo Ricci, Giulio Aleni, Johann Adam Schall von Bell, Ferdinand Verbiest, Allessandro Valignano, Francisco Cabral, Luis Froís and Alexandre de Rhodes. The Jesuit Epoch in Asia continues to be a favourite object of study and admiration. Johannes Meier wrote recently:

> From the very beginning the Jesuit Order was a global player, bringing Christianity to the most remote corners of the world and facing strange cultures, languages and religions with flexibility and competence. Their high educational level, tight organisation, spiritual motivation, their mobility and internationality made them strong promoters of cultural contact between Europe and the other continents, of spiritual encounter, of controlled cultural change (Wolfgang Reinhard) and of the propagation of information concerning other cultures (Meier 2000:5, from the German).

However, some scholars in mission history and theology studied the quality of this spiritual encounter and were convinced that it was strongly influenced by Western theology, by the theory of accommodation and even by a colonist attitude. In this contribution I intend to go deeper into this matter by studying three great missionaries of the Sixteenth and Seventeenth Centuries: Jerome Xavier who may be considered to be the real founder of the Mogul Mission in India; Matteo Ricci who introduced a new approach in China; and Roberto de Nobili, the pioneer among the Brahmins in India. My intention is not to belittle the achievements of these pioneers, but to reduce them to their proper proportions. By doing this I hope to illustrate that the passage from a theology in Asia to an Asian theology was reserved to modern Asian theologians (Camps 1991:1-21).

2 JEROME XAVIER S.J. (1549-1617) AND THE PRINCIPLE OF GRADUAL REVELATION

This grandnephew of Saint Francis Xavier arrived in 1595 in the Mogul Empire in northern India and he stayed there till 1614. He served at the court of the Emperors Akbar and Jahangir. He became the real founder of the Mogul Mission. He mastered the Persian language, the language of the court and of the ruling class. He had the Koran translated from the Arabic into Persian and most probably he was the author of the Portuguese translation of the Persian text. Xavier created important works of Persian Christian literature and proved to have acquired a detailed knowledge of mainly Muslim doctrines, traditions and customs. He attended many religious disputations at the court, in the church, the mosque or at his residence (Camps 1957:179-226).

In this contribution I am especially interested in the controversial works Xavier wrote in Persian. The most important was *A'ina-yi haqq-numa* (The Truth-showing Mirror) of which a Spanish text exists in the Jesuit Archives in Rome: *Fuente de Vida* (Fountain of Life) (Camps 2000b:33-46; 1957: passim). Xavier also wrote an Abridgement in Persian (cf. Camps 2000b:37-39 and appendix 2). The work is divided into five books and is composed as a kind of dialogue between three partners: a Father, a Philosopher and a Mullah. Beginning with the ninth chapter of the third book the interlocutors are nearly exclusively the Father and the Mullah. In this most important part of the entire work the discussion is restricted to a comparison of Islam and Christianity. Since in Islam it was accepted that the Qu'ran substituted the Gospel, Xavier had to deal with the question. Therefore, he introduced a new principle: the gradual revelation:

> If God would introduce a change, it ought to be not from better to worse or from perfect to less perfect, but from worse to better and from imperfect to perfect. And, as it is proper to the devil to pull and lure away from the good and the sublime to the bad and the base, so it is proper to God to raise His creatures from the base to the sublime. As the perfect teacher gradually instructs his disciple in a more profound doctrine, so when God again sends prophets to the world He always makes them means of a new light in the world and He declares His will more fully with the aid of spiritual and perfect precepts and commandments. Therefore He elevated Abraham above Noah, Moses above Abraham, Jesus Christ our Lord above Moses and the Gospel above the Old Law (Camps 1957:124-125).

Xavier applies this principle of gradual revelation to a comparison of Islam with Christianity:

> Two things, therefore, remain for the Muslims: firstly that their law is more perfect than that of the Gospel, and secondly, that Muhammed was greater in the eyes of God and the world, and more qualified and authorized by God; if these are not true, the assertion that Muhammed abolished the Gospel of Christ by his own law is not exact. For it is God's custom that the more perfect abolishes the imperfect as the light of the sun obscures that of the stars, and that a more perfect and more authorized prophet brings the more perfect law (ibid.:125).

In the fourth and the fifth book of the *Fuente de Vida* this comparison between both religions and their founders is elaborated in detail. Whereas the discussion in the first three books is artificial and scholastic and most probably based on a number of works of Thomas Aquinas (ibid.:163), the two last books betray the real authorship of Jerome Xavier himself. This part of the work is based on a study of the Qu'ran, of the traditions and of communications received from Islamic scholars in the Mogul Empire. We know that Xavier had the Qu'ran at his disposal and he quoted the holy book of the Muslims extensively and frequently. His arguments are devoid of inventions of fantasy and distinguish themselves from the controversial writings of the early Middle Ages. Xavier tried to be as objective as possible and several times he mentioned the good things that can be found in the Qu'ran. He professes not to be incited by malevolence or hatred. In this respect the works of Christian writers of the thirteenth and fourteenth centuries could have influenced Xavier, as for example William of Tripoli, Ramón Martí, Ricoldo da Montecroce and Ramón Lull.

They wrote their works after prolonged acquaintance with Islamic scriptures and traditions and after having acquired experience of the Muslim way of life by staying in Muslim countries. Xavier continues this new school of thought, but a direct dependence on this new trend cannot be proved. Moreover, as Jerome Xavier had the same instruments and context at his disposal, he was not in need of having access to earlier writings. It must be concluded that the second part of the *Fuente de Vida* is an original contribution of Xavier to the Christian literature dealing with Islam (ibid.: 170-175).

This is certainly also true in the case of the thesis of gradual revelation introduced by Xavier as a guiding principle in his work. It gives a great consistency to the second part of the *Fuente de Vida,* but unfortunately it does not lead to a dialogical character of the discussion. Xavier does not really enter into the mind and the heart of his interlocutor. He was a child of his time and did not rise above the polemic level. His notion of revelation did not make room for an answer to the question whether Islam and the prophet Muhammad had a place in God's dealings with humankind.

3   MATTEO RICCI S.J. (1552-1610) AND PRE-EVANGELICAL DIALOGUE

When two Jesuit Fathers, Michele Ruggieri and Matteo Ricci, took up their residence at Zhaoqing in 1583, the third attempt to introduce Christianity in China started (Camps 2000c; Mungello 1999). Ruggieri left China in 1588 and Ricci became the Father of the China Mission. Ricci moved in 1589 from Zhaoqing to Shaozhou and in 1594 he changed out of his Buddhist dress into the dress of the Chinese class of the Literati. He had already started translating the four classic Chinese books into Latin and from then onward he fixed all his attention on the meeting between Christianity and Confucianism. Moving again he took up his residence in Nanchang (1595) and in Nanking (1599), finally reaching Beijing in 1601. He played an important role at the court of the Emperor and among the Literati by publishing philosophical, religious and profane books. Moreover, he introduced certain Chinese Rites into the Christian way of life. When he died in 1610, there were about 2.500 Catholics in China and some 16 Jesuits (Ducornet 1992; Gisondi 1999). For a study of the quality of the spiritual encounters between Ricci and the Chinese Literati a work published by Ricci in 1603: *The True Meaning of the Lord of Heaven* (*Tianzhu shiyi*) is essential (Ricci 1985).

In the introduction to this voluminous work Ricci states that his intention is to correct the erroneous doctrines concerning the Lord of Heaven and to enter into a dialogue with Chinese scholars.[1] The discussion is a kind of duologue between the Chinese scholar, who starts asking questions, and the Western scholar, who answers. A variety of topics is brought up, as for example: creation, the nature of the human soul and spiritual beings, reincarnation, fasting, the taking of life, reward or punishment, the fundamental goodness of human nature, Western customs, the history of celibacy and the birth of the Lord of Heaven in the West. The Chinese scholar is certainly not a Buddhist, for both he and the Western scholar agree that India is a low and lowly nation possessing no arts of civilisation and standards of moral conduct. Ricci wrote that the Buddhist religion came from India to China and that the canonical wri-

---

[1] Ibid.:59-61. The Chinese and English text of this work is to be found on pages 55-458.

tings of the Buddha contain the erroneous doctrine of reincarnation and a hundred other lies (op.cit.:241-243). Both the Buddhist and the Chinese scholar also attacked the teachings of Taoists and Neo-Confucians (op. cit.:99-103; cf. Kern 1992).

As stated, Ricci's intention was to correct the erroneous doctrines concerning the Lord of Heaven. From the very beginning he promised to use explanations based solely on reason. He also stated that the doctrine about the Lord of Heaven is universally known to all nations from the West to the East and is to be found in their canonical writings. Using scholastic philosophy Ricci explained the nature and the uniqueness of the Lord of Heaven. Challenged by the Chinese scholar, Ricci gave his view of the three religious ways of China:

> The 'nothing' spoken of by Lao Tzu and the 'voidness' taught by the Buddha are totally at variance with the doctrine concerning the Lord of Heaven; and it is therefore abundantly clear that they do not merit esteem. When it comes to the 'existence' and 'sincerity' of the Confucians, however, although I have not heard a complete explanation of the meaning of these words, they would seem to be close to the truth (Ricci 1985:99).

According to Ricci, the three schools should "return to the one and only correct Way" (ibid.:101). After a short discussion of the teachings of Laozi and Buddha, full attention is paid to the question in what respect the Confucians are close to the truth. It is Ricci's conviction that the true doctrine of the Lord of Heaven was present in the ancient Chinese writings:

> Although I arrived in China late in life, I have assiduously studied the ancient records of China and discovered that the superior men of ancient times worshipped and revered the Sovereign on High, [the Supreme Lord] of Heaven and earth, but I have never heard of them paying respect to the Supreme Ultimate. If the Supreme Ultimate is the Sovereign on High and ancestor of all things, why did not the sages of ancient times say so? (ibid.:107).

Ricci did not consider the Supreme Ultimate to be personal. After a long philosophical discussion of such an impersonal Supreme Ultimate, the Chinese scholar acknowledged that this Neo-Confucian doctrine was incorrect and he said: "You have argued the matter exhaustively, Sir, and your views are the same as those of the sages and worthies of ancient times" (ibid.:121). The Western scholar, Ricci, affirms this statement by saying that Our Lord of Heaven (*Tianzhu*) is the same as the Sovereign on High (*Shangdi*) in the ancient Chinese canonical writings.

He proves this by giving eleven quotations taken from the *Doctrine of the Mean,* the *Book of Odes*, the *Book of Changes*, the *Book of Rites* and the *Book of History* (123ff.).

The Chinese scholar is very grateful for this new insight concerning the harmony of the Christian God with the God of ancient China:

> I am ashamed that we Confucian scholars have not been able to see clearly the important matters in life. We have investigated other things in detail, and we have been unaware of that learning which is concerned with the end of human existence. Our parents give us the various parts of our bodies, and we ought, therefore, to be filial towards them. Our sovereign and his ministers give us land, places to live, trees, and animals so that we can practice filial piety towards our elders, and instruct and nurture our children. We ought therefore to honour them as well. But how much more should we honour the Lord of Heaven who is the great Father and Mother, the great Sovereign, the first Cause of all first ancestors, the One from whom all sovereigns derive their mandate and the Producer and Sustainer of all things? How can one be mistaken about Him or forget Him (ibid.:131).

Jonathan D. Spence summarises Ricci's way of thinking as follows:

> In choosing the Chinese characters that should be used to translate the Christian monotheistic concept of God, Ricci took another characteristically ingenious yet compromising stance. He decided that the two Chinese characters *Shang-di,* connoting something approximating the 'Lord-of-All' or 'Highest Ruler', could be retained for use in the new context. This was partly because current Chinese use of *Shang-di* was not religious in the Christian spiritual sense. Ricci also urged that in the far recesses of the Chinese past such a concept of the one true God had existed, although the knowledge of that God had subsequently faded from Chinese consciousness with the reediting of the cultural past by the Buddhist-influenced Neo-Confucians of the twelfth century. Yet to balance these interpretations, Ricci suggested that a new coinage—*Tian-zhu* or Heaven's Lord—might also be used by missionaries and their Chinese converts to avoid the confusing cultural overlays of *Shang-di* (Spence 1998:34f.).

Concerning the quality of Ricci's reasoning Spence remarks that Ricci applied the same principle to Chinese science: ancient Chinese science and culture were better than the present:

> He did suggest—and this was later to become a fateful argument—that Chinese science had somehow fallen behind that of the West by failing to develop its full potentials, once so strongly part of Chinese culture. The Chinese, wrote Ricci, 'have no conception of the rules of logic', and consequently 'the science of ethics with them is a

series of confused maxims and deductions'. Similarly, though 'at one time they were quite proficient in arithmetic and geometry, in the study and teaching of these branches of learning they laboured with more or less confusion'. The implication was clearly that with a more rigorous system of logic, and a renewed concentration on mathematics and science, which the West was in a position to offer, China would become a better place (ibid.:35).

It may be clear from the foregoing that Ricci's approach was a very special one. His work *The True Meaning of the Lord of Heaven* was definitely not a catechism treating all the doctrines of the Christian faith. Revelation has no place in it, for it is Ricci's intention to help the Chinese to use the Western way of reasoning, a strong part of ancient Chinese culture that faded away in the course of history. He applied this theory to theodicy, ethics, mathematics and sciences like geometry and arithmetic. This is why the editors of this important work of Ricci call it a preparation for the gospel, or a pre-evangelical dialogue (Ricci 1985:23, 51).

Ricci adapted his teaching to the mentality of the Chinese Confucian scholars by discussing the discipline of self-cultivation, God as creator and ruler of the universe, the basic theories of Taoism, Buddhism and Neo-Confucianism, the nature and condition of man, the way to eternal life by becoming a good and virtuous person and some additional topics like the social organisation of the Western world and the practice of celibacy. Only at the end of his work did Ricci touch upon the person of Jesus, his preaching and ascension to Heaven, without mentioning his death on the cross (ibid.:449,453-455). And he concludes:

> Our purpose is not to be teachers of men. It is simply that because we feel pity for men's mistakes we wish to lead them back to their original path and into the holy Church of the Lord of Heaven. We are all brothers who share the same father; how dare we accept the title of 'teacher' and offend against the rites which govern teachers of men? The script used in the canonical writings of the Lord of Heaven is different from Chinese script. Although I have not finished translating them, I have complete translations of the essential parts. But what I have discussed earlier are all key elements of this teaching. I hope that those who study the Way will go home and savour the teachings which I have propounded in the several foregoing chapters. If you have no further doubts about what I have said, what is there to hinder you accepting the canonical writings, receiving the sacred water and entering the Church? (ibid.:456f.).

Looking back Ricci wrote:

> This catechism does not treat of all the mysteries of our holy faith,
> which need be explained only to catechumens and Christians, but only
> of certain principles, especially such as can be proved and understood
> with the light of reason. Thus it can be of service both to Christians
> and to non-Christians and can be understood in those remote regions
> which our Fathers cannot immediately reach, preparing the way for
> those other mysteries which depend upon faith and revealed wisdom
> (ibid.:43).

The intention of Ricci's efforts is quite evident: to prepare the way for
a fuller introduction into Christianity by making exclusive use of reason,
by studying the ancient Chinese writings and by proving that both the
Christian and the ancient Confucian canonical writings agree in matters
belonging to theodicy and ethics. It was not Ricci's intention to prove
how the original Confucian thought could be of interest to Christian
thinking or in what way the treasures of Confucianism and Christianity
could merge. On the contrary, he tried to prove that the original Confucianism was in agreement with the philosophical Western approach of
the doctrine concerning the idea of God. Making use of scholastic doctrines and being dependent on contemporary outright rejection of other
religions he was not in a position to enter into a real and theological dialogue with Buddhism, Taoism and the later developments of the Confucian teachings.

Ricci was forced to interpret Confucianism in such a way that it—as
a philosophical system—was understandable for Christians and Confucian scholars. It is good to remember that Michele Ruggieri had written a
catechism in Chinese and that he gave an excellent account of the heart
of Christian faith: incarnation and redemption. It is also good to remember that Ricci intended to replace the work of Ruggieri by his own: *The
True meaning of the Lord of heaven.* The catechism, composed by Ruggieri in the form of questions asked by a Chinese man and answered by
a Christian, was published in 1584. Ricci together with a Chinese scholar had revised the text before publication. Ruggieri and Ricci referred
to themselves as bonzes from India and made use of Buddhist terminology, paying little attention to Confucianism and ignoring the religious
aspects of Taoism.

When Ricci abandoned this approach by joining the ranks of the
Chinese Confucian literati in 1594, and had completed his first draft of
The True Meaning of the Lord of Heaven in 1596, the earlier work of
Ruggieri was destroyed (Gisondi 1999:95-101; Ricci 1985:12). A copy
of the first printing of Ruggieri's work: *A True Record of the Lord of
Heaven—A New Compilation from India*—is kept in the Jesuit Archives

in Rome. A revised edition: *True Record of the Sacred Teachings Concerning the Lord of Heaven* was published by João Monteiro S.J. some time after 1637 and a copy of a later reprint was preserved in the Jesuit Library of Zikawei in Shanghai.A detailed comparison of Ruggieri's and Ricci's works is still lacking, but we know that the more philosophical parts of Ruggieri's writing were preserved by Ricci and that sections treating God's revelation were removed by him.

There can be no doubt that by making a sharp distinction between the philosophical and the theological dimension of the Christian faith and by classifying early Confucian thought as being only philosophical, Ricci confirmed the current opinion that other religions had no place in the history of salvation. He explained his view of Christian thought with the aid of his view of the original Confucian thought. A real dialogue would have tried to enter more deeply and more comprehensively into China's and Europe's religious convictions (Ricci 1985:12-15: Standaert 1998: 219ff.).

4   ROBERTO DE NOBILI S.J. (1577-1656) AND THE TWO STAGES OF REVELATION

This Roman nobleman entered the Society of Jesus in 1597 and was ordained a priest in 1603. He arrived in India in 1605 and reached Madurai in the south in 1606. He stayed there till 1645. From there he was transferred to Jaffna in Sri Lanka and he died in 1556 in Chennai (Madras). He mastered Sanskrit, Tamil and Telegu, the first being the classical language of Hindu India and the others ancient South-Indian vernaculars. He studied the religious texts in both languages. His intention was to prove that the Christian faith was not a foreign religion. Living as a real Sannyasi he made contact with the highest Hindu caste, the Brahmins. They should be accepted as Christians while remaining Brahmins. De Nobili wrote many works in both languages and discussed with members of the highest caste. He met with much opposition mostly from other Christians, and he had to defend himself even to the Roman authorities. He is considered to be one of the most important and interesting missionaries India ever knew (Bachmann 1972; Sauliére 1995; Rajamanickam, 1972; Neill 1984:279-300).

Roberto de Nobili was a prolific writer of letters and treatises. Sauliére gives the most complete list: Italian, Latin, Portuguese, Sanskrit, Tamil and Telegu were the languages De Nobili used (Sauliére 1995:462-484). Three treatises of Roberto de Nobili have been translated recently and published in English (2000). They are: *Report concer-*

ning certain customs of the Indian nation (1613), *The dialogue on eternal life* (1610) and *Inquiry into the meaning of 'God'* (around 1610). Our study will make use of these three important works. The first was written in Latin, the two others in Tamil. *The Report* is by far the longest of the treatises. As was the case with Jerome Xavier and Matteo Ricci, it is our intention to study how Roberto de Nobili related Christianity and Hinduism.

De Nobili made a sharp distinction between what he called the sacred portions and the profane and merely social matters. Religious and cultural aspects were separable. The first had to be rejected, the second not:

> My only intention is to caution against extending our condemnation beyond what is proper, and to allow the truth to have its say in any subject whatsoever (De Nobili 2000:105; see also 99, 103ff.).

The distinctive badge of the brahmin class, the thread, the tuft of hair, the use of sandal paste on the body, the sandal mark on the forehead, the common badge used by a learned man, the square-shaped frontmark, all these customs have a social and ornamental purpose and by their nature free from any religious implication (ibid.:147, 171 175, 179,185). De Nobili repeatedly makes this statement, though he is writing about the idolaters and the heathen. This implies that he accepts social and ornamental customs, but not the religion wherein these customs are practised. De Nobili refers to the *Summa Theologiae*, Part II.II, question 3, of Thomas Aquinas and concludes:

> in the use of any object, we should keep an eye on the specific end inherent in it, either of its own nature or by man's assignment. For every human undertaking is governed by its end. Hence, if the whole substance of an action apart from any superimposed intention has an honest end, there is no reason why the action itself should be condemned and forbidden. Only the objectionable form, if any, is to be rejected (ibid.:211).

We may conclude that *The Report* is an apology written by de Nobili to defend his thesis of the distinction between customs and religion. He was a great observer of Hindu customs and we are obliged to him for the amount of information. We now turn to the study of the two other treatises dealing with religious matters. In *The Dialogue on Eternal Life,* a master and a disciple enter into a discussion. This is called a dialogue:

For 'dialogue' means 'raising questions and answering them.' This is
a dialogue 'on eternal life,' since we are inquiring together into liberation, which is eternal life" (ibid.:233).

The question is: where is knowledge of liberation to be found? The answer of the master is: in the Veda of the Lord:

> The true statements spoken by the Lord in various ways are said to be
> 'Vedic utterances'. Thus the Lord revealed different truths to different
> great persons with the intention of saving the world. Thus the Lord
> himself wrote the Veda using their tongues as pens, so these great
> persons did not teach merely according to their own right thinking
> (ibid.:235).

The master then distinguishes the basic truths from the higher truths.
The first category can be grasped by natural human intelligence: the
world as creation, the Lord as its cause, the oneness of the Lord and the
Lord's perfect goodness. To the basic truths belong also the moral and
ethical norms. The higher truths are inaccessible to the human intelligence and cannot be comprehended by the human mind:

> When the human mind knows the transcendent-and-immanent Being
> through created things, it becomes clear that the created world is very
> perfect, but that the glory of the Lord is still more perfect. But howe-
> ver much the human mind has understood, and how much created
> things can make known other truths, they cannot reveal certain truths,
> e.g., that the Lord is three though one. Were this not revealed, it could
> not be known by the human mind on its own. Therefore, among the
> things that we ought to know about the Lord, there will always be so-
> me truths about the Lord which remain inaccessible to human reason
> (ibid.:249).

If certain truths are inaccessible to human reason, the disciple asks, how
can they then enter human consciousness? The master answers that the
mind has to take them in faith, based on the words of one who has seen
them. It is the Lord, who reveals these words and they are called the
Veda. There are two stages in this revelation:

> What the Lord revealed to people with less maturity in knowledge can
> be called the 'old Veda', while what he granted to those with full ma-
> turity in knowledge can be called 'new Veda'. But both were revealed
> by one and the same Lord, and there is no contradiction between
> them. Both are true. The difference between them is like the differen-
> ce between the stages of childhood and old age, nothing more. This is
> why we said that the Lord taught the commandments in a manner
> which was appropriate to a world that for some time was like a child.
> Then, after he became human, the Almighty graciously taught the path

of the highest righteousness to those who were longing for righteousness and who, like elders, were in possession of full maturity in knowledge (ibid.:260).

The disciple continues the discussion by observing that there are many
Vedas or belief systems in the world. As they are not in harmony with
one another, he wants to know whether they are all composed by the
Lord or not. The master applies the principle of non-contradiction and
states that the Lord cannot teach mutually contradictory viewpoints.
There is only one true Veda, though there can be many paths leading to
the same truth. De Nobili or the master explains the origin of the many
religions:

> The Veda which the Lord gave to the world as a help to human beings
> was known [in the beginning]. But in the course of time and in certain
> places great sinners, due to their sinful behaviour, began to dislike the
> Veda given by the Lord, [misusing] the freedom which the Lord had
> given them in order that they might accept truth and righteousness.
> The reason they disliked and gave up the Lord's Veda was that in this
> Veda deeds of righteousness are taught, deeds repugnant to them,
> which exclude the sinful deeds in which they indulge. Thus, earlier
> generations did not teach the Veda to the next generations. By now a
> long period of time has intervened, and in some places the Veda of the
> Lord has entirely ceased to exist. In the absence of the Lord's revealed
> Veda, some people very much steeped in sin and mentally warped due
> to it fashioned numerous completely false religious viewpoints
> (ibid.:267).

It now becomes clear that according to de Nobili there is only one true
religion or Veda which appears in two stages of childhood or maturity.
There is progress within this one religion and the highest is the stage of
maturity, which is the new Veda. This stage appeared when the Lord
became human. Other religious systems were considered by de Nobili to
be false. It is also striking that he did not explain the truths inaccessible
to human reason, but restricted himself to mentioning commandments,
deeds, righteousness and sinful behaviour. He also gave a lengthy discourse on idolatry, the worship of false images of the Almighty, and
considered this to be the essence of other religious systems.

One would expect an answer to the question about the truths inaccessible to human reason and contained in the only true Veda, in de Nobili's treatise entitled: *Inquiry into the Meaning of 'God'*. However, he
develops some philosophical viewpoints concerning the idea of God and
he refutes a great number of Hindu religious systems as being idolatry.
At the end he sums up the Ten Commandments, revealed by God. He

ends by writing: these ten are contained in two: Love God above all things, and: Love others as you yourself (ibid.: 323; cf. Arokiasamy 1986.)

Concluding, there can be no doubt that Roberto de Nobili was a true follower of Saint Thomas Aquinas, the great thinker of the Middle Ages. For him too the use of reason, including the knowledge of God, was a preparation for accepting revelation. Proper religious thinking and submission to revelation should have ethical and moral effects. False religion is known by idolatry. De Nobili was a scholar and expert in the many customs of Hindu India, but he considered them to be ornamental and social characteristics, entirely separated from religious implications. He was convinced that only one true religion existed and this came into being when the Almighty became human. In the three treatises we have studied this reference to the Incarnation of the Lord together with a very brief mention of the Lord being three though one is the only time that the inaccessible mysteries or truths are touched upon. Finally, the use of the word 'dialogue' has nothing to do with the modern use of that term. The religious system of the Hindus is idolatry and de Nobili was not able to learn from them.

5   JEROME XAVIER, MATTEO RICCI AND ROBERTO DE NOBILI COMPARED

It is striking that these three great Jesuit missionaries of the 16th and 17th centuries wrote important works in the form of a dialogue, or a discussion between a Father, a Western scholar or a master and a Mullah, a Chinese scholar or a disciple. In this way all three proved that they had studied thoroughly the religious systems they met: Islam, Chinese religions and Indian religions. Moreover, they took care to learn the language of the country they lived in: Persian, Chinese, Sanskrit, Tamil and Telegu. All three were strongly influenced by the scholastic doctrine of the Church in Europe.

Jerome Xavier wrote explicitly on the life, passion, death and resurrection of Jesus as well as on the Holy Trinity, as he was challenged by the critical views of his Muslim interlocutors. Ricci and de Nobili had no such challengers, because in China and in India these Christian mysteries and doctrines were not known. That is why in the treatises studied the discussion is limited to truths accessible to reason. For all three it is true that they considered the religious systems they encountered to be false or idolatrous. This may be the real reason why they did not engage in a theological dialogue understood in the modern sense: to be partners in dialogue on the ways and roads God has given to all human beings in order to strive together towards the coming of the Kingdom of God.

Jerome Xavier, Matteo Ricci and Roberto de Nobili were theologians in Asia, not Asian theologians. They were strongly influenced by Father Alessandro Valignano S.J. (1539-1606), the chief administrative inspector of the Jesuit Missions extending from India to Japan. His real title was Visitor and he was forceful, talented and hard working. Valignano was a good observer and he wrote long reports to Father General in Rome. His missionary principles were famous in his days and he worked them out in constant consultation with his fellow Jesuits (Moran 1993; Valignano 1583; Alden 1996:155f., passim). Especially for the members of the Society of Jesus in Japan he wrote a voluminous work of missionary principles (Schütte 1951-8). In them we find the same method of approaching other cultures and religious systems.

Valignano defended an exterior adaptation: the missionaries should study the language and they should accept the customs of the people they lived with. This was not inculturation or a kind of dialogue as advocated by the *Declaration on the Relationship of the Church to Non-Christian Religions (Nostra Aetate)* of the Second Vatican Council. Moreover, Valignano wrote a catechism: *Catechism of the Christian Faith, in which the truth of our religion is proved, and the Japanese sects are refuted.* Using scholastic methods he attacked other religions as being nothing more than idolatry (Valignano 1586).

All the same, these Jesuit missionaries were pioneers in exploring foreign languages, cultures and religions. More than others they came232 close to the realities of Asia. But they had to use the learning and instruments proper to their time. This they did with great courage and competence. It was not their mistake that the context of our time is different and asks for further courageous steps.

BIBLIOGRAPHY

Alden, Dauril. (1996). *The Making of an Enterprise. The Society of Jesus in Portugal, its empire and beyond 1540-1750*. Stanford.
Arokiasamy, Soosai (S.J.). (1986). *Dharma, Hindu and Christian, according to Roberto de Nobili. Analysis of its meaning and its use in Hinduism and Christianity*. Roma.
Bachmann, Peter R. (1972). *Roberto Nobili 1577-1656. Ein missionsgeschichtlicher Beitrag zum christlichen Dialog mit Hinduismus*. Roma.
Camps, Arnulf (OFM). (1957). *Jerome Xavier S.J. and the Muslims of the Mogul Empire. Controversial works and missionary activity*. Schöneck-Beckenried.

—. (1991). "Das dritte Auge. Von einer Theologie in Asien zu einer asiatischen Theologie". In: *Zeitschrift für Missionswissenschaft und Religionswissenschaft* 75. Pp.1-21.

—. (2000a). "Das Christentum aus chinesischem und japanischem Blickwinkel während der Jesuitischen Epoche der Missionsgeschichte Asiens (1549-1773)". In: A. Camps, *Studies in Asian Mission History 1956-1998*, Leiden-Boston-Köln. Pp. 122-138.

—. (2000b) "Persian Works of Jerome Xavier, a Jesuit at the Mogul Court". In: A. Camps, *Studies in Asian Mission History 1956-1998*, Leiden-Boston-Köln. Pp. 33-46.

—. (2000c) *Studies in Asian Mission History 1956-1998*. Leiden-Boston-Köln. Pp.105-121.

De Nobili, Roberto (S.J.). (2000). *Preaching Wisdom to the Wise. Three Treatises*. Translated and introduced by Anand Amaladass (S.J.) and Francis X. Clooney (S.J.). St. Louis.

Ducornet, Étienne. (1992). *Matteo Ricci*. Paris.

Gisondi, Francesco Antonio. (1999). *Michele Ruggieri, missionario in Cina e primo sinologo europeo*. Milano.

Kern, Iso. (1992). *Buddhistische Kritik am Christentum im China des 17. Jahrhunderts*. Bern-Frankfurt a.M.-New York-Paris-Wien.

Meier, Johannes (ed.). (2000). *Usque ad Ultimum Terrae. Die Jesuiten und die transkontinentale Ausbreitung des Christentums 1540-1773*. Göttingen. Pp.5-9.

Moran, J.F. (1993). *The Japanese and the Jesuits. Alessandro Valignano in sixteenth-century Japan*. London-New York.

Mungello, D.E. (1999). *The Great Encounter of China and the West, 1500-1800*. Lanham-New York-Boulder-Oxford.

Neill, Stephen. (1984). *A History of Christianity in India. The beginnings to AD 1707*. Cambridge-New York- New Rochelle-Melbourne-Sydney.

Ricci, Matteo (S.J.). (1985). *The True Meaning of the Lord of Heaven (T'ien-chu Shih-i)*. Translated, with introduction and notes by Douglas Lancashire and Peter Hu Kuo-chen (S.J.). A Chinese-English edition by Edward J. Malatesta (S.J.). St. Louis-Taipei.

Schütte Josef Franz (S.J.). (1951-1958). *Valignano's Missionsgrundsätze für Japan*. Roma.

Spence, Jonathan D. (1998). *The Chan's Great Continent. China in Western Minds*. New York-London.

Standaert, Nicolaas. (1998). *Yang Tingyun, Confucian and Christian in Late Ming China, His Life and Thought*. Leiden-New York-København-Köln.

Saulière. A. (S.J.). (1995). *His Star in the East*. Revised and re-edited by S. Rajamanickam (S.J.). Madras.

Rajamanickam, S. (S.J.). (1972). *The first oriental scholar*. Tirunelveli.

Valignano, Patre Alexandro (S.J.) (ed.). (1586). *Catechismus christianae fidei, in quo veritas nostrae religionis ostenditur, et sectae japonenses confutantur*. Olyssipone. (A facsimile edition was printed in Tokyo 1972).

Valignano, Alexandre. (1583). *Les Jésuites au Japon. Relation missionaire.* Traduction et présentation et notes de J. Bésinau (S.J.). Paris 1990.

16 Directions in Vatican Documents on Interreligious Dialogue

Willi Henkel, OMI

1 INTRODUCTION

The Second Vatican Council promoted a new attitude of Roman Catholics toward the followers of other religions. The new orientation began with the first encyclical of Paul VI *Ecclesiam Suam* (ES) (1964).[1] Sometimes this encyclical has been called the "Magna Charta" of dialogue. Paul VI required as characteristics of dialogue: 1) *clarity*: what is explained must be intelligible; 2) we must lead dialogue in the spirit of Christ which is *meekness*; 3) *trust* is necessary in both partners of dialogue; 4) *prudence* takes into account the moral and psychological circumstances of the partner. In dialogue "*truth* is wedded to *charity* and understanding to love" (ES 81f.). Dialogue lives from friendly relations and service. Therefore genuine dialogue does not silence truth; it does not weaken or suppress it; but rather it allows for the profession of Christian faith (ES 88). It aims at listening to and learning from each of the other partners. Another quality is the disinterest of any temporal or political gain (ES 98). Paul VI enumerates all men who worship one supreme God, as Christians do. He then speaks of the Jewish people who have in common with Christians the Old Testament. He proceeds to mention the monotheistic religions, especially Islam. Finally, he mentions those who follow the African and Asian religions. Obviously, we need not to adopt an uncritical attitude in relation to other religions. But we can also open ourselves to their spiritual and moral values and join them in defending religious liberty, social welfare and peace.

On Pentecost 1964, Pope Paul VI instituted the Secretariat for Non-Christians as a distinct body from the Congregation for the Evangelization of Peoples. In 1988 it was named the Pontifical Council for Interreligious Dialogue. Paul VI indicated its tasks to be to search methods and ways of promoting the dialogue with non-Christians in order "that non-Christians be known honestly and esteemed by Christians and that

---

[1] Abbreviations: AG (Ad Gentes; 1965), DM (Dialogue and Mission), DP (Dialogue and Proclamation), EN (Evangelii Nuntiandi; 1975), ES (Ecclesiam Suam), GS (Gaudium et Spes; 1965), LG (Lumen Gentium; Sec. Vatican Council), NA (Nostra Aetate; 1966), OT (Optatam Totius; 1965), RM (Redemptionis Missio; 1990). See for the documents of the Vatican Council II: Flannery (1998).

in their turn non-Christians can adequately know and esteem Christian doctrine and life" (Kroeger 1997:233).

2   VATICAN COUNCIL II AND WORLD RELIGIONS

The Second Vatican Council offers a new and positive approach to non-Christian religions. It states clearly the uniqueness of Jesus Christ and of his revelation. The declaration *Nostra Aetate* (NA) deals in five paragraphs with the relation of the Catholic Church to the religions of the world. The fathers of the Council begin with what Christians share with non-Christians (NA 1), expressing a new attitude of the Catholic Church. They ask for respect for the religions (Neuner-Dupuis 1990:33-39). The Council mentions the great religions of the world as well as the primitive religions (NA 2). Judaism has a special place for Christians as they consider the Old Testament to be a part of the Christian revelation. The Council affirms the values in the religions contained in the rites of these religions.

The Council does not offer a theology of the religions. The religions are, however, a true "preparation of the Gospel" (AG 9); they contain "seeds of the Word" (AG 11; LG 17); a "ray of truth" (NA 2); the seeds are planted before the preaching of the Gospel (AG 15, 18). World religions are a response to the self-manifestation of God (GS 16, 22). "The Holy Spirit was already at work before Christ was glorified" (AG 4; cf. Neuner-Dupuis 1990: 33). World religions have their place in the universal design of God for salvation (AG 3). This plan includes all who believe in the Creator (LG 16). Muslims

> profess fidelity to the faith of Abraham, and with us adore the one and merciful God who will judge mankind on the last day...as Saviour desires all men to be saved. For those also can attain eternal salvation who without their fault on their part do not know the Gospel of Christ and His Church, but seek him with a sincere heart, and under the influence of grace endeavour to do His will as recognized through the promptings of their conscience. Nor does divine Providence deny the help necessary for salvation, who without fault on their part have not yet reached the explicit knowledge of God and yet endeavour, not without grace to live a good life, for whatever goodness or truth is found among them is considered by the Church as a preparation of the Gospel, a gift from Him who enlightens every man that he may finally have life (LG 16).

3   MILESTONES IN INTERRELIGIOUS DIALOGUE

Kroeger speaks of milestones that have been reached after Vatican Council II in interreligious dialogue (1997:232-237). Some of these are: the Apostolic Exhortation *Evangelii Nuntiandi* of Paul VI (8 December 1975); the document *Dialogue and Mission* (Pentecost 1984); the Encyclical *Redemptoris Missio* (7 December 1990) of John Paul II and the document *Dialogue and Proclamation* published by the Pontifical Council for Interreligious Dialogue together with the Congregation for the Evangelization of Peoples (Pentecost 1991).

Following Vatican Council II, Paul VI expressed a great respect for non-Christian religions. These are "living expressions of the soul of vast groups of people... they have taught generations of peoples how to pray... they are impregnated with innumerable 'seeds of the Word' and constitute a 'true preparation for the Gospel'. The Church needs to offer to the missionaries of today and of tomorrow new horizons in their contacts with non-Christian religions (EN 53).

4   DIALOGUE AND MISSION (DM)

After the Plenary Assembly of the Secretariat for non-Christian religions, the Secretariat (now called Pontifical Council) published this document, *Dialogo e Missione* (DM), with the approval of the Pope. It explains the nature of dialogue and of mission. In the first part, the document expounds the foundations of dialogue based on personal and social needs in a world of rapid change (DM 21). For Christians, the foundations of dialogue are rooted in faith in God the Father, in God the Son who illuminates every man and is united to every person as the redeemer in every human encounter, and in God the Holy Spirit who is at work also "outside the visible confines of the Mystical Body" (RM 6; AG 15). "The reign of God is the final end of all persons. The Church is to be 'its seed and beginning' (LG 5, 9), and is called from the first to start out on this path towards the end, along with the rest of humanity to advance toward that goal" (DM 25). This duty includes the struggle over evil and sin.

Dialogue and Mission incorporates the positive elements in world religions in a new panorama. In non-Christian religions exist "elements which are true and good" (OT 16); "precious things both religious and human" (GS 92); "seeds of contemplation" (AG 18); elements of "truth and grace" (AG 9); "seeds of the Word" (AG 11,15); "rays of the truth which illuminate all mankind" (NA 2; DM 26).

Dialogue and Mission asks for a "sincere and patient dialogue" , in which partners are willing to share the "treasures a bountiful God has distributed among the nations of the earth... (and) try to illuminate these treasures with the light of the Gospel" (DM 27).

5   FORMS OF DIALOGUE

Dialogue and Mission offers as special contribution the forms of dialogue of every day life:
  • The dialogue of life is an attitude and a spirit, which demands concern for persons, respect, and hospitality (DM 29).
  • Every Christian is called to bring the spirit of the Gospel into the environment.
  • It is a dialogue of action and collaboration with others on various levels for an integral development and liberation (DM 31) and social justice and peace.
  • The dialogue of theological exchange where they try to understand the religious heritage and appreciate spiritual values (DM 33).
  • The dialogue of religious experience, where persons share in their experiences of prayer and contemplation in the search of the Absolute (DM 35).
  • We must add a dialogue of culture, because religious traditions are linked with cultures in various ways (Zago 1995:107).

6   DIALOGUE AND PROCLAMATION

The document *Dialogue and Proclamation* points out that these forms of dialogue are not the privilege of specialists only. Dialogue can be practiced on many different levels of religious experience. It "can give more life to theological discussions" (DP 43). The document explains the nature and the relationship between both. Interreligious dialogue can give a valuable contribution "to eliminate tensions and conflicts" (DP 46). It can purify cultures from dehumanizing elements.

The document *Dialogue and Proclamation* is the result of a broad consultation with the purpose of pastoral orientation, especially for those "who have a leadership role in the community and are engaged in formation work" (DP 7). The document has a "didactic style" and "focuses only these two aspects of the evangelizing mission" (Tomko 1991:108).

Interreligious dialogue is presented in an extensive manner (DP 14-41) on the basis of conciliar statements (cf. DP). Reasons are given why the religious traditions are viewed positively and "are to be approached with great sensitivity" and great "respect" (DP 14). One of the reasons is that these religious traditions have borne witness to the efforts to find answers "to those profound mysteries of the human condition" (NA 1). Finally they are a living expression of millions of people during centuries and they continue today (DP 14).

Dialogue requires from both partners a balanced attitude, which avoids being ingenious or overcritical (DP 47). Both enter into it with the integrity of their own faith; both must be open to truth. Christians as individuals have no guarantee that they already possess the fullness of truth. They must be ready "to learn and receive from others the positive values of their traditions" (DP 45). In this process, they may have to give up prejudices and their faith will not be weakened but purified and deepened through dialogue.

Dialogue has a specific method, which "includes all forms of mutual knowledge, harmony and enrichment" (Zago 1992:22). Obstacles may arise from various human factors (DP 51-54):

- Difficulties may be due to insufficient grounding in one's own faith (DP 52), or to insufficient knowledge and understanding of the non-Christian religions.
- They may result from cultural differences, and socio-political factors.
- They may be due to self-sufficiency and lack of openness. A lack of the perception of the value of interreligious dialogue; there may be suspicions about the other's motives; a polemical spirit, a spirit of intolerance (DP 52).
- There may be a wrong understanding of conversion, baptism, dialogue.
- From these concrete circumstances we may conclude that dialogue requires persons with an open mind and heart willing to learn from the religious experience of other religions.

7   REDEMPTORIS MISSIO (RM 1990)

The encyclical *Redemptoris Missio* of John Paul II intends to relaunch the missionary activity of the Church oriented towards the proclamation of the mystery of Jesus Christ. Dialogue plays an important role in this activity. According to the encyclical dialogue is not in opposition to the mission *ad gentes*:

> The Church sees no conflict between proclaiming Christ and engaging in interreligious dialogue. Instead, the Church seeks to link the two in the context of her mission ad gentes. These two elements must maintain their intimate connection and distinctiveness. Therefore they

should not be confused, manipulated or regarded as identical as
though they were interchangeable (RM 55).

According to Dupuis this means "that dialogue cannot be reduced to
being a means for proclamation" (Dupuis 1992:151). Indeed, the encyclical affirms clearly that "dialogue does not originate from tactical concerns or self-interest but is an activity with its own guiding principles,
requirements and dignity" (RM 56). Through dialogue, the Church seeks
to uncover the seeds of the Word, "a ray of that truth which enlightens
all men" (RM 56). The Church does this under the guidance of the Holy
Spirit who operates outside its boundaries also in the religions. The encyclical reaffirms the qualities of true dialogue: truth, humility, frank-
ness, the mutual witness, and purification. On the other hand, it asks for
the elimination of prejudice, intolerance and misunderstandings. Dialogue constitutes "an integral element of mission in the sense that all missionary activity is realized in and for individuals and cultures and can be
a specific activity where proclamation is possible and dutiful and when
it is impossible" (Zago 1992:95).

8   CONCLUSION

Christians who enter into dialogue with non-Christians must be aware of
their own spirituality that is based on the Holy Trinity. They have been
baptized in the name of the Holy Trinity and they make disciples of
Christ, baptizing in the name of the Holy Trinity. Vatican Council II
documents present a Trinitarian vision of the Church (LG 1-9) and of the
missionary activity of the Church (AG 1-5). The Trinity is also the basis
for the Church as communion, a key concept of Vatican II. Both attitudes favour a greater awareness of one's own identity and of openness.

Christian partners who enter into dialogue must keep the integrity of
their own faith and at the same time must be open to learning positive
values of other religions and traditions. They keep their own Christian
identity. While presenting and explaining on the one hand their Christian
values, they are also ready, on the other hand, to learn values of
non-Christian religions as their non-Christian partners explain those to
them. All partners must respect the values of the other. Learning these
they grow in mutual knowledge and enrichment. At the same time, they
must avoid all forms of fundamentalism and separatist divisions. "God
is for everyone...In its interior life and external mission, the Trinity provides the basis for attitudes and works of dialogue with everyone, while
always retaining one's own identity which is the full acceptance of
God's gift, with a universal openness adopting God's very manner with

everyone" (Zago 2001:16). Paul VI requires from the dialogue of the missionary complete faithfulness to his faith: "Only the man who is completely faithful to the teaching of Christ can be an apostle. And only he who lives his Christian life to the full can remain uncontaminated by the errors with which he comes into contact" (ES 88). In the Vatican Council II documents we find the twofold attitude of identity and openness relating dialogue to proclamation.

In his encyclical *Ecclesiam Suam* Paul VI presents religion as a dialogue between God and humans. He calls it a "dialogue of salvation" that has its origin in God's love. No one is forced to accept the "incredible invitation" of God's love, that has entered the world through the incarnation of Jesus Christ. God invites and enables the real man to accept his love and answer it. Accepting this dialogue takes on the qualities of charity: it becomes universal, it is without limits and calculations, gradual and disinterested, respectful and adapted to the concrete persons.

In the Encyclical *Redemptoris Missio* John Paul II calls love "the soul of all missionary activity...which has been and remains the driving force of mission, and is also the sole criterion for judging what is to be done or not done, changed or not changed. It is the principle which must direct every action and the end to which that action must be directed" (RM 60). In discussing spirituality he concludes that the missionary must love persons as Jesus loved them; he must be the universal brother (RM 89). This charity for all "which inspired Jesus' own charity... takes the form of concern, tenderness, compassion, openness, availability, and interest in people's problems"; it includes also dialogue (RM 89).

Christians believe in the working of the Holy Spirit also outside the visible Church. Engaging in dialogue, they are open to accepting whatever is good and true in non-Christian religions. Since the Holy Spirit is the principle agent of mission, Christians try to discover his working also outside the Church.

On all the levels where dialogue is practised the partners of dialogue have to take into account the moral and psychological circumstances of the other partner. Dialogue is a friendly encounter of mind and heart with persons of different world religions (Arinze 1990:21).

BIBLIOGRAPHY

Arinze, F. (1990). "The Christian commitment to interreligious dialogue". In: J.H. Kroeger (ed.). *Interreligious Dialogue*. Davao City.
"Dialogo e Missione". (1984). In: *Acta Apostolicae Sedis* 86. Pp. 816-828.
"Dialogue and Proclamation". (1991). In: *Catholic International* 2. Pp. 805-823.

Dupuis, J. (1993). "A theological commentary: Dialogue and Proclamation". In: W. Burrows (ed.), *Redemption and Dialogue*. Maryknoll (N.Y.).

Flannery, Anthony. (ed.). (1998). *Vatican Council II*. Vol. 1: *The conciliar and post conciliar documents*. Dublin: Dominican Publications. New rev. ed.; 4th edition.

Kroeger, J.H.. (1997). "Milestones in interreligious dialogue". In: *Studies in Interreligious Dialogue* 7. Pp. 232-237.

Neuner, J., and B J. Dupuis. (1990). "Vatican II and World Religions". In: J.H. Kroeger (ed.), *Interreligious Dialogue*. Davao City. Pp. 33-39.

Paul VI. (1964). "Ecclesiam Suam". In: *Acta Apostolicae Sedis* 56. Pp. 609-659.

Tomko, J. (1991). "Excerpts from Cardinal…analysis of Dialogue and Proclamation". In: *Catholic International* 2.

Zago. M. (1992). "Dialogue and Proclamation: an explanatory document of great importance". In: *Omnis Terra* 26.

—. (1995). "Interreligious dialogue". In: S. Karotrmprel (ed.). *Following Christ in Mission*. Rome.

—. (2001). "The Spirituality of Dialogue". In: *OMI Documentation*. No. 240.

17 Dialogue is Evangelism: Evangelism is Dialogue

Kenneth Cracknell

1 INTRODUCTION

In 1979 the *Guidelines on Dialogue with People of Living Faiths* and Ideologies was sent by the Central Committee of the World Council of Churches (WCC) to member churches asking for "their consideration and discussion, animated testing and evaluation, and for their elaboration in each specific situation." Many different parts of the world have produced their own versions of the *Guidelines*, adapting them for their own contexts.[1] Through various programmes the *Guidelines* have indeed animated new and profound discussions on the theology of religions and of the challenges that religious plurality brings to Christian self-understanding.[2] Within the WCC itself the *Guidelines* have helped further development of "Ecumenical Considerations" for relations to specific religious traditions.[3] The *Guidelines* were revised and re-issued in a revised form in 2002. What was it about these *Guidelines* that made them acceptable to such a wide section of the WCC membership? Re-reading them in 2002, one is struck by such key phrases as "community," "vulnerability," "sensitivity," "humility," "integrity," "risk-taking,"and "joy." Such words struck a chord with the feelings of many Christians living in the aftermath of a long period of aggressive imperialism and colonial exploitation on the part of the West. Missionary activity was deemed by many to have been both the result of feelings of cultural superiority and also the willing tool of economic and political hegemonism. In addition, the world religious traditions had come no longer to be considered as the realm of heathenism and paganism, as we can see from the way in which non-Roman Catholics welcomed the themes of *Nostra Aetate* (1965). By the mid 1970's member churches of the WCC were looking for ways of affirming a positive theology of religions, and a new kind of relationship with people of different faith.[4] This new rela-

---

[1] One of these was the British *Guidelines on Dialogue: Relations with People of Other Faith*, British Council of Churches 1981.

[2] *My Neighbour's Faith and Mine*, a five year long study project, was influential in discussions and declarations of the WCC.

[3] Particularly in regard to Judaism and Islam.

[4] The British Council of Churches, for example, had affirmed that the presence of people of other faiths in Britain was "within the gracious purposes of God." See Cracknell 1985: 452-61.

tionship would, however, have to maintain the Christian distinctives, and avoid mere concessions to the proposition that all paths were equally valid ways to God, or worse to a secularistic notion that all religions were "equally valid and equally false." Contrary to any such propositions, the writers of the statement said immediately that there was no desire to escape the Christian responsibility, re-emphasized in the Nairobi assembly of the WCC in 1975 to "confess Christ today" (2). Rather the *Guidelines* needed to be seen as an exploration of other ways besides mission and evangelism of "making plain the intentions of Christian witness and service," for "Christian integrity includes an integrity of response to the call of the risen Christ to be witnesses to Him in all the world" (3).

Thus reassured, member churches were able to receive these *Guidelines*, hearing clearly their unambiguous assertion that dialogue and witness are intrinsic to one another. As the document states:

> In dialogue, Christians seek "to speak the truth in a spirit of love," not naively "to be tossed to and fro, and to be carried about with every wind of doctrine" (Eph. 4:14-15). In giving their witness they recognize that in most circumstances today the spirit of dialogue is necessary. For this reason we do not see dialogue and the giving of witness as standing in any contradiction to one another. Indeed, as Christians enter into dialogue with their commitment to Jesus Christ, time and again the relationship of dialogue gives opportunity for authentic witness (11).

To be sure authentic witness goes both ways. Even in 1979 the churches had much experience of learning from their Jewish, Muslim, Hindu or Buddhist friends. So the 1979 *Guidelines* added, "at the same time we feel able with integrity to assure our partners in dialogue that we come not as manipulators but as genuine fellow-pilgrims, to speak with them what we believe God to have done in Jesus Christ who has gone before us, but whom we seek to meet anew in dialogue".

This understanding of witness most certainly includes personal and individual faith, but it also embraces the great themes of God at work in history. As the Chiang Mai precursor document from 1978 said it, "Throughout the Christian history, witness has also meant the setting up of the signs of God's reign over all of human life; witness has much to do with bringing healing and wholeness to a world that is torn apart by rivalries and wars, social disparities and economic injustices." "Witness" is therefore a stronger and more inclusive term than "evangelism," and suggests why the latter term is not much used in the *Guidelines*. In what follows I want to explore how the formulation: "the relationship of dialogue gives opportunity for authentic witness," in both the 1979 *Guidelines* and their current revision offer rich insights to what has traditionally been denoted by evangelism. The WCC *Guidelines for Dialogue in Britain* (1981) put the principle rather more succinctly: "Dialogue becomes the means of authentic witness." I want to argue that in its essence dialogue is evangelism and evangelism is dialogue.

2   EVANGELISM

But first a word about the term evangelism. As I have written elsewhere the contemporary English usage of this word is but a recent phenomenon: "The terms evangelism and evangelisation are comparative latecomers in Christian vocabulary. Rare indeed are the sightings of either word before the mid-nineteenth century. An "evangelist" was one of the writers of the four Gospels or a title of an office in the early church, and that virtually was it!" (Cracknell 1992:3).This fact can be placed alongside the equally important observation that the so-called Great Commission in Matthew 28:16-20 played hardly any role in the homiletic tradition of the Protestant churches until the time of William Carey at the end of the eighteenth century.[5] In 1752, John Wesley commented on Matthew 28:16-20 only because he was writing his *Explanatory Notes* on every part of the New Testament. And he failed even then to use the word evangelism in any form in describing the missionary task (Wesley 1752:138; cf. Logan 1995:21ff.).

It behoves us therefore not to allow conceptions from the nineteenth and twentieth centuries to dominate our thinking about evangelism, still less to provide us with norms and patterns. Large meetings led by professional revivalists are not necessary to evangelism. Neither are house-by-house visitations through a particular town or village. Nor is the invasion of other people's privacy in an airport or market place. No, rather we have to fix upon the root meaning of *euangelion* and *euangelizomai* in the New Testament.

According to Mark 1:14 Jesus began his ministry by saying to his hearers: radically turn round your thoughts (*metanoeite*) and have faith in (*pisteuete*) the good news (*en toi euangeliooi*). From the preceding words and the remainder of the Gospel narrative, we learn that the content of that good news is the arrival of the Kingdom of God. The verbal

---

[5] Of course, in the *Enquiry into the Obligation of Christian to Use Means for the Conversion of the Heathen* (1792), which begins with "An Enquiry whether the Commission given by our Lord to his Disciples be not still binding on us?," 1961: 7.

form does not require us to add "preach" or "teach" or "proclaim" to make sense of it. It is a verbal form "to good-news," or "to good-message," as in, for example, "I remind you, brothers of the good-news which I good-newsed to you," (*to euangelion ho euèngelisamèn humin*, 1 Cor 15:1). (See the similar expression in Gal. 1:11: *to euangelion to euangelisthèn hup' emou*.) Accordingly, we get the remarkable expression "teaching and good-newsing" Jesus Christ (*didaskontes kai euangelizomenoi ton Christon Ièsoun*) in Acts 5:42. Good-newsing can take innumerable forms, and is not solely determined by such words as preaching and proclaiming. This is why Michael Green was so right in saying that the early church "gossiped the Gospel" and why the famous Franciscan injunction adorns the wall of many churches and seminaries: "Preach the Gospel always: sometimes use words."[6]

3 DIALOGUE

In the New Testament "good-newsing" certainly includes forms of interfaith dialogue. In the gospels these range from the conversations of Jesus with Samaritans, with a Syro-Phoenician woman, and with the centurion of Matthew chapter 8. Paul's encounter with the people of the Areopagus was clearly dialogical, since it arose out of Paul's conversations in the Athenian synagogue, streets and market places. This is described as a daily dialogue: *dielegeto...kata pasin hemera* (Acts 17:17). To be sure, since in Acts 17 there is just the one set speech to the Epicurean and Stoic philosophers, the Areopagus incident sounds as if it was a one-way proclamation, ending with a resounding challenge to repent and to believe. Many hearers rejected that challenge with mockery. But the record tells of those who expressed their wish to go on with the debate, "we will hear you again about this" (Acts 17:33).[7] According to the Acts narrative such philosophers did indeed have another opportunity. This eventually took place in Ephesus, in the School of Tyrannus, against the

---

[6] See Green 1970: 173. His actual sentence is: 'They went everywhere gossiping the gospel; they did it naturally, enthusiastically, and with the conviction of those who are not paid to say that sort of thing.'

[7] The homiletical tradition of the church has habitually presented the *Areopagitica* sermon as a failure (cf. John Wesley 1976: 467: "Paul departing from Athens: He did not stay there long. The philosophers there were too easy, too indolent and too wise in their own eyes to receive the gospel"), but this overlooks the presence in the record of Dionysius and Damaris and others who attached themselves to Paul and had faith (*kollethentes auto epistuesan*, Acts 17:34)

background of the ongoing dialogue with the Jewish community. The incidents in question are conveyed to us in just three verses:

> 8. And he entered the synagogue, and for three months spoke boldly, arguing and pleading about the kingdom of God 9. but when some were stubborn and disbelieved, speaking evil of the Way before the congregation, he withdrew from them, taking the disciples with him, and argued daily in the school of Tyrannus. 10. This continued for two years, so that all the residents of Asia heard the word of the Lord, both Jews and Greeks. (Acts 19:8-10 Revised Standard Version).[8]

"Arguing and pleading" in verse 8 is a rendering of *dialegomenos kai peithon*, and "argued" in verse 9 is also translated *dielegomenos*.[9] In both cases the use of some form of "dialoguing" would much better help contemporary readers. Both in the synagogue and the school of Tyrannus the method of "good-newsing" the Gospel that Paul used was "dialogue." These three verses tell us much more about the "good-newsing" approach of Paul to these people of faith, whether Jews or philosophers. First and foremost we should observe the period of time involved. Paul is described as virtually stationary for considerably more than two years. This is not a man who must hasten from place to place lest souls pass into eternity and the torment of hell-fire without even hearing of Jesus Christ. For two years and three months it is worth his time to engage in reasoning and persuading. This activity takes place across boundaries, in places where other people feel at home. For Paul had to be first in the synagogue. To be sure there was no clean break between his ancestral faith and his new discovery of Christ. Even so, Paul deliberately put himself under the Law (see I Cor 9:20) and observed every one of the synagogue customs that he might be able to "good-news" the Gospel to his own people. He remained there for many weeks, a welcome dialogue

---

[8] I agree with the comment of Ernst Haenchen (1971:588) who says that "We can estimate Chapter 19 aright only when we understand it in the total design of Luke's work." But a cursory glance at Haenchen's Commentary, will show that while he allows that Luke must have taken the historical details over from tradition (he adds "what creates life out of this chronological-topographical skeleton goes back to Luke himself, whose style here is unmistakable"), he pays insufficient attention to what Luke means in telling us the stories recorded here.

[9] In English translations in common use a whole range of words are used as variants: "disputing" (Authorized Version), "reasoning" (Revised Version), "using argument" and "continued to hold discussions" (New English Bible), "held discussions" (Good News Bible), "argued persuasively" (Jerusalem Bible).

partner, until some of his enemies made trouble for him, speaking evil of the Way. Out of courtesy to the Jewish community Paul left and moved to his second location, the "hall of Tyrannus." The word translated "hall" in the RSV, is *scholè*, a place where a philosopher held his sessions.[10] Paul thus moved deliberately into the physical environment of the Greek philosophers. In neither place does Paul's "good-newsing" take place on his own terms and in a neutral environment. The agenda and terms of reference of the conversations are set by the other parties to the dialogue. This is very different from the usual modes of operation, where Christians invite people to come into our structures (in both the physical and metaphysical senses of this word) and where they set the agenda.

Having crossed those boundaries, having moved to the other persons' world, Paul models both a deep courtesy and a joyous engagement with that world. There are two clues in the three verses as to the content of the dialogue. In the synagogue, the conversations turn, we are told, on the meaning of the Kingdom of God. Paul is clearly not understood as offering a take-it-or-leave it set of proof-texts showing that Jesus is the Messiah, and therefore closing down any further possibility of discussion. The dialogue, Luke tells us, was about the shape of God's sovereign rule in the earth. How are the human facts of suffering and impotence to be related to the rule of God in the light of the death on the cross of the Righteous Servant? This continues to be a central issue of Christian-Jewish dialogue.

The second clue is embedded in the somewhat odd expression "All the residents of Asia, both Jews and Greeks heard the word of God." Either Luke is carelessly exaggerating a very small-scale success or he has something else in mind. "All the residents of Asia" simply did not hear, in a literal or physical sense. The Christian mission to Asia Minor persisted for several centuries. It seems to me that Luke is suggesting something more profound. As a result of the daily intellectual struggles, in the hours-long discussions, month in and month out, with Greek philosophical and theological concepts, Paul brought all the resources of his disciplined mind to engaging their underlying thought-patterns. How could what he had glimpsed of Christ be expressed in words that resonated with the systems and doctrines held by those who frequented the School of Tyrannus? Could such Hellenistic concepts as *eikon, prototo-*

---

[10] It is incidentally fascinating to see that some manuscripts of the New Testament say that Paul taught in the School of Tyrannus "from the fifth hour to the tenth", i.e. "from eleven o'clock to four", that is, at siesta time when the school was not otherwise in use.

kos, archè, pleroma, theotès be used as means for Christological statement? In Paul's own letters, some of them from this period in Ephesus, we can see Stoic, Platonic and Epicurean thought forms being used to express the meaning of Jesus Christ.[11] Paul had put himself in the position to "tell the story properly" to the mind of Asia. I suggest that it is Luke's view that the Christian movement was being prepared here for the thrust into the Hellenistic world whereby Christianity out-thought the pagan philosophies. Here, Luke is suggesting, is the part for the whole: a kind of "first-fruitage" of Hellenistic Christian theology. Now, he implies, "all Asia" is in a position "to hear the gospel in a language addressed to its mind as well as to its heart." As I have written elsewhere, "Were we Christians more generally to take this model seriously, we would be far more concerned than we often appear to be to find ways of expressing our faith so that Muslims or Marxists, Hindus or Humanists could really be said to have 'heard the Word of God'. For many people of other faiths the gospel story just has not yet been properly told" (1986:28).

4   DIALOGUE AS EVANGELISM IN THE HISTORY OF THE CHRISTIAN MISSION

This general understanding of dialogue as the most appropriate means to evangelism has persisted through the long centuries of the church.[12]

---

[11] There are some grounds for supposing Ephesus to be the place of origin of the Letter to the Colossians, where such expressions are used, see Dunn1996:40. An earlier N.T. scholar Moule wrote once that the identification of Jesus, "the crucified Nazarene," within thirty years of his death as the subject of such terminology is "staggering, and fairly cries of for some explanation" (1957:19). It could well be that part of the explanation is the two year period spent in the school of Tyrannus.

[12] Andrew Walls suggests that one watershed in the rediscovery of dialogical methods in missionary work can be found in the different circumstances of the Spanish and Portuguese sea-borne empires. "The Spanish presence was concentrated in America and the Philippines. The Portuguese presence stretched like a thread along the coasts of Africa, along the Persian gulf and across the Indian Ocean, into South India and Sri Lanka and the coasts and islands of Southeast Asia and offshore China and on to Japan—not to mention Brazil." With only limited resources and confronted by resistant Islam, Hinduism, and Buddhism the Portuguese-type missionary necessarily became dialogue and persuasion, exemplified in such figures as Robert de Nobili and Giuseppe Beschi. As Wall remarks, "In this strange way, interfaith dialogue was born of frustrated colonialism. Putting it another way: in the mercy of God, the king of

Despite woeful diversions into the use of coercive methods: forcible baptisms, mass conversions, crusades, economic and cultural bribery, psychological manipulation, the great tradition of "reasoning and persuading" has never been wholly lost. As Jerald Gort remarks: "Coercive mission is not consistent with salvation history and certainly does not accord with a truly effective Christian testimony."[13]

The second half of this essay will point to some striking figures in the Protestant missionary movement of the past three centuries who have lived out the proposition that "dialogue is evangelism: evangelism is dialogue."[14] Each of these was in some degree both a theoretician and a practitioner. Their convergent and complementary insights, ranging over the last three hundred years, are immediately relevant to our theme.

5   THE PASSIONATE STUDENT OF HINDUISM

The first Protestant missionary in India was Bartholomaeus Ziegenbalg (1683-1719).[15] He arrived in Tranquebar on July 9th, 1706 and immediately set out on the path of unremitting labour that led to his early death at the age of thirty five. His achievements focussed on the study of Tamil language and culture. He prepared dictionaries, published a Tamil grammar, and collected Tamil manuscripts. Steadfastly opposed to the westernisation of Indian Christians, Ziegenbalg was assiduous in teaching Tamil schoolchildren their own language and customs. To do this he set out on a self-appointed task of understanding Hinduism from within. Unfortunately, some might say, his informants were not the great pandits of Thanjavur or Madurai but rather the ordinary citizenry of Tanquebar. The latest study of Ziegenbalg by Brijraj Singh affirms another point of view about Ziegenbalg's achievements:

Portugal never had enough servants to go out into the highways and byways and compel them to come in" (2002:40f.).

[13] Gort writes that the church "has a duty to insure that its witness is not shaped wrongly, in such a way that it hinders God"s action and blocks the kingdom. Looking at the practice of the past one is struck by the fact that church has frequently given witness to the gospel with might and main, exhibiting a crusading rather than a crucified mind. And in many situations this remains true even now" (1995:208).

[14] For other examples see Cracknell 1995.

[15] Two important studies are Jeyaraj 1996 and Singh 1999. In these brief remarks I am not so concerned about the coming to being of an Indian indigenous church as about the evangelistic process.

For it turns out that his ignorance of the historical element of Hinduism, his less than perfect understanding of the abstract and philosophical nature of Hindu reformers and sages are matched by an unparallelled knowledge of the populist gods and vernacular forms of worship, his very detailed observation of Hindu rituals, a thorough familiarity with legends associated with various god and their feasts and festivals, and accurate descriptions of phenomena that are of very great ethnological interest. These include the tilaks and other caste marks of various sects, the special prayers used by them, the musical instruments in use at the time, or the arrangement of folk deities around a major god in a temple complex.[16]

Equipped with such a mass of information, and speaking Tamil fluently, Ziegenbalg turned to what Brijraj Singh calls "interfaith dialogue." In so doing, though he was not aware of it, Ziegenbalg was entering into India's living tradition of interfaith colloquies, a pattern set in the previous century by the great Mughul emperor Akbar (1556-1605). To be sure, Ziegenbalg's motives included a desire to defeat Hinduism and Islam by showing up their errors, but he was not of a violently polemical spirit, and was quite without the taint of racism or imperialism manifested in other eighteenth-century pioneers of study of Indian language and customs.[17] On the contrary he believed, as Brijraj Singh writes, "in a genuine spiritual conversion" which could only be gained through a process of "reading, learning, meditation, thought and prayer" (121). His profound Lutheran pietism led him to emphasize the importance of books. So he attempted to start a printing press and to build a library. He was deeply committed to educational work and establishment of schools. His

---

[16] Brijraj Singh (1999:105) is basing this assessment on a manuscript that Ziegenbalg completed in 1711. The English version of the title can be read as *The complete description of the heathendom of Malabar* wherein, from their own writings, their precepts and doctrines in theology as well as philosophy are set out in detail and are communicated for the useful instruction of beloved Europe. He sent this home to A.H. Francke in Halle who refused to print it. Only in 1927 was the full text published and it has never been translated into English. There is also a later document, completed in 1713, that did appear in English as *The Genealogy of the South-Indian God* (1868). Francke also refused to publish this, writing that "Missionaries were sent out to extirpate Hinduism, and not to spread heathenist nonsense in Europe."

[17] I think, for example, of Sir William Jones (1746-94) working in Calcutta. His references to Indians are full of condescending remarks about their "supineness" and "indolence".

work in dialogue was characterized by a profound respect for "the intellectual achievements of Tamil people whom God has liberally blessed with strength of thought and readiness of apprehending the various aspects of and mutual relations of all sublunary things" (298f.). Elsewhere he praised their skill in debate and argument, affirming that talking with them had led him into a "deeper consideration of many subjects, and in both theology and philosophy learned much of which neither I nor other students had thought before" (122f.).

This concern with winning arguments by fair means was not conducive to church growth. It has been estimated that at the time of his death in 1719 Ziegenbalg left behind him only 250 converts. He was one for whom evangelism was dialogue and we are left to speculate what might have been if he had lived another thirty years.

6   THE MAN WHO LOVED MUSLIMS

Henry Martyn (1781-1812), like Ziegenbalg, suffered a tragically early death. Martyn died at the age of thirty-one.[18] His story is well-known and has recently been reassessed by Clinton Bennett in his *In Dialogue with Truth: a Critical Biography of Henry Martyn* (1994). Strictly speaking Martyn was never a missionary, but rather a Chaplain with the East India Company, posted by the company to Dinapore and then to Cawnpore. In both places his refusal to regard Indians as inferior and his respect for Indian culture annoyed and alienated the English. He annoyed the general at Dinapore by suggesting that Indians were not fools and "ingenuity and clear reasoning were not confined to England and Europe" (Padwick 1922:95). Though suffering from tuberculosis, he began a long journey home through Shiraz, where he wanted to present his Persian translation of the New Testament to the Shah. Martyn recorded in his Journal, "I am sometimes led on by the Persians to tell them all I know of the recesses of the sanctuary, and these are the things that interest them."[19] But then he attracted the attention of the more strictly orthodox Muslims and was lured into controversy with the Mullah Mirza Ibrahim, and other members of the local scholarly class. These encounters were later published as *Controversial Tracts on Christianity and Mohammedanism* (1824) and have left an impression that Martyn was an ardent polemicist. In fact he confided to his Journal that while a

---

[18] For a brief but cogent introduction, see Bennett 1994.

[19] By "the recesses of the sanctuary" Martyn means the deepest spiritual experiences, normally never discussed by Englishmen.

debate might "entice a spirit of enquiry" he did not overvalue "much stress upon clear argument: the work of God is seldom wrought in this way."[20]

7   THE FIRST THEORETICIAN OF MISSION AS DIALOGUE

Thomas Ebenezer Slater (1840-1912) had the benefit of many decades of London Missionary Society work in India and elsewhere when he began publishing influential works on the theory of mission and the Christian understanding of Hinduism. His earliest major work *The Philosophy of Modern Missions: a Present Day Plea* (1882) showed the profound influence of the Anglican theologian F. D. Maurice (1805-1872), especially his seminal work *The Religions of the World* (1846).[21]

Quoting Maurice directly Slater wrote that missions revealed "Christ as the organic Root and Head of the human family, the representative of the race, in whom every tribe is interested and towards whom every soul stands in vital relation." Missions, Slater continued, pointed "to Him as the light of the world, as the fountain of all the truth and goodness, that gleamed out in the ancient world, as the fulfiller of all pre-Christian hopes and aspirations, as the central truth that reconciles the systems of men" (47f.). As early as 1882 Slater affirmed that "All other religions await for their fulfilment in Christianity" (112). Though the fulfilment theory is often attributed to J.N. Farquhar and his *The Crown of Hinduism* (1913), it is here that we have its beginnings. This view was to dominate missionary understanding of other religions at least until 1938, and does so still in some circles. Slater believed that this was the most philosophic of the grounds "on which the claims of mission could be based" (112).

Slater's own long career in India began in educational work, but later centered upon extensive work with college graduates, where he had already formulated this principle in addressing them: "The aspect in which I would set Christianity before you is not an aspect of antagonism but consummation."[22] In this spirit he wrote many books about Hindu thought, culminating in his most influential work, *The Higher Hinduism in Relation to Christianity* (1902). In this book Slater's theme is that the "revelation of the Gospel will be in complete accord with the best senti-

---

[20] Wilberforce 1837:55.

[21] For more about Slater see my 1995:108-119. See Slater 1882 and 1902.

[22] *In God Revealed*, a series of public lectures published privately in Madras in 1876.

ments of [India's] best minds, the true realisation of the visions of her seers, the real fulfilment of the longings of her sages" (291). The last words of *The Higher Hinduism* are "We shall never gain the non-Christian world until we treat its religions with justice, courtesy and love" (291).

8   THE MISSIONARY AS THE LOCUS OF DIALOGUE

By1910 the missionaries who responded to Commission Four of the World Missionary Conference in Edinburgh had come to feel that their task could only be carried out if they treated the religious traditions of other men and women with profound respect by showing how all their best thought pointed to Christ.[23] The outstanding Dutch missionary practitioner and thinker, Hendrik Kraemer (1888-1965) was to challenge this position in a fundamental way in 1938. The thesis of his Tambaram Conference book, *The Christian Message in a Non-Christian World*, is well known. Kraemer's book was a complex and profound theological statement in which he made the distinction between "Biblical realism" and all other forms of religious experience, emphasizing a profound discontinuity between human religion and Christian revelation. For Kramer there were no "points of contact" in the other religious tradition upon which missionaries could build and thus fulfil the longings of Hinduism or Buddhism.[24]

Despite his reputation for making harsh decisions about the status of these other religious traditions,[25] Kraemer endorses sharing religious

---

[23] See Van Lin 1974. An English version of this valuable work is in preparation. Also see Cracknell 1995:191-202. The title was borrowed from T. E. Slater. When I wrote that book I acknowledged regretfully the absence of serious testimony from the continent of Africa about the "fulfilment" of African religion in Christianity. It is now possible to point to the study of the pioneering Africanist Edwin W. Smith by Young (2002). Young shows Smith to have been firmly of fulfilment theology persuasion. That he was a man of dialogue is affirmed by the name Africans gave to him: Chitutanano, "the quiet wise spirit".

[24] Kraemer is a complex and multi-layered thinker and he went on writing for almost another thirty years. For an excellent brief introduction see Hoedemaker, who also highlights the idea of "the missionary as point of contact" remarking that this concept connects Kraemer's thought "very fruitfully to later developments in the theology of religions and of dialogue" (1994:514).

[25] This reputation is often justified. See, for example, his references to Islam as "a great syncretistic body" and to its "iron rigidity," (1938:215, 353) and to Hinduism as

experience as "valid and very valuable" and shows himself fully aware of why Christian missionaries should take such an approach. He refers to a "haunting dread of all superiority" and to "the delicate and justified desire to have real human contact" which should be "on the footing of spiritual give and take." Kraemer also refers to an understandable aversion from "dogmatic" religion and speaks of a "too one-sided stress on preaching." This he says is often in reality "mere annoying interference" (298). Equally valid is the path of social service, which he sees as a noble insistence to demonstrate in practice that being a Christian means a new quality of life.

Kraemer therefore was adamant concerning the need for "faith, hope and love" in the hearts of those who wish to "good-news" the Muslim world. Any missionary, he wrote, who has fallen "a victim to the attitude of fear or disgust or hatred of Islam, does better to go home and never come back" (354f.).

In these and many other ways, Kraemer is advocating an attitude of dialogue, with its attendant attributes of deep interest in the other person, its repudiation of interest in "systems" and in winning arguments, and its desire for the deepest well-being of the other. These go along with the opportunity to bear authentic witness. Elsewhere in the book is a dictum parallel to my own title, "witness has to be conceived as real ministry and ministry as real witness" (405). In bearing witness to people of different faith commitments the central issue is the attitude of the missionary. After a long chapter in which Kraemer demonstrated the inadequacy of the "points-of-contact" approach, he stands his argument on its head and insists that there is in fact a "point-of contact":

> This point of contact is the disposition and attitude of the missionary. It seems rather upsetting to make the missionary the point of contact. Nevertheless it is true, as practice teaches. The *strategic and absolutely dominant point in this whole important problem is the missionary worker himself.* Such is the golden rule, or if one prefers, the iron rule in this whole matter (140).

9   THE THEORIST OF WORLD RELIGIOUS DIALOGUE

Our last witness to the theme that evangelism is dialogue and dialogue is evangelism is Wilfred Cantwell Smith (1916-2000), whose career ranged from educational missionary work in Lahore with the Canadian Mission in the early 1940's to professorships of Comparative Religion

---

"exclusively individualistic and essentially eudaemonistic" (140).

in McGill, Dalhousie and Harvard Universities.[26] He retired from Harvard in 1983. For the last half of the twentieth century he was both an interpreter of the significance of religion in human life and the importance of inter-religious encounter, and has some claim to be the most quoted of the scholars referred to by contemporary practitioners of dialogue.

His own experience of the ordinary people of the Muslim world in northwest India in the 1940's suggested to him that what human beings had in common was the quality of faith. To illustrate this proposition he tells a story of climbing in the Himalayas. He came across a fruit seller, "a humble and poor and loveable old man with a stack of oranges that he was selling by weight." For scales, Smith tells us, he had a rough and ready balance.

> He put oranges in one pan and weighed them with some rocks that he had there, a middle sized one and two smallish ones the three of which made up one sir (two pounds). He was too poor to own metal weights stamped and standard. That the three stones actually weighed a sir was an unverified presumption, though I personally believe that they did. I watched him for a while, as he made occasional sales to passers-by, and afterward fell into conversation with him. He was far from any possibility of having his dealings checked, and there was no external measure of his honesty, which I found was sustained rather by a verse from the Qur'an which runs, "Lo, He over all things is watching" (Smith 1967:89).

To this humble Muslim the Qur'an had become the word of God, and his response was for Smith quite simply: faith. This kind of faith, says Smith, is a universal quality. Human beings everywhere, he contends, have always lived out of, or from "faith," losing it only when they have been ultimately overtaken by what can be called nihilism or existential despair. Consequently, any appreciation of beauty; any striving for good; any pursuit of justice; any recognition that some things are good, some are bad, and that it matters; any feeling or practice of love; any love of what theists call "God;" all these are examples of personal, and communal faith. Because all human beings work within this common dimension of faith, human discourse about religion is not only possible, it is essential. It takes place at human levels of mutual personal disclosures. Certainly there are the doctrines, the ethics, rituals, of the world religious traditions but these serve to under gird and build up faith. They are, in his language, the "mundane cause" of faith. At the same time the response of men and women within these traditions is normally a res-

---

[26] For a convenient Introduction, see the Reader: Cracknell 2001.

ponse to "transcendence", as those traditions bear their own testimony to the "divine" and to the "beyond."[27]

Smith frequently offered pointers to enable Christians to move forward in their always-slowly-changing conception of mission. Recognizing that mission must involve a sense of concern and responsibility for the spiritual life of all humankind, Smith wrote a major programmatic statement entitled "Participation: the Changing Christian Role in Other Cultures" (Smith 1969). Participation becomes the key concept: the role of the missionary is now to act as an agent in bringing into reality a world-wide community. "The missionary assignment," he insists, "for the next phase in human history is to take the leadership in this participation." Such a vocation will have immediate consequences for the self-image of missionaries. They will become people who feel "that Christianity has caught a certain vision of God, has seen an aspect of ultimate truth, which is to be communicated to the general search for God and truth in which people of other communities are also engaged." In his or her new guise the missionary becomes a person who is committed to the way of dialogue, or in Smith's own preferred terminology, colloquy. The idea of colloquy indeed stands at the heart of Smith's controlling vision of a single world community in which "we," that is, "all of us," talk about "us all" in the twenty-first century.

10   CONCLUSION

These five thinkers are very different in their approaches to mission and evangelism, but they have one central and profound insight in common. Ziegenbalg's extraordinary willingness to listen to and record different points of view; Henry Martyn's modelling of friendship and empathy; Slater's interpretation of the religion of other men and women that turned upon justice, courtesy and love; Kraemer's insistence upon patience and genuine interest in other people and their religion and their whole range of life; Smith's insistence that the evangelist must become a participant in other people's cultures: all bear their testimony that evangelism is dialogue and dialogue is evangelism. By sitting where other people sit, by engaging them in conversation, behaving with courtesy and friendship, by offering gentle information and reasonable arguments, more is accomplished for the "good-newsing" of the Gospel than by all the coercive and crusading tactics of other forms of proclamation and preaching.

---

[27] For all this see most conveniently chapter 7 of Smith 1979.

Dialogue and the giving of witness do not stand in any contradiction to one another, as the WCC *Guidelines* affirmed in 1979. On the contrary a dialogical attitude must be seen to be an indispensable ingredient of evangelism. The *Guidelines* were doing no more than referring to this tradition when they said "as Christians enter into dialogue with their commitment to Jesus Christ, time and again the relationship of dialogue gives opportunity for authentic witness." Christians everywhere may be grateful that the WCC has just republished the *Guidelines* in a revised and updated form. In the immensely complicated and often dangerous world of the twenty-first century we need as much help as we can get to determine how we may bear witness to Christ.

BIBLIOGRAPHY

Bennett, Clinton. (1994). "Henry Martyn 1781-1878 Scholarship in the Service of Mission". In: Gerald Anderson, Robert T. Coote, Norman A. Horner and James M. Phillips (eds). *Mission Legacies: Biographical Studies of the Leaders of the Modern Missionary Movement*. Maryknoll: Orbis Books. Pp 264-270.

The British Guidelines on Dialogue: Relations with People of Other Faith. (1981). London: British Council of Churches.

Carey, William. (1792). *Enquiry into the Obligation of Christian to Use Means for the Conversion of the Heathen*. Facsimile edition. London: Carey Kingsgate Press.

Cracknell, Kenneth. (1985) "Within God's Gracious Purposes: Interfaith Dialogue in Britain". In: *The Ecumenical Review* 37. Pp. 452-61.

—. (1986). *Towards a New Relationship: Christian and People of Other Faith*. London: Epworth.

—. (1992). *Protestant Evangelism or Catholic Evangelization?* London: Methodist Sacramental Fellowship.

—. (1995). *Justice Courtesy and Love: Theologians and Missionaries Encountering World Religions, 1846-1914*. London: Epworth.

—. (2001). *Wilfred Cantwell Smith: a Reader*. Oxford: Oneworld.

Dunn, J.D.G. (1996). *The Epistles to Colossians and Philemon*. Grand Rapids: Eerdmans.

Gort, Jerald D. (1995). "Distress, Salvation and the Mediation of Salvation". In: Frans J. Verstraelen *et al*. (eds.), *Missiology, an Ecumenical Introduction: Texts and Contexts of Global Christianity*. Grand Rapids: Eerdmans. Pp. 194-210.

Green, Michael. (1970). *Evangelism in the Early Church*. London: Hodder and Stoughton.

Haenchen, Ernst. (1971). *The Acts of the Apostles*. E.T. Oxford: Blackwell.

Hoedemaker, Libertus. A. (1994). "Hendrik Kraemer, 1888-1965: Biblical Realism Applied to Mission". In: Gerald Anderson, Robert T. Coote, Norman

A. Horner and James M. Phillips (eds.). (1994). *Mission Legacies: Biographical Studies of the Leaders of the Modern Missionary Movement.* Maryknoll: Orbis Books. Pp 508-515.

Jeyaraj, Daniel. (1996). *Der Beitrag der danische-halleschen Mission zum Werden einer indisch-einheimsche Kirche.* Erlangen: Ev-Luth. Mission Verlag.

Kraemer, Hendrik. (1938). *The Christian Message in a Non-Christian World.* London: Edinburgh House Press.

Logan, James C. (1995). "The Evangelical Imperative: a Wesleyan Perspective". In: James C. Logan (ed.). *Theology and Evangelism in the Wesleyan Heritage.* Nashville: Kingswood.

Moule, C.F.D. (1957). *The Epistles of Paul the Apostle to the Colossians and to Philemon.* Cambridge: Cambridge University Press.

My Neighbour's Faith and Mine. (1979). Geneva: WCC.

Padwick, Constance. (1992). *Henry Martyn: Confessor of the Faith.* London: SCM Press.

Singh, Brijraj. (1999). *The First Protestant Missionary to India: Bartholomaeus Ziegenbalg (1683-1719).* Delhi: Oxford University Press.

Slater, Thomas Ebenezer. (1882). *The Philosophy of Modern Missions: a Present Day Plea.* London: James Clarke.

—. (1902). *The Higher Hinduism in Relations to Christianity: Certain Aspects of Hinduism from a Christian Standpoint.* London: Elliott Stock.

Smith, Wilfred Cantwell. (1967). "Can Religions be True or False?". In: *Questions of Religious Truth.* London: Gollancz.

—. (1969). "Participation: the Changing Christian Role" In: *Other Cultures.* Occasional Bulletin of the Missionary Research Library 20. No.4. New York. Pp 1-13. Also published in: Gerald H. Anderson and Thomas F. Stransky (eds.). *Mission Trends* No.2. New York: Paulist Press / Grand Rapids: Eerdmans 1975; and in: Willard G. Oxtoby (ed.). (1982). *Religious Diversity.* New York: Crossroad.

—. (1979). *Faith and Belief.* Princeton: Princeton University Press.

Van Lin, J.J.E (1974). *Protestantse Theologie der Godsdiensten van Edinburgh naar Tambaram 1910-1938.* Assen: Van Gorcum.

Walls, Andrew. (2002). *The Cross-Cultural Process in Christian History.* Edinburgh: T. and T Clark / Maryknoll NY: Orbis.

Wesley, John. (1752). *Explanatory Notes upon the New Testament.* Reprint: London: Epworth 1976.

Wilberforce, S. (1837). *Journals and Letters of Henry Martyn.* Vol. 2. London: R. B. Seeley and W. Burnside.

Young, W. John. (2002). *The Quiet Wise Spirit: Edwin W. Smith (1876-1957) and Africa.* London: Epworth.

18 Indonesian Muslims And The North-American West

1 INTRODUCTION

Relations between Christians and Muslims have often been defined as an affair between an imagined cultural and territorial unity of an Islamic world and an undetermined Christian West. The standard book on the relation has already the title *Islam and the West. The Making of an Image* (Norman 1960). For Indonesia, the world's largest country with a Muslim majority of 87% (i.e. 194 million out of a population of some 220 million in 2002), the relation with Christians was for the largest period in history with European Christians. The Portuguese initiative of trade and colonial expansion started in 1511, and was taken over by the Dutch around 1600. Because of the arrival of Muslims in various regions of the vast archipelago at about the same time, there are various studies describing "the Race between Islam and Christianity " (cf. Azra 2000; Steenbrink 2002).

Only in the 20th century some North-Americans came in. They were not important until Indonesian independence in 1945. Since that time the North-American influence has gained momentum in Indonesia and America-originated missionary Christianity has become more a counter-part for Indonesian Muslims. This contribution wants to present some aspects of this encounter Indonesian Muslims and Christians of North-America. From a few cases we want to draw some conclusions about the growing role of North-America as world leader and the impact of Muslims meeting people from the United States and Canada in person.

2 HAMKA IN NORTH-AMERICA, 25 AUGUST - 25 DECEMBER 1952

Haji Abdulmalik bin Abdulkarim Amrullah, better known under his acronym Hamka (1908-1981) was one of modern Indonesia's best known religious authors. Born in a family of Muslim clergy, he developed not as a traditional Muslim scholar, leading a school in the countryside, but he became a pioneer in a new style of religious leaders, founding magazines for people in the big cities, where he mixed religious teachings with romantic stories and more worldly wisdom. In 1935 Hamka moved to Medan, the booming capital of North-Sumatra, where the rubber and copra plantations created a society of rich Western colonial planters and Malay Muslim traditional rulers, of the coolies from

Muslim Java and from Buddhist China. Here Hamka started in 1935 the weekly *Pedoman Masyarakat* (Guidance for the People). The magazine became extremely popular through the romantic novels that were published in weekly episodes as a feuilleton. In quite sentimental stories, Hamka fought against polygamous marriage and against local pre-Islamic customs that still influenced many Indonesian societies.

After 1950 Hamka came to the capital of the independent Republic of Indonesia as a member of the national parliament and a senior advisor to the Ministry of Education, while continuing his activities as an important thinker for the formulation of a modernised and confident Muslim community. He wrote some very solid books: the most impressive result is a 30 volume Quran commentary, counting some 10,000 pages. Among his writings is also a 1,200 pages long History of Islam. But Hamka also continued to write many shorter contributions for newspapers and magazines.

In 1952 Hamka was invited to America by the US Government, and he wrote some lengthy articles about this trip. They were collected in two small volumes of 127 and 144 pages. In the following we will give a selected reading of this impression. In this reassessment we keep in mind the later development of Hamka as leader of Indonesian Muslims. After a period of intense and optimistic nationalism, following the declaration of Independence in 1945, the late 1950s saw an increasing clash between communists and religious groups. The communists were eliminated from the political podium in 1965 and even physically from many regions as well: the coup of 30 September and its aftermath probably cost 500,000 lives. After 1966 the relations between Muslims and Christians gradually became more tense. The anti-communist policy of the Suharto period (1966-1998) urged all Indonesians to register their religion. Quite a few former communists now opted for Christianity and the Christian presence in Central Java became more and more visible, although Christians remained a small minority: up to 9,5% for the whole country, but never more than 1-2% on the most populous island of Java.

This stronger presence of Christianity, among other reasons, caused an increased competition between the two major religions of the country. In 1975 Hamka was elected as the General Chairman of the highest religious body of Indonesia, the *Majelis Ulama* or High Council of Muslim Clerics. Hamka's position in this body ended in 1981 with a religious decision (*fatwa*) that Muslims were not allowed to attend Christmas celebrations with their neighbour Christians. The *fatwa* was defended by Hamka as a move against too easy relations between the two religions and especially against the danger of syncretism and easy conversion. In the aftermath of the uproar about this issue Hamka died on 24th July 1981. Since then, besides being considered a popular writer on religious issues, he is mostly known as the fierce defender of Islam against communism, against the quite liberal state philosophy of Pancasila and most of all against the growing influence of Christianity. What was Hamka's view on Christianity in the early 1950s? What was his perception of North-America at that time? This we will read from his description of a close contact with North-American cultural and religious life in 1952.

The first impression of America for Hamka was that of a country of progress. He knew the Middle East, Egypt and Arabia from several visits. His first visit to the region was in 1926-7, when he went to Mecca for the pilgrimage of the *hajj*, but also with the aspiration to do thorough religious studies in Mecca. At that time, an older and very respected Indonesian cleric, like Hamka also originating from the Minangkabau lands of Sumatra, Haji Agus Salim, warned him that Mecca was not good for pursuing studies. "This country [Arabia] is suited for worship, but you should not look for science or even wisdom here. You should instead look for education and develop yourself in your own country."[1] This same look on Arabia and the Middle East is found in this impression of North-America. The West (also the Netherlands during a short stopover on his way to New York), but especially America is much more advanced (*lebih maju*, literally "further ahead") than the Muslim world. It is even stated bluntly that "Arabia is good for one's soul, but the United Stated much better for one's intelligence" (Hamka 1954: I,5). The Egyptians built in twenty years their highest pyramid of 415 feet, but the Empire State Building, with its height of 1250 feet, was constructed in only one year! (I,9). There is not much resentment about colonialism in his remarks. The small Dutch country could manage to be the colonizer of Indonesia, twenty times its size, during 350 years. But now the ties are dissolved, "because that was the will of history" (I,7).

Hamka recognised much of North-American Christianity as quite similar to the religion of Islam in his own country. While telling about the big city of crimes and nightclubs, Chicago, he emphasized the noble work done by the YMCA that had opened seven hotels in the city, scores of restaurants, and courses for workers and youth. The YMCA is compared with the reformist Islamic movement of Indonesia, Muhammadiyah (I,28). Quite interesting is his observation that Muslims pray five times per day, but Christians four times. He observed in families where he

---

[1] See Steenbrink 1994: 131, in a quote from Hamka's autobiography, that he wrote in the late 1940s.

joined the meals that "North-Americans said their prayers four times per day: at breakfast, at lunch and dinner and before going to bed" (I,98). Another interesting comparison was his understanding of the term "Pilgrim Fathers". Hamka knew little English and had always a translator with him. These guides were sometimes North-Americans who taught Indonesian (like Echols), returned missionaries, but mostly Indonesians who lived in the United States. His interpretation of Thanksgiving Day may have originated in a too literal translation. About the "Pilgrims" who arrived in America with the Mayflower, he writes:

> Pilgrims means people that go to the *hajj*, because they wanted to migrate to America, because on that continent they wanted to found a pure and clean Christian community and free themselves from the influence of the religious struggles in Europe. Every year this spirit is commemorated, so that their offspring should not forget this origin. The holiday of Thanksgiving is specific for America (I,83).

When looking for an Islamic parallel to the journey of the people on the Mayflower, the hijra or move from troublesome Mecca to the warm welcome in Medina that was a great break in the career of the Prophet Muhammed, would have been a much more reasonable story. Now the pilgrimage to Mecca was probably chosen because of the translation of the literal meaning of pilgrim into the religious vocabulary of Muslim Indonesians.

Also the issue of the many denominations in America did not give negative feelings about Christianity in America. He calls the different Protestant denominations *mazhab* after the word used for the various schools of Islamic law. Although Muslims may follow a different *mazhab*, they have no difficulty in recognizing other people as true Muslims (I,84f.).

In Buffalo, New York, Hamka was the guest of the Quaker family of a Mr. Brill, a friend of the professor of Indonesian Studies at Cornell University, John M. Echols. With both families he really felt at home and his comment was, "The differences of colour, nationality and religion, disappeared, were replaced by feeling of sympathy and mutual respect." This author of sentimental novels, remains the romantic author in describing that he received a kiss from a young girl before she went to bed, in the same style she kissed her parents. Hamka started weeping, and Mrs Brill said to him: "You must feel homesick now" (I,25f.).

As a writer and editor of journals, Hamka of course was interested in the Christian press. In Chicago he had a meeting with the editor of the magazine *Christian Century*. Without further comment, Hamka noted down the information that the great progress of society in the twentieth century was made thanks to the Christian civilization. Hamka, of course, really agreed with the North-American criticism of the tight bounds between colonialism and mission: "Several colonizing nations, including the Netherlands, gave large sums to churches, not directly for the propagation of their faith, but for the spread of civilization and maintenance of religion on their colonies, and this has only resulted in hatred towards Christianity" (I,72).

In Salt Lake City Hamka was invited to give a lecture at a Mormon College on the theme of "Brotherhood". He discussed the relation between the Muslim world and the West in a very broad perspective:

> The Lord has given the Western part of the world very deep philosophical thinking. The West has produced Socrates, Plato and Aristotle. But the Western mind would have remained poor, when the doctrine of Jesus Christ about love would not have arrived from the East into the West. On the other hand, when the religion of Islam grew through Muhammed and the Muslim civilization rose in Baghdad, Spain and other parts of the world, the sophisticated tradition of thinking that was the legacy of the Greek philosophers, also was used by Muslim scholars.
>
> Some centuries later, the relation between East and West became dominated by hatred. This was caused by the arrival of people of the West in Eastern territory, because of the epidemic of colonialism. This hatred has damaged both sides. People from the East hate the West because of colonialism, and because they could not obtain their knowledge. The people from the West were arrogant because of the sophisticated knowledge and technology, and their soul turned empty. But now the situation has changed and the people of the East have opened their eyes again, although they are still in a poor condition as to technology and are in need of much help in order to overcome their poverty...
>
> The religions of the world are in fact not in conflict. Only the passionate characters of many of their adherents are in conflict. The Christians are brothers and sisters of the Muslims. Muhammed recognized that his work only was an extension of the efforts of Jesus, but the Muslim and the Christian communities once started the crusades. The solution that we have to find nowadays, is not the solution of a conflict of people who believe together in One God, because basically they are already united. The solution that we have to find is to solve the problem of how we can reach all those who believe in One God, in order to call them back to real and full belief. (I,39f.).

Among the various denominations in America, the Unitarians received the warmest sympathy of Hamka. They could be considered a religion of their own, because the basic elements of their religion are quite far away from the common doctrine of Christians. They do not accept a hereditary character, attached to Adam's sin. This was only his individual mistake. Therefore Jesus was sent only as a messenger. He was not a Son of God and not a redeemer for all humankind. "But, unfortunately, they do not recognize Muhammed as a messenger. And some of them also do not accept the Last Judgement. Although they are close to Islam, the Unitarians remain a Christian sect" (I,85).

In general, Hamka was quite surprised about the great importance given to (Christian) religion in the United States. He saw that virtually all major academic institutes had started from a theological school, that religion played an important role in the daily life of the army personnel (with good periods of silence for prayers at their meals, and with army chaplains) and most striking of all, that the doctrines of Marx and Sartre had few adherents in America: "Many students in the Middle East who suffer from an inferiority complex are influenced by these philosophers, even more than in Europe or America. Also in Egypt and Lebanon we may see a much bigger influence of Sartre than the city of Paris" (I,88).

Even the often criticised free contacts between males and females, especially among the youth, were signalled in a positive way by Hamka.

> The free social contact that we can observe here also has clear moral boundaries. They call this etiquette, subtle rules that one has to obey strictly. People who do not abide by these rules are considered as not civilised. This free social contact originates from a philosophy of life and good education. Our ban on free social contact in the Eastern countries finds its origin in our backwardness. In many countries the women are excluded from society and prevented from free communication because they are not trusted and have no self-confidence. But in the West this feeling of self-confidence is promoted (II,30).

Hamka's impressions of America were published more than one year after his journey. They are probably based on notes, written down while he was still travelling. There was, however, time enough for him to reflect and to reorganize his notes according to themes and topics. They are not just simple passing notes. It is the ripe observation of a well-travelled, middle-aged man who writes down his true admiration for North-American society, including its practice of Christian religion. Hamka, of course, also gave some special attention to the rather few expressions of Muslim life he could see in the United States. He describes and even presents a beautiful photograph of the great mosque of Washington (I,114f.). He felt an honoured guest and never felt threatened or in competition with North-American society. His country was still young and promising and apparently he had good hope for a better future.

In 1962 Hamka was put in jail because he considered the policy of Indonesia's first President, Soekarno, too much in favour of communism. In 1966, at the beginning of the 'New Order' regime of General Soeharto he was set free and in 1975 appointed chairman of the *Majelis Ulama*, the prestigious Council of Muslim Clerics. After that he turned into a much more active partisan for the Islamic community against the expanding Christian mission. In 1978 the Government took some measures to limit the number of foreign missionaries and to regulate foreign aid given through churches. As chairman of the *Majelis Ulama*, Hamka strongly supported these measures. In early 1981 this Council took a decision to issue a *fatwa*, a religious decision, that forbade Muslims from participating in Christmas celebrations together with Christians. The considerations of this *fatwa* recognised that Muslims join the Christians in their belief about the virgin birth of Jesus from Mary, that they accept Jesus as Spirit and Word of God and as one of the Prophets. Nevertheless these common beliefs do not supersede the great differences between the two major religions of Indonesia. Therefore Muslims should not attend the common celebrations. The Indonesian government was disappointed with this decision of the Muslim clerics and urged the *Majelis Ulama* to withdraw the *fatwa*. Hamka reacted in an emotional and outspoken style: "Religious scholars are indeed the heirs of the prophets. From these they inherit the slander and contempt that they received... Are religious scholars only teachers that can be ordered or dismissed arbitrarily? And if a meeting must be closed, he may be summoned: Hey, nice man, just say a prayer."[2] Hamka did not withdraw the *fatwa*, and saw no other solution than to resign from his position at the *Majelis Ulama*, on 19 May, 1981. He died two months later on 24 July, 1981.

If we look at the career of Hamka as a whole under the perspective of inter-religious relations, we may notice a growing frustration and also an increase in animosity. During the colonial period, Hamka mostly lived in regions with an overwhelming majority of Muslims. Christians did not play an important role in his thinking and writing. His post-colonial report of his voyage to America is in this sense an exception, because he wrote numerous pages about Christians and nearly always in a very sympathetic and positive way. Apparently Hamka felt respected and honoured in America and definitely never threatened.

---

[2] From an editorial in his own magazine, *Panji Masyarakat*, 1 May 1981. See also Steenbrink 1994: 143.

In 1950 Hamka wrote in a book for common people on religious psychology, called *Pribadi*, [Personality]:

> Anyone who has become totally absorbed in his own belief, whatever religion (belief) he embraces, certainly has no more time to hate the followers of other religions. How can there be hatred in the heart so close to God? .. In this religion it is as if we get born twice, and the first birth is in Islam. But after we have grown up, we must be born again (once more). We study the religion as deeply as possible and we adjust our lives to it. Then we begin to study other religions as well, so that, as Muslims, we will know our similarities as well as our differences (Hamka 1950:121).

In *Pribadi*, Hamka is very generous in his praise of people from other religions: Abraham Lincoln, General Eisenhower, Tolstoy, Martin Luther, the Protestant medical doctor and politician dr. Leimena: they are all praised for their strong religious personalities. We must read these positive judgements within the perspective of the time: the gloomy expectations after the struggle for independence, 1945-1949, when Muslims and Christians were united in the ideal of the new nation. Here the North-Americans are praised too, while the Dutch only are criticised because during the colonial period they had tried to establish the idea of Islam as a backward religion, not suited for modern times (ibid.:143).

3   SIDE-WAY: THE SPIRITUAL QUEST OF HAMKA'S BROTHER WILLY AMRULLAH

Hamka had a younger half-brother who had migrated to the United States, and had adapted his name as Willy K. (Karim) Amrullah (adapted from his earlier name of Abdul Wadud). Willy/Wadud had settled in San Francisco before 1952 and accompanied his brother when Hamka was in California.[3] On 10 June, 1981, one month before Hamka passed away, Willy was baptised a Christian in Bali. Since then he has been active as a Christian preacher and minister, occasionally in Indonesia. The conversion to Christianity of this brother of one of the most famous Muslims of Minangkabau has caused much trouble.

---

[3] Photograph in Empat Bulan di Amerika, I,40. See also Hamka, Ayahku, Jakarta: Jayamurni, 1967, 224-224. More information about this travel and also the later development of Amrullah in the "Open Letter by the Rev. Willy K. Amrullah", August 2, 1999, in English translation published through www.geocities.com/athens/ Acropolis /1082/ Rac_Padg.htm

Willy's conversion was not the only incident in Minangkabau, related to Christian mission. In the 1950s North-American Baptists built a hospital in the town of Bukittingi. In the 1990s a Bible translation into the Minangkabau language (by many people considered only a dialect of Malay or common Indonesian) brought much criticism from the Muslims. All Minangkabau people can understand the common Indonesian language and therefore are able to use these translations. The Minangkabau translation was considered an act of aggressive proselytism because of the close connection between this language/dialect, the local culture and Islam The number of converted Minangkabau people remains small: about 100 out of 2 million Minangkabau people in the original Indonesian province and some 400 living in other provinces of Indonesia or abroad. Yet some leaders try to suggest that the overall Islamic character of Minangkabau society is threatened by the Minangkabau translation of the Bible.

After the fall of President Suharto in May 1998, protests against corruption and army control of the country have called for greater autonomy of the provinces. For the Minangkabau province of West Sumatra, this autonomy could most easily be realised by the introduction of Islamic law or *shari'a* as the local law. Its introduction in 2000 has caused trouble. In this strongly Islamic region, for centuries there had been many exceptions to Islamic rulings. Best known was the exceptional position of women. Land ownership in Minangkabau was passed on exclusively to the female heirs. Much of trade was also in the hands of women who freely went out to markets early in the mornings in order to be there at sunrise, at daytime, and late into the evening. All this would be prohibited by the introduction of the *shari'a*. The defenders of the proposal to introduce the Islamic law neglected these feminist issues and stressed the danger to the Islamic character of Minangkabau represented by the 'aggressive' Christian missionary activities. The issues of the hospital built by North-American Baptists, the Bible translation and the activities of the North-American Minangkabau minister Willy Abdul Hadad Karim Amrullah were used by Muslim leaders to start an anti-North-American and anti-Christian campaign of mobilisation against a danger that in the eyes of outsiders was much exaggerated.

4   ABDUL MUKTI ALI IN MONTREAL, 1955-1957

Abdul Mukti Ali was born in 1923 in Cepu, East Java. Unlike Hamka he was not born in a family of Muslim clerics. While Hamka's father was an independent religious teacher, with a rather large school, Mukti Ali's father was a rich trader who could afford to send his son to a European style school, the Dutch-language HIS, *Hollandsch-Indische School*, followed later by a secondary school, the proper education to become an official in the colonial administration. In 1940, after Mukti Ali finished that part of his education, he was sent to an Islamic school, the college (pesantren) of Termas, 180 kilometers from Cepu. The strict discipline in the closed compound should lead this eager student to the knowledge of the sacred sciences. In August, 1945, the nationalist spirit permeated the Pesantren of Termas and Mukti Ali enrolled in the military ranks of the Hizbollah, to fight against Dutch colonialism. His father objected to this activity: "I sent you to Termas not to become a soldier, but to study, to become somebody."[4] So Mukti Ali attempted for a time to pursue his studies while also assuming some political tasks in the Blora District as a representative for a reformist political party. After the struggle for independence, Mukti Ali performed the *hajj* in 1950 and then went to Karachi to pursue higher Islamic studies. He obtained a PhD, specializing in Islamic History. Through some of his professors in Karachi, but also by way of some of his former Indonesian contacts, Mukti Ali learned about the initiative of Wilfred Cantwell Smith to open a department of Comparative Religion and Islamic Studies at McGill University in Montreal. At the beginning of the fall term of 1955 he enrolled at McGill, where he obtained his MA in 1957. The sequence of his academic pursuits may sound odd to Westerners and has at times been debated. But it is also a sign of the great difference in style and mutual appreciation between religious studies in the East and the West.[5] Although Mukti Ali only stayed for two years in Canada, this was the most important and decisive part of his intellectual formation as a religious scholar spanning some seventeen years. The lasting influence of his Canadian experience can be seen in the following.

Mukti Ali came back to Indonesia from his formative travelling to become the founder of the chair of comparative religion at the first institute of academic study of Islam in a modern style in Indonesia, opened in Jakarta in 1957. This institute was later transferred to Yogyakarta to eventually become the IAIN, *Institut Agama Islam Negeri* or State Institute of Islamic Studies. Mukti Ali broke with the normative and apologetic style that dominated the classical tradition of comparative

---

[4] From the biography by Mukti Ali written by several of his younger students, in Widyakusuma 1993, 24. See also Ali Munhanif 1996: esp. 89.

[5] The conservative opponent of Prof. Mukti Ali in Indonesia, Prof. Muh. Rasjidi in several articles doubted the academic degree of Doctor for Mukti Ali. This was continued by Ali Munhanif 1996:123 note 13.

religion in Islam, introducing a number of elements from his Canadian courses. One of his favourite ideas was the close link between the "spirit of puritanism and the rise of capitalism" as described by Max Weber. Mukti Ali hoped to establish a link between reformed Islam and a prosperous and economically strong Indonesia. In this sense he admired Canadian and North-American society. He also hoped to renew the scientific spirit in Muslim societies. When he was invited to deliver a speech on the occasion of the Prophet's Ascension in the mosque of the President's palace in Jakarta on 2 January, 1962, his subject was the harmony between "Faith and Science". The speech is a fierce attack against a unproductive and even harmful apologetic that avoids the real problems and seeks only emotional satisfaction. For the solution of the question Mukti Ali referred to Dutch Protestant Dick Mulder, at that time a lecturer in philosophy and comparative religion at a Protestant college and the Gadjah Mada State University of Yogyakarta.[6] For Mukti Ali inter-religious cooperation was needed first of all for a prosperous Indonesia. Muslims should seek science from the most developed countries of the world. That was similar to seeking science in the West.

In order to develop a religious tradition that would be in harmony with this modern development, Mukti Ali wanted to expose the elite Islamic thinkers of his country to Western culture and science. He was nominated Minister of Religion for the period 1971-1978. At the end of his period as a minister he succeeded in starting a programme of cooperation between the Dutch and Indonesian governments. In September 1978 he was able to send the first group of ten lecturers from the State Institute of Islamic Studies from Jakarta, Yogyakarta and other places to Leiden for a confrontation with "orientalism". In his opinion, Muslim scholars in Indonesia could not compete with intellectuals in other fields like science, medicine, social science and economics if they studied only in traditional Muslim centres like Mecca, Cairo or Baghdad. In secular fields all prominent specialists of his country had for some time pursued education in Europe or America. The religious elite would be considered backward if they could not use the same language and academic culture as their secular colleagues. Therefore he sought development projects, financed by the Dutch, Canadian and other Western governments. The programmes initiated by Mukti Ali were quite successful. Today a number of students are still involved in similar programmes in Leiden at the

---

[6] Dr. A. Mukti Ali 1969, reference to Mulder on p. 31. For other references of Mukti Ali to apologetic see B.J. Boland 1971:225-230.

INIS, *Indonesian-Netherlands Cooperation in Islamic Studies.*[7] In 1987 a similar programme involving more fellows was started in Montreal at McGill University, where every year between 15 and 20 graduate students for religious studies were accepted.[8] Smaller programmes were set up in France, in the United Kingdom at the SOAS in London, at several universities in the United States (involving Fulbright fellowships) and in Australia. By 2000, a majority of those who held the top of academic positions in Islamic theology had benefited from the experience of at least some years of study in a non-Muslim country in the West.

Before the start of these programmes, in 1978, besides Mukti Ali, scores of Indonesian Muslims had pursued degrees in McGill. The most prominent probably were Dr. Harun Nasution, rector of the Islamic Institute (IAIN) of Jakarta and A. Timur Djaelani, secretary general of the Ministry of Religion. There were so many McGill graduates in the higher echelons of the religious bureaucracy, that some people in the early 1980s talked of "McGill Mafia" in Indonesian Islam.

Mukti Ali stimulated renewal in Islamic thinking and considered contact with Western science as a very important method. He even stimulated the idea of an academic discipline of Occidentalism as an equivalent of Orientalism. As scholars from the West had acquired their knowledge about eastern societies, so Mukti Ali believed Muslims should make serious study of the western societies and develop a branch of knowledge that could be labelled Occidentalism. One major contribution in this field was done by Mukti Ali himself in a book written about Muslims in America (Mukti Ali 1990).The book was partly the result of a visit to America in July-August 1986, where he visited the Islamic Center of Washington and Hartford Seminary Foundation. Yvonne Haddad's studies on Muslims in Canada and the United States, besides information from the magazine *The Bulletin of the Islamic Center*, Washington D.C. are the major sources for this book.

Mukti Ali never developed a comprehensive theory or view on modern Islam. He remained quite eclectic. In the words of a young student who wrote in his diary in early 1970:

---

[7] For a list of the 49 Indonesian Muslim scholars involved in programmes in Leiden between 1969 and 1988, see *INIS News Letter* Vol 1, 1989:5-9. In the 1990s about 100 scholars followed programmes in Leiden.

[8] Fifteen graduates from McGill published *Pengalaman Belajar Islam di Kanada* [Experience of Studying Islam in Canada, by Yudian W. Asmin (ed.), 1997].

Throughout [Mukti Ali's] intellectual career in Indonesia, as a Muslim scholar, he seems not to have had a strong desire to integrate his contradictory ideas. Mukti Ali, if I may describe him, is a thinker in the process of transition, but, unfortunately, he lets the transition itself go on for ever. Therefore, he looks like a person who has put one foot across the bridge but left the other behind. This is because he does not realize that transition has to evolve (beyond the) contradictions. Oh, (pity) the man who experiences contradictions, but does not try to solve them.[9]

These are words written by a radical and impatient student who died shortly after writing them. They show both the strength and weakness of the contacts made by Mukti Ali. He saw the importance of the new ideas collected in Canada, but was not able to integrate these into a comprehensive unity.

Alongside the fascination of Mukti Ali for fresh ideas from the West, there remained a firm frontier, not to be crossed: that of missionary efforts of Christians. In this field, Mukti Ali, like Hamka, remained open as long as he did not feel threatened and was accepted as an equal to Western Christians. But as soon as he became aware of anything that looked like proselytising, he could become staunch and angry. In 1972, as Minister of Religion, he was invited to give an address to a National Christmas Ceremony. Mukti Ali, who had joined several meetings of the World Council of Churches,[10] accepted the invitation (different from Hamka in 1981, when this participation was considered as forbidden or *haram*). Besides many friendly words, Mukti Ali also made clear where the boundaries were:

It is impossible to convert someone who has embraced a religion, or to leave one's religious belief to embrace another religion by compulsion or by offering material gifts. It is unworthy to exploit the weakness of the uneducated, the sick and the young to embrace a certain religion... It is unworthy as well for religious people like us to try to convert a person by attacking his religious belief and duties.[11]

In this matter Mukti Ali differed absolutely from his Yogyakarta colleague and long-time Chairperson of the Interfaith Programme of the World Council of Churches, Dr. Dick Mulder. The latter considered Islam and

---

[9] From the diary of Ahmad Wahib 1984:63.

[10] Mukti Alli attended a.o. the following meetings, organized by the WCC: Ajaltoun, April 1970, Broumana, July 1972; Colombo, April 1974; cf. Stuart Brown 1989:18, 28, 46.

[11] Quoted after Munhanif 1996:109.

Christianity both as missionary religions that had the duty to preach their message and even to develop programmes and strategies for this active and missionary preaching. Hamka and Mukti Ali saw the basis for the relation between the two religions to be not a missionary approach, but a mutual recognition. Finally, both missed this honest and true recognition from the Christian side, at least from missionary circles.

5   FREQUENT TRAVELLERS

Above we have analysed two prominent modern Indonesians and the impact of their contact with North-American and Canadian society. They are just a few of many others. Religious transition proceeds not only through missionaries moving from one land to another. Often the believers themselves are actively incorporating new ideas. The quest for religious knowledge has always been a major reason for frequent, intense and long travelling. In Indonesian religious history this began during the Hindu and Buddhist periods, when many Indonesians travelled to India to study at religious schools. In the theories of conversion of Indonesia to Hinduism and Buddhism, these Indonesian students are now considered more important than Buddhist monks or Hindu sages who went to Indonesia from other foreign countries. The same phenomenon can be observed after the first encounter with Muslims. After the arrival of Islam, Indonesians no longer went to India, but to the countries of the Middle East, most of all to Mecca and other towns of the Holy Land, in search of knowledge (Steenbrink 1988). After 1910, Cairo became the most popular place for Indonesian Muslim students to seek knowledge. But since the 1950s Western countries have been the favourite place of study, also for Islamic sciences. This has caused some tension with Cairo graduates in Indonesia (Abaza 1994).

In 1984, *Prisma*, the most prominent journal of socio-economic science in Indonesia, published a special issue on young Muslim scholars. One third out of the twelve examples of promising Muslim scholars had pursued their studies in the United States.[12]

---

[12] Ahmad Syafi'i Ma'arif, now chairman of the Muhammadiyah; Amien Rais, now speaker of the united two chambers of parliament, and general chairman of the Muhammadiyah (until 1998); Nurcholis Madjid, Kuntowijoyo.

6   A GLOBAL CLASH OF RELIGIONS?

One of the most difficult questions in the long debate about inter-religious conflicts, is the definition of a religious conflict: is it economic, political, social, personal or 'religious'? What conclusions can be drawn from the biographies and personal experience, sketched above, most of all, from the Muslim experiences with America and North-Americans?

First, we must take note that non-religious social affairs like economics and politics are part of the complex pattern of inter-religious sensitivity that leads to conflict. But much also depends on personal factors. Some people may just change their opinion in different situations. They may find some situations suitable to be exploited for political or strictly personal gain. Under some personal conditions, relations may be easier to establish than might otherwise be the case. Many Muslims show genuine openness when they are studying in Western countries (especially when they are receiving more or less generous fellowships or subsidies from people in these countries). A difficult question is how in this case the relation between giver-receiver can be maintained as a balanced and equal relationship. Sympathy cannot be bought and a humiliating generosity never will create a true friendship. In our examples we did not meet any overt example of a negative side effect of this kind of generosity.

Secondly, we might question whether there is any special impact of the North-American style of Christianity in Indonesia. The Portuguese Catholics were the first to establish Christian communities. They were suppressed by Dutch colonialism that fiercely opposed any work by Catholic priests during the period 1605-1808 and turned the new Christians into Protestants in the Moluccas. After the 1830s, some Germans were allowed to preach in Borneo-Kalimantan and later in the successful Batak mission in Sumatra. Only after 1930 did North-American missionaries arrive, representing mostly Evangelical and Pentecostal traditions. Several Christians who were questioned by me about this matter openly confessed their opinion that Evangelical and Pentecostal Christianity usually is more exclusive and more negative towards Islam than mainstream Christianity. Therefore the recent increase of problems between Christians and Muslims in Indonesia seems to be related by them to the growing presence of this "North-American-style" Christianity in the country, especially on the island of Java. Today it is estimated that about half of the 6.5% Protestant Christians in Indonesia belong to an Evangelical or Pentecostal denomination. Most Muslims have a vague idea about the difference between Catholics and Protestants. But they have little understanding of the differences between classical or mainstream and evangelical Christianity. However, in the Moluccan conflict this difference did not play any role. Therefore I do not see any specific role played by "North-American Protestantism" in the recent conflicts between Christian and Muslims.

Third, in *The Clash of Civilizations*, the North-American social scientist, Samuel Huntington, suggests that major clashes between political or religious rivals will occur on the edges or border-regions of their spheres of influence. Our examples above suggest rather that religious leaders are ready to start complaints and conflicts when national governments are weak. When political leadership fails or is ostensibly weak, religious leaders may see this as an opportunity to enhance their influence, authority, and grip on their communities.

Fourth, whatever the case or circumstances, Muslims are willing to give up missionary claims if they are recognised as a religion with equal rights and value as that of Christians. The idea that there could be an agreement on the issue that both Islam and Christianity are missionary religions is not a very realistic and fruitful one. Both Christianity and Islam need to give up the pretension to some kind of world hegemony. It would be very good if both quite clearly and repeatedly professed the idea that they have given up the idea of ruling the world or the dream of an exclusive religious superiority. Power and authority over the world belong only to God. To Him is the Judgement.

BIBLIOGRAPHY

Abaza, Mona. (1994). *Indonesian Students in Cairo*. Paris: Archipel.
Asmin, Yudian W. (ed.). (1997). *Pengalaman Belajar Islam di Kanada* (*Experience of Studying Islam in Canada*). Yogyakarta: Titian Ilahi.
Azra, Azyumardi. (2000). "The Race between Islam and Christianity theory revisited. Islamization and Christianization in the Malay-Indonesian archipelago 1530-1670". *Documentatieblad voor de Geschiedenis van de Nederlandse Zending en Overzeese kerken* 7 . Pp. 26-37
Boland, B.J. (1971). *The Struggle of Islam in Modern Indonesia*. The Hague: Nijhoff.
Brown, Stuart E. (1989). *Meeting in Faith*. Geneva: WCC.
Hamka (1954). *Empat Bulan di Amerika* [Four Months in America]. Jakarta: Tintamas, 2 Vols.
—. (1950). *Pribadi*. Jakarta: Bulan bintang 1962. 6th edition.
—. (1967). Ayahku. Jakarta: Jayamurni.

Mukti Ali, H.A. (1969). *Bagaimana Menghampiri Isra' Mi'radj Nabi Besar Muhammad s.a.w. atau Iman dan Ilmu Pengetahuan.* (*An Approach to the Miracle of Muhammed's Ascension or faith and Science*). Yogyakarta: Nida.

—. (1990). *Muslim Bilali and Muslim Muhajir di Amerika Serikat. (Bilali and Muhajir, Black and Immigrant Muslims in the USA*). Jakarta: Haji Masagung.

Munhanif, Ali. (1996). "Islam and the Struggle for Religious Pluralism in Indonesia: A Political Reading of the Religious Thought of Mukti Ali". *Studia Islamika* 3. Nr.1. Pp. 79-126.

Norman, Daniel. (1960). *Islam and the West. The Making of an Image.* Edinburgh: Edinburgh University Press.

Steenbrink,Karel. (1994). "Hamka and the Integration of the Islamic Ummah of Indonesia." *Studia Islamika* Vol I/3. Pp. 119-149.

—. (1998). "Indian Teachers and their Indonesian Pupils. On Intellectual Relations between India and Indonesia 1600-1800". In: *Itinerario* 1. Special Issue: *The Ancien Regime in India and Indonesia.* Pp. 129-141.

—. (2002). "Another Race between Islam and Christianity: the Case of Flores. Southeast Indonesia, 1900-1920". *Studia Islamika.* Pp. 63-106.

Wahib, Ahmad. (1984). *Pergolakan Pemikiran Islam. (The Struggle for Islamic Thinking*). Jakarta LP3ES.

Widyakusuma, Abdurrahman (ed.). (1993). *Agama dan Masyarakat. 70 Tahun H. A. Mukti Ali.* Yogyakarta: IAIN Sunan Kalijaga Press.

19 *Kevalaṃ Khiṭṭhassa puññena mutti* (Salvation through the Merit of Christ Alone):

An Attempt to Translate the Central Theme
of Protestant Christianity into the Language of
Theravada Buddhism

Rein Fernhout

1   INTRODUCTION

The theme of this chapter has to do with the question of how to preach
Jesus Christ within the context of other religions. On the one side we
need to avoid the Scylla of a Gospel which becomes unintelligible because the idiom of that other religion is not taken into account. On the
other side we encounter the Charybdis of *traduttori sono traditori*: the
Gospel is adapted to such a degree that it can no longer be called Gospel.

I once made an attempt to steer clear of both this Scylla and this
Charybdis in the concrete context of a dialogue with Thai Buddhists,
among whom were some monks.[1] With concepts from Theravada
Buddhism, as adhered to in Thailand, and terms borrowed from its
church language (i.e. Pali, nearly cognate with Sanskrit). I tried to make
clear what salvation by Jesus Christ means to us, without "buddhizing"
this salvation. The aim of this attempt was not in the first place immediately a missionary one. My primary aim at the time was to give them
some understanding of the central theme of Protestant Christianity. But
who does not become something of a missionary when matters of ultimate concern are at issue?

In this paper I shall try to explain the significance of Jesus Christ for
Christians, using as my starting point the Buddhist concept *puñña*, a
term which is generally translated by 'merit'. *Puñña* is a very important,
if not the most important concept in the daily lives of Buddhists.
Christianity, however, contains something conceptually analogous to the
term *puñña*. In the sixteenth century the Protestant branch of Christianity separated from the Roman Catholic Church. The reason for this separation can be described as a conflict concerning merit. The place of Jesus
Christ in salvation was the central issue in this conflict. Over against
Roman Catholicism, Protestantism connected merit with the person of
Jesus Christ alone. I realize that this sounds rather enigmatic to Buddhist

---

[1] At the Mahidol University, Salaya, Thailand, June 1991.

ears, but I hope to make clear how this exclusive connection between
Jesus Christ and merit came about and what the consequences are for the
daily lives of Protestant Christians, insofar as they live according to the
classical Protestant tradition.

I will begin by exploring the concept *puñña* in Theravada
Buddhism, after which we will treat the analogous concept in Roman
Catholic doctrine. I will then look at the break the monk Martin Luther
(1483-1546) made with Roman Catholic teaching; this break is the origin of Protestant Christianity. In the end I will draw some conclusions
concerning the function of *puñña* in Theravada Buddhism and Protestant
Christianity.

2   *PUÑÑA* IN BUDDHISM

I realize that trying to define the nature of a Buddhist concept such as
puñña without being a Buddhist oneself, is hazardous. In the first place,
there is the risk of imprecise formulations due to incomplete knowledge.
Moreover, the concept *puñña* is not only a matter of doctrine but above
all something that is experienced in everyday Buddhist life. As a consequence, it undoubtedly possesses shades and overtones which a religious
outsider will not recognize and even find difficult to comprehend. It is
quite possible that even if my formulations are as such flawless
Buddhists may not recognize themselves in them, because the formulations lack the emotional value that for them is indissolubly connected
with *puñña*. I hope they will correct my observations in both cases: that
of imprecise formulation and that of the lack of emotional value.

Puñña, to my thinking, can be defined as the positive lasting quality
of a human act; lasting because the quality remains after the act is finished. Such a positive lasting quality causes happiness in the future, especially in a following existence. The opposite of *puñña* is *papa*, a word
that can be translated by 'sin'. *Papa* is the negative lasting quality of a
human act and causes unhappiness in the future. The nature of one's
rebirth is dependent on the proportion of *puñña* to *papa* acquired during
preceding life. When *puñña* dominates one will be reborn into a better
existence; if *papa* tips the scale one's next life will be worse.

It is possible to transfer the acquired *puñña* to another person. King
Mongkut wrote an impressive poem about this:

> May the *puñña* made by me now or at some other time
> be shared among all beings here infinite, immeasurable;
> those dear to me and virtuous as mothers or as fathers are,
> the seen and the invisible, others neutral, hostile too;

beings established in the world upon three planes, of four kinds of birth,
of five, one or four constituents, wandering in realms small and great,
my *puñña*-dedication here
having known, may they rejoice
and those who do not know of this,
may deities announce it to them.
By rejoicing in this cause, this gift of *puñña* given by me
may beings all forever live
a happy life and free from hate,
and may they find the Path secure
and may their good wish succeed![2]

This possibility of transference of the positive lasting quality of one's
act to another strikes a modern Westerner as very strange. For modern
Western consciousness every person is a more or less isolated individual
who should bear the responsibility for his or her own acts. The quality
of an act reflects only upon the agent of the act and cannot be transferred
to another nor can another receive it from someone else. The Buddhist
concept of *puñña* is at variance with such modern individualism. According to Buddhists, transference of *puñña* is possible even to different
categories of beings, including the spirits of the dead. After the ordination of a *bhikkhu* (monk) or *samaṇera* (novice) the congregation sings:
"Just as the rivers full of water fill the ocean full, even so does that here
given benefit the dead."[3]

Puñña is acquired in various ways. The most productive field from
which *puñña* can be reaped, however, is the monastic order, the Sangha.
The Sangha is called *anuttaraṃ puññakhettaṃ lokassa*: 'the incomparable field of *puñña* for the world'. That is one of the reasons why the
Sangha occupies such a central position in the life of Buddhist laity. The
Sangha offers the most eminent opportunities to earn *puñña*. This earning of *puñña* can take place, if I understood it properly, in two ways:
actively and passively. One acquires *puñña* in an active way by doing
something for the Sangha or giving something to the Sangha. For instance, one can give monks food or one can collect money for the building
or enlargment of a monastery. *Puñña* is passively received by means of
the blessings which flow from the Sangha, for example, during
preaching and in a number of ceremonies.

---

[2] Text and translation from Somdet Phra Mahā Samaṇa Chao Krom Phrayā
Vajirañāṇavarorasa 1973:72. King Monkut (1851-1868) had been a monk before he
became king.

[3] Vajirañāṇavarorasa:77.

Ultimate salvation in *nibbana* (Sanskrit: *nirvana*), however, is not acquired by *puñña*. *Puñña* belongs to the sphere of ignorance (*avijja*), which is characterized by the chain of cause and effect. *Puñña* itself is affected by an act and it is the cause of rebirth into a better existence. Ultimate salvation, however, consists in the complete fading of ignorance and the breaking of the chain of cause and effect.

By way of summary we can say, that *puñña* is the positive lasting quality of human acts. As such, *puñña* is the cause of rebirth into a better existence. *Puñña* can be transfered to other persons, even to the dead. The Sangha is the most important field where *puñña* can be harvested, actively and passively. But it is impossible to reach *nibbana* by means of *puñña*.

3   *MERITUM* IN ROMAN CATHOLIC DOCTRINE

The word *puñña* is usually translated into English by 'merit'. This word is of Latin origin: it is the English form of the Latin word *meritum*. Latin was the church language of the Roman Catholic Church, as Pali is the church language of Theravada Buddhism. Roman Catholic doctrine includes the concept *meritum*, which bears a remarkable resemblance to the Buddhist *puñña*. I do not know whether this resemblance is the reason behind translating *puñña* as 'merit', but this translation is in any case fully justified.

Like *puñña*, *meritum* can be described as the positive lasting quality of a human act, over against sin as the negative lasting quality. Christianity does not teach the idea of *samsara* as the cycle of births but does, indeed, teach existence after death. According to Roman Catholic thinking, the nature of that existence was dependent on merit acquired during one's life on earth. There were three possibilities in this respect. A person who had committed sins so serious that his eventual merit paled into insignificance beside them went to hell. Those who had excelled in merit, so that their sins were fully compensated, entered heaven. Most people, however, had earned too little merit to go directly to heaven and too much merit to be condemned to hell. They therefore went to the purgatory where their sins were expiated under horrible vexation. The expiation could take a very long time. In an earlier stage of Roman Catholic history it was said that this could sometimes take millions of years, but in the end one was granted entry into heaven.

One's stay in heaven, in contrast to the Buddhist view, is not a transitory but a permanent state. Therefore, one's entry into heaven can be compared with the attainment of *nibbāna* in Buddhism, which is also permanent. Some years ago I saw in a Sri Lankan newpaper two mourning notices, one beneath the other, of two boys, one Christian and one Buddhist. The first notice expressed the hope "Till we meet in Heaven with Jesus." And the second, "May you attain Nibbana".

According to Roman Catholic doctrine, some people had earned more merit than they themselves needed to reach heaven. These were the saints, whose surplus merit could benefit others. Thus the notion of transference of merit can be found in Christianity as well as in Buddhism. However, in Christianity such transference occurred in a different way. Merit was not transferred directly but through the medium of the Church.

The Roman Catholic Church was charged with the disposal of the treasure of merit, which had been left by the saints. It could distribute this merit among those who had done something good for the Church: for instance, those who had given money to the Church. Like the Buddhist Sangha, the Church was in a certain sense "the incomparable field of merit for the world." The Church distributed the merit by means of so-called indulgences, which made it possible to reduce one's punishment in purgatory. Persons could use the indulgence for themselves or they could use it for a deceased relative who was supposedly in purgatory. Thus, as in Buddhism, transference of merit to a deceased person was possible. The concept merit transcends the separation between the living and the dead. This, however, did not obtain for people in hell; their sins were so serious that no indulgence could help.

This transference of the surplus merit of saints was, however, subordinate to an entirely different kind of transference of merit. This concerns the pre-eminent place of Jesus Christ in Christianity. Jesus Christ is the Son of God who became human to expiate human sin on the cross. Through his death and resurrection He acquired inexhaustible merit, which could benefit others entirely, because, being without sin, Jesus Christ did not need merit for himself. Roman Catholic doctrine teaches that the merit of Jesus Christ is also distributed by the Church, especially by means of ceremonies known in Christian terminology as sacraments: holy acts, such as baptism and the Lord's Supper. There is quite a difference between this sacramentally distributed merit and that of the indulgences that were mentioned above. The latter effected only reduction of punishment, whereas the sacraments enable people to gain their own merit. Due to the inexhaustible merit of Jesus Christ, the sacraments are fountains of divine energy, by means of which the believer is able to do meritorious works. The total amount of merit earned by these works determines whether one goes to heaven or to purgatory. If the merit is nullified by very serious sins, the so-called deadly sins, then nothing other than hell is left.

What are those meritorious works? Roughly speaking, we can reduce them to the same denominator: love. I realize that in a Buddhist environment the word love can very easily arouse misunderstanding. Discussing this matter here would take us too far afield. Misunderstanding can be avoided if we bear in mind that the Christian concept love should not be translated into Pali by *kama* but by *metta*. It is not emotional or sensual love, but, in agreement with one of the translations of *metta* in the dictionary of Rhys Davids and Stede, "active interest in others." Merit is earned by works of love to God and to one's neighbour.

In the beginning of the sixteenth century, however, many people felt that, notwithstanding the use of sacraments, they were lacking in such love, especially in love to God. Therefore they chose to enter the monastery in order to become a monk or a nun. They expected that they would be in a better position in the monastery to lead a holy life full of love. By means of such a holy life they hoped to earn the merit that would open the gates of heaven, if not immediately after death then after a comparatively short stay in purgatory. Monks and nuns were, we may say, super merit-makers.

Thus the concept merit played a great role in classical Roman Catholic thinking, a greater part still, strictly speaking, than in Buddhism. In Buddhism it is impossible to reach ultimate salvation in *nibbana* by means of *puñña*. In Roman Catholicism, however, to enter heaven is the ultimate salvation for humans and the acquired merit enables a person to enter heaven. According to Roman Catholic doctrine, the transference of merit was possible in two ways and in both of them the Church was the indispensable medium. By means of indulgences the extra merit of the saints was distributed to reduce punishment in purgatory. These indulgences could be obtained for deceased relatives as well. In the sacraments the merit of Jesus Christ was communicated to believers as a kind of divine energy by means of which they could gain their own merit in deeds of love to God and to the neighbour. Those who wanted to dedicate their whole life to this became monks or nuns.

4   MARTIN LUTHER AND THE RISE OF PROTESTANTISM

The name of Protestantism suggests that this branch of Western Christianity originated in a protest movement. It did, in fact, but the name as such was due to another reason which has no direct relation to our subject. Protestantism began with a conflict between Martin Luther and the Roman Catholic Church. For a better understanding of this conflict it is necessary to relate something of the biography of this man. Luther was a German who, as a young man, went to university to study law. He was not only gifted intellectually but musically as well; the Protestant churches owe many hymns to him. During his study he experienced a severe religious crisis. As to his own conscience, he lacked so much merit that he despaired of ever entering heaven. It seems that the sudden death of a friend made a very deep impression on him. At the same time, on the way back to the university from his home, Luther travelled through a forest in which he was surprised by a heavy thunderstorm. Terribly frightened, he made a vow to become a monk. As we saw above, the monastery was the pre-eminent place for an person to gain merit.

For Luther, however, monastic life turned out to be a bitter disappointment. Exert himself as he would, he could not get rid of his feeling of despair that his merit added up to nothing and that he was much too sinful to have any hope of salvation. The existential deadlock at which he arrived can best be illustrated by the tension that is present between the concepts merit and love, by means of which merit was to be acquired. The Buddhist concept *metta* is defined as active interest in others. As stated above, the same definition could obtain for the Christian concept love. Interest, however, in others—God or human beings—is not to be combined with longing for merit, for then one's interest is not in others but in oneself. As a matter of fact, love for another is meritorious, but not if one's aim is to gain merit for oneself, for then it is no longer love. The problem becomes twice as serious if love for God is the issue. Luther observed that it was impossible for him to love God. True love for God does not require merit and if one desires merit, one does not truly love God. In the monastery Luther was confronted with this irresolvable question. Luther saw his own sinfulness as the reason why this problem could not be resolved: he was too sinful to be able to love God without longing for merit.

Amid his distress, a breakthrough took place in Luther's life. Explained in terms of the concept merit, this breakthrough was a fully new understanding of the significance of the inexhaustible merit of Christ for a sinful human being. The Roman Catholic Church taught that with the help of the merit of Christ the believer was able to gain his own merit. In the monastery Luther discovered that he did not succeed in earning sufficient merit—indeed, that he never would be able to do this. As a sinful person, he always would remain stuck in the opposition between merit and love. However, he gained new insight into the merit of Jesus Christ. When Jesus Christ died on the cross there was a radical exchange between Him and sinful human beings. He took over their sins: that was why He had to die. Thus he gave them his merit. This merit is so all-encompassing that it does not enable sinful people to gain their own merit but gives them eternal salvation. The way in which, according to Luther, a human being receives this merit is through faith (*saddha*), i.e. personal confidence in Jesus Christ. Therefore Luther and, with him Protestantism, teaches that a human being is not saved by his own merit but by 'faith alone'. This expression may be translated into Pali by '*kevalaya saddhaya*'.

I want to illustrate the impact of Luther's discovery by means of part of a letter he wrote to a fellow monk, who had moved to another monastery. Some Pali equivalents are added between brackets. In this letter, however, the central concept is not so much merit (*puñña*) as righteousness (*dhammikatta*). Therefore, some explanation is needed first. According to Roman Catholic doctrine merit is the converse of righteousness. When a person possesses merit he is righteous and, conversely, when he is righteous he possesses merit. Looking for one's own righteousness, the subject of the letter, is tantamount to looking for one's own merit, as the monks especially were wont to do. Luther says the following to his fellow monk:

For the rest I should like to know how it is with your spiritual state. Have you had enough of your own righteousness (*sakad-hammikatta*) at last and have you learned to trust in the righte-ousness of Christ (*Kiṭṭhassa dhammikatta*) drawing new life from that? In our days the temptation to pride comes upon ma-ny people like a violent fever, especially those who are eagerly striving for righteousness and virtue. But they are fully ignorant (*avijjabharita*) of the righteousness of God which is given to us abundantly and for nothing in Christ. Therefore they are trying to do good works (*dhammikani kammani*) through their own strength for so long that, adorned by virtue (*sila*) and merit (*puñña*), they will have the joyful confidence of being accepta-ble to God. This, however, is not to be achieved by any means or in any way. When you were with us, you lived in this fallacy too—more correctly, in this delusion. I myself was ensnared in it as well. At the moment, however, I'm fighting against this delusion, but I have not yet brought the fight to an end.

Therefore, my beloved brother, take your refuge in Christ (*Kiṭṭham saraṇa m gaccha*),[4] namely in the crucified Christ! Learn to sing his praise and to despair of yourself. And say to Him: Lord Jesus, You are my righteousness (*dhammikattam mam' asi*) and I'm your sin (*papam tava 'mhi*). You took over what was mine and gave me what was yours. You received what you were not and gave me what I was not.

Beware of striving for such a blameless life that you do no longer want to appear a sinner in your own eyes—indeed to be a sinner altogether. For Christ lives among sinners only. He came from heaven, where he lived with righteous people, to take up his residence among sinners as well. Consider this love of his again and again and you will experience the very swee-test comfort of that. When we could achieve peace of conscien-ce by our own troubles and vexations, why then did He die? No, you will find peace with Him only by despairing of your-self and your own works; in this you surely will not be without comfort! Moreover you will learn from Him, that as He accep-ted you and made your sins his sins, so He made his righteousness your righteousness as well.[5]

---

[4] Compare the first part of the *tiratana* (Three Jewels) or *tisaraṇa* (Three Refuges), the Buddhist 'confession of faith': I take refuge in the Buddha (*Buddham saraṇam gacchimi*), I take refuge in the Dhamma (Sk. Dharma), I take refuge in the Sangha.

[5] Transl. from Luther, *Letters* I:35).

So far Luther. The letter shows a bewildering radicalism which in later Protestantism has not always been maintained. The idea that the merit of Christ is the impulse for earning one's own merit often returned, even though the word merit was not always used. With Luther no room is left for one's own merit. The merit of Christ is all.

Anything that a person could add to this would detract from the merit of Christ. This merit can only be received by faith and is destined for sinners, that is, for those who realize that they are wholly without merit. A believer therefore remains a *bhikkhu* all his life, not in the later sense of monk but in the original meaning of mendicant, a person who has to receive everything from another—in this case from Jesus Christ. When Luther died a scrap of paper was found close to his deathbed, on which the following words were written: "We are mendicants; that is true (*bhikkav' amha, taṃ saccaṃ*)!"

It is not difficult to guess what the criticism was that broke upon Luther and those of his way of believing, even up to now. If someone no longer has to earn merit, why would he exert himself any longer to do good? This reproach is, alas, not without foundation. Some do, indeed, embrace Luther's doctrine as a ready excuse for spiritual laziness. Of such people, however, it must be said that they clearly do not understand what it is to be wholly without their own merit and to be allowed to live on the basis of the merit of Jesus Christ. In a text booklet produced by some Protestants somewhat later than Luther we read the following question and answer: Question: Does not this teaching make people careless and sinful? Answer: No, for it is impossible for those who are ingrafted into Christ by true faith (*saccaya saddhaya*) not to bring forth the fruit of gratitude.[6]

True faith makes the believer grateful. The Pali word for gratitude is *katavedita* (literally: consciousness of what has been done). *Katavedita* makes what is at issue more clear than the English 'gratitude': the believer is conscious—not so much intellectually as existentially—of what Christ has done for him of her. Such gratitude can no longer strive for merit, for how could I desire my own merit when Jesus Christ has merited all for me? It does, however, produce fruits: the believer shows God and other people his or her gratitude.

What is new in the teaching of Luther is not that Jesus Christ died for sinful people, but that He expiated *all* sin and that sinful people can find *all* the merit they need in Him alone. This radicalism had consequences for every point of Roman Catholic doctrine that was discussed

---

[6] Heidelberg Catechism: Q.& A. 64

above. Indulgences based on the surplus merit of the saints became superfluous and even impossible. Purgatory disappeared, because the sins for which Christ died need not be expiated again. Deceased believers are with Jesus Christ and no longer need remission of punishment. Hell remained, but hell is less a punishment for deadly sins as the consequence of unbelief, that is, refusal to accept the merit of Christ. The sacraments obtain a quite different function. They no longer serve to grant divine energy for acquiring merit, but to strengthen faith in Jesus Christ. Monastic life had lost its purpose for Luther: he left the monastery and married. In the meantime the Roman Catholic Church condemned the ideas of Luther and excommunicated him. This was the beginning of Protestantism as a separate branch of Christianity.

5 PROTESTANT CHRISTIANITY AND THERAVADA BUDDHISM

We saw that in contrast to the modern individualistic conception of humankind, the possibility of the transference of merit from one person to another can be found in Buddhism as well as Christianity. Christianity knows the reverse possibility too, namely, the assuming of another's sin upon oneself. I did not find this last possibility in Theravada Buddhism, but perhaps there are examples in the stories of the Bodhisattva (future Buddha) from the Jatakas.[7] The peculiar characteristic of Protestant Christianity is that both possibilities are due exclusively to Jesus Christ. In Him both belong indissolubly together as well: because He expiated the sins of others, He earned inexhaustible merit for them. We share in this merit through faith (*saddha*) alone.

Concerning the relation between ultimate salvation and merit or *puñña* there is a profound difference between Theravāda Buddhism and Protestant Christianity. According to Protestant Christianity salvation is achieved through merit, though not through the merit of the believers themselves or of deceased saints but through that of Jesus Christ alone. Ultimate salvation for the Theravada Buddhist lies on the other side of the opposition between *puñña* and *papa*. *Puñña* may grant a person the highest attainable bliss in *samsara*, a place as a divine being in heaven, but never *nibbana*.

This leads to the following consideration. With Luther we observed a tension between merit and love. In principle, to my thinking, this tension is present in the relation between *puñña* and *metta* as well. This is not to deny by the fact that many Buddhists as well as many Christians are

---

[7] Stories about former lives of the Buddha (very popular among Buddhists).

not always or perhaps never conscious of this tension. One person, however, for whom this tension does not hold, or in any case holds much less, is the Buddhist monk. For it is not his intention to earn merit but to reach *nibbana*. Therefore his *metta* and the conveyance of *puñña* can be entirely pure, for he does not need merit for himself. The same purity of love we find with Jesus Christ, although for quite different reasons. As the sinless Son of God, He did not require any merit for Himself. The merit of his expiation of sin is entirely destined for sinful human beings.

As I remarked at the beginning of this paper *puñña* plays an important part in Buddhist daily life. The analogous concept merit has been even more important for Christianity as well in doctrine and in life. In the daily life of Protestant Christians, however, it lost its significance, at least ideally. I hope that I have made clear what the reason for this is. In view of the unique merit of Jesus Christ one's own merits had to give way for 'fruits of gratitude (*kataveditaya phalani*)'.

6   CONCLUSION

How did the Buddhists react to my lecture? As far as I can remember, it resembled to some extent the reaction of the Athenians to Paul's address on the Areopagus. There was an exchange of courtesies, some questions were asked and that was all. To be honest, I had not expected much more. The setting was not suited for that. Nevertheless, one hopes that something of the *mysterium fascinans* of the Gospel has been left behind.

On rereading my paper it strikes me that I used the Roman Catholic Church at that time to a large extent as the dark side in order to shed light on the radicalness of salvation through Jesus Christ alone. On the other hand I myself am much more dependent on the medieval theologian and philosopher Anselm than many present-day Protestants will appreciate. In both cases I described classical positions. The same goes for my description of Theravada Buddhism: it is the classical form as adhered to in Thailand. There is, however, a modern existential and hermeneutical interpretation of Buddhism, initiated by the monk Buddhadasa, which has gained much impact in Thailand. A dialogue with adherents of this new interpretation should not start with Luther but with Rudolf Bultmann.[8] This would require a totally different setting. Possibly Roman Catholics and Protestants of the more conservative type both would

---

[8] The striking similarity between Buddhadasa and Bultmann is pointed to by Louis Gabaude, *Une herméneutique bouddhique contemporaine* 1988: 385-389. It is the more remarkable as Buddhadasa in all probability knew nothing about Bultmann.

even discover that they themselves feel more affinity with classical Theravada Buddhism than with 'bultmannian' Christianity. Modern age brings along its reshuffles!

BIBLIOGRAPHY

Gabaude, Louis, *Une herméneutique bouddhique contemporaine de Thaïlande: Buddhadasa Bhikkhu.* (1988). Paris: École Française d'Extrême-Orient.
Heidelberg Catechism.
Jackson, Peter, *Buddhadasa: A Buddhist Thinker for the Moderne World.* (1988). Bangkok: The Siam Society
Luther, Martin. *Werke, Briefe* 1. (Weimar edition).
Vajirañanavarorasa, Somdet Phra Maha Samana Chao Krom Phraya, *Ordination Procedure.* (1973). Bangkok: King Maha Makuta's Academy.

PART VI

THE CHALLENGE OF ECUMENICAL RELATIONS

20 Liberative Ecumenism at the African Grassroots

Marthinus L. Daneel

1 INTRODUCTION

Jerald Gort and I have shared strong interests in ecumenism ever since the time we studied and later worked together at the theological faculty of the Free University of Amsterdam. As an outstanding scholar in missiology, Jerry studied and published on this subject as it evolved in the context of the World Council of Churches and international ecclesiastical developments. By way of contrast, my own interests were geographically limited to the situation of Zimbabwe where I attempted as a White African and missiological activist to engage in an ecumenical ministry at the grassroots for and with the African Initiated Churches (AICs).

Despite the difference in approach, there was a way in which our ecumenical endeavours were complementary and mutually beneficial. Jerry's depth of insight and well-defined theological orientation enabled me to evaluate more accurately and critically the complex ecumenical processes in which I was involved in the field. And my trial and error attempts to foster African Initiated Church (AIC) ecumenical leadership opened a window for him in Africa, and an excuse to occasionally escape the rigours of Western indoor academia and briefly exchange them for the vibrant celebration of life of the AICs under the African sun.

I was privileged to found and direct for some time two ecumenical movements in Zimbabwe. The African Independent Church Conference, called *Fambidzano yemaKereke avaTema*, (lit.: Cooperative of Black Churches) in Shona, was the first ecumenical movement of African Initiated Churches in Zimbabwe. Established in 1972, it focused mainly on the provision of theological education by extension (TEE) and on socio-economic development work for the benefit of the AICs involved. ZIRRCON (Zimbabwe Institute of Religious Research and Ecological Conservation) founded in 1988, is a religiously based earthkeeping institution encompassing a massive "green army" composed of a traditionalist unit, called AZTREC (Association of Zimbabwean Traditionalist Ecologists), which includes large numbers of chiefs, tribal elders, headmen, and senior spirit mediums; and a Christian unit, named AAEC (Association of African Earthkeeping Churches), which has a membership of some 180 AICs. ZIRRCON represents a combined force totaling some two million adherents. On the whole, ecumenism in the Fambidzano context entailed collaboration between Christian churches. By way of contrast, ZIRRCON's earthkeeping endeavours added a dimension of mutually approved and sustained interaction between African Christian and non-Christian (i.e., African traditional religious) counterparts. The latter type of ecumenism, though not less meaningful, is obviously more complex and in some respects more controversial than the former. The liberative dimension in both types of interfaith encounter will be featured in this paper.

Through a number of visits to Zimbabwe, Jerry familiarized himself with the emergent patterns of ecumenism over an extensive period of time. During these visits, as a representative of the Free University of Amsterdam and the Protestant Dutch mission councils (Gereformeerd and Hervormd), both of which sponsored the Zimbabwe venture, Jerry patiently observed TEE classes at outlying extension centers, attended meetings with Fambidzano leaders, and spent hours with me discussing developments in the new movement. I could not have wished for a better-qualified and dedicated ecumenical envoy to assess the work in the field and report back to the sponsoring institutions abroad. In this paper I am in a sense still reporting to the Dutch agencies whose substantial investment in an AIC mission in Africa enabled me to develop a rewarding lifetime ministry beyond all early expectations.

In presenting a few brief reflections on the ecumenical nature of this ministry, I am paying tribute not only to a respected fellow ecumenist and friend but also to the leadership of these institutions for providing the required resources. Had it not been for the generous support of the Free University and the African Studies Center in Leiden, I would not have had the opportunity to live among the Shona Independents for nearly three years from 1965 to 1967. This period of research provided me with the necessary insights into the needs of the AICs and the network of contacts with AIC leaders which formed the platform for launching Fambidzano. Subsequently, both the Free University and the Reformed mission councils of the Netherlands subsidized the budding AIC movement in Zimbabwe. In later years ZIRRCON was funded mainly by EZE (*Evangelische Zentralstelle für Entwicklungshilfe*) in Germany, with additional grants made by the Dutch embassy in Harare. I salute all these institutions without whose support the chapter on AIC ecumenism in Zimbabwe's twentieth-century ecclesiastical history could not have been written.

It is fitting that the caption of this paper, which signals my ongoing discourse with Jerry on AIC ecumenism, is similar to the one he used for an essay entitled "Liberative Ecumenism: Gateway to the Sharing of Religious Experience Today" (1992). In this essay Jerry searches for an entrée to interreligious sharing of experience. He proposes that "an eminently promising means of bridging this gap [between religions] and of discovering possible areas of overlap of religious experience is the practice of liberative ecumenism, i.e., interreligious cooperation and identification with the poor" (ibid.:88). It is no coincidence that two of the major components implicit in the proposed agenda for liberative ecumenism, namely interreligious cooperation and identification with the poor, were also focal points in the two Shona grassroots movements: Fambidzano and ZIRRCON. For, although the same terminology was not necessarily prominent in the policy and development of these movements, the liberationist thrust was clearly in evidence in the collaborative encounter of diverse religious partners in the achievement of common objectives and the empowerment of the poor to initiate and con-trol their own interreligious endeavour.

Given the valuable insights developed in Jerry's reflections on "liberative ecumenism," it seems appropriate that I start with a brief discussion of the salient features in his essay before I attempt an evaluation of these African grassroots movements through the ecumenical perspective he provides.

2   GORT'S THEORETICAL CONSIDERATIONS

In a discussion of the modes and dynamics of sharing, a distinction is made in the underlying theology of religion between the two extreme positions of inclusivism and exclusivism. The former assumes that all religions are essentially the same, ruling out the possibility of ultimate revelational particularity and thus eliminating the principle of fundamentally or constitutionally diver-gent religious identity. The latter fails to recognize the saving presence of God throughout all the world in that it ignores the telling teachings of many religions. These views are mutually exclusive and preclude meaningful inter-religious sharing (ibid.:93). To avoid the impasse of these extreme positions Gort suggests a form of theologizing which incorporates the more flexible concept of religious "distinctiveness" as proposed by Kenneth Cragg. This concept allows more generous scope for the similarities and differences between religious faiths than does "uniqueness," inasmuch as the latter qualification, as usually employed, leaves little or no room for "overlap of meaning and experience between faith-concerns" (ibid.:94). An acknowledgment of the "distinctiveness" of religions allows for the various dimensions of sharing distinguished by Gort: participation, witness, and conversion. In this connection he contends that José Miguez Bonino's telling observation concerning interaction between Christian denominations, namely, that "plurality may not be sacralized at the expense of coherence," while "coherence must not be sacralized at the expense of diversity," is equally applicable to interreligious relations (ibid.).

A condition for meaningful interreligious sharing lies in the genuine nature and authenticity of the religious experience of the partners concerned. Rootedness in the Eternal, as opposed to satanic or idolatrous encounter, remains a yardstick in this field, which cannot be compromised. "The quest for full sharing," adds Gort,

> ought to be viewed as valid between and among religions whose beliefs and practices demonstrate that they "contain dreams of the new order and a new humankind, which are both a vision and motivating force" [Dornberg, 112] for the lives of their adherents (ibid.:95).

Moreover, the articulations of the sharing faith-partners should reveal their understanding that the final purpose of divine revelation is the reflection of light into the world so that darkness may be overcome.

As for the motives and aims of interreligious sharing, the main objective, as in all religious activity, lies in honouring God. Gort singles out a deteriorating global situation in which all religions share responsibility for the dividedness of human communities, a division that precludes world peace, justice, and the integrity of creation. Herein lies the penultimate aim and motive of religious sharing. He contends that "in the new situation of globalized pluralization all have a shared responsibility for defining those terms [i.e., peace, justice, integrity of creation] and for combatting injustice, division and enmity, and the shameless exploitation of nature" (ibid.:98).

Dialogue and mission represent two of the major responses of religion to the needs of the contemporary world. Within Christianity, those who con-sidered dividedness as the more urgent challenge tended to advocate dialogue as solution. In turn, those who identified poverty and the brokenness of humanity as priority opted for mission with its liberative thrust and gospel for the poor as prime task. Gort argues, however, that both options were based on a flawed hermeneutic. Dialogue did not pay sufficient attention to the poverty of the majority of religious believers, while mission neglected the religiosity of the poor. Instead of the two strategies operating autonomously or interrelating only in unresolved tension, they should, according to Gort, interact in a mutually beneficial manner.

> Dialogue must allow itself to be thoroughly informed by the liberative thrust of mission in the realization that justice is the ultimate aim and purpose of communication.... Likewise, mission must let itself be shot

through with the communicative thrust of dialogue in the awareness that religion lies at the basis of liberation (ibid.:101).

At this point Pieris is quoted as saying: "No true liberation is possible unless people are 'religiously' motivated toward it" (ibid.).

The insight that "mission cannot be properly exercised in the absence of dialogue" was developed largely within the context of the missiological reflection that emerged from the consultations of the Ecumenical Association of Third World Theologians (EATWOT) since about 1985 (ibid.). To achieve a new methodology that integrates dialogue and mission, an orientation is required which allows "cooperation with those religions or movements within religions that have a liberative aim and force" (ibid.:102).[1] This new approach, says Gort, can appropriately be called "liberative ecumenism." The positive potential of the hermeneutic implicit in this methodology is such that Gort suggests, as a practical implication, the merging of the two departments in the World Council of Churches dealing respectively with dialogue and mis-sion into one division of Liberative Ecumenism.

Gort qualifies the envisaged ecumenism in terms of cooperative relations between people of different faiths, identification with the poor, and interreligious involvement in movements of creativity, innovation and renewal. A degree of risk is involved here because this ecumenism requires that stagnant discourse based on so-called "objectivity" or "neutrality" be replaced by living and working together. But it is only in this way that an existential situation can be achieved which engenders fresh understanding and shared impulses for renewed dialogue. From a Christian view the main condition for participation in interreligious innovation remains commitment to the ministry and gospel of Jesus Christ. In this connection Gort interprets Samartha's assertion that "Christ is at work wherever people are struggling for freedom and renewal, seeking for fullness of life, peace and joy," as follows:

> If a religious movement or praxis has a genuinely liberative thrust toward human justice and peace, Christians may feel free to align themselves with it and seek to relate to it in the form of cooperative participation, even though in doing so they will have to take "certain risks" and might "not know where [they] are being led" [Samartha, 243].... [And] joint interreligious praxis among and on behalf of the poor will yield not only the enhancement of a greater measure of justice but also an increase of communication and understanding (ibid.: 103).

---

[1] See also Mbiti's essay in this volume.

3   INTERCHURCH (AICS) AND INTERFAITH (AICs AND AFRICAN TRADI-
     TIONAL RELIGION) ECUMENISM AT THE AFRICAN GRASSROOTS

This brief chapter covering more than 30 years of ecumenical endeavor
(18 years in Fambidzano and 15 years in ZIRRCON) obviously cannot
incorporate a full evaluation of the wide range of ecumenical activities
involved. Moreover, the autobiographical dimension that inevitably
pervades this account as a result of the leading role I played as founder
of and full participant in both movements, introduces elements of subjectivity which may subtly distort aspects of the overall picture. Other
theologians and church historians may well judge the AIC ecumenism in
Zimbabwe of the past few decades in an entirely different light than I do.
The privilege I was afforded throughout most of my working life to
partake in an enriching ministry among African Independents and traditional religionists necessitates the sharing of insights, particularly if such
sharing relates to a friend and colleague whose ecumenical pilgrimage
so meaningfully interacted with mine.

    If nothing else, my observations below will illustrate an uneven
passage in the formation of African ecumenism. The trial and error
process I was involved in reflects something of the difference between
the activity of neat theological formulation (often wrongly seen, as Gort
argues, as the sole arbiter in the process of defining the parameters of
ecumenism) and the challenging, if unpredictable, praxis of living and
implementing ecumenism in Afri-can rural society. Bengt Sundkler and
Harold Turner, the trailblazers of AIC studies in South and West Africa
respectively, tried to dissuade me from engaging in such ministry. They
were familiar with the failures of early attempts to unite AICs and argued that the independent nature of AIC leader-ship was bound to form a
near insurmountable barrier. Thus, I was aware from the outset of the
odds against AIC ecumenism. But after three years of experiencing the
generosity and support of the AICs for my field research, I was strongly
motivated to give them something meaningful in return.

3.1 Interchurch ecumenism

In 1972, when I began visiting AIC leaders and office-bearers with
proposals for an ecumenical movement, they had little or no educational
background or experience to help them interpret all the ramifications of
ecumenical interaction. The kind of sophisticated theological discourse
based on the polarized positions of inclusivism versus exclusivism, as
described by Gort, was of course nonexistent in the rural village context
where the AICs were operating. The majority of AIC leaders were barely literate, had received little schooling and, with a few exceptions, had

no theological training in a Western sense. Most were subsistence farmers, owning hardly any literature apart from their Bibles and some hymnals. Excepting a few impressive church headquarters with schools, church buildings and/or clustered healing centers, the bulk of AICs had only small buildings or extended huts for churches, with a few Bible texts painted on the hut of a bishop, as indicators of AIC administrative centers. Poverty-ridden homesteads of small-scale farmers did not have telephones. Communication by mail was sporadic. As a result, sustained contact with the rural AICs in Zimbabwe required endless travel, much of it over badly rutted dirt roads. Thus, during the first year of preparatory talks with individual leaders, group consultations and conferences leading to the formation of Fambidzano (Daneel 1989:30), I lived for long periods of time in rural villages.

Resistance to ecumenism was generated by group attitudes of exclusivism. AIC leaders feared that they could jeopardize their positions in relation to their followers if they were seen in an interchurch situation to compromise on issues that touched on the very identity of their churches. In a field of intense religious competition there was uncertainty about the impact of the proposed ecumenism on ingroup loyalties and cohesion. Processes of out-reach and group formation hinged largely on solidifying internal identity via criticism of rival church groups. Thus the Spirit-type churches (Zionists and Apostles) were inclined to look down on the Ethiopian-type or non-prophetic movements (the First Ethiopian Church, the African Reformed and African Congregational Church, etc.) as "non-Christian" because of their so-called neglect of the Holy Spirit. The Ethiopian type churches, in turn, accused the Zionists and Apostles of aligning themselves to ancestral and demonic spirits rather than to the Holy Spirit of the Bible. In both instances the Christian nature of the churches concerned was called into question.

Even within those churches that shared the same features, such as the Pentecostal-oriented Spirit-type churches, the claims of founding leaders in group-consolidating traditions over the years tended to set trends of exclusivism. Thus the visionary experiences of Johane Maranke, founder of the largest AIC in Zimbabwe, the African Apostolic Church of Johane Maranke, became the center of widely held Apostolic claims that this church is the only divinely sanctioned church of Christ in the country, if not in all of Africa. Johane was said to have been transported to heaven where he was commissioned directly by Christ to establish His true church in Africa. In like manner, Bishop Samuel Mutendi, founder of the Zion Christian Church in Zimbabwe, became known as "man of God" to his followers, in his case, too, in consequence of divine legitimation. In this instance the leader claimed a divine calling through dreams and performed numerous healings and successful rain requests in the name of the Christian God. To many of his followers God was nowhere more truly present than at Mutendi's headquarters, Zion City. It is not surprising, therefore, that when Johane Maranke and Samuel Mutendi met to see if they could find common ground for cooperation, they came to the conclusion that they did not serve the same Holy Spirit, whereupon they parted company.

Against this background it was clear to me that the development of inter-AIC ecumenical ties, the move from inward-looking exclusivism (which according to Gort "fails to recognize the saving presence of God throughout all the world") to a more tolerant and open-ended distinctiveness within participant churches, would amount to a long-term up-hill effort. The challenge in the first year was to persuade at least some of the churches to join the envisaged movement. Fortunately, I had built friendships of mutual trust with most of the AIC leaders during the preceding period of research. The publi-cations I brought with me from The Netherlands, books with their own histories and pictures, persuaded the AIC leaders that our joint efforts to record the development of their churches had not been in vain. One bishop, when he saw his own picture next to the historical sketch of his church in one of the books, sighed with relief and said: "Now I can die in peace because the world out there will know and recognize me." Another important factor was that I was not employed by any of the local mission churches, so my endeavours could not be interpreted as an attempt by any of the so-called mainline churches to gain control over the AICs. Despite some lingering suspicions about my motives in AIC quarters during the preparatory phase, the majority of the AIC leaders accepted at an early stage that I had returned to work for and with them. The new movement was to be seen as an independent entity, owned and run by the AICs themselves. Those were the conditions I negotiated with the sponsoring Dutch mission agencies in recognition of AIC autonomy and the sensitivity of these churches to any form of mission-church interference or manipulation.

The main objectives of the envisaged ecumenical body were: (1) that it would provide much-needed theological education for the AIC leadership; and (2) that it would provide a platform from which member churches could acquire respect and recognition from the mainline churches. It was clear at the time that these were major considerations for the first twelve, mainly Zionist and Ethiopian-type churches which joined hands in forming Fam-bidzano during the first major conference held in

July, 1972. The delegates of many more AICs attended, but they wanted time to reflect on the matter and seek consensus in their own churches. Thus, far from starting on a large scale, the working out of Fambidzano's constitution, the establishment of a TEE program, and the development of an administrative center were under-taken by a small core-group of churches, who called themselves the "Fam-bidzano pioneers,"and myself. Hesitation and suspicion in the non-affiliated AICs was overcome over time as the comprehensive benefits of ecumenism unfolded. A groundswell of recruitment then followed, until the movement peaked with an overall membership of some 90 churches.

In an attempt to safeguard the Christian nature of Fambidzano, specific conditions for membership were constitutionally defined. In order to qualify a church had to: (1) be based on the word of God (both Old and New Testaments); (2) believe in God the Father, Jesus Christ His Son, and the Holy Spirit; (3) practice baptism in the name of the triune God; (4) practice holy communion; and (5) have a church council to deal with disciplinary issues. Evident in these conditions are the Reformed *notae ecclesiae*. The implementation of these conditions by prominent AIC leaders in Fambidzano's executive board opened a new chapter among the AICs. Leaders of formerly opposing Spirit-type and Ethiopian-type churches were now required to evaluate other AICs applying for membership. These criteria represented a deeper level of theological reflection than the old prejudices of the past that revolved around Holy-Spirit manifestations. At this point the isolationist and exclusivist traits in participant churches started to break down as the search for an overarching ecumenical identity gained momentum. That the AIC leaders of the fledgling movement, despite their attempts to achieve greater interchurch tolerance, were serious about safeguarding the Christian nature of their new venture was reflected in the deliberate exclusion of Mai Chaza's *Guta raJehovah* (City of Jehovah) Church. It was felt at the time that Mai Chaza's posthumous integration with the God of the Bible, as propounded in a church handbook, was an unacceptable aberration of the understanding of the triune God of Scripture.

The sustained experience of meaningful interaction was more important for the elimination of the barriers of exclusivism between the Fambidzano churches than the theological search for scriptural, doctrinal and sacramental equivalence. Through regular annual conferences, administrative board meetings, participation in TEE classes on a weekly basis, regular visits to member churches by the Fambidzano president and a host of spontaneously organized interchurch worship ceremonies, an interactive exposure took place that contributed to the development of mutual responsibilities between leaders, women and ordinary church members. As new friendships were forged and new projects were launched, introspective claims of religious uniqueness and superior custodianship of biblical truths receded into the background for each participant church. In the annual graduation ceremonies involving hundreds of students, TEE tutors, and AIC supporters from a host of churches, it became particularly clear that the focus had shifted from introspective churchism to an emphasis on the African churches, including the Western-initiated mission churches whose members were also participating in the TEE and correspondence courses. Service within God's Kingdom through advanced church leadership, spiritual growth, women's advancement and socio-economic uplift superseded the narrow preoccupation of individual leaders with their own ecclesial kingdoms. When Bishop Gavhure, leader of the First Ethiopian Church and widely respected president of Fambidzano, passed away, for instance, a leadership succession ceremony in his church to install his successor son, Ishmael, was conducted by the leaders of a large number of both Ethiopian-type and Spirit-type churches. What formerly would have amounted to an intimate ingroup ceremony in a specific church became an ecumenical event with wide-ranging inspirational sharing in Fambidzano's ranks and consolidation of leadership in the bereaved church.

Events of this nature did not signal a relativistic trend in terms of individual church identities. But the growing tolerance and respect between churches rendered unnecessary an insistence on ingroup uniqueness. The change in interchurch attitudes, although not subject to precise theological definition in Fambidzano circles, was indeed a move away from doctrinal rigidity toward the recognition of group distinctiveness, the acknowledgment of ecclesial pluriformity in the participant church communities. This pluriformity contributed toward enrichment and creativity in sharing rather than conflict and withdrawal. What Gort postulates as essential for ecumenical theologizing was being acted out in at least a rudimentary fashion at the African grassroots by the AICs.

Positive as the ecumenical undercurrent in the bonding of Fambidzano member churches tended to be, the process was by no means ideal or without flaws. Leadership jealousies and squabbles over finance flared up from time to time. Invariably, when internal cohesion was threatened by dissent, the necessary effort was put forth to assure the preservation of unity. The ecumenicity we shared hinged to a large extent on significant non-theological factors like friendships that remained steadfast during crises and the preparedness to risk crossing new frontiers when there were no guarantees of success, i.e., the willingness to operate on the basis of trial-and-error. At bottom, we clung in faith to the words of John 17:21-23, which we chose as cornerstone for our movement. As Christ prayed for his disciples to be united so that the world could see and believe in his mission, so we grew in the conviction that our unity in acceptance of his Lordship mandated Fambidzano's mission of equipping member churches for growth in self-interpretation, Bible knowledge, holistic ministry and the work of extended outreach in witness to the world so that it might see and believe that Jesus is Lord.

3.2 Interreligious Ecumenism

When it came to the development of ecumenical ties between the AICs and practitioners of African Traditional Religion (ATR) in the ZIRRCON context, the obstacles of exclusivist attitudes, isolationist religious rituals within the two camps, and rivalry for the religious allegiance of potential members were even more daunting than the inter-AIC antagonisms referred to above. The Ethiopian-type churches were more lenient in allowing their members to occasionally attend traditional rain rituals in honour of the senior tribal ancestors or to visit a traditional doctor (*nganga*), even if such visits implied the prescription of ancestral veneration for a cure. But the Spirit-type churches on the whole forbade all forms of ATR participation, publicly rejecting on all counts ancestral veneration and the high-god cult as incompatible with Christianity. Deliberate attempts were made to replace all key traditional rituals— such as the home-bringing *kugadzira*, which elevates the spirit of the deceased into ancestorhood; the *mukwerere* rain rituals; the rain requests at the high-god cult shrines of Matonjeni; and traditional healing praxis, including exorcism and dealing with wizardry—with Christianized parallel ceremonies within the church. By replacing the roles of the traditional doctors (*nganga*), spirit mediums (*masvikiro*) and high-god cultists with the inculturated ministries of healing prophets, the Zionist and Apostolic churches were relating the good news of the Gospel at an existential level in African society, where it interacted forcefully with the deeper vestiges of indigenous worldviews and cosmologies. In this respect the Spirit-type churches provoked stronger reactions from opposing traditionalists than did the mainline mission churches. The latter's rejection of traditional belief systems and customs as heathenism was often not strongly backed by contextualized internal church ministries that could serve as an attractive alternative to ATR. Consequently, the members of mainline churches seemed to be more inclined than those of the Spirit-type churches to lead a double religious life, attending church events as recognized Christians, but reverting to traditional religion in times of individual affliction or family crises.

One of the bitter interreligious conflicts between AICs and traditionalists, which lasted many years, was that between Bishop Samuel Mutendi of the Zion Christian Church and the *Mwari* cult in the Matopo hills. The Zionist bishop posed a direct threat to the traditional oracle's influence in the central south-eastern regions of Zimbabwe. Not only did Mutendi successfully supplant the annual rain-request ceremonies at the shrines of the Shona high-god with Zionist rituals, leading many tribal chiefs to shift their allegiance from the traditional cult to the Zionist church, but he also publicly denounced the core of ATR as satanic. During a paschal service in 1965, for instance, Mutendi called on his audience to reject the old religion:

> [A] family under Satan's guidance [referring to *Mwari* cult and ancestral veneration] has no peace. You must therefore cast away all that was prac-ticed by your forebears. They believed in and worshipped their ancestors. This kind of worship is the same as believing in demons. Cast away all these things and believe in Him who is in heaven (Daneel 1970:65).

Mwari, the Shona high-god, retaliated with oracular reprimands. Soon after the bishop's pronouncements were reported at the Matonjeni shrines, *Mwari* told the senior cult messenger from Bikita district (where Mutendi's Zion City was situated),

> You people of Bikita believe in Mutendi's power to make rain. I do not like this and I shall send but little rain for the next six months. If you want rain, go and ask Mutendi! Let us see if he succeeds. I will punish the people [with droughts] because the Zionists call me Satan! (ibid.: 69).

Not all the Spirit-type churches were as radical as Mutendi's ZCC in their condemnation of the god of Matonjeni. The robed *Ndaza* Zionists of the Holy Cord, for instance, provoked less bitter comments from the Matonjeni shrines than did Mutendi. Nevertheless, the Zionists generally were considered more disruptive of traditional beliefs and customs than other churches. Consequently it was not uncommon during the 1960s to hear complaints from the high-god shrines and from conservative traditionalists that "the Zionists disrupt the known order" (*vaZioni vanoputsa nyika*: literally "the Zionists break up the land/country"). Given this tradition of interreligious conflict, how was it possible to forge a breakthrough and move from antagonistic exclusivism toward collaborative distinctiveness? Some of the major factors that conditioned this process were the following.

First, the years of liberation struggle *(chimurenga)*, 1965-1980, saw some of the religious barriers break down between Christians and traditionalists. The cause of liberation from the yoke of colonialism, fueled by a rising African nationalism, required united action. Cadres of guerrilla fighters were composed of traditionalists and Christians who fought side by side in a com-mon cause. Zionist and Apostolic prophets found themselves collaborating during *pungwe* meetings (political night vigils) with traditionalist *masvikiro* (spirit mediums) in the search for traitors to the cause and the protection of innocent individuals who faced the threat of death in heated situations rife with false allegations. Conditions in the war front were far from homogeneous, however. Some *vaPostori*, for instance, were forced by guerrillas to drink sacrificial beer and venerate the ancestors in direct violation of their church laws. Quite a few AIC members were martyred for refusing to burn their Bibles or stop worshipping Jesus Christ, whom some guerrillas branded as the God of the white oppressors. Despite such diversity, *chimurenga* had in a sense set the stage for traditionalist-Christian ecumenism, especially in contexts of national or regional crisis that required the transcendence of petty religious rivalry and prejudice.

Second, my research program in the mid-1980s on the role of religion in the *chimurenga* struggle enabled me to identify with spirit mediums, *Mwari* cultists, and former guerrilla fighters under rather unusual circumstances. Together we visited the *poshitos* (observation posts) and mountain hide-out caves they had used during the struggle. From those positions we looked down on the "lost lands" that had been recovered politically from the colonial powers through Independence but which, through overuse and deforestation, was ecologically as "lost" as before. It was here, in the mountains of Zimbabwe that we started to share the suffering of an afflicted creation, the urgency of the needs of the earth-community for remedial action. It was here that we started sharing resolve to act, to engage in a new *chimurenga* which in due course was to be appropriately called "the war of the trees." Once I reciprocated by inviting some twenty spirit mediums, most of them *chimurenga* veterans, to come and stay for a weekend at my house in Masvingo town, the first phase of Christian-traditionalist breakthrough toward ecumenical interaction began in earnest. For twenty rural spirit mediums to converge on an urban home in their traditional attire, including skins of wild animals, ostrich plumes as headgear and battle-axes and spears as symbols of warfare, was quite unusual. But the commitment and determination of these earthkeepers-to-be prevailed over any religious and cultural prejudices that may have existed. A constitution for the militant new green movement, initially called the Association of Zimbabwean Spirit Mediums, was drafted. A basic strategy for tree planting, wildlife conservation and the protection of water resources, in terms of African traditional worldviews and conservationist praxis, was adopted. The first appointment of a leading spirit medium, Lydia Chabata, as nursery keeper was made, a move which in due course led to the cultivation of some 17,000 seedlings in my backyard. This became our first nursery that led to numerous tree-planting ceremonies by a growing band of traditionalist earthkeepers throughout the communal lands of Masvingo Province.

Third, interfaith ecumenism was born in liberative ecological action from the outset. My home-based research offices became the movement's first headquarters, with my research staff, several of whom were Zionists, forming the core of administration and planning alongside their traditionalist counterparts. Despite a degree of dependence on my fundraising activities and catalytic input toward united action, the spirit mediums, chiefs, tribal elders and ex-guerrilla combatants retained sufficient initiative to expand and consolidate a fast-growing movement. Significantly, their confidence and experience as earthkeepers grew over a period of three years prior to the formation of the Association of African Earthkeeping Churches (AAEC) as their Christian counterpart. Against the backdrop of Fambidzano's wide-ranging projects and influence in the preceding years, it was psychologically important to the traditionalists at this point to hold the advantage as trailblazers and trendsetters in the new earthkeeping struggle. Thus, the numerical advantage of the AICs as they came in as a green force, many of them already steeped in a tradition of Christian ecumenism, did not pose a serious threat to the cohesion and internal equilibrium already achieved by the cadres of AZTREC.

Fourth, the overt enthusiasm of the AICs for the pioneering contribution of the traditionalist earthkeepers and their willingness to look beyond the rivalries of the past toward a united cause went a long way toward alleviating fears of religious incompatibility and strife in the ecumenical endeavour. In the initial encounter as fellow earthkeepers the traditionalist leaders certainly did not treat their Christian counterparts as intruders in their coveted field of action. The AIC bishops, in turn, welcomed the tree-planting chiefs and spirit mediums as expert green advisers during the meetings preceding the formation of the AAEC.

The move from religious exclusivism toward cooperation-friendly distinctiveness was not the result of careful theological planning and definition, of conference proceedings with meticulously drafted documents or preplanned progress based on clear-cut guidelines. Rather, it

was more a visceral thing, rooted in mutual trust and goodwill and shared unquestioned love for the land. The spirit-mediums were convinced
that *Mwari* (to them both the God of the Bible and the pre-Christian
Creator of Africa) was guiding me and eventually also the AICs to commit to the new struggle, and I was equally convinced that they themselves were genuinely prepared to respond to what they considered the
promptings of their guardian ancestors of the land (*varidzi venyika*) to
restore the denuded earth. Religious consensus was not set as condition
for meaningful cooperation between the traditionalist and Christian
partners. Instead, consensus regarding the nature of religious ecumenism
grew out of mutual trust and respect in interpersonal relationships as
new patterns evolved for joint engagement in earthcare.

3.3 Requirements for Interreligious Sharing
According to Gort, authenticity of religious experience as a condition for
multifaith sharing should be "rooted in the Eternal," as opposed to deliberate "satanic or idolatrous encounter." In addition, the religions of the
sharing partners should, he says, reflect awareness ("dreams") of belonging to a new order in which divine revelation inspires people to counteract darkness and evil by radiating light and truth in society.

Even though these characteristics of authentic religious experience
were not in all respects explicit in the deliberations preceding ecumenical sharing in the Fambidzano context, they were inherent in the evol-
ving process of AIC ecumenism. For the participant churches, rootedness in Scriptures meant rootedness in the Eternal. Fambidzano's ecumenism was a response to Christ's call to mission and unity. The context
and inspiration for such response was the Kingdom of God, a theme that
repeatedly featured on the agenda of Annual General Conference meetings. Improvement of scriptural knowledge through theological education, with its resultant benefits for church leadership and church life, was
considered to be the work of God's Kingdom. Progress in the new dispensation included a holistic approach that not only targeted spiritual
improvement but also intensified the struggle against poverty and injustice through community development, income generation and water
distribution.

To assess the traditionalist counterpart's "rootedness in the Eternal"
in the ZIRRCON context was obviously a more complex matter than
establishing common ground among the Scripture-oriented churches of
Fambidzano. Sustained contact and friendships over many years between myself and numerous traditionalists (*Mwari* cultists, spirit mediums, *nganga* doctors and tribal elders) enabled me to integrate to a large
extent my own theological viewpoint of ATR as a product of God's

general revelation with empirical observations of African religion. Unlike the more rigid Barthian theology that could find no trace of Christ in non-Christian religions, I had little difficulty in viewing ATR as a manifestation of the fact that the universal God, the God of Scriptures, has not left Himself without witness throughout the entire world. To me this viewpoint did not imply religious relativism but rather the obligation to relate the good news of the Gospel to the religious world of Africa in a meaningful way .

What impressed one from the outset about the core-group of spirit medi-ums in our earthkeeping movement was that they shared an overriding sense of dedication to the new religio-political dispensation of independent Zim-babwe. They had dreamt their dreams about and fought for the liberation of the lost lands in a struggle which had as goal the establishment of a just society, free from the yoke of colonialism. Moreover, they were fully prepared to extend the *chimurenga* of yesteryear into the realm of earthcare, to engage in the new struggle of protective liberation of God's creation. There was no satanic intent in the constructive mobilization of traditionalist forces toward earthcare. Thus the conditions for interfaith ecumenism, as envisaged by Gort, were in some ways being met from the outset.

It should be pointed out, however, that initially the urgency of environ-mental destruction and our determination to fight it overrode to a large extent any religious prejudices that may have been present. There was simply no time to attempt the achievement of full consensus on the details of religious interaction, save for the basic facts that we were prepared to face the environmental challenge together and that we agreed on a form of collaboration which would include mutual respect for each other's religious traditions and identity. One had no illusions about the divide between Christianity and African Traditional Religion and about the frictions and misunderstandings that this could generate. The risks of controversy, of churches objecting to far-reaching identification with traditionalists, of accusations from Christian quarters that the Christian faith could be compromised by so-called religious syncretism, of traditionalists misinterpreting Christian collaboration with them as a form of endorsement of all aspects of their religion, etc., were inevitable. There was simply no way of resolving all these and other anticipated problems in advance.

In light of the burning conviction that ultimately all God's people, irre-spective of race, culture or religion, share responsibility as keepers of crea-tion, it was more important to move into environmental action despite the potential risks involved than to accept inertia in anticipation of possible roadblocks ahead. Thus, mutual "rootedness in the Eternal' was not an explicit prerequisite for joint endeavour in the area of earth-keeping. Nevertheless, the experience of such rootedness grew once the partners began responding consciously to the promptings of the wise African sages of the past and a biblically related divine commission, behind both of which they sensed something of the mysterious movement of God's Spirit.

4   MOTIVES AND AIMS OF INTERRELIGIOUS SHARING

Gort stipulates that all interreligious sharing should focus primarily on "the honour of God." This central motive for ecumenism is placed in the context of increased societal polarization on a global scale. Honouring God in such a deteriorating situation inevitably translates into all religions sharing responsibility for peace, justice and the protection of natural resources. The gravity of such responsibility makes it incumbent upon religions to join forces and reconcile their differences.

4.1 Fambidzano Motives

Honoring God certainly was a pervasive underlying motive in Fambidzano's ecumenism. This was to take shape in service to and worship of God against the backdrop of an Africanized Kingdom theology. God's reign and Christ's healing presence was already an experienced reality in the ministries of iconic and prophetic leaders at AIC headquarters and healing colonies prior to the existence of Fambidzano. Subsequently, united AIC action was to find realization in improved church leadership, a deepening of spirituality and biblical-theological knowledge, and general church progress through outreach, growth and organization. The hub around which all this revolved was Fambidzano's TEE program. Thus our interchurch ecumenism as such was never an end in itself. Instead, it was a vehicle for purposeful theological advancement and holistic mission so that the world might see and believe in the Lordship and Saviourhood of Christ.

At its peak Fambidzano's TEE work encompassed regular weekly train-ing at 40 extension centers throughout Masvingo Province, at Chivhu and in Harare. Several teams of tutors taught up to 600 AIC and mainline mission church students at these centers each year. Certificate courses lasted for two years and included basic biblical studies, church history, homiletics, ethics, and theology of religions, all in the vernacular. More than a thousand students annually also participated in the correspondence courses.

The impact of theological education on students and participant churches was gauged in an extensive survey (Daneel 1989: chapters 6 and 7). Old Testament studies facilitated an understanding of AIC prophetic praxis in relation to biblical Hebrew prophets, while New Testament studies strengthened the Christological basis of church life, triggered a spate of student conversions and, in combination with homiletics, led to improved sermon preparation and exegetically sound preaching in the place of fragmented text interpretation. Church history lessons contributed significantly toward advanced self-interpretation in the ranks of AICs in relation to world Christianity and provided an interpretive basis for the parallel development of Fambidzano in joining first of all the Rhodesian Christian Conference and then the National Christian Council affiliated with the WCC. As the knowledge of the dynamics of church schisms worldwide grew in the ranks of participant AICs, the leadership placed a deliberate curb on schismatic fragmentation through sustained negotiations with prospective defectors. The result was startling: hardly a single schism occurred in Fambidzano's member churches during the more than twenty years of its existence.

The motive of honouring God also found expression in Fambidzano's response to the comprehensive needs of its church constituencies. Poverty was fought through a host of income-generating, community-development and water-supply projects (Daneel 1989). Moreover, after years of opposition by male bishops Fambidzano took the bold step of promoting female emancipation and women's leadership in the churches through the formation of an ecumenical Women's Association which closely linked the Ruwadzano (Women's Leagues) of participant churches. Such developments constituted a kind of realized-eschatology thrust among most AICs, the attempted concretization of God's salvation in the here and now through the agency of holistic healing ministries aimed at relieving the physical, mental, social and economic maladies of Africa.

4.2 ZIRRCON's Motives

The interreligious ecumenism of ZIRRCON revolved around the basic principle of the liberation of God's creation and the shared conviction that the Creator's call to people to "care for his garden" (as found in the Genesis story) implies a divine charge of earthkeeping for all humanity.

Traditionalists and Christians alike shared from the outset an awareness of urgency in the need for environmental reform, an urgency that required the mobilization of all human resources irrespective of religious, cultural and related intergroup patterns of exclusivism. Although there was a consensus that the Creator is the initiator of all earthkeeping endeavors and that a rejuvenated earth would witness first of all to His honor and glory, the intuition was strong that God entrusted the task of earthcare to all his people as active agents. My own inclination was to interpret human stewardship and responsibility for the environment within the framework of scriptural references to the coming of a "new heaven and new earth." In other words, these biblical prophecies should be understood as involving more than exclusively divine intervention in ushering in a new dispensation. Somehow our tree-planting activities could be seen as symbols and signposts of the new heaven and earth, already present, yet still to come.

How did these motives translate into ecumenical practice? A network of nurseries was developed in the districts surrounding Masvingo town: fifteen main nurseries cultivating up to 50,000 seedlings a year, and a host of satellite nurseries, managed by leaders of Women's clubs, youth clubs and students at ZIRRCON's theological (TEE) training centers. A total of well over 500,000 seedlings were cultivated annually by traditionalist representatives of AZTREC and Christian members of AAEC working side by side for modest salaries as nursery keepers. Just before the rainy season the seedlings were distributed in rural areas and ceremonially planted in woodlots owned communally by participant communities. During the past fifteen years an estimated total of eight to nine million seedlings have been planted in several thousands of woodlots. Traditionalists tended to look upon their woodlots as a modern version of the traditional area of conservation, the ancestral "holy grove" (*marambatemwa*, lit. "refused to have the trees felled"), while the Christian earthkeepers called theirs the "Lord's Acre" in recognition of Christ as healing Earthkeeper.

Ritualization of the holy "war of trees" was of the utmost importance. It took place mainly in the context of all-day tree-planting ceremonies, called *mafukidzanyika* ("clothing the land") by the traditionalists and *maporesanyika* ("healing the land") by their Christian counterparts. The former were opened by the tribal elders of AZTREC appearing in their traditionalist attire. They would invoke their senior ancestral "guardians of the land" (*varidzi venyika*), inform them of the plan to use the day to restore their land with new trees, engage in beer libations and celebrate the event with war and *shavi* dances. The proceedings would often take on the character of *pungwe* meetings, i.e., political reorientation vigils such as those held in the *chimu-renga* years. In this instance inspiration for the green struggle would be drawn from narratives about ancestral guidance and divine intervention during the pre-Independence war, thereby linking the military and environmental struggles. Christian earthkeepers attending the *mafukidzanyika* ceremonies would listen reverently to the speeches and ritual addresses to the ancestors. At times they added their own accounts of *chimurenga* experiences. But they would refrain as a group from drinking the sacrificial beer of the ancestors as a witness to their Christian identity. Sharing across the religious divide became more distinctly manifest at the point when traditionalist and Christian earthkeepers without reserve joined hands in planting the seedlings reserved for the new woodlot.

Toward the end of the tree-planting season when a large delegation of chiefs and spirit-mediums traveled some 300 km to the distant Matopo hills to report to *Mwari*, the oracular deity, regarding the latest progress and to request rain particularly for the newly planted trees, a number of AIC bishops and Christian ZIRRCON officials accompanied them as observers. In a rare show of goodwill, the *Mwari* priests allowed the Christian delegates to attend the secretive oracle sessions in the deep of the night. Thus a new chapter of interfaith dialogue and mutual religious tolerance and understanding was written in Zimbabwe. This development was a far cry from the interreligious conflicts of the past. The sharp edges of religious differences were not necessarily overcome in such interchange. Yet Christian leaders achieved an invaluable form of rapport with their non-Christian roots. As a result they were able to relate meaningfully to their traditionalist counter-parts from a vantage point of assessing and respecting the manner in which their fellow earthkeepers "honour God" from within the green struggle.

The Christian "land-healing" ceremonies, in turn, were developed into tree-planting Eucharists with extensive liturgies. These included public confessions of ecological sins and partaking of the sacramental elements with a seedling in the hand to illustrate symbolically that "in Christ all things are held together" (Col. 1:17). Then followed the sanctification of the new Lord's Acre with holy water and soil, the planting of the trees with elaborate addresses concerning them, and concluding healing ceremonies with a blessing for the earthkeepers by the laying on of hands. Thus, the essence of such tree-planting events is Christ's holistic mission to this earth, the proclamation of his salvation as good news, manifest in this instance as the healing and restoration of both humans and their fellow members of the earth-community.

Unlike the conventional Eucharist taking place within the secluded con-fines of a church building, the ecumenical tree-planting Eucharist was open-ended in its relatedness not only to human beings but also to all the animate and inanimate members of nature. It incorporated the attendance of a wide variety of church members, not only of the earthkeeping AICs but also of the mainline churches. Invariably, a large contingent of chiefs, spirit mediums and traditionalist elders attended the proceedings, sitting as a distinct group of AZTREC representatives not far from the communion table. Just as the Christian earthkeepers did not drink the sacrificial beer of the ancestors during *mafukidzanyika* ceremo-nies, the traditionalists (excepting a few Christian chiefs) did not partake in the sacrament of the *maporesanyika*. But they listened attentively, often with overt approval, to the Eucharist sermons of AIC bishops. At times Christian chiefs added their own sermons, some of which revealed a remarkable mix of African wisdom, Christocentrism and commitment to ZIRRCON's emergent ethic of earthcare.

Subsequent to the sacramental use of the bread and wine, the traditionalist earthkeepers would join their Christian counterparts in planting and addressing the trees as "sisters" and "brothers" in the woodlot, the Lord's Acre. This was done in union, with joyous celebration, laughter, dance and song. As the sun set and the last rays shone through the young leaves of newly planted and watered seedlings, the earthkeepers (Christians and traditionalists alike) would kneel in front of healing prophets of the AICs for the sustenance and healing of tired or broken bodies, through the power of the Father, the Son and Holy Spirit.

Thus, in the combination of *maporesanyika* and *mafukidzanyika* ceremo-nies, Christian-traditionalist ecumenism acknowledges the religious divide or, as stated above, the "distinctiveness" of the participant parties. However, the sharing of a common goal de-emphasizes the differences. Suspicions and judgmental attitudes fade as the green struggle is given a more humane and caring face. In the shared service of earthkeepers to God's creation, a sense of vocation and common destiny grows. New friendships and respect across the religious divide reveal the presence of a loving God whose power and grace spans and overcomes the distance of human divisions.

5   DIALOGUE AND MISSION

To overcome the flaws of one-sidedness in the strategies of dialogue and mission, "the former tending to neglect the poverty within religions and the latter the religiosity of the poor," Gort pleads for meaningful interaction and integration of both strategies. Following the new methodology of "liberative ecumenism," he argues, as already indicated above, that stagnant discourse between religions on the basis of "neutrality" or "objectivity" should be replaced by cooperative relations of living and working together with a liberative thrust. While Gort reminds us, on the one hand, that a basic condition for Christians in all forms of ecumenism remains full adherence to the ministry and gospel of Christ, he contends that Christians should feel free to align themselves with other religions involved in struggles for freedom, even though such alignment inevitably involves risk.

Considering the two brands of African grassroots ecumenism we are surveying, the similarities between their existential realities and Gort's pro-posals for liberative ecumenism are so striking that someone may well feel tempted to ask whether Gort wrote the script for these movements. Perhaps his observations of a spontaneously enacted 'script' at the African grassroots also impacted the development of his ecumenical theology.

5.1 Dialogue and Mission in Fambidzano

Unsurprisingly, Fambidzano's main focus on interchurch ecumenism entailed an understanding of dialogue as consisting, in the first place, of communication between AIC denominations in a wide variety of newly-created contexts such as conferences, executive meetings, gatherings of women's associations, theological training centers, joint services, Eucharists, funerals, and ordination ceremonies. The sharing of Bible interpretations, spiritual insights, experiences in church growth, different church histories and traditions, the latest congregational developments and personal issues in these contexts was of great value in heightening the sense of unity and spiritual renewal in the ranks of Fambidzano.

As time went on, however, Fambidzano began to promote interreligious dialogue between Christians and traditionalists as well. Some TEE courses were specifically crafted to deal with and assess the patterns of interaction in healing contexts between Spirit-type faith-healers and people (both Christian and non-Christian) still adhering to African religious belief systems. This led to lively debates among students during classes and occasioned reflective self-assessments by church leaders of the varied processes of religious interchange taking place in Zionist and Apostolic healing colonies where a truly indigenous *theologia religionis* was taking shape in praxis. In addition, Fambidzano's eventual involvement in attempts to arrest poverty in rural villages through religiously open-ended community-development projects also stimulated comprehensive Christian-traditionalist ecumenism or, in Gort's words, a "living and working together with a view to the alleviation of human suffering."

Unfortunately, Fambidzano proved to be insufficiently equipped to handle the pressures of community development. At the time, everyone involved was confident about expanding Fambidzano's activities in this direction. The movement had proved itself to be a stable organization, standing on its own feet for several years. Financial transparency and accountability appeared to be in evidence in accordance with built-in constitutional safeguards. But given the needs of the poor, the demands and expectations of AIC bishops were disproportionate to the available means. Impressed at first by the efficiency of Fambidzano's administration and wide-ranging influence, Western development agents tended to overburden the movement's infrastructure with ambitious projects. Supervision of project implementation at the grassroots was inadequate. The agents had their own agendas, not all of which were realistically aligned to the religio-cultural background and leadership potential of Fambidzano.

Fambidzano kept limping along for a few years. Preoccupation with more development projects and funds than it could properly manage took its toll on TEE work. Once this mainstay of the movement's ecumenical endeavour crumbled, disintegration set in and finally, for reasons that are too complicated to set out within the limits of this essay, Fambidzano collapsed. But not all was lost. Fambidzano made a lasting contribution to AIC ecumenism that is still in evidence in widened and constructive interchurch relations. Without the Fambidzano background, for instance, it would not have been possible for ZIRRCON to mobilize the AICs in the Association of African Earth-keeping Churches (AAEC) as quickly and effectively as was the case. In addition to the lasting influence Fambidzano's TEE work has had on AIC leadership, one of the most outstanding features of the movement's legacy is the innovative emphasis it has had on the integral relationship between ecu-menism and mission.

In the pre-Fambidzano era some AICs, especially Bishop Mutendi's Zion Christian Church, tended to use the Eucharist during paschal celebrations as a flash-point, a 'launching pad' for large-scale countrywide missionary cam-paigns. Fambidzano extended this tradition by refashioning ecumenical paschal celebrations into missionary events in themselves. Eucharistic sermons focused on Christ's good news, reminded audiences of the witnessing character of Christian unity, called for repentance and, as a result, triggered conversions and baptisms. Thus, the ecumenical witness given during joint sacramental celebrations resulted directly in baptismal ceremonies in which the leaders of participant churches would together enter the "waters of Jordan" (any dam or river suited for the occasion) to baptize new converts in the church of their choice.

The prime representative of Fambidzano's new approach to an ecumenical Eucharist-in-mission was Bishop Forridge, who fashioned his entire ministry to accommodate the conviction that ecumenical

endeavour in Christ quite literally spelled mission. For years he propaga-
ted this conviction in the eastern regions of the Gutu district until he
eventually succeeded in drawing the widest possible cross section of
mission churches (Dutch Reformed, Roman Catholic, Full Gospel, Methodist, Church of Christ, etc.) and AICs into a regular program of joint
paschal celebrations. His success in persuading large numbers of non-
affiliated *VaPostori* (Maranke Apostles), the church with arguably the
strongest anti-ecumenical bias in Zimbabwe, to participate underscored
the far-reaching ecumenical impact of his ministry.

Concerned with the witness character of *paseka* against the background of Fambidzano's interpretation of John 17:21-23, Bishop Forridge molded his ecumenical Eucharist into a ceremony in which internal
reorientation, cleansing and spiritual upliftment in the church's visible
unification as the body of Christ was combined with the outbound witnessing movement of the church into the world. In this way he engendered a spirit of interecclesial altruism, whereby the preoccupation of
individual AIC leaders with membership recruitment for and preservation of the influence of their own churches shifted to the more broadly
conceived understanding of Christ's salvific dispensation for all the
world.

Bishop Forridge was only a semiliterate man, but at the African
grassroots he featured as an outstanding Christian leader of great compassion and integrity. His ecumenical achievements live on in the
churches of eastern Gutu, and his legacy—which is the legacy of Fambidzano—challenges the church in Africa and beyond to commit itself
afresh to mission in unity, where denominational self-interest pales in
the blaze of the demands and promises of God's Kingdom.

5.2 Dialogue and Mission in ZIRRCON

Cooperative interaction between traditionalist and Christian earthkeepers
in the 'war of trees' necessarily makes dialogue an integral part of the
entire ZIRRCON enterprise. Much of this dialogue is informal and spontaneous where Christians and traditionalists share their religious convictions while working together in nurseries or woodlots. ZIRRCON's
eighty women's clubs, engaged in both ecological (nurseries, tree-planting and gully reclama-tion) and income-generating (clothing manufac-
turing, gardening, cattle-feeding, bakeries, soap and cooking oil production, etc.) activities, are religiously loosely knit organizations. The
AZTREC / AAEC distinctions are somewhat less prominent in the activities of these clubs, which allows the women a certain flexibility and
latitude for improvisation in dialogue according to the personal and
ritual needs of each situation. In clubs where Christians and traditiona-

lists are well represented in the leadership, ceremonies can alternate between the different religious poles per occasion or be allowed to incorporate Christian or traditionalist features in succession in one ceremony. Whatever the variation in religious interaction, however, care is taken to honor and respect the religious identity of all role-players, in accordance with the policy and general trend set by ZIRRCON.

Much dialogue about religious interface in the ceremonial contexts of the above-mentioned 'land-clothing' and 'land-healing' tree-planting ceremonies took place between AZTREC and the AAEC before the formal rules for pub-lic collaboration took shape. At no stage did the retention of religious identity by the earthkeepers—for instance, the abstention on the part of Christians from drinking sacrificial beer during *mafukidzanyika* ceremonies and on the part of traditionalists from partaking of the sacramental elements of the *maporesanyika* Eucharist—obstruct mutual commitments to earthcare. It was actually in the repeated ritual acknowledgement of religious pluriformity and the growing motivation of cooperating partners to learn more about each other's faith that the shackles of suspicion and fear were cast off in favor of informal sharing of religious experience during the activities, meals and pri-vate conversations that formed part of each tree-planting event.

Commitment to a common cause in ZIRRCON did not, of course, guarantee harmonious interreligious encounter in all dialogical situations; far from it. At times tempers flared as spirit mediums ribbed Christians for their putative 'pride' or 'hypocrisy,' while AIC bishops targeted the evils associated with heavy beer drinking during ancestral rituals. Critical attitudes and public criticisms seldom provoked alienation, however. The chiefs and spirit mediums themselves curbed beer drinking in the tree-planting context and adopted the oft repeated slogan during their *mafukidzanyika* speeches: "forward the war of trees; down with those who idle at the beer pots!"

The classical case of dialogue turning into radical confrontation in ZIRRCON's history occurred during a conference meeting attended by more than a hundred AZTREC and AAEC delegates. The topic of discussion was the fencing of ancestral holy groves, particularly Mt. Rasa in the Gutu district, for the purpose of the reintroduction and protection of wildlife. Fencing, as a symbol of white encroachment on African lands, has always been a sensitive issue among African subsistence farmers. On this occasion the subject touched a raw nerve and ignited strong mystical protest as spirit mediums fell possessed, shaking and shouting, while the ancestors in guttural or booming voices lodged their dissatisfaction. Some ancestors complained that game fences would obstruct their passage from their 'dwellings' (graves) in the holy mountain to their living descendants in the villages down in the surrounding plains. They objected vehemently to the Christian earthkeepers' support of the fencing proposals. Pandemonium broke loose. AIC bishops and prophets started singing their exorcism songs, suggesting that they needed to drive off the intruding 'demons.' That only further aggravated the situation. For a while it appeared as if the 'war of the trees' was threatening to erupt into a real 'war' between opposing religious factions. Conference proceedings ground to a halt. The entire afternoon was spent in informal group discussions. Intensified dialogue on religious issues significantly led to a 'truce,' or, perhaps better, reconciliation. The salient point in this event was that the deeper religious sentiments surfaced by way of fierce confrontation, then led to extensive discussions and finally culminated in reaffirmation of commitment to united earthkeeping action. To my knowledge the fencing issue remained unresolved, but group catharsis through dialogue led to greater understanding of disparate sentiments as the green army once again closed ranks for the struggle ahead.

The empowerment of the poor for purposes of economic upliftment also featured prominently in ZIRRCON's strategies of dialogue-in-mission. From the outset ZIRRCON and the women's clubs engaged in income-generating projects tried valiantly to accommodate the myriad of requests from within earthkeeping circles and wider rural communities for development support. ZIRRCON's appeals for funding to this end coincided with policy changes at EZE (*Evangelische Zentralstelle für Entwicklungshilfe*) headquarters in Bonn. EZE, our main sponsor, introduced a new program called PSP (Par-ticipatory Strategic Planning) which implied far-reaching restructuring for ZIRRCON as virtual condition for ongoing support. Insistence on community involvement at all levels of planning, implementation and financial control impeded decision-making processes at the executive level and facilitated unrealistic expectations at the grassroots, causing disaffection when the expected support did not materialize. This insistence also threatened to convert ZIRRCON—even though that may not have been the intention of EZE—into a development NGO in which the original quest for earthcare ran the risk of being overrun by other considerations. Once again, just as was the case with Fambidzano, the wrackful poverty of the African masses and their grievous need for economic improvement drew a movement not fully equipped to deal with all the development issues imposed on it into a destructive vortex.

In my view ZIRRCON, as originally conceived, was being forced to take on a shape it had never dreamt of or planned for at the outset. The battle cry of the "war of the trees" grew fainter during the PSP phase, and the number of trees planted during the annual rainy season plummeted from nearly a million to only 400,000. I pleaded with EZE representatives and ZIRRCON staff to allocate poverty-alleviation issues to a development desk alongside the existing ecology, women's, youth and other desks, which would have been a relatively easy way to restore the movement's equilibrium. For some years, however, these entreaties fell on deaf ears. Currently ZIRRCON appears to be on an even keel in spite of some uncertainty about its financial future and despite the current political upheaval and environmental destruction taking place in Zimbabwe. It is to be hoped that the movement's innovative contribution to earthkeeping will endure and grow in the future.

ZIRRCON's mission, intertwined as it is with dialogue, has an essentially twofold thrust: environmental, which can be measured in terms of secular ecological criteria; and religious, which, insofar as the motivation behind environmental endeavor is of a mystical nature, can be assessed in terms of African traditionalist or Christian theological criteria. I have argued that it is appropriate to speak of AZTREC's work as African traditionalist mission. African religion admittedly lacks the dimension of witness, the call to conver-sion and recruitment which characterizes Christian mission. Yet AZTREC's green warfare resembles Christian mission because, in contrast to normal ATR practice, Mwari, the oracular deity, is believed to send traditionalists into the world for a purpose wider than the interests of their own clan or tribe. They, too, measure the relative success or failure of their mission of ecological stewardship in direct relation to the mystical source of their endeavour; hence the repeated appeal to the ancestral guardians of the land to observe, inspire and recognize the tree-planting work of their living descendants, and AZTREC's annual deliberations on the progress and problems of the green struggle at Mwari's Matopo shrines (Daneel 1998: 269-271)

With regard to ZIRRCON's mission in the Christian sense, the question arises whether it is at all possible to share a mission of earthca-re as closely as the AAEC churches and AZTREC traditionalists are doing and still retain the true spirit and essence of New Testament missionary outreach. Does the Christian–non-Christian ecumenism evinced during tree-planting ceremonies and Matonjeni visits necessarily jeopardize the distinctive nature of Christian witness? My own verbal interaction with the ancient Mwari of Africa during oracular sessions, I realized, could be the cause of confusion in Christian circles. My overall impression in this respect was that, despite my experience during Matonjeni visits of walking a knife-edge between two religious worlds, the challenge of Christian mission, of proclaiming and enacting the good news of Christ's salvific work in this world, was never absent, never obstructed, never entirely unheeded during these activities. Christian mission, it appeared, could maintain its Christ-centered focus, its concern for both human and cosmic salvation, even while extending its energies to the field of earthcare in close collaboration with fellow, traditionalist earthkeepers.

The AAEC's tree-planting Eucharist, like Fambidzano's ecumenical *paseka* celebration mentioned above, is in itself a missionary event. In the proclamation of the good news of the Gospel by several AIC preachers in the run-up to the use of the sacraments a strong Christocentric emphasis is unmistakable. This is the occasion for witness, as both the Christian earth-keepers and their dialogical partners—the chiefs and spirit mediums, devotees of the Mwari cult at Matonjeni—are called upon either to renew their conversion to Christ or to accept his Lordship over all creation (Mt. 28:18) and his role as Earthkeeper, which is the fulfillment of the protective function of the ancestral guardians of the land. This is also the occasion for qualifying the church's ecological mission. Bishop Wapendama, leader of the Signs of the Apostles Church, for instance, roused his multireligious audience during such a ceremony as follows:

> We, deliverers of the stricken land, were sent by Mwari on a divine mis-sion. Deliverance, Mwari says, lies in the trees. Jesus said: "I leave you, my followers, to complete my work." And that task is the one of healing! We, the followers of Jesus, have to continue with this healing ministry. So let us all fight, clothing, healing the earth with trees! It is our task to strengthen this mission with our numbers of people. We shall clothe and heal the entire land with trees and drive off affliction. I believe we can do it.

In delivering this message during an ecumenical Eucharist Wapendama implied that where the union between Christ and His disciples—cutting across all denominational boundaries—is sacramentally confirmed, the mission of earth-healing integral to it is visibly acknowledged and revitalized. God certainly takes the initiative in the deliverance and restoration of the ravaged earth, but He calls the Christian body of believers, i.e., the church, to help rescue the stricken earth from its malady here and now (Carmody 1983:78). In the ZIRRCON context the ecological *missio Dei* of course encompasses all human beings prepared to accept the divine earthcare mandate. Bishop Wapendama's insights hint at Africa's vision that the church has been called to mission, not as a privileged community of mere soul-savers but as a fellowship which, in Bishop Anastasios of Androussa's words, understands that "the whole world, not only humankind but the entire universe, has been called to share in the restoration that was accomplished by the redeeming work of Christ" (quoted in Messer 1992:69-70).

Due to the tendency in AICs to interpret salvation as comprehensive healing and liberation in the here and now, the AAEC's tree-planting Eucharist functions as a vehicle for the proclamation and realization of just this kind of all-encompassing "good news." It is conducted as integral part of the church's struggle for justice. Through the recurrent presence of church leaders and traditionalists who played prominent roles during the *chimurenga* struggle the sacrament of the war of the trees is directly linked to the country's and the AICs' history of liberation. Bishop Machokoto, first president of the AAEC, said:

> There is absolutely no doubt about the connection [between our tree-planting and former liberation struggle].... This war of the trees is the most important war, following the first *chimurenga*. We are all committed to this struggle to restore the vanquished land through afforestation.... Trees are our life-line! A ward with dense forests knows no death!

This combination of *chimurenga* experience and holistic views about the interaction of human beings and nature contributes toward a potent message of God's mysterious and protective presence in all of life, in all of creation. It emphasizes, moreover, the restoration of justice through responsible land husbandry which includes concerted opposition to over-exploitation of natural resources.

One of the most poignant features of the enactment of Christ's salvific message in the tree-planting sacrament is the inclusion of the earth's inanimate members—the trees, water and soil—in the sacred communion between Christ and His disciples. By virtually standing in embrace with trees at the communion table, earthkeeping communicants are admitting to God that they are incomplete as individuals, that their humanity is informed and qualified by and in nature, and that in this "widening" of their communion they are not interfering with but recognizing Christ's Lordship over all the earth (Mt. 28:18) by paying to all "members" of creation the respect originally required of humans by the Creator God. This is how the AICs reinterpret the Genesis story, and it is on the basis of this reading that their members are called to replace exploitive forms of human dominion over nature with a ministry of humble stewardship of the earth. The earth is 'liberated' in the liturgical acknowledgment that it can retaliate legitimately as *ngozi* (vengeful spirit) when abused, in the address of trees as 'brothers' and 'sisters' in a kind of dialogue that recognizes the value and dignity of the tree and allows 'him/ her' to respond in the liturgy, and in the request to the soil to receive and protect the seedlings entrusted to it.

Even though non-Christian earthkeepers attending the Eucharist do not partake of the sacramental elements, they are party to an event which en-riches interreligious sharing. Their identification during the Eucharist with Christian earthkeepers at the personal level and their affirmation of numerous spiritual and eco-ethical issues raised during the sermons—as is reflected in their own speeches and conversations—are pointers of collaborative interchange between mission and dialogue which breathes, at the existential level in rural Africa, the very kind of meaning, hope and love, envisaged in Jerry Gort's plea for liberative ecumenism.

6   LIBERATIVE ECUMENISM: CONCLUDING REMARKS

Toward the end of my discourse on the two forms of African ecumenism I have been engaged in—interchurch and interreligious—I realize that their liberative features have been mentioned in passing rather than forming the subject of closer scrutiny. In conclusion, therefore, I wish briefly to highlight a few liberationist trends lest their significance as landmarks of a very speci-fic type of ecumenism remain obscure.

Probably the most important aspect of Fambidzano's ecumenism was the liberation of member AICs from ecclesial obscurity, geographical isolation and non-recognition by the local mainline churches. Geographical isolation, due to poverty-imposed limitations on modern means of communication, long-distance travel and ecumenical opportunity, was substantially responsible for the introverted and exclusivist trends which characterized the above-mentioned, pre-Fambidzano attitudes among AICs, especially the Spirit- and Ethiopian-type ones. Fambidzano's infrastructure ensured extensive and sustained encounter among member churches, leading to improvement of their self-knowledge, to fresh understanding of their Fambidzano counterparts, and to new interpersonal relations and friendships within the wide range of churches of which they were a part. And of course all of this heightened the individual and communal sense of self-respect, intrinsic value and dignity. Liberation from ecclesial obscurity extended much further than local inter-AIC relations. Fambidzano's associate membership in the Rhodesian Christian Conference and later the National Christian Council also provided a liberative breakthrough from rural isolation. Regular meetings with representatives of the mainline churches, visits by church leaders from overseas and attendance by Fambidzano delegates at a number of ecumenical conferences in Europe engendered a sense of belonging to the world church and provided encouragement for local ministry.

Considering the need of the AICs for recognition of their validity as Christian churches by their local 'mother churches'—the very mission churches from which many of their members seceded—without a loss of their new-found autonomy, there was only one model of ecumenism that could possibly succeed. Fambidzano had to affirm and expand the liberation already achieved by the AICs when their leaders took distance from the tutelage of white leadership in the mission churches. Hence our insistence from the outset that the funding from abroad should have no stringent denominational strings attached, that even though the origins of such sources might be Netherlands Reformed, British Congregational, Swedish and German Lutheran, the control and administration of funds would be entirely Fambidzano's responsibility, free from any control or supervision by Zimbabwean mission churches. Thus, we built the TEE institution not as a form of mission at the behest of a mainline mission church but as an AIC enterprise, the ownership of which was vested firmly at the core of the emergent AIC movement. Liberation from the stigma of theologically ill-equipped leadership in the AICs therefore evolved as a process controlled by the AICs on their own behalf, relatively free from external control. This form of empowerment of poverty-ridden churches did much for the reinforcement of their hard-won autonomy, for their self-esteem, as well as their growing ability to interact with the local mainline churches from a platform of strength rather than from the former inferior position of being branded as separatists or heretics, unworthy of recognition as Christian churches.

The tree-planting Eucharist of ZIRRCON signals much more than the liberation of nature through the greening of a barren countryside. It under-scores with ritual regularity the empowerment of the poor and marginalized people of this part of the two-thirds world to make a contribution that is of such significance that it captures, for once, the imagination of the nation, the recognition and approval of the government. It also incorporates quality of life for the earthkeepers; their liberation from obscurity in a remote part of Zimbabwe; their overcoming of social marginality and futility as news media repeatedly report on their work; and their escape from the hopelessness of poverty as their nursery-keeper salaries, budding woodlots and small-scale income-generating projects revive some hope for a better future. Thus the good news of engagement in sacramental service to nature is that the dehumanizing shackles of decades of colonial rule and environmental desecration, caused for the most part by disproportionate land allocation, are shaken off in the quest for holistic healing for all life on earth.

There can be little doubt that the soteriology at the base of ZIRRCON's eucharistic mission model is wider in its conception of healing and liberation than the original Zionist model and the one developed by Bishop Forridge in the Fambidzano context. Salvation remains basically human salvation. God's free gift of grace still requires the human response of conversion, spiritual growth and church-planting. Imbedded in this interaction between Savior and humanity, however, is the prophetic promise of a new heaven and new earth, the salvation of all creation. ZIRRCON's ecumenical theology challenges all God's people to be active in the enactment and realization of such salvation by working for, among other things, the empowerment of the poor.

The two stories narrated above, incomplete as they are, represent a contextualized African endorsement of the main tenets of Jerry Gort's ecumeni-cal theology. They illustrate something of the richly varied weave of the fabric of liberative ecumenism in rural Africa. They also reflect institutional dilemmas, failures and vulnerabilities alongside the sheer adventure and joy of Africans exploring new avenues of contextually relevant ecumenism, new ways of proclaiming and living Christ's good news where the pain of poverty converts into the celebration of hope and liberation.

My own pilgrimage into the inscape of African spirituality is inseparably linked to the narrative above. That journey has in many respects been an un-charted, unconventional and controversial passage in which Africa taught me to become a storytelling rather than an analytical theologian. This explains in part the relative absence of theoretical theology and wide-ranging source references in my narrative: stories tend to avoid abstractions due to the story-teller's fascination and bond with the players 'on stage.' But it also explains my gratitude to friends and colleagues like Jerry Gort whose more precisely defined theologies remind me of my Calvinist roots and inform the course I steer in Africa as footloose storyteller and tree planter in the midst of dancing prophets and beer-libating traditionalist elders. Given the inventiveness and originality of African AICs in crafting their own version(s) of liberative ecumenism in Zimbabwe, the church in Africa and beyond may benefit from heeding the challenge implicit in this story for the renewal of its ministry in contextual mission, dialogue and comprehensive liberation within the orbit of local, continental and global ecumenism.

BIBLIOGRAPHY

Carmody, J. (1983). *Ecology and Religion : Toward a New Christian Theology of Nature*. New York: Paulist Press.

Daneel, M.L. (1970). *The God of the Matopo Hills*. The Hague: Mouton.

—. (1974). *Old and New in Southern Shona Independent Churches*, Vol. 2: *Church Growth: Causative Factors and Recruitment Techniques*. The Hague: Mouton.

—. (1987). *Quest for Belonging: Introduction to a Study of African Independent Churches*. Gweru: Mambo Press.

—. (1989). *Fambidzano: Ecumenical Movement of Zimbabwean Independent Churches*. Gweru: Mambo Press.

—. (1998). *African Earthkeepers*, Vol. 1: *Interfaith Mission in Earth Care*. Pretoria: Unisa Press.

—. (1999). *African Earthkeepers*, Vol. 2: *Environmental Mission and Liberation in Christian Perspective*. Pretoria: Unisa Press.

Dornberg, Ulrich. "Development and Interreligious Dialogue: Some Preliminary Remarks for Discussion." *Mission Studies: Journal of the IAMS*, VI-2:12 (1989). Pp. 108-116.

Gort, Jerald D. (1992). "Liberative Ecumenism: Gateway to the Sharing of Religious Experience Today." In: J.D. Gort, H.M. Vroom, R. Fernhout and A. Wessels (eds.). *On Sharing Religious Experience: Possibilities of Interfaith Mutuality*. Currents of Encounter Vol. 4. Amsterdam: Rodopi / Grand Rapids: Eerdmans. Pp. 88-105.

Messer, D.E. (1992). *A Conspirancy of Goodness: Contemporary Images of Christian Mission*. Nashville: Abingdon Press.

Samartha, Stanley J. (1976). "Mission and Movements of Innovation." In: G.H. Anderson and T.F. Stransky (eds.). *Third World Theologies*. Mission Trends Nr. 3. New York: Paulist Press / Grand Rapids: Eerdmans. Pp. 233-244.

Sundkler, Bengt. (1948). *Bantu Prophets in South Africa*. London: Oxford University Press.

Turner, Harold. W. (1963). *Modern African Religious Movements: An Introduction for the Christian Churches*. Nsukka: University of Nigeria. Rev. ed. 1965.

21 "Go Slow Through Uyo":
Dialogue as Missionary Method

Wilbert R. Shenk

1 INTRODUCTION

On November 14, 1959 Edwin and Irene Weaver, veterans of twenty years of missionary service in India, disembarked from the freighter "African Pilot" in Lagos, Nigeria. Their commission from the Mennonite Board of Missions (MBM), Elkhart, Indiana, was to relate to a group of churches in southeast Nigeria that a year earlier had assumed the name "Mennonite Church Nigeria, Inc."[1] These churches presented themselves as comprising sixty congregations with 2,832 members "under leadership and founder Rev. A.A. Dick, B.Th." They requested "resident missionaries" and identified these needs: 1) Bible school for training ministers; 2) high school; 3) hospital; 4) scholarships for college-level study in America; and 5) financial support for ministers.[2]

As the Weavers approached their destination on November 21, they noticed a warning on the outskirts of the town: "Go Slow Through Uyo!" They would ponder this sign often in the days ahead.

Weavers set about getting acquainted with the leaders who had issued the invitation and their churches. In his first report to the mission board on December 8, Edwin Weaver observed: "It is impossible to attempt to relate the feelings and experiences of the past eighteen days. They have been days filled with emotions of many kinds. We have been fearful, encouraged, disappointed, thrilled, discouraged, and at times sick at heart, wondering why we came—all these in turn."[3] As he sized up the situation, Weaver noted they had to confront two "big problems." The first was the urgent request of these church leaders to be recognized as ordained pastors and receive certificates of ordination. Weaver had already discovered that a number of these men had been ordained by A.A. Dick who now presented himself as founder of the Mennonite

---

[1] Initial contact had come by way of correspondence in response to the "Way to Life" radio program sponsored by Mennonite Broadcasts, Inc., and broadcast from ELWA, Monrovia, Liberia.

[2] MBM IV-18-13 Nigeria 1956-59, A.A. Dick to Rev. and Mrs. S.J. Hostetler, Nov. 23, 1958. All correspondence cited here is in the Mennonite Board of Missions collection, Mennonite Church Archives, Goshen, Indiana.

[3] MBM IV-18-13, Edwin Weaver to MBM, Dec. 8, 1959.

Church Nigeria but was an erstwhile Mormon bishop and a man of questionable repute. Quick resolution of the issue seemed unlikely. Weaver observed: "Our [Mennonite Church Nigeria] pastors are very untrained. And shocking to say, almost entirely illiterate. This includes the vice-president of the conference."[4] By this time Weaver also realized some of the pastors were polygamists. A central issue in coming years would be church leadership.

The second, and more pressing, problem was "our relation to all the other Churches with which we are surrounded." Sounding a note of despair Weaver asserted: "Never in my life have I seen a place so full of Churches and their institutions.[5] Church and school buildings everywhere. Never have I been in a religious situation so pathetically confused."[6] The churches readily divided into two groups. The first consisted of the "established churches," including the Presbyterian (Church of Scotland), Anglican, Qua Iboe, and Methodist. These churches cooperated in the Christian Council of Nigeria (CCN). The Roman Catholic Church was a strong influence in the region also but did not seek relations with other Christian bodies.

The second group was a mixed multitude that did not recognize comity agreements and was not interested in cooperation with other churches. This group included Mormons, Seventh Day Adventists, Jehovah Witnesses, Salvation Army, (Missouri Synod) Lutherans, Church of Christ, The African Church, The Church of God, various kinds of Pentecostals, "and many others too numerous to mention."

Southeastern Nigeria was rife with religious confusion and proselytizing activity. A spirit of competition characterized inter-church relations. The established churches sharply criticized the indigenous churches as "breakaway groups" in which individuals under discipline were received into membership with no questions asked. The indigenous churches complained they experienced ostracism and censure at the hands of the established churches and missions. Weavers found these conditions distasteful and were tempted to withdraw. "Go Slow through Uyo" rang in their ears.

---

[4] E.I. Weaver to J.H. Yoder, Dec. 14, 1959.

[5] It was commonly asserted that 95 percent of the population was "Christian." In fact, no reliable statistical information was available; but a survey in 1963 revealed, for example, there were 225 Christian congregations within a five-mile radius of Uyo representing some forty different denominations.

[6] Cf. E.I. Weaver to J.H. Yoder, Dec. 14, 1959.

As Weavers visited other missions in the area they quickly learned that they were by no means the first missionaries to have answered the "Macedonian call" from a self-designated denominational affiliate in Nigeria. One missionary confided "that in the past two years six other proselyting groups had entered this town."[7] The Lutherans arrived in 1936 under similar circumstances and had managed to stay; but typically missions left as quickly as they had come. On the one hand, Edwin Weaver acknowledged "we still know very little about the whole situation," but, on the other, "already we do know that there is hard work to be done." Their resolve to stay was growing.

Yet the way forward was beset with daunting obstacles. The leaders of the established churches and missions in the area spoke with one voice: "You are not needed here. Please leave." They urged the Weavers to find another place to work, possibly in northern Nigeria or Cameroon.[8] More ominous still was the notice from the Immigration Office in February 1960 that the Weavers must leave the country since the Government of Nigeria did not recognize their mission. Furthermore, they were told that such recognition would not be forthcoming.

Into this confusion and uncertainty a glimmer of light appeared. When the Weavers met with R. M. Macdonald, leader of the Church of

---

[7] Cf. E.I. Weaver to J.H. Yoder, Dec. 14, 1959.

[8] E.I. Weaver to J.H. Yoder, Dec. 24, 1959, reports on a visit to W.H. Graddon, head of the Qua Iboe Mission. When the Weavers pressed Graddon concerning their coming to the area, he replied: "There is no open door for another mission in Uyo...To start a new work would simply add to the confusion." Weaver contacted W.J. Wood, secretary of the Christian Council of Nigeria (CCN) and received a reply Jan. 5, 1960: "No approach was made by your Mission Board to the Christian Council, I regret to say. Had they asked for information, they would have been told that the Uyo-Eket-Abak area is notorious for the number of invitations emanating from it to Mission Boards overseas. Rarely, if ever, do they arise from a genuine need. Usually the origin is some disgruntled person or group who is not prepared to accept the standards of Christian discipleship of the Church or Mission working in that area. Not infrequently the motive is even less commendable, being nothing more than a desire on the part of the person concerned to get what he can for himself, both out of the local people he can persuade to support him, and any agency overseas which will swallow his story." Wood advised Weaver to get in touch with R. M. Macdonald, secretary for the Eastern Region of the CCN (E. I. Weaver to J.H. Yoder, Jan. 15, 1960).

Scotland Mission and officer of the CCN, he told Weavers of his burden.[9]

Over the course of many years he had watched the church situation
in southeastern Nigeria deteriorate. He was convinced that a fresh initiative was needed that would constructively address this complicated
circumstance—one that would improve relations among churches by
bringing them together. Any solution had to include the many independent churches in the region that heretofore had been held at arms length
by the established churches.[10] At the same time Macdonald began to
explore the possibility of the Mennonite missionaries securing visas under the Church of Scotland Mission since CSM urgently required assistance with their schools and hospitals. On March 31, 1960 Macdonald
wrote offering the Weavers a CSM house in which to live and recognition as workers under their mission. This opened the way for Mennonite
workers to be placed in Presbyterian-related medical and educational
institutions in Eastern Region, thus solving the visa problem.

Six weeks after they arrived in Uyo, the Weavers had identified
three main themes that had to be addressed if the church and mission
status quo in southeastern Nigeria were to be changed: 1) the established
churches and all other Christian missions and churches had to find a
basis for communicating with one another; 2) leadership training was the
key to transforming the confused pastoral and theological conditions in
many churches; and 3) the Mennonite Church Nigeria, itself a part of the
independent church phenomenon, had to be worked with responsibly.

---

[9] The Weavers met Macdonald on January 14, 1960. Writing to Yoder and Graber
(Jan. 15, 1960) Weaver says: "Our visit with Mr. Macdonald was the beginning of a
new day for us. Before my visit with Mr. Macdonald we could see no light in this
whole situation…Now there is some light shining in the darkness… In reply to my
question if there is not some way for us to work here to bring harmony and unity into
the atmosphere of confusion and mistrust, he responded by saying, 'that is the very
thing we have been looking for and hoping could happen.'"

[10] Macdonald proposed to call the ER Council executive together immediately to
consider this embryonic proposal. He contacted his executive and announced a
meeting with the Weavers present in early February (Macdonald to Weavers, Jan. 24,
1960). In the event, this initial meeting on February 6 did not go well. Though the
Weavers were received courteously and sympathetically, the ER executive committee
advised them strongly to leave the area! But Macdonald was undeterred.

2 The Situation in 1959

The church and mission situation in southeastern Nigeria in 1959 can be summarized in terms of three dimensions: religious, ecclesiastical, and missions.

1. *Religious.* In 1959 the study of what was then called religious independency in Africa was not yet fully established. Bengt Sundkler's pioneering study of *Bantu Prophets in South Africa* (1948) and Efraim Andersson's *Messianic Popular Movements in the Lower Congo* (1958) were scholarly works that gradually were winning a hearing.[11] Journals such as *International Review of Missions* had published several articles since the 1920s dealing with "independent," "prophetic," or "separatist" churches in South Africa and Congo; but no scholarly studies had been carried out in southeastern Nigeria, one of the areas where this phenomenon had flourished since the late nineteenth century. In summary, an accurate description of the religious situation in southeastern Nigeria was not yet available.

2. *Ecclesiastical.* The existing systems for ecclesiastical relations in southeastern Nigeria institutionalized fragmentation and made it difficult to envisage change. Mainline Protestants relied on the Christian Council of Nigeria to organize cooperative projects but neither the considerable number of non-cooperating Conservative Protestants nor African independent churches contemplated joining the CCN. The former were averse to "ecumenical" relations and the CCN did not recognize the latter as bona fide churches. Furthermore, the Anglican, Presbyterian, and Methodist churches in Nigeria were absorbed in negotiating the union of their three churches and this would preoccupy them until those conversations broke down in 1967.

3. *Missions.* The older missions had established their work on the basis of comity agreements whereas the newer missions ignored such conventions. Unlike other countries where an inter-mission council that provided services to mission agencies of all stripes was established early on, Nigeria had no such structure. Over the years the situation had

---

[11] A historiographical account of this field of study would be instructive. E.g., *International Review of Missions* published a review of Sundkler's book (58:2 [April 1949]:230-33), but Andersson's was ignored. An appreciative review of Andersson's book was written by Fehderau, a missionary linguist in the Congo, concluding with five implications of Andersson's analysis (1960). An overview of early developments and the underlying issues is given in Shepherd (1937). Nothing comparable for Nigeria had appeared by 1959. A noteworthy article was Dougall (1956).

grown increasingly crowded and confused as missions proliferated and so-called independency flourished.

3   WORKING OUT A RESPONSE

From the beginning Edwin Weaver spoke of the need for a new kind of post-colonial mission strategy for southeastern Nigeria. Motivated by his experience in India where after 1949 his mission had systematically dismantled "colonial" structures, he envisaged developing a strategy that would address the root causes of the fragmentation that was deeply embedded in the history of the missions and churches of that region. Special care had to be taken to understand the historico-cultural context.

1. *The strategists.* Three people played key roles in defining a new strategy: Edwin I. Weaver, John H. Yoder, and Harold W. Turner. Weaver (1903-1989) was a man of warm and deep piety who met people easily, was impatient with archaic structures and instinctively brought people together. He was a person of action. He was impatient with the status quo and believed concrete and practical solutions could be found; but he understood that careful study of the history, culture and inter-church relations of the region were indispensable prerequisites.

Yoder (1927-1997) had joined the administrative staff of Mennonite Board of Missions (MBM) in 1958 while teaching part-time at Goshen Biblical Seminary. Yoder's gifts of penetrating analysis, theological acuity, wide acquaintance with both ecumenical and evangelical missions, and awareness of the literature of the day were crucial to the process. One of Yoder's special interests was the theory of ecumenism, a theme with particular salience in southeastern Nigeria.[12] In *The Ecumenical Movement and the Faithful Church* Yoder argued "that Christian unity is just as clearly a Biblical imperative as are evangelization, nonresistance, and nonconformity ...and that however delicate the question

---

[12] Reacting incisively to the attitude projected by representatives of the CCN (fn. 8 above), Yoder commented to Weaver: "As I said in a previous letter, we will have to know much more about the terms under which these independent churches broke with the larger body before being sure that they do not have just as much spiritual right to invite us into Nigeria as the Council of Churches has to invite us out. Somehow, Mr. Wood seems to have forgotten the ecumenical dimension of his office, when he reprimands you for having fraternal relationship with Christian churches, when actually such fraternal relationships should be his own responsibility" (Yoder to Weaver, Jan. 15, 1960).

may be, it demands open discussion and action."[13] From both the New Testament and sixteenth-century church history, he affirmed "[It] is the duty of the evangelical Christian to seek to establish and maintain brotherly relationships with anyone who confesses Christ" (ibid.:35).

Turner (1911-2002) came to West Africa in 1955 as lecturer in Old Testament at Fourah Bay College, Sierra Leone. By 1957 he had begun a major study of the Church of the Lord (Aladura), an African-initiated Church in Nigeria that was spreading to other African countries (Turner, 1967). Turner adopted a phenomenological methodology that required scrupulous attention to the empirical evidence and empathy for the subjects being studied. When the Weavers and Turner chanced to meet in a guesthouse in Lagos in 1961, he had already published several articles based on his findings and was developing a typology of these new religious movements (Turner 1960; 1961:106-10; 1963; cf. 1978). They immediately discovered their common passion. In 1963 Turner moved to the new University of Nigeria, Nsukka, and this made possible regular collaboration with Weavers. An assiduous researcher, Turner had a clear eye for what this situation required. The mutual prejudices of the established churches and the indigenous churches could only be dissolved on the basis of accurate information. Raw data had to be gathered in the field.

2. *Defining the problem.* The first challenge was to define the situation in southeastern Nigeria in the light of mission theory and practice. One of the seminal influences in missions thought in the 1950s and 1960s was the journal *Practical Anthropology*. This modest publication was geared to the needs of the field missionary to clarify issues and provide new insight. The main contributors to the journal were anthropologists and linguists often associated with the Bible Societies and translation projects. In the late 1950s a frequent theme in *Practical Anthropology* was the "indigenous church." Yoder had kept abreast of this literature, especially the contributions by Eugene A. Nida and William A. Smalley and suggested various articles to the Weavers (Smalley 1958; 1959a: 1959b). Yoder's supervisor at MBM, J. D. Graber, had also served in India and was a direct contemporary of Donald A. McGavran. Initially, Graber thought the Weavers might get needed guidance from McGavran's recent book, *The Bridges of God* (1955). Experience dicta-

---

[13] Yoder (1958). Weaver wrote to Yoder Dec. 14, 1959, noting inter alia: "The other day I opened one of our barrels containing books. The first I got out to read again was your *The Ecumenical Movement and the Faithful Church.* I was very much impressed. I didn't lay it aside until I had completed it. Your booklet has applications and implications for us here.

ted otherwise. McGavran's ideas on strategy did not anticipate the Nigeria situation.[14]

Yoder's reply to Weaver's initial report of December 8 was crucial. Writing on December 18, he comes to grips with the pivotal question quickly. Weavers' key concern was that they not add to the present confusion. Yoder responds: "I would argue that the only justification for our moving into a place like Nigeria, with such a large percentage of Christians of varying shapes and kinds, is that we help to decrease the confusion. *In a sense this is more an ecumenical than a missionary task*, if those two concepts can be separated."[15] Yoder went on to argue that the present situation was the result of the conflict between two types of church: the established churches that arrogated to themselves a controlling ecclesiastical role and the rest of the churches that had little regard for order and structures. The two ecclesial types could not be separated. But in the end the problem turned on the quality of leadership. The established churches assumed the right to control ecclesiastical affairs and other churches deeply resented this. The conflict was like a festering sore.

Thus, from the beginning Yoder encouraged the Weavers to view their context with a different lens than that of classical missions, precisely so that the response made to the spiritual needs of the people in southeastern Nigeria might be relevant to their reality.[16] The *missional* could not be separated from the *ecclesial*. Such scandalous disunity was destructive of both church and mission.

---

[14] E.g., J. D. Graber to E. and I. Weaver, May 3, 1960, #7, and JDG to EIW, July 13, 1960. Cf. Weaver's response to Graber (July 21, 1960): "It is my impression that UYO does not quite fit what Mac (sic) is trying to say in that book, the thesis of which I wholeheartedly accept." Finally, EIW to JDG Sept. 17, 1960. McGavran and the Weavers were acquainted from India. Later, in teaching Church Growth, he used the Weavers' approach in Nigeria as a case of a "wrong strategy" that resulted in a "missed opportunity."

[15] J. H. Yoder to E. I. Weaver, December 18, 1959 (emphasis added).

[16] The complexities of the situation are reflected in E.I. Weaver to J.H. Yoder, March 6, 1961: "Many of the African missions still seem to be of the old style; little adjustment seems to have been made to changing times...Though Christianity has been here for over a hundred years, there is still so much paganism within the Church. There is ritual killing, ritual cannibalism and everything pagan in more pagan areas without the church... I could move much faster by taking the old line of mission program and methods. But I do not feel this is wise. The Church must be theirs. I must be here simply to work with them and help them and not to control them or to dominate the scene."

3. *Programmatic principle.* One searches the written record in vain for a concise statement of what is here termed the "programmatic principle." And yet anyone observing the unfolding program will be impressed with its coherence.[17] It was propelled by an "axial principle" embodied in people guided by this principle. This principle was *dialogue.* Edwin Weaver spoke often in terms of fostering "cooperation and reconciliation," but these goals could only be realized through dialogue based on mutual respect, careful listening to each other, and working together to solve common problems. The various initiatives that came to fruition were the result of this programmatic principle.

4   MULTI-FACETED PROGRAM RESPONSE

Over the course of several years Edwin Weaver was at the center of creating five projects designed to bring the churches of the region together at several levels, including Inter-Church Study Group, Independent Churches Fellowship, United Independent Churches Bible School, scholarship program, and Inter-Church Team. Each of these projects was practical and focussed on acknowledged needs. Each one brought together people and groups who otherwise would not have cooperated with one another. The goal was to lay the foundation for trust and respect while meeting concrete needs. Three of these initiatives will be described briefly.

1. *Inter-Church Study Group.* Undoubtedly, the ICSG was crucial to the entire undertaking. The steps involved in getting it set up, however, indicate just how difficult it was to overcome the deep-seated mistrust that characterized relations among the churches of the region. Had it failed, other initiatives would have been more difficult, if not impossible to launch.

Weaver reported to Yoder on February 11, 1961 that representatives from the three ecclesiastical streams met in late March in a Quao Iboe church near Uyo to discuss the "confused" church situation.[18] Macdonald and Weaver hoped this meeting would lay the basis for a continuing conversation between the various groups—established churches, Conservative Evangelicals, and independents. A week after the meeting

---

[17] Cf. Edwin and Irene Weaver, 1970; for an engaging account of their experiences in Nigeria, 1959-1966. Appendix II, "A Mission Strategy for Uyo" conveys essential features of Weavers' approach.

[18] Represented were Lutherans (Missouri Synod), Salvation Army, Pentecostals, Church of Christ, Mennonites, World Crusade, and Council of Churches members.

Weaver wrote to Yoder: "Our Mar. 28th meeting was not too encouraging... The strongest voice in the meeting cut right across what both Macdonald and I are interested in trying to accomplish." Although eighteen people attended, the old mentality was in control. The dominant people were not yet prepared to think in new terms.

However, in September decisive action was taken during the annual meeting of the "CNN" Regional Council. A Special Study Committee was authorized "which Mr. Weaver could call from time to time for consultation" with the following purposes: 1) promote fellowship and understanding and ways of working cooperatively; 2) attempt to understand and reach more effectively any indigenous churches who are without good leadership and standards; 3) conduct periodic study and discussion conferences; 4) appoint selected persons from within and without our committee to prepare and present papers for discussion on various problems of common interest. In broad strokes this minute gives a programmatic statement of Edwin Weaver's vision of what had to be done.[19] It was announced that the first meeting would be held the following March.

The first meeting of the Inter-Church Study Group took place March 3, 1962 with seven denominational groups represented. A paper by H. W. Turner on "The Significance of African Prophet Movements" was the basis for discussion. Discussants identified several issues: 1) the need to clarify the problematic term "indigenous churches" and find a non-pejorative alternative; 2) the lack of reliable church statistics for the region; 3) indigenous church-missions relations; 4) recognition of the wide spectrum of beliefs and practices among indigenous groups; 5) lack of cooperation among missions that opened the way for free-lancing among the indigenous groups.

This marked the beginning of a pattern of quarterly meetings that ran until 1967 when the civil war disrupted all civilian life. The composition of the group was increasingly comprehensive and it became a forum where representatives of both established and independent churches presented papers on their faith, practice, and theology followed by fruitful dialogue.[20] This brought together people who otherwise would not

---

[19] Edwin Weaver wrote this as a statement of "Purpose of the Special Study Committee." The status of the document is unclear. It appears Weaver made notes and then wrote this up as a record of the meeting afterwards. But he does not sign it as recorder or chair of the committee.

[20] Sample papers presented to study sessions: "Early History of the Apostolic Church," I.B.I. Ita; "The History and Contribution of the Mount Zion Mission," A.J.

have met and ensured that participants would hear each group interpret itself. This built rapport among the group members. Edwin Weaver began compiling "The Uyo Papers," consisting of presentations to the ICSG and relevant papers from elsewhere in Africa. By 1967 this collection included some fifty items.

2. *Inter-Church Team.* Auxiliary to the ICSG was the Inter-Church Team organized to gather statistics on the churches in selected districts. The Department of Religious Studies, University of Nigeria, Nsukka, under A. F. Walls and H. W. Turner, provided expert help in organizing the data-gathering and processing it. Out of this came several surveys. *The Abak Story* was the first one completed. It documented the varieties of churches, the locations and number of churches, membership, and leaders for that area. The comprehensive nature of the process and the fact that the research team was composed of members from various churches was an important confidence-building measure.

3. *Independent Churches Fellowship.* While Edwin Weaver's initial concern was to bridge between the established and independent churches, it soon became evident that the independent churches themselves had no means of meeting each other and working together. Weaver convened representatives of five of these groups December 16, 1963 and organized the United Independent Churches Fellowship. A primary concern of this group was to address the needs for leadership training. In 1965 the United Independent Churches Bible School was opened in Uyo with teachers drawn from both established and independent churches.

5 Conclusion

The civil war, 1966-1970, disrupted everything. Foreigners were forced to leave and properties seized. Even the large amount of Inter-Church Study research materials Edwin Weaver and I. U. Nsasak, his Nigerian associate, had collected were confiscated and destroyed by the military. Following the war no one stepped forward to revive the promising initiatives of 1961-1967. When Edwin and Irene Weaver applied for visas to visit Nigeria after the civil war ended, they were denied. From all accounts, in the absence of leadership the old culture of "independency"

Eminue; "Church of Christ in Africa (Johera)", A. Matthew Ajuoga; "Modern African Religious Movements", H.W. Turner; "Theological Education for Independent Churches," E.I. Weaver; "The Present-Day Prophets and the Principles upon which they work," J.A. Aina; "Prophecy," S.I. Etuk; and "Divine healing in Independent Churches," D.U. Otong. From "Index to Inter-Church Study Papers, Uyo." Undated.

rebounded. Between 1968 and 1971 the Weavers helped establish projects in other West African countries based on the model developed in Nigeria. Subsequently, they assisted in establishing similar projects in Botswana, Lesotho, and Swaziland.

The most intriguing question posed by this case study is why southeastern Nigeria has produced such vigorous religious innovation for nearly a century. That question remains unanswered.

BIBLIOGRAPHY

Andersson, Efraim. (1958). *Messianic Popular Movements in the Lower Congo*. Studia Ethnografica Upsaliensia XIV. Uppsala: Almqvist and Wiksells Boktryckeri AB.
Dougall, J.W.C. (1956). "African Separatist Churches". *International Review of Missions* 45:3. Pp. 257-66.
Fehderau. Harold W. (1960). "Review of *Messianic Popular Movements in the Lower Congo*". *Practical Anthropology* 7:6 (Nov.-Dec.). Pp. 279-283.
McGavran, Donald. (1955). *The Bridges of God*. London: World Dominion Press.
Shepherd, R.H.W. (1937). "The Separatist Churches of South Africa". *IRM* 26:4. Pp. 453-63.
Smalley, William. R. (1958). "Cultural Implications of an Indigenous Church". *Practical Anthropology* 5:2. Pp. 51-65.
—. (1959a). "What Are Indigenous Churches Like?" *PA* 6:3. Pp. 135-39
—. (1959b). "Vocabulary and the Preaching of the Gospel". *PA* 6:4. Pp. 182-85.
Sundkler, Bengt. (1948). *Bantu Prophets in South Africa*. London: Oxford University Press. Second edition 1961.
Turner, H.W. (1961). "Searching and Syncretism: A West African Documentation". *Practical Anthropology* 8:3 (May-June). Pp. 106-10.
—. (1963). *Modern African Religious Movements: An Introduction for the Christian Churches*. Nsukka: Department of Religious Studies, University of Nigeria. Rev. ed. 1965.
—. (1967). *African Independent Church*. 2 vols. Oxford: Clarendon Press.
—. (1960). "The Litany of an Independent West African Church," *Practical Anthropology* 7:6. Pp. 256-262.
—. (1978). *Religious Innovation in Africa: Collected Essays on New Religious Movements*. Boston: G. K. Hall.
Weaver, Edwin and Irene. (1970). *The Uyo Story*. Elkhart, Ind.: Mennonite Board of Missions.
Yoder, J.H. (1958). *The Ecumenical Movement and the Faithful Church*. Scottdale, Penna.: Herald Press.

A SELECTION OF RELEVANT PUBLICATIONS
BY JERALD GORT

ARTICLES, CHAPTERS AND MONOGRAPHS

The Concept of 'Mutual Assistance' at the 1928 World Missionary Conference in Jerusalem: Relations Between the So-Called 'Younger' and 'Older' Churches. Bound mimeograph. 1971. 68 pp.

"The Problem of Taiwan." With L. de Jong, D. Kooiman, B.M. Velema, J. Verkuyl. *Lutheran World*, 20, 2 (1973). Pp. 167-176.

Also published as "Das Problem Taiwan (Formosa)." Translated by Jürgen Roloff. *Lutherische Rundschau*, 20, 2 (1973). Pp. 222-234.

"Geloven in een vesting van rijkdom," and "Ontwikkelingslanden hebben geen welvaart nodig." *Voorlopig*, 6, 7/8 (1974). Pp. 229-236.

Anonymous Christianity and Other Recent Roman Catholic Contributions to Theologia Religionum: Their Context in Catholic Theology and Their Implications for Mission. Bound mimeograph. 1976. 104 pp.

"Jerusalem 1928: Kingdom, Mission and Church." *International Review of Mission*, 68, 266 (1978). Pp. 273-298.

"Gospel for the Poor?" In: *Zending op Weg naar de Toekomst* (see further 'CO-EDITED VOLUMES' below). 1978. Pp. 80-109.

Also published in: *Missiology: An International Review*, 7, 3 (1979). Pp. 325-354; in Spanish, French and English as resource document for the International Missionary Conference in Melbourne, May 1980, Geneva: CWME/WCC, 1980; and as a monograph in Korean, Seoul, 1990, 36 pp.

"The Contours of the Reformed Understanding of Christian Mission: An Attempt at Delineation." Mission Focus, 7, 3 (1979). Pp. 37-41.

Also published in: *Calvin Theological Journal*, 15, 1 (1980). Pp. 47-61, and *Occasional Bulletin of Missionary Research*, 4, 4 (1980). Pp. 156-162.

Your Kingdom Come: Melbourne, Australia, May 12-25, 1980. Amsterdam: Free University Central Reproduction Service. 1980. 30 pp.

"Melbourne: A Missiological Interpretation." *International Review of Mission*, 69, 276/277 (1980), 557-574.

"Melbourne: evangelikalen en oekumenikalen." *Wereld en Zending*, 9, 4 (1980). Pp. 334-345.

"Is het evangelie slecht nieuws voor de rijken?" *VU Magazine*, 9, 10 (1980). Pp. 34-39.

"Christenen moeten partij kiezen voor verdrukten en kanslozen." *VU Magazine*, 9, 11 (1980). Pp. 34-37.

"De markante ontwikkeling in het missionaire denken." *Rondom het Woord*, 22, 4 (1980/81). Pp. 2-11.

The Role of the Christian Study Centers. Consultation Report, Singapore, December 2-8, 1980. With Pontus Nasution and Peter Lee. Geneva: CWME/WCC. 1981.

"Mag het evangelie aangepast worden?" In: (eds.) Dick C. Mulder *et al. Staalkaart van de Theologie*. Amsterdam: Free University Bookstore and Publishing. 1982. Pp. 77-99.

"Bezinning op zending." In: Beleidsnota van het Zuid Azië Orgaan van de zending der Gereformeerde Kerken in Nederland. Lunteren: Dienstencentrum. 1982. Pp. 2-11.

"Buitenkerkelijken als randkerkelijken?" De theorie van het 'anonieme christendom' en 'werkers der gerechtigheid' buiten de kerk." In: J. Vlijm (ed.). *Buitensporig geloven*. Kampen: Kok. 1983. Pp. 137-152.

Waar haalt u de moed vandaan? Zaandam: Classis Noord-Holland (GKN). 1984. 21 pp.

"African Christian Independency." With Marthinus L. Daneel. In: *Christian Mission and Human Transformation*. Report of the Sixth International Association of Mission Studies Conference, 8-14 January 1985, Harare, Zimbabwe. Gweru: Mambo Press. 1985. Pp. 76-82.

"De christelijke beweging in de Indiase kontekst." *Wereld en Zending*, 14, 2 (1985). Pp. 98-111.

"De wisselvalligheden van 150 jaren zending in China." *Wereld en Zending*, 16, 4 (1987). Pp. 330-339.

"Onheil, Heil en Bemiddeling." In: F.J. Verstraelen, A. Camps, L.A. Hoedemaker, M.R. Spindler (eds.). *Oecumenische Inleiding in de Missiologie: Teksten en Konteksten van het Wereldchristendom*. Kampen: Kok. 1988. Pp. 203-218.

"Syncretism and Dialogue: Christian Historical and Early Ecumenical Perceptions." In: *Dialogue and Syncretism: An Interdisciplinary Approach*. (see further 'CO-EDITED VOLUMES' below). 1989. Pp. 36-51

Also published in: *Mission Studies: Journal of the International Association for Mission Studies*, VI-1 (1989). Pp. 9-23, and in Indonesian in: *Peninjau*, 14, 2 and 15, 1 (1990). Pp. 39-55.

"Foreword." In: Marthinus L. Daneel. *Fambidzano: Ecumenical Movement of Zimbabwean Independent Churches*. Gweru: Mambo Press. 1989. Pp. 7-12.

"Van Edinburgh 1910 naar San Antonio 1989: Een doorlopend verhaal." *Wereld en Zending*, 18, 4 (1989). Pp. 359-365.

"Liberative Ecumenism: Gateway to the Sharing of Religious Experience Today." *Mission Studies: Journal of the International Association for Mission Studies*, VIII-1 (1991). Pp. 57-77.

Also published in: *On Sharing Religious Experience: Possibilities of Interfaith Mutuality* (see further 'CO-EDITED VOLUMES' below). 1992. Pp. 88-105.

"The Christian Ecumenical Reception of Human Rights." In: *Human Rights and Religious Values: An Uneasy Relationship?* (see further 'CO-EDITED VOLUMES' below). 1995. Pp. 203-238.

"Human Distress, Salvation, and Mediation of Salvation." In: Frans J. Verstraelen, Arnulf Camps, Libertus A. Hoedemaker, Marc R. Spindler (eds.). *Mis-*

siology, An Ecumenical Introduction: Texts and Contexts of Global Christianity. Translated by John Vriend. Grand Rapids: Eerdmans. Pp. 194-210.

"Theological Issues for Missiological Education: An Ecumenical-Protestant Perspective." In: J. Dudley Woodberry, Charles Van Engen, Edgar J. Elliston (eds.). *Missiological Education for the 21ˢᵗ Century: The Book, the Circle, and the Sandals.* Essays in Honour of Paul E. Pierson. Maryknoll: Orbis Press. 1996. Pp. 67-76.

"General Introduction." With Hendrik M. Vroom. In: *Holy Scriptures in Judaism, Christianity and Islam: Hermeneutics, Values and Society* (see further 'CO-EDITED VOLUMES' below). 1977. Pp. 7-11.

"Johannes Verkuyl." In: Gerald H. Anderson *et al.* (eds.), *Biographical Dictionary of Christian Missions.* New York: Macmillan Reference. 1997.

"Listening to All the Saints: Precondition of a Responsible Hermeneutics for Mission." In: Marthinus L. Daneel (ed.). *African Christian Outreach.* Vol. I: *The African Initiated Churches.* Pretoria: Southern African Missiological Society, 2001. Pp. 47-60.

"Johannes Verkuyl 1908-2001: Een bijzonder leraar, vriend en missioloog." *Gereformeerd Theologisch Tijdschrift,* 100, 2 (2001). Pp. 47-53.

Also published in shorter form in: *Soteria,* 18, 1(2001). Pp. 47-51.

"Religion, Conflict and Reconciliation." With Hendrik M. Vroom. In: *Religion, Conflict, and Reconciliation: Multifaith Ideals and Realities* (see further 'CO-EDITED VOLUMES' below). 2002. Pp. 3-10.

"Religion, Conflict, and Reconciliation: Ecumenical Initiatives Amidst Human Brokenness and Community Division." In: *Religion, Conflict, and Reconciliation: Multifaith Ideals and Realities* (see further 'CO-EDITED VOLUMES' below), 2002. Pp. 117-133.

Also published in: *Mission Studies: Journal of the International Association for Mission Studies,* 19, 2 (2002). Pp. 90-112.

"De vis en het water: Enkele inleidende notities inzake contextualiteit." In: *Veelkleurige christendom: noord, zuid, oost, west* (see further 'CO-EDITED VOLUMES' below). 2003. Pp. 13-31.

"Reconciliation-Related Research at the Free University, Amsterdam." In: John Hulst (ed.). *The Word of God and the Academy in Contemporary Culture(s).* Budapest: Károli Gáspár University. 2003. Pp. 219-229.

"Religions View Religions: A Brief Position Paper." In: *Religions View Religions: Explorations in Pursuit of Understanding* (see further 'CO-EDITED VOLUMES' below), publication in 2003.

"Theology of Religion: The Case of Christianity from the Perspective of Ecumenical Thought." In: *Religions View Religions: Explorations in Pursuit of Understanding* (see further 'CO-EDITED VOLUMES' below), publication in 2003.

CO-EDITED VOLUMES AND READERS

Lowland Highlights: Church and Oecumene in the Netherlands. Edited by J.A. Hebly and Jerald D. Gort. Kampen: Kok. 1972.

Zending op Weg naar de Toekomst. Essays in Honor of Johannes Verkuyl. Edited by Jerald D. Gort, Herman Westmaas and Dick C. Mulder. Kam-pen: Kok, 1978.

Black Theology. A Documentary Reader. Edited by Jerald Gort, Anton Wessels and Corien Veenhuizen. Amsterdam: Free University Central Reproduction Service, 1979, 438 pp.

African Christian Theology. A Documentary Reader. Edited by Jerald Gort, Anton Wessels and Corien Veenhuizen. Amsterdam: Free University Central Reproduction Service. 1980. 734 pp.

Gospel for the Poor. A Documentary Reader. 3 Parts. Edited by Jerald Gort, Anton Wessels and Corien Veenhuizen. Amsterdam: Free University Central Reproduction Service, 1981, 2155 pp.

"Who Do People Say That I Am?" Western, Jewish, Asian, African, Latin American Images of Jesus Christ. A Documentary Reader. Edited by Jerald Gort, Anton Wessels and Corien Veenhuizen. Amsterdam: Free University Central Reproduction Service. 1981. 564 pp.

Living with Christ among People: Evangelical and Ecumenical Views on Evangelism. A Documentary Reader. Edited by Jerald Gort, Anton Wessels and Harm Lanting. Amsterdam: Free University Central Reproduction Service. 1982. 560 pp.

Theology in Asia. A Documentary Reader. Edited by Jerald Gort, Anton Wessels and Harm Lanting. Amsterdam: Free University Central Reproduction Service. 1983. 640 pp.

Africa – Born in Zion: Developments in Church and Theology in Africa. A Documentary Reader. Edited by Jerald Gort, Anton Wessels and Gerard van Viegen. Amsterdam: Free University Central Reproduction Service. 1984. 615 pp.

The Christianization of Europe: Interaction between Gospel and Culture. A Documentary Reader. Edited by Jerald Gort, Anton Wessels and Gerard van Viegen. Amsterdam: Free University Central Reproduction Service. 1985. 582 pp.

Religies in Nieuw Perspektief. Essays in Honour of Dick C. Mulder. Edited by Remmelt Bakker, Rein Fernhout, Jerald Gort and Anton Wessels. Kampen: Kok. 1985.

Dialogue and Syncretism: An Interdisciplinary Approach. Currents of Encounter Vol. 1. (eds.) Jerald D. Gort, Rein Fernhout, Hendrik M. Vroom and Anton Wessels. Grand Rapids: Eerdmans / Amsterdam: Rodopi. 1989.

On Sharing Religious Experience: Possibilities of Interfaith Mutuality. Currents of Encounter Vol. 4. (eds.) Jerald D. Gort, Hendrik M. Vroom, Rein Fernhout and Anton Wessels. Amsterdam: Rodopi / Grand Rapids: Eerdmans. 1992

Human Rights and Religious Values: An Uneasy Relationship? Currents of Encounter Vol. 8. Edited by Abdullahi A. An-Na'im, Jerald D. Gort and Hendrik M. Vroom. Amsterdam: Rodopi / Grand Rapids: Eerdmans, 1995.

Holy Scriptures in Judaism, Christianity and Islam: Hermeneutics, Values and Society. Currents of Encounter Vol. 17. (eds.) Hendrik M. Vroom and Jerald D. Gort. Amsterdam-Atlanta: Rodopi. 1997.

Religion, Conflict, and Reconciliation: Multifaith Ideals and Realities. Currents of Encounter Vol. 17. Edited by Jerald D. Gort, Henry Jansen and Hendrik M. Vroom. Amsterdam-New York: Rodopi. 2002.

Veelkleurige christendom:Contextualisatie in Noord, Zuid, Oost en West. Essays in Honour of Anton Wessels. Edited by Corstiaan van der Burg, Jerald Gort, Lourens Minnema, Reender Kranenborg and Henk Vroom. Zoetermeer: Meinema. 2003.

Religions View Religions: Explorations in Pursuit of Understanding. Currents of Encounter Vol. 20. Edited by Jerald Gort, Lourens Minnema, Hendrik Vroom. Amsterdam-New York: Rodopi. 2003.

Personalia

Gerald H. Anderson is director emeritus of the Overseas Ministries Study Center.

G. Jan van Butselaar, is the General Secretary emeritus of the Netherlands Missionary Council.

Arnulf Camps is professor emeritus of Missiology and Third-World Theology at the Catholic University, Nijmegen.

Kenneth Cracknell is professor of Theology and Global Studies at the Brite Divinity School, Fort Worth, Texas.

Marthinus L. Daneel is professor emeritus of Missiology, University of South Africa, and Professor of African Studies, Theological Faculty, University of Boston

André F. Droogers is professor of Religious Anthropology, Faculty of Social-Cultural Studies, Vrije Universiteit, Amsterdam.

Rein Fernhout is associate professor emeritus of Comparative Religions, Faculty of Theology, Vrije Universiteit, Amsterdam.

Roger S. Greenway is professor of Missiology, Calvin Theological Seminary, Grand Rapids (Michigan)

Willi Henkel is the director and archivist emeritus of the Missionary Library of the Pontificia Universita Urbaniana, Rome.

Henry Jansen, PhD. PhD. Vrije Universiteit, is minister of the Reformed Church of Opperdoes, Netherlands.

Jan A.B. Jongeneel is professor of Missiology at the Facutlty of Theology at the University of Utrecht.

Anne-Marie Kool is director and Professor of Missiology, Protestant Institute for Mission Studies, Budapest.

Piet Meiring is professor of Missiology, Pretoria University.

John S. Mbiti is professor of the Science of Mission and Extra-European Theology at the University of Bern

Robert J. Schreiter is professor of Doctrinal Theology at the Catholic Theological Union, Chicago, and professor of Christianity and Culture at the Catholic University at Nijmegen.

Wilbert R. Shenk is professor of the History of Mission at Fuller Theological Seminary, Pasadena (California).

Marc Spindler is professor emeritus of Missiology, Faculty of Theology, Leyden University.

Karel Steenbrink is Senior Staff Member, Interuniversity Institute for Missiology and Ecumenics, Utrecht.

Charles Van Engen is professor of the Biblical Theology of Mission, Fuller Theological Seminary, Pasadena (California).

Frans Verstraelen is professor emeritus of Religious Studies, Faculty of Theology, University of Zimbabwe.

Hendrik M. Vroom is professor of Philosophy of Religion and Apologetics, Faculties of Philosophy and Theology, Vrije Universiteit, Amsterdam

INDEX OF NAMES

INDEX OF SUBJECTS

CURRENTS OF ENCOUNTER

GENERAL EDITORS: Rein Fernhout, Jerald D. Gort, Henry Jansen,
Lourens Minnema, Hendrik M. Vroom, Anton Wessels

──────── VOLUMES PUBLISHED OR AT PRESS ────────